D1597105

Teaching Music through Performance in Jazz

Also available from GIA Publications, Inc:

Teaching Music through Performance in Band, Volume 1

Teaching Music through Performance in Band, Volume 2

Teaching Music through Performance in Band, Volume 3

Teaching Music through Performance in Band, Volume 4

Teaching Music through Performance in Band, Volume 5

Teaching Music through Performance in Band, Volume 6

Teaching Music through Performance in Beginning Band

Teaching Music through Performance in Beginning Band, Volume 2

Teaching Music through Performing Marches

Teaching Music through Performance in Orchestra, Volume 1

Teaching Music through Performance in Orchestra, Volume 2

Teaching Music through Performance in Orchestra, Volume 3

Teaching Music through Performance in Choir, Volume 1

Teaching Music through Performance in Choir, Volume 2

Teaching Music through Performance in Jazz

G-7268

Teaching Music through Performance in Jazz

Ronald Carter

Wynton Marsalis

Ronald C. McCurdy

Ron Modell

Reginald Thomas

Compiled and Edited by Richard Miles
and Ronald Carter

GIA Publications, Inc.
Chicago

Teaching Music through Performance in Jazz
Ronald Carter, Wynton Marsalis, Ronald C. McCurdy,
Ron Modell, Reginald Thomas
Compiled and edited by Richard Miles and Ronald Carter
www.TeachingMusic.org

GIA Publications, Inc.
7404 S. Mason Ave., Chicago 60638
www.giamusic.com

Printed in the United States of America.

G-7268
ISBN: 978-1-57999-713-7

Table of Contents

PART II: The Jazz Band Ensemble Conductor as Teacher

ACKNOWLEDGMENTS

The following Research Associates are gratefully acknowledged for outstanding scholarly contributions to the Teacher Resource Guides:

Leon Anderson, Jr.
Director of Jazz Studies
Florida State University • Tallahassee, Florida

Tim AuBuchon
Director of Jazz Studies
Truman State University • Kirksville, Missouri

Doug Beach
Director of Jazz Studies
Elmhurst College • Elmhurst, Illinois

Thomas Bough
Director of Athletic Bands
Northern Illinois University

Cecil Bridgewater
Professor of Music
Manhattan School of Music, New School Jazz and Contemporary Music,
William Paterson Jazz Program • New York, New York

Joren Cain
Assistant Professor of Music
Valdosta State University • Valdosta, Georgia

Ronald Carter
Director of Jazz Studies
Northern Illinois University
DeKalb, Illinois
Vice President • International Association For Jazz Education

Reuben Cooper, Jr.
Director of Bands
DeKalb High School • DeKalb, Illinois

Brian W. Copping
Jazz Coordinator
School of Instrumental Music • Perth, Western Australia

Brian Coyle
Director of Jazz Studies
Hope College • Holland, Michigan

Raleigh Dailey
Lecturer in Jazz Studies
University of Kentucky • Lexington, Kentucky

Art Davis
Assistant Professor of Jazz Studies
Northern Illinois University • DeKalb, Illinois

John Davis
Director of Jazz Studies
University of Colorado • Boulder, Colorado

Jose Antonio Diaz
Director of Bands
MacArthur High School • Houston, Texas

Thomas Dust
Associate Professor
Secondary Music Education
University of Alberta • Edmonton, Alberta, Canada

Curtis Essig
Director of Jazz Studies
Associate Director of Bands
Youth Performing Arts School • Louisville, Kentucky

Ricky L. Fleming
Director of Bands
Buffalo State College • Buffalo, New York

Jim Gasior
Associate Professor of Jazz and Instrumental Studies
New World School of the Arts • Miami, Florida

Victor L. Goines
Artistic Director of Jazz Studies
The Juilliard School
New York, New York

Robert Griffin
Director of Bands
Howard W. Blake
High School of the Arts • Tampa, Florida

Scott Hall
Director of Jazz Studies
Columbia College Chicago • Chicago, Illinois

Jay Hildebrandt
Professor of Music
University of Delaware • Newark, Delaware

Ben L. Huntoon
Director, Otterbein College Jazz Ensemble
Jazz Education Consultant, Stanton's Sheet Music
President, Ohio IAJE • Columbus, Ohio

Adam Hucke
Director of Jazz Ensembles
McKendree College • Lebanon, Illinois

Jeff Jarvis
Director of Jazz Studies
California State University, Long Beach • Long Beach, California

Susie Jones
Jazz Studies
Mt. Hood Community College • Gresham, Oregon

James Kaczmarek
Band Director/ General Music Instructor
James Shields Elementary
Co-Director South Shore Youth Jazz Ensemble • Chicago, Illinois

Randall Key
Director of Bands
Hartselle High School Band • Hartselle, Alabama

Steve Kirby
Director of Jazz Studies
Faculty of Music
University of Manitoba • Winnipeg, Manitoba

Joe Lill
Director of Bands
North Park University • Chicago, Illinois

Pete Madsen
Coordinator of Jazz Studies
University of Nebraska at Omaha • Omaha, Nebraska

Stephen C. Massey
Director of Music
Foxboro Public Schools • Foxboro, Massachusetts

William T. McDaniel
Professor of Music and Director of Jazz Studies
The Ohio State University • Columbus, Ohio

Mike McMann
Instrumental Music Director
North Scott High School • Eldridge, Iowa

Scott Mertens
Sycamore, Illinois

Thara Memory
Artistic Director
Pacific Crest American Music Program • Portland, Oregon

Robert Meunier
Director of Bands
Drake University • Des Moines, Iowa

Aaron Moe
Jazz Director
Normandale Community College • Bloomington, Minnesota

Robert Morgan
Director of Jazz Studies Emeritus
High School for Performing and Visual Arts • Houston, Texas

Peter M. Muller, Jr.
Graduate Assistant
Northern Illinois University • DeKalb, Illinois

Larry Nelson
Assistant Professor of Jazz Studies, Saxophone, and Musicology
Eastern Kentucky University • Richmond, Kentucky

Kevin Norton
Graduate Research Assistant
Morehead State University • Morehead, Kentucky

Nicola van Onselen
Capetown, South Africa

Larry Panella
Director of Jazz Studies
The University of Southern Mississippi • Hattiesburg, Mississippi

Mary Jo Papich
Fine Arts Department Chair
Highland Park High School • Highland Park, Illinois

Don N. Parker
Assistant Professor of Music (Percussion/Jazz)
Fayetteville State University • Fayetteville, North Carolina

Robert Parton
Associate Professor of Jazz Studies
Chicago College of Performing Arts
Roosevelt University• Chicago, Illinois

James H. Patterson
Associate Professor and
Clark Atlanta University Jazz Orchestra Director
Clark Atlanta University • Atlanta, Georgia

Marco Pignataro
Director of Jazz & Caribbean Music Studies
Puerto Rico Conservatory of Music • San Juan, Puerto Rico

Saul Richardson
Director of Jazz
North Sydney Boys' High School
Crows Nest, New South Wales Australia

Paul Scea
Director of Jazz Studies
West Virginia University • Morgantown, West Virginia

Eddie Severn
Freelance Trumpeter and Composer
Saylorsburg, Pennsylvania

Todd Shiver
Director of Bands
Georgia College & State University • Milledgeville, Georgia

Murray F. A. Smith
PhD Candidate, Secondary Education
University of Alberta • Edmonton, Alberta, Canada

Tom Smith
Senior Fulbright Professor
Fulbright Professional Specialist Program

Steven Snyder
Associate Professor of Music
Morehead State University • Morehead, Kentucky

Dave Stamps
Managing Director, The Center for Jazz Composition
Visiting Assistant Professor
University of South Florida • Tampa, Florida

Roxanne Stevenson
Director of Bands
Chicago State University • Chicago, Illinois

Janis Stockhouse
Director of Bands
Bloomington High School North • Bloomington, Indiana

Thomas W. Streeter
Professor of Music/Director of Jazz Studies
Illinois Wesleyan University • Bloomington, Illinois

Steve Sveum
Director of Bands and Jazz
Sun Prairie High School • Sun Prairie, Wisconsin

Russell Thomas, Jr.
Director of Jazz Studies
Department of Music
Jackson State University • Jackson, Mississippi

Jerry Tolson
Associate Professor
Jazz Studies/Music Education
School of Music
University of Louisville • Louisville, Kentucky

Gordon Towell
Professor of Music
Jazz Studies/Music Education
Morehead State University • Morehead, Kentucky

Chris Vadala
Director of Jazz Studies
Professor of Saxophone
University of Maryland
School of Music • College Park, Maryland

Rodrigo Villanueva
Assistant Professor of Jazz Studies
Northern Illinois University • DeKalb, Illinois

Robert Waggoner
Director of the Community Music School Jazz Lab Ensemble
Adjunct Instructor of Jazz Education
Webster University • St. Louis, Missouri

Mark Webster
Graduate Research Assistant
Morehead State University • Morehead, Kentucky

Rick White
Director of Instrumental Music
Olympic College • Bremerton, Washington

Ira Wiggins
Director of Jazz Studies
North Carolina Central University • Durham, North Carolina

Introduction

Ron Carter

The American art form of jazz has become a major component of music programs in the United States and the world. As I travel around the country as an education consultant for Jazz at Lincoln Center in New York, directors with outstanding concert and marching band programs are continually expressing an interest in getting their jazz programs on the same level. They realize the training in great schools of music education all over the country has still left a void in their preparation for selecting quality jazz literature and teaching specific jazz concepts. Due to the tremendous success of the *Teaching Music through Performance* series, it was inevitable that the entire music education community would begin to inquire about and welcome a text focused on jazz.

I was fortunate to be able to study with some of the greatest music educators and conductors of the twentieth century: Samuel C. Berry, Mary Hoffman, Daniel Kohut, Charles Leonard, John Paynter, and Harry Begian—these are but a few that have added to my knowledge base over the years. My jazz education, however, has grown through research, performance, and interacting with such jazz greats as Clark Terry, George Hudson, Jimmy Heath, Ed Thigpen, and many others. I have had to opportunity to grow daily and be given the opportunity to share my knowledge and experiences.

Jazz has the ability to teach music concepts but also stretch the boundaries of creativity in rehearsal, improvisation, and cultural relevance. Jazz requires a personal relationship with music that makes music education not just work but *fun*! The concepts of cultural relevance to vocalization, dance, and the study of theory are continually stressed as integrated aspects of this text. The new world order is that, as musicians, we are all educators, and as educators, we are all musicians. Therefore we teach and continually search for knowledge that will make us most effective in our rehearsals and classrooms.

I am excited about the authors of the introductory chapters and the outstanding jazz educators and musicians from all around the world that have agreed to be part of this first step of research. This first text is only the beginning, and includes only a small portion of materials available for teaching music through performance in jazz. However, the effort has been made to include chapters that will immediately assist educators on all levels as well as provide reviews of literature on all levels.

This book is for everyone who values the importance of jazz as an integral part of our music education system. I attended a recent presentation by Barry Harris, a great jazz pianist and educators and he was specific about passing on the love for music and the power of the triplet swing feel. His passion for teaching and performing jazz will hopefully be passed on through the study of this text and the journey to the next edition.

A Note about Pitch Designations

There is no uniform practice for indicating different octaves without musical notation. Some refer to the line or space of the staff; others use various combinations of capital and lower-case letters with super- or subscript numerals and/or prime marks (').

Throughout this volume, each author's system is left intact. Octave designations are followed, however, by a letter name in parentheses using this system:

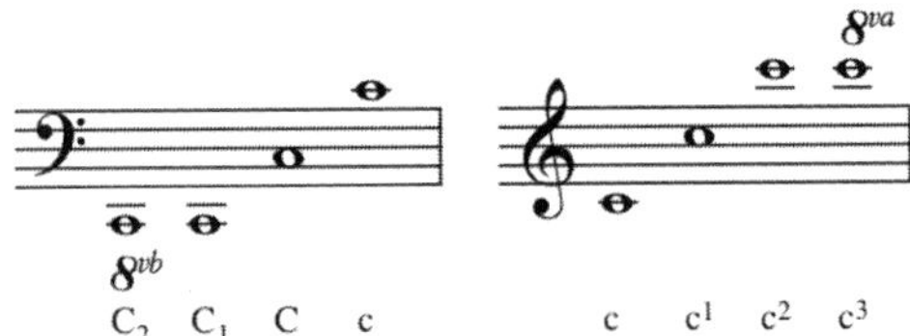

It is hoped that this will provide a consistent reference point as the text is read.

PART I

THE TEACHING OF MUSIC

CHAPTER 1

Why Teach Jazz?

Wynton Marsalis

Excerpted from the keynote address at Jazz at Lincoln Center's Inaugural Band Director Academy, June 14, 2000, Snowmass, Colorado

Thank you all very, very much for coming out here. It's a pleasure to be here. This has been a dream of ours for quite some time—to get some band directors together to talk about the music and our kids. I've had many years of experience in schools around our country. Those years taught me one thing: the band director is the primary musical influence on kids. When going to a school, I was always careful not to interfere with the band director in any way or attempt to usurp his or her authority. And over the last twenty years, I've never encountered a band director who didn't say, "Hey man, just help my students. It's not really about me; help them, and then maybe I'll take you to lunch or something and you can leave. Don't worry about me—just do what you can do."

So today I'm going to talk about why we're teaching jazz, and what makes jazz music an important tool of education. At its most basic, education provides students with a greater sense of the possible. Jazz music expands a kid's horizon of aspiration. We want students to be aware of what's possible and to feel they can attain the possible. I remember when I first heard Maurice Andre play; I'd be in the front room of my house, trying to figure out how to get piccolo trumpet notes on a regular B♭ trumpet. Bill Fielder, then the trumpet professor at Mississippi Valley State told me, "Man, that's a piccolo trumpet that man is playing. You're not ever going to get that [B♭ trumpet] to sound like that."

Even though I was ignorant, Mr. Fielder made me understand that I could do it; but I needed a piccolo trumpet to do it. Then he said, "You know what I'm going to do? I'm going to get you a piccolo trumpet, and I'm going to let you keep it, and I'll be back in two months, and if you can play it, you can keep it. But if you can't play it, I'm taking it back." So boy, I practiced that piccolo trumpet, squeaking and squawking; and I really couldn't play it that well, but he let me keep it, so I kept practicing it.

Jazz music gives us an opportunity to teach our students a respect for history in a painless way. A lot of the time students memorize facts for tests but never really digest information. Well, if you're learning Louis Armstrong, or you're learning Duke Ellington, you develop an active conception of history. These were real people. And you start to realize that, while technology may change, the technology of our souls doesn't change. That's why we can still read Homer or see Michelangelo and be moved, inspired, and enriched. The basic human concerns of their day still exist today. Their solutions still work. The best of our music is the same. It doesn't get old. Our music shows us the effect an individual can have in and on their time—this is what Booker Little played, or this is what Charlie Parker did. The music gives you a frame of reference for your experiences. I can remember when someone called me to play in the New Orleans Civic Orchestra. I was thirteen and I didn't really want to go, because I thought black people didn't play orchestra music. To not be alone, I called an afro-wearing friend of mine and said, "Please come to the Jewish Community Center and save me from being the only black person at this rehearsal." So we get there and everybody's setting up, and I see the weatherman standing behind the timpani—so I thought it's probably going to be sad. But even though my father was a musician and I had heard orchestral music, I really didn't understand that people wrote it down and you played it. It seems like something very basic to understand, but I didn't have a complete conception of what it was. It was just something that people played, that your parents made you go to once or twice in your life, and you were so bored that you couldn't believe it; you just slept and you left.

So, we get into the rehearsal and we're playing the music of Beethoven. Well, it was the worst thing you had ever heard. Our orchestra was very amateurish. But beyond all of that poor execution and bad intonation was the mind and the conception, the feelings and the thoughts and the aspirations of Ludwig Van Beethoven.

So I start to just listen, and then it dawned on me: this man *wrote* this—he had to know what they're playing, the notes, and so on. I started to understand the organization of the music.

You know, in orchestra rehearsal, if you play trumpet, you only have one note every forty-five measures or something. You come in, "duh-dum." Most of the time you're just listening to the strings play. If you don't know how to listen, most of the time, you're bored.

But in the course of these rehearsals, I began to understand just how the music was organized, and I began to develop a feeling for and an understanding of this music. I became unbored through listening. And this really stuck with me when I started to be a part of jazz bands. When we would play in a big band, the music was so sad, you couldn't really figure out anything about jazz from playing it. Most of it sounded like a funk tune with a marching band on top of it. So, I would always wonder to myself, "Why is it when I play in youth orchestra, we're playing Ravel's *Bolero*, I mean, we'd murder it, but we're playing it, or we're playing Mussorgsky's *Pictures at an Exhibition*, or Beethoven's Fifth, all of these great pieces, but when we come in to jazz band, we're playing something so trite that there's no way you could understand the meaning of the art by playing that version of it?

Sometimes I go into a band, and the band will be playing some of the most insubstantial music in the world. I ask the band director, "Why y'all playing this music?" "Oh, the kids want to play this," he'll say. And I'm thinking, man, I missed out. Do they do that in math class? Are they doing that in English? Or the football, or even the debate team? Where else in the school are the kids determining what they're doing? They have colleges like that? I want to work on my Ph.D., you know, in free throw shooting. So it's very important to make the kids understand that this is part of an educational experience.

Now a lot of the times, the band directors also have the pressure of the parents or the pressure of the principal. The kids in the school, they don't want to hear this; they don't want to hear that. But when the band sounds good, they don't mind hearing it. Sometimes it's important to utilize your individual power: the power of one. As the band director, you almost always know much more about music than anyone else in the school. Decisions about music should be made to your taste, not be the choice of those who don't have any.

• • •

I think it's important to realize that our music is the best art to teach the most basic of democratic relationships—the rights and responsibilities of individuals to the larger group. This is something that's sadly lacking in our culture in general. We can see it in the polarization that pollutes our national dialogue, and we see it in the level of selfishness that is exhibited constantly. It's always, me, me, me, me, me.

I once went on a tour of colleges. I asked the college students for an example of a democratic act. It was always something that was given to them: I can vote, I can buy what I want, I can live where I want, I can do this. It was never: I have the opportunity to participate in this and give someone else this opportunity; I have the responsibility of providing this.

I think the most mature conception of adulthood can be found in that balance between rights and responsibilities. The more immature you are, the more rights you want. The more mature you are, the more responsibilities you have and the more you are providing rights for others. The most obvious example of this, of course, would be parenthood. Parenthood is all about sacrifice. I have to do this because I want my children to have this. Many times teenagers are allowed to miss this central and basic fact. And it's something that my father was always great with teaching. He would say, "Man, I want y'all to rebel more than anything in the world, because the greatest rebellion is one that you finance yourself. I want you to get out and finance your own rebellion, and I'm going to sit in your house and let you pay my bills while *I* tell *you* what *you* should be doing.

In jazz you're always put in a position to make responsible choices: How loud are you going to play? How are you going to balance in the section? When it's time for a solo, who's going to solo? How long are you going to solo? How will you correct a mistake during an improvisation?

Our music also demands that we develop our hearing. Teaching students some scientific method of playing on chord changes that deemphasizes hearing the harmonic progression takes them further away from jazz. Even though it's an area that we might not be comfortable with, it's our job to empower students and to teach them to listen and to hear. We should encourage them to get with the harmony, get to the piano, learn three or four basic chords, a blues—it's a great tool to encourage hearing, encourage them to learn solos off of recordings. A lot of them might not want to spend much time working on stuff, and, well, we all have been in that position. We know that feeling. But the philosophy comes from us; we're the directors, and we have much more influence over our kids, no matter how hardheaded they are, than we think we have. In our rehearsals, sometimes we need to stop and say "Okay, this is what happened in this moment of music. The student played this, and you did that to respond, and you did that, and on the drums, did you hear what the soloist was doing?" "Oh no, I wasn't really listening." "That's why it sounded sad." It's important for us to go through the progression of choices that makes a performance succeed or fail.

We have to teach them how to hear, just like you have to be taught to listen in a conversation. Don't run away from training their ears just because we, ourselves, may be deficient in this arena. Teaching hearing also gives us the opportunity to develop our own ears to a higher level.

It's like the experience you have as a parent. How many times do your kids come home and teach you how to use some new technology or beat you at chess, and they're nine or ten years old, and then you start working on your chess game. You don't want to be beat by a nine-year-old. Maybe you take them to a museum, or somewhere you really would never go on your own, but because you have this experience with them, you start to learn new things that enhance your life. We can think of many instances in which parenting forces us to develop aspects of ourselves that hadn't been cultivated.

• • •

I want to stress to all our directors the importance of improvisation. We have to teach our students how to improvise, no matter how sad they sound at first. You don't chastise a baby for not being able to speak correctly. But when they say two or three little phrases that you can't distinguish one word from "doo-doo-ba-boo-boo"—"Did you hear what he said?!" So we're always encouraging and supporting their attempts. We have to extend that elementary school band conception into high school and sometimes into college. We have to encourage the students so they'll get over that shyness and learn how to speak this language.

You know, we all can remember the elementary school band or the high school band Christmas concert that was just unbelievably sad. The band all out of tune, you had to play a solo and you messed it up, you were nervous, and yet your mom was still, "Oh, my baby sounded so good." You know you didn't sound good. But it made you *feel* good. We have to continue that tradition, which is not to say any and everything is great, but to say we recognize that each student struggles in some way. We know when one is lazy or one is working hard, and we should encourage all of our students to play and make choices, even when they are not the best choices. Do something.

Improvised music provides a great life lesson for students. Through improvising, kids learn to handle the unforeseen with grace. Musically, group improvisation teaches the individual to adjust circumstances beyond her control and use her portion of influence to create something cohesive that sounds good. That's the beauty of Louis Armstrong and the thing that was so startling to everyone first hearing him.

There's a great account of Bix Beiderbecke saying that when he first heard Louis Armstrong, it was unbelievable, because here was a guy improvising a solo, and playing what Bix called "like phrases," so that one phrase led logically to another phrase led to another phrase. Through Armstrong he understood that you could improvise and make a complete artistic statement. Well, now here we are, eighty years later, and we're trying to teach our students how to create coherent improvised solos, to understand the importance of creating and developing ideas through the harmonic form.

You know, you don't have to create the Sistine Chapel; but let's concentrate on developing our solos and understanding the value of improvisation. How many times in the lives of our students are they going to be called upon to improvise? It might just be basic improvisation in the kitchen, or it could be some serious personal crisis. But the art of improvisation and the fact of improvisation is something that is essential to living a confident, modern life. That's why it's very, very important: soloing and improvisation.

• • •

Jazz, because it allows us to interface with the greatest minds in American music, empowers our students to make honest and personal statements. In our music there's a premium on integrity. First, just the integrity of playing your instrument. When you hear someone like Clifford Brown, or Art Tatum, or Charlie Parker, you know they had to practice that instrument with integrity: every day being serious about it, addressing deficiencies. They were willing to do that, and do it over and over and over again. Second, jazz demands that our students to be confident enough to express how they're feeling, to develop their personal identity and to play what they are hearing in the moment they hear it.

The roll call of innovators we have produced is not the greatest achievement of jazz. That amateurs and professionals could play together in the streets of New Orleans and create great music is an extraordinary expression of communal creativity the likes of which had never been seen in music. This is our greatest achievement. The music was constructed in such a way that a genius like Louis Armstrong could perform with someone who could barely play, and they could make up something that satisfied them and an audience.

Jazz music affords every musician an opportunity to find and develop his or her individual sound and identity. They don't have to create an entirely new form of music to be successful. How many trumpeters were influenced by Dizzy Gillespie? Miles Davis, Fats Navarro, Clifford Brown, Booker Little, and so on and so forth. We could just go on and on and on. But we know when we hear Booker or Freddie; we know that's not Dizzy. Though none of those trumpeters invented bebop, the creation of their *own* sound was enough to make legions of fans happy and send musicians to the practice room.

• • •

An important aspect of jazz is the blues. When jazz musicians applied the sophistication of other forms to the sound of the blues, they created a language that was universal—sophisticated and down home. All bases were covered.

The best example I can think of is Louis Armstrong's version of *Star Dust*. You think about the distance between some fundamental country blues progression and the complex harmonic progression of *Star Dust*, and realize that Pops could hear blues implications in that song. His solo and singing on *Star Dust* is a great musical achievement of natural integration. And from this we have musician after musician after musician. Charlie Parker said he tried to put the blues in everything he played. Blues expression raises the soul quotient of our playing; something we need to raise in the worst kind of way.

We often confuse having an "edge," or strange hairstyle, with being soulful, and it's just because of a lack of education. Many times I see kids and they're caught in the gap; they don't really know how to develop the expression of who they are. So they're naturally going to go toward the thing that is sold to them most frequently: where the most commercial money is, cloaked in fake irreverence, pornography and profanity. We live in that environment and it is incumbent upon us to teach our students about these things like we have to do with our own kids. We can't act like it's not there; it is. And it affects our bands, because music is the most common method of delivery of this cocktail of ignorance.

So we have to raise the soul quotient of our students, so that they understand what the world of human feeling affords you. And when you pick up your horn to play, you're entering the world of human feeling. And the question of soul is always, "How do you want to make somebody else feel?" Yes, the blues is a very important aspect of our music that should not be run from. Instead of running from it, we should run towards it.

It's like dealing with the most hardheaded, difficult kids. You want to really run from them, but most of the times, these are the kids you've got to run toward, because they are looking for something—they need to be loved or have a foot put in their butt. It's best to keep those kinds of kids in the band and work with them. But you have to walk that thin line. If they step across that certain line, you got to send them home. That's just my experience. As much as you don't want to send them home, you have to be firm. It's very important for them to be clear about your authority. It's better to have a sad band that you can teach than to have one or two kids that are a disruptive influence just because they play better than others. Try to bring those kids in; but if they don't want it, let them go, and the other ones will step up.

• • •

Jazz is romantic music. It is a music that exudes a sensuality that can't be reduced to pornography. A lot of stuff that I see and hear—I don't even know how to address it. We are in a crisis situation due to the proliferation of vulgar videos and music. Sexuality *is* a part of life. You can't teach jazz music and avoid that, because the sale of sex to kids through music affects their taste. Believe it or not, jazz can counter state the hyper-sexuality of this forty-year downward spiral.

The whole history of the American popular song runs through jazz. Most of that material is very romantic. Kids can learn from checking out Billie Holiday, Sarah Vaughan, Frank Sinatra. That generation had a certain conception of adult romance, and it's important for us to understand that this is an important part of life, not something to be awkwardly avoided. By the time kids get into high school, they're old enough to understand love songs. We can't take kids, fourteen, fifteen, sixteen, whose sexuality is being exploited everyday by companies, and by people with half of their clothes on, and talk to these students like they're six years old, 'cause they're not.

• • •

I always remember we were in Chicago once, and this is a story that I really keep with me, and I think about this when I'm playing my horn.

A group of kids had come in; it was a lunch with the mayor and everybody was sitting up with their suits on. You know kids; they come into that situation wondering, "When is this going to be over?" So the kids come out, they play mallet instruments, and there's one little bitty kid maybe eight years old in the middle. He doesn't play one note the whole time they're playing, and I'm kind of looking at him wondering, is he going to play? So the whole band is playing, and he's just sitting there, but he has his mallets up, and he's ready. He's looking at the music like he's trying to translate the Rosetta Stone or something. I've never seen a look with this type of intensity.

So Wes Anderson and I started watching him, and we were saying, "Do you think he's going to play?" He said, "I don't know, it's almost over man!" So he just kept looking and then when he got to the very last note, he hit this note; he was so nervous, "BING!" And right, as soon as he hit the note, he looked across the room at a bigger kid (about twelve or thirteen), who was probably his brother, and the big kid gave a solemn nod of approval, and the eight-year-old just started gushing with satisfaction.

I said to myself and Wes, "That's how we ought to be playing. One note. He looked at that note like it was St. Peter. And I think about that sometimes when I want to stand up and not give a hundred percent. What about that little kid? And that's a feeling we should try to give our bands. Because a lot of kids just don't have it. We have to bring that type of energy and feeling to them, even if we must overdo it sometimes. That's a big part of our job.

• • •

Now there are many pitfalls, of course. I've been to many bands where the greatest one is apathy. We have to keep our kids interested in the music. It's very hard sometimes. I remember when I was in high school, my band director, who had directed bands for forty years and was a little out of touch with kids of the seventies, said: "I remember when I had great bands. Now I just have uninspired bands with kids that don't want to play. What can I do to get through to these kids?" And I said, "Man, I don't think you can really do anything with these kids, because they are so spoiled, they aren't interested in being in the band. This is just a way to get out of a *real* class." I think sometimes you have to just outlast kids and counteract their apathy with your enthusiasm.

And then there are many problems—no acoustic bass player, bad feeder schools, etc. It's very important for band directors to develop good relationships with all those middle school directors and elementary schools; get to know the people and make them a part of what you are doing. How many band directors with a great band say, "Man, I have a great band, but I have great feeder schools." Keep recruiting kids; bring them and their parents into the world of music. And if you maintain a positive attitude and feeling, your band program will flourish. But you can't do it by yourself.

One thing I learned from Ron Carter when he was at East St. Louis—I actually did my first clinic for him in 1980. He called me, he said, "Man, you're playing with Art Blakey." I think I was nineteen. He said, "I want you to come talk to my trumpet players." I said "Yeah, man, I'd love to come talk to your trumpet players." I went over to the school; his school was in the middle of one of the most challenging areas in America. When you go into the area, you'd be saying, "Man, it's going to be a sad band." But when you get his band room, his kids were in there playing great!

But then, he'd bring his kids to our concert. He'd have a big parent booster organization. He achieved that. We have to keep recruiting. When you have a strong parent booster organization and a good relationship with the feeder schools, you know the people you're dealing with, and when you have good relationships with the other band directors in your area, your programs will flourish.

Even though success may seem a long way off, you have to try to flourish in difficult situations. It's like what I call a "humanity gig"—you are really disgusted, the band is arguing, you don't feel like playing, you're tired, you been on the road, you had to get on a plane and you're scared to fly, the iron burned your suit, on and on. And you walk out on the gig and there are only seventy people in a five-hundred-seat hall. You want to go home. But that's when you have to play like you're playing the greatest gig of your life. That's when you find out if you want to play or just be seen playing.

Those are some of the things I think about—things about our music that can help a young person grow into mature adulthood, and things that we can deal with when teaching this music. We're all trying to do the same thing— create a better environment for our kids. But it's important for us to take that moral high ground in this time and say, "We don't want the audience to train people in music; or the record companies or popularity polls, or any of this other stuff that has nothing to do with music." Let's deal with practicing and playing together and swinging and the things that make music so great. Let's remember all the reasons we got into it and enjoy it, and that's why we're here today.

Written and delivered by
Wynton Marsalis, Artistic Director
Jazz at Lincoln Center, www.jalc.org
at Jazz at Lincoln Center's Inaugural Band Director Academy
June 14, 2000, Snowmass, Colorado.

Edited by Todd Stoll and Jazz at Lincoln Center.

CHAPTER 2

A Multicultural Approach to Jazz Education

Ronald Carter

The melting pot of cultures that have come together to allow this great music we call jazz to develop covers the entire globe. It is important to understand that everyone should share in the pride that jazz is a true gift to the world and is truly American in origin. Many cultures continue to contribute to its growth and development through inclusion and expansion. Jazz developed from cultural traditions that were part of the Afro-American cultural tradition in America, along with the many other cultural traditions that developed in this country. Noted jazz scholar, Lewis Porter states:

> So when we are looking for residuals of African culture in jazz, and I believe they exist, we are not looking for African melodies or instruments, but African concepts—concepts of sound quality, of structure, and of the role of music in a cultural life.[1]

The role of music in the culture has embodied itself in all Black American music, including jazz. This has become my lifelong quest: to search for creative and cultural ways to continually pass on aspects of jazz that are more culturally based.

The traditional approach to teaching jazz in our conservatory system includes learning an instrument well, scales, arranging, composition, listening, history, and performing in large and small groups. This approach has proven itself as a catalyst to get many students interested and informed about jazz. These concepts, which are linked to the Western European logic, are very important and taught well in our music education system. However, the foundation of the jazz tradition is firmly rooted in the cultural diversities of many people. The cultural concepts passed on through the West African tradition through the Black American culture is still evolving in our educational system.

There are always students and directors looking to make a connection with the real deal of jazz, which involves concepts that are much more difficult to teach. The concepts of jazz feel, blues feel, swing feel, sound quality, and emotional intent—simply put, what makes one want to really listen.

I was a high school band director at Lincoln High School in East St. Louis, Illinois for over seventeen years. There were cultural traditions present that allowed me to grow as an educator and jazz musician. Of course, this is the high school Miles Davis attended and where he played in the high school band. Miles makes it a very big point to discuss and applaud the great music and cultural traditions in St. Louis and East St. Louis. Miles stated:

> They were serious about their partying and listening to music.[2]

Even in the late 1970s through the 1990s there was still a special relationship with music in East St. Louis. Music was still an important part of every aspect of the community, especially in church. Students spent many hours in church singing and playing. Many of the more talented students played by listening and responding to the music without any formal music training. My job with these students was getting them to learn and connect with the logic of concepts they had already mastered: the Aural Tradition.

Dr. Eileen Southern states that

> Equiano the African reminds us that music, poetry, and the dance were inextricably interlinked, and as we have seen, poet and musician typically one and the same person.[3]

The concept that music, poetry, and dance being completely linked is a cultural concept that allows students to become personally involved in experiencing jazz. This leads to a concept that I have used for many years: that jazz, even the foundation of jazz, ragtime, is a dance-oriented tradition. This allows students to truly appreciate the necessity for a strong rhythmic foundation that led to a dance-oriented feel. This also set the foundation to realize the importance of using the human voice to learn style, phrasing, and interpretation in my jazz rehearsals. Of course, we have to realize that Black American music culture involves more than just jazz. William Grant Still states in a letter to *Music Journal* in February of 1971:

> In actual fact, American Negro music (which is a fusion of African and various European elements) encompasses a great deal more than jazz, and any teacher who claims to teach the subject should be aware of all its forms, from the Negro folk product to the advances now being made in serious music.
>
> The only reason there has been such great emphasis on jazz is that it has been pushed by commercial interests, and this doesn't mean that it is the only, or even the most important, form in existence.[4]

Jazz, because of its development as dance and popular music, has enjoyed a great deal more promotion and commercial interest than other genres. The concept of its relationship to dance still motivates, and easily relates jazz to all popular styles of music. I believe this was a key reason for the success of the jazz program I had at Lincoln High School many years ago. All the students felt they could dance, even though they were not really great dancers. Professor Eileen Southern states:

> One of the most striking features of the African life was the importance given to music and dance.[5]

It is very easy to research and understand how much of the music that evolved into jazz was dance-oriented music. I have always searched for more definitive ways to allow students to personalize their awareness of the importance of rhythmic feel. This awareness does not mean each student will be able to actually dance at conclusion of a great performance of an Ellington composition; however, they should be able to internalize the pulse and inner feel of the music that leads to movement, either outwardly or internally. The use of dance as a logical approach to teaching jazz rhythm, style, and articulation is very important to learning the true essence of all music.

There have been many books written about how to play jazz, but jazz is truly an aural tradition. This simply means that if you really want to learn to play jazz, you have to listen to it. Wynton Marsalis states:

> The only way to learn jazz is by playing, and listening to those who can play.[6]

This states how this music has been passed culturally from one generation to the next. We have to continually remind ourselves how language is passed on from one generation to the next by listening. An example of this concept is the process of listening to a Miles Davis recording of *Freddie The Freeloader*, learning an idea, and then using call and response to teach this idea to a jazz class. I can remember teaching my students at Lincoln school many jazz standards using this process repeatedly. Southern states:

> Jazz is primarily an aural kind of music; its written score represents but a skeleton of actually what takes place during a performance.[7]

Jazz has distinct advantages over many other types of music we study and perform, as the original composers of the music record it. This allows the listener to hear the actual intent of the music in that moment. The emotion and the stylistic complexities are there for us all to study and re-create if we choose to do so. Musicologists have continually studied and researched to provide relevant information about the performance of the music of Bach, Beethoven, Mozart and many of our great composers. However, jazz recordings allow us to connect with the composer and the intent of the performance. Wynton Marsalis states:

> There are many ways to listen, and as for musicians, if we don't listen, we can't play.[8]

I spend a considerable amount of time trying to find new listening material on all levels to teach jazz concepts. Listening to learn is very important and should be maintained on all levels of jazz education. There has to be a constant effort to use and connect the logic part of the brain with the intuitive, creative side. Many great players, such as John Coltrane and Miles Davis, were able to make the connection and develop as key jazz artists from whom we listen and learn.

I have just completed my thirteenth year at Northern Illinois University in DeKalb, Illinois. The students there have developed a very strong connection to the desire to learn and experience jazz from a multicultural perspective. Northern is a little different from most traditional music schools, because all students, regardless of major, get an opportunity to experience music from diverse cultures. In other words, they only need to pass the audition to be able to play in the world class NIU Steel Pan Orchestra, NIU Wind Ensemble, NIU Philharmonic, Gamelan Orchestra, NIU Jazz Bands, NIU Latin Jazz, and many chamber groups. Many of the performing groups depend on reading music capabilities, while others require a combination of specific cultural concepts, as does jazz. I normally ask students if they sing, and most say no. Eileen Southern states,

> The most salient features of jazz derive directly from the blues. Jazz is a vocally oriented music; its players replace the voice with their instruments, but try to recreate its singing style and blue notes by using scooping, sliding, whining, growling, falsetto effects.[9]

Vocalization, or the oral tradition, such as poetry, singing, and/or rapping is a very important aspect to learning jazz through a multicultural perspective. Wycliffe Gordon, jazz trombonist states, "If you can't sing it, you can't play it."[10] I have heard musicians go back and forth about this specific idea, but I can assure you that most agree that vocal call and response—sing it, then play it—has played a very important role in their jazz journey. I teach an Introduction to Jazz Studies class at Northern, and all students have to sing the melody and one chorus of an instrumental blues piece. The next part of the assignment involves recording the singing of the solo to listen for style, blues effects, articulation, vibrato, and other stylistic inflections as they internalize the rhythmic feel. The recorded vocal version is then compared to the original instrumental version to make sure the imitation is exact.

Students are then required to play the transcription on their specific instruments by memory. The final phase of the assignment is to notate the entire portion of the transcription with chord notations. This has made a big difference as students experience a new approach to learning jazz. I have concluded that using the voice to learn jazz makes the experience very personal for the student. The hope is that making the experience of learning jazz more personal enables students to become lifelong supporters and consumers of this great music without having to become professional musicians. This is another reason I always start beginners on the blues, and then eventually move to more advanced tunes once specific cultural aspects of the music are understood. I encourage students to sing along with all types of music, not just jazz. I am a member of the Chicago Jazz Philharmonic, and I see how effectively Orbert Davis, the conductor, uses voice and other means to help the entire orchestra understand specific jazz styles concepts in the arrangements and original music the group performs.

The great efforts made by the pioneers of jazz education, such as, the Stan Kenton workshops, dance bands at historically Black colleges, North Texas, Berklee, and publications and research by Dr. David Baker, Jamey Aebersold, and many others are very important. Jazz has been given an opportunity to be used as a perfect vehicle to pass on musical concepts as well as creativity, feel, and attitude. The entire world needs to embrace the importance of cultural diversity and understand how jazz has evolved through this concept. The idea of jazz being aural (listening) and oral (voice), culturally linked to the music through dance have allowed me to develop the following concepts. These concepts will hopefully allow many others the ability pass on the intrinsic aspects known as swing and groove. Just as Duke Ellington stated, "It don't mean a thing, if it ain't got that swing!"[11]

Teaching Jazz Using the Vocal Tradition

I have presented clinics and workshops at Midwest Clinic, International Association for Jazz Education, and many all-state conferences for over fifteen years. Every effort has been made to stress the importance of not just relying on information taken from publications at that time, but developing concepts that were less obvious.

I remember attending a clinic with the great Clark Terry in 1981 at the Elmhurst Jazz Festival, where he talked about the need to understand that there is a different language and articulation going on when teaching and playing jazz. I immediately went home and tried to apply these concepts to my teaching. The flute was an obvious choice when experimenting with these concepts since it related more to the brass instruments. He talked about a system for jazz articulation called *doodle tonguing*. I was already using vocalization as a means of teaching jazz style phrasing and articulation, but Clark's system made everything much more transparent. I could actually hear the difference as he demonstrated on his trumpet.

The possibility of combining Clark's ideas about doodle tonguing with my concepts of vocalizing jazz phrasing and articulation meant no remediation. The lips for the brass players stay in a similar playing position and the tongue is in a proper position as well. In other words, when singing or actually playing jazz phrases things are in the correct position. The off-on tongue placement of the saxophone is also in place for correct jazz style and phrasing. The fact that jazz is a vocally oriented art form relates to the proper use and placement of the tongue. It really made sense. Try talking without using your tongue; not so easy, is it?

Here is basic outline of the system for getting acquainted with teaching jazz using the oral or vocal approach.

Clark Terry's Basic Concept of Doodle Tonguing: (as I heard it)

1. Use a *D attack!*
2. Say the basic vowels: A, E, I, O, U.
   Sing the basic vowel sounds.
   Note: Constant, supported air stream is very important!
3. Combine the *D attack* with each vowel.

Example 1

Note: Sing with one breath of air with full support throughout the entire phrase.

4. Combine the full *ddle* to each phrase.

Example 2

Notes: The final "e" is silent on the end of each word.
Sing with one breath of air with full support throughout the entire phrase.

Add an accent to the middle *dd* sound of the phrase.

Example 3

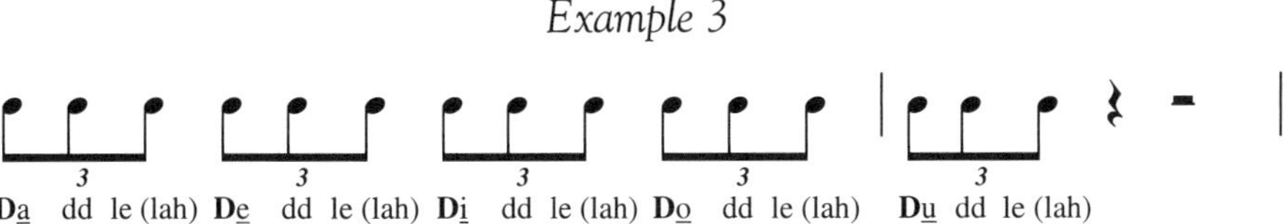

Notes: To create the triplet feel, *le* is pronounced *lah*.
Sing with one breath of air with full support throughout the entire phrase.

6. Develop your own exercises to drill and have fun with these ideas until air support and tongue placement feels natural.

7. *Duddle* becomes *Doodle*.

Combining Doodle Tonguing With Basic Jazz Articulation Syllables

Do not be afraid to adapt any articulation syllable to your own style and what you hear when you listen to jazz greats interpret jazz phrases. Making this system fit your comfort zone is very important. Start recording yourself as you sing jazz phrases, and always work for improvement.

The basis system of jazz articulation is as follows:

SYLLABLE	MEANING	NOTATION
Doo or Du	long notes, legato	
Dah	long accented notes	
Daht	fat, heavy, accented sound	
Dot	short accented notes	
Dit	short, spaced, non-accented notes, staccato	
Da (day)	smooth eighth notes	
De	smooth eighth notes	
Di	smooth eighth notes	
Do (doe)	smooth eighth notes	
Un	smooth eighth notes	

Triplets

Example 4

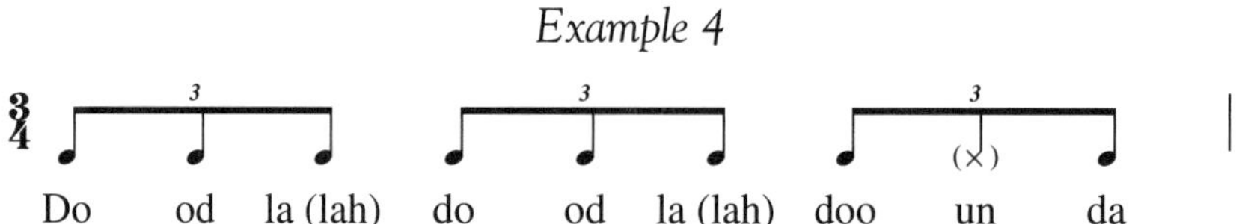

Syllables for Common Jazz Swing Phrases:

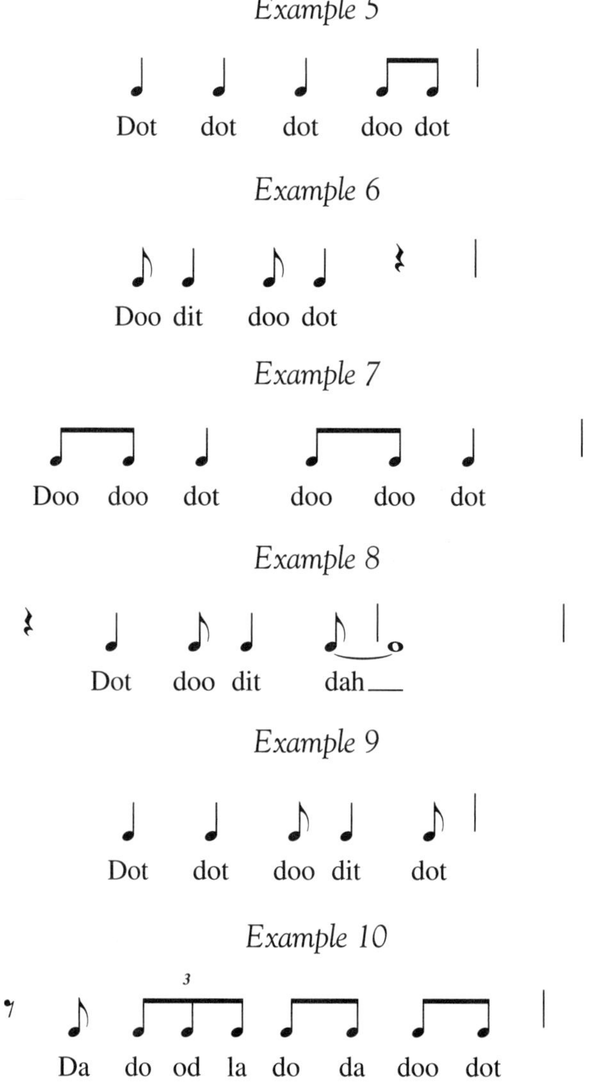

SYLLABLES FOR A SELECT GROUP OF JAZZ STANDARDS:

Example 11
In a Mellow Tone – Duke Ellington (try to sound like Duke)

Example 12
Shiny Stockings, Count Basie Orchestra (try to sound like Basie)

Start Encouraging Students to Sing for Fun!

I have found it is very important to make singing a necessary part of the culture of learning concepts in music. Not only should the voice be a part of every aspect of learning jazz, but all music in a music education curriculum. Encourage students to sing commercials, video game music, ring tones, popular music, and melodies from wind ensemble, orchestra, and even marching band literature. Vocalization should become as natural as speech and conversation. I have worked with people of all ages and have never encountered students who couldn't eventually vocalize jazz phrases. The idea that you do best what you do most is definitely true.

During the opening session of the *Jazz at Lincoln Center* Band Director Academy I encouraged all directors attending to:

1. Sing bass lines and imitate the length and attack of the bass notes with specific recordings of Ray Brown, Milt Hinton and others.

Example 13

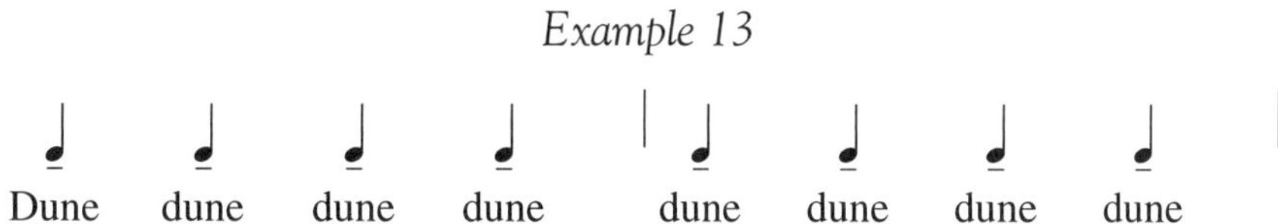

2. Sing piano comping lines along with specific recordings.

Example 14

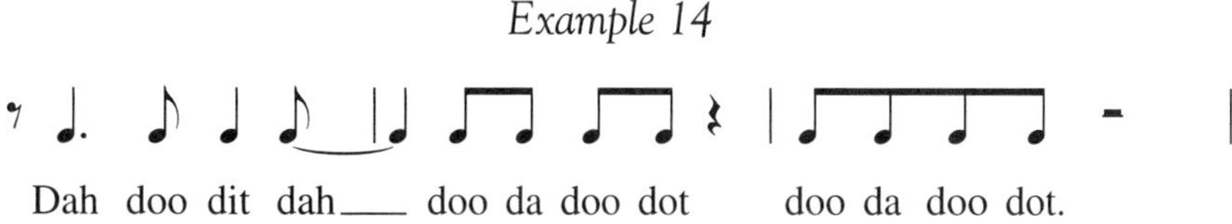

3. Sing guitar rhythms and styles *a la* the Freddie Green style.

4. Sing Drum Fills, set ups, and ride patterns:

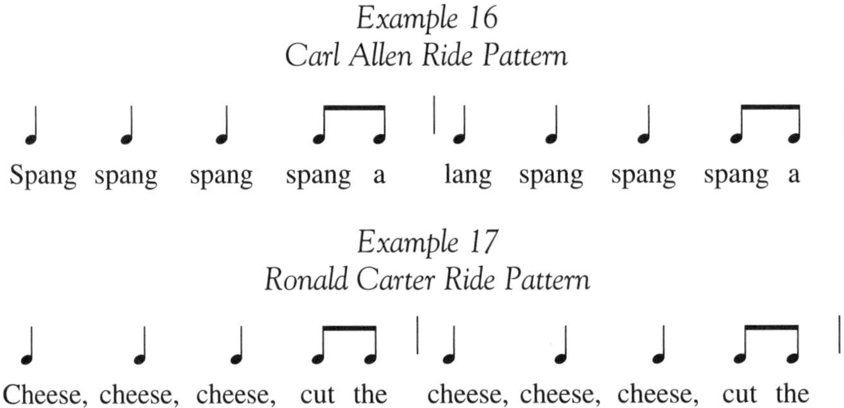

As you develop your program it is very important to create a culture of singing the melody first to every jazz arrangement rehearsed. This is very important as more time is allocated to jazz improvisation. Learning the melody makes adding the logic of chords and progressions to improvisation much easier; it also speeds individual success. As students become much more comfortable with this process they become self learners—something improvisation demands. The eventual goal is to give everyone in the jazz band the tools to improvise and function as creative musicians. The voice is very personal, and is quite effective in leading to confidence and understanding in improvisation.

Internalizing the Jazz Rhythmic Feel: Why Dance?

In the East St. Louis community, there was a constant emphasis on movement to music in church, in the marching bands, and at home. The relationship of music to dance was never talked about, but always assumed by everyone. We spent as much time in the marching band working on the latest dance steps as we did working on music and marching drills. I would get a student in every now and then with whom I had to spend time talking about rhythmic feel and dance. The choirs at all the local churches were a sense of pride and all the music was learned aurally without notation. Students that had been culturally inspired to use the ear to learn complex rhythms, styles and harmony and make it seem so easy.

I had spent my many years in college learning to teach the logic of music and felt very confident. However, this allowed me to take for granted the many aspects of teaching jazz that were already part of that East St. Louis culture. Students would learn a concept, melody, or composition and still remember it many years later. The importance of the ability to hear a phrase and play it back immediately, internalize rhythm and sing complex ideas was always part of every rehearsal.

At Northern, students vocalized and sang jazz articulations and styles, but I realized that without the relationship to movement and dance, something was missing. I began to have students find the pulse of the music we were playing and move as we sang the phrases. I even asked students that were able to dance to invite others in the band to their homes to groove and dance to jazz music, both traditional and nontraditional. I also started to research and study and the development of jazz to find creative ways to make that cultural aspect an integral part of jazz pedagogy at Northern.

The use of dance as a logical approach to teaching jazz styles and articulation became an important part of our program. In the West African cultural tradition, polyrhythms, cross-rhythms, and syncopation are felt and not logically written out. Students had to feel and internalize these complex rhythms.

When I attended the University of Illinois in Champaign, Illinois, I performed in a West African High-Life group with Dr. Oscar Sully. He was from Ghana, West Africa, and taught that the complexity of jazz foundations stems from the ability to feel *duple* versus *triplet* pulses in the beat of jazz. In fact, Dr. Sully never used time signatures in his complex compositions; instead, he used bar lines to group music in duple or triplet feel. We listened to the foundation of the feel set up by the rhythm section and were able to play exactly what he had intended in his compositions. This became a very important aspect of the pedagogical approach to teaching different types of jazz feels I developed.

I met Ed Thigpen, a great jazz drummer, many years ago. He toured locally with the Northern Illinois University Jazz Ensemble and went to Europe with us in 2001. As we worked together, we discovered that our philosophies and approaches to teaching jazz feel were very similar.

Ed published many of his concepts in *Rhythm Bought To Life*, available from Alfred Publishing. In the book he talks about the need to develop the ability to distinguish between duple and triple pulses in music. The primary foundation beat doesn't change; only the micro beats or pulse.

There have been many discussions about knowing rhythms and having good rhythmic feel. A metronome has good tempo, but who wants to dance to a metronome? Body movement or dance is essential in order to have good rhythmic feel. There has to be an internalization of the pulse that leads to a feeling of movement and motion. It seems that that vocalization without understanding and internalizing rhythmic feel does not go far enough. Only when I combined both concepts was I able to give my students a true multi-cultural approach.

TRIPLET PULSE
A traditional swing feel that is divisible by three.

Example 18

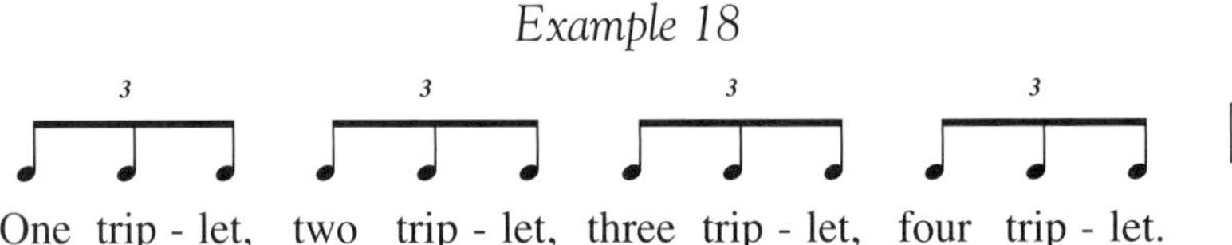

Each quarter note or primary beat has the feel of three equal pulses.

Example 19

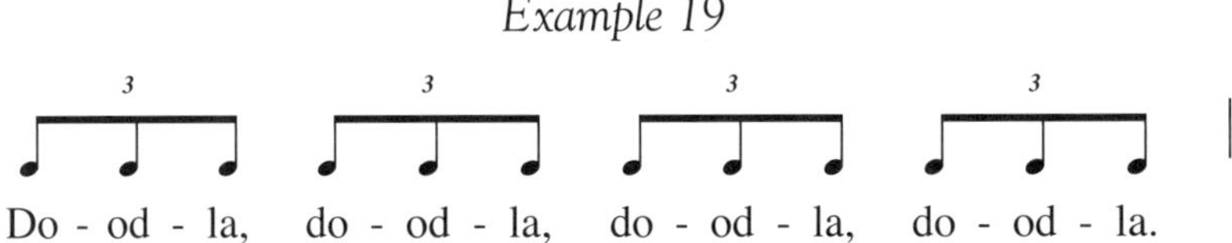

- Add vocal syllables, singing and internalizing the triplet pulse.
- Note that the triplet pulse has an upward feel motion.
- Repeat the example above until students are able to internally feel the triplet pulse.

ADDING MOVEMENT
Move the right heel of the foot up and down so that the heel strikes the floor on every primary beat. Use the *la* (lah) of the beat as preparatory for the primary downbeat of one, two, three, or four.

MOVEMENT EXERCISE
Have every student stand and do the traditional gospel church step while singing *Do od la* while feeling a triplet pulse:

BEAT	MOVEMENT
One	Step to the left
Two	Slide and place the right foot next to the left foot
La of beat two	Lift the right foot
Beat three	Return the right foot to the starting position
La of beat three	Lift the left foot
Beat four	Place the left foot next to right foot

Next start the gospel church step while feeling the anticipation of the triplet using the following pattern:

Example 20

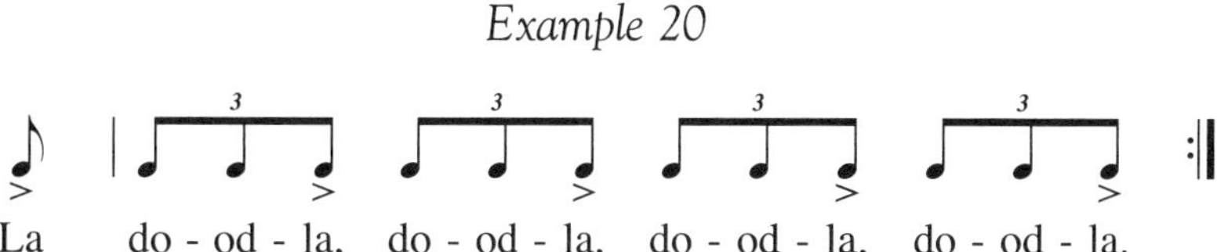

Do this with both hands together, as if you were praying, while moving in a subdivided motion in the same direction as the heels of your feet. Keep your hands in front so that the motion and direction can be seen.

Use the heels for movement instead of the front of the feet. The heel prompts the movement of the pelvic area and the entire body, creating the illusion of dancing.

Sample Exercise
Fly Me To The Moon by Count Basie.

Listen, sing, move, and dance to the recording until the feel is internalized.

Example 21

Duple Pulse:
Traditional rock and Latin styles that are divisible by two.

Example 22

Each quarter note or primary beat has the feeling of two or four equal pulses.

Example 23

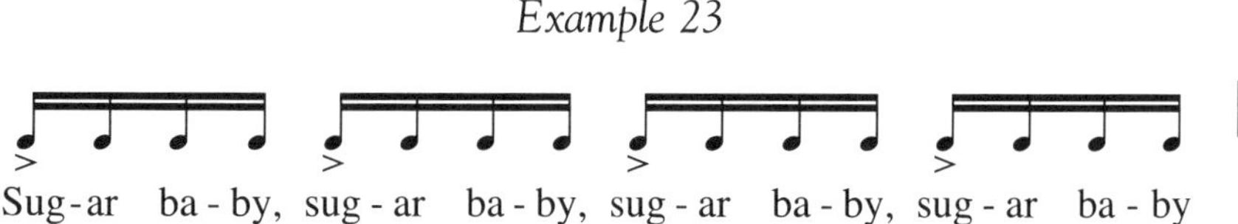

- Add vocal syllables, singing and internalizing the duple pulse.
- Note that the duplet pulse has an downward feel motion with the accent on the first
  (primary) part of the beat.
- Repeat the example above until students are able to internally feel the duple pulse.

ADDING MOVEMENT
Move the heel so that it is up on <u>Ba</u> (the "and" of the beat) and down *Su* (the primary beat).

MOVEMENT EXERCISE
The same as with triplet movement. Prepare to move each foot on the upbeat (the "and") of each beat.

SAMPLE EXERCISE
St. Thomas by Sonny Rollins.

Listen, sing, move, and dance to the recording until the feel is internalized.

Example 24

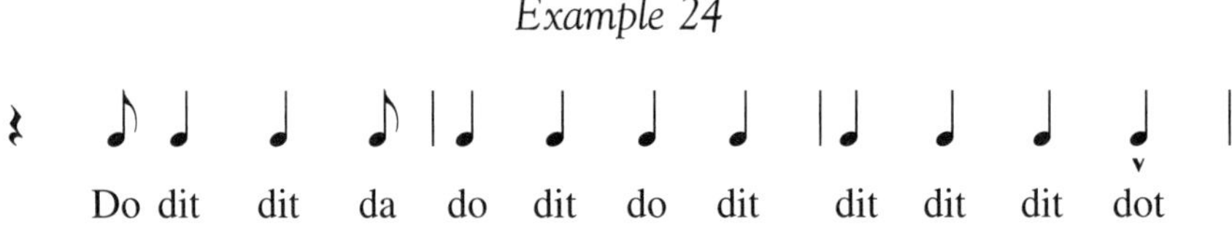

Notes

1 Lewis Porter, *Jazz: A Century of Change* (New York, 1997), 87.
2 Miles Davis with Quincy Troupe, *Miles* (New York, 1989), 38.
3 Eileen Southern, *The Music of Black Americans: A History* (New York, 1983), 18.
4 Duke Ellington, *Music Is My Mistress* (New York, 1980), 471.
5 Eileen Southern, *The Music of Black Americans: A History* (New York, 1983), 6.
6 Wynton Marsalis and Frank Stewart, *Sweet Swing Blues On The Road* (New York, 1994), 137.
7 Eileen Southern, *The Music of Black Americans: A History* (New York, 1983), 363.
8 Wynton Marsalis and Frank Stewart, *Sweet Swing Blues On The Road* (New York, 1994), 16.
9 Eileen Southern, *The Music of Black America's History* (New York, 1983), 363.
10 Wycliffe Gorgon, Lecture presentation, Iowa All-State Conference, May 11, 2007.
11 Duke Ellington, *Music is My Mistress*

CHAPTER 3

Rehearsal Techniques: A Holistic Approach Intregrating Composition, Improvisation, Theory and Cultural Considerations in the Rehearsal

Ronald C. McCurdy

One of the most important aspects of directing any musical ensemble is to maximize rehearsal time and run the rehearsal efficiently. This is especially true with jazz ensembles. In many middle and high schools, the jazz ensemble is not always part of the daily schedule. The jazz ensemble meets either before or after school two or three days a week for a few hours.

If the ensemble and the musical experience are to be successful, the daily rehearsal must be well planned. Often there is not enough room in the curriculum or time in the school day to have classes in jazz improvisation, jazz theory, and jazz history. But for any ensemble to perform with depth, integrity and sophistication, all of these need to be addressed.

The question becomes: How do you incorporate all of these things within an abbreviated rehearsal schedule? How do you ensure that your students will have a sense of the history and knowledge of the evolution of jazz? How do you teach theoretical principles that will help develop aural skills? How do you facilitate the students' development of jazz improvisation? These are questions directors have searched for years to answer. Unfortunately, something ultimately is omitted or left for students to figure out on their on. As we know, some will, but most will not.

The purpose of this chapter is to offer a series of teaching strategies that allow the director to maximize her rehearsal period. These ideas that incorporate theoretical principles, present relevant historical information, and ways of introducing improvisation within the context of the rehearsal.

Some of these ideas may lead you wonder why so much precious rehearsal time spent on techniques rather than rehearsing charts. The answer is: If you apply these techniques, you will save much rehearsal time. Your ensemble will perform on a higher level with integrity and soulfulness. In short, your students will perform with a true understanding of how to correctly play the music we call jazz.

• • •

Most jazz ensemble directors tend to spend the majority of time preparing for concerts by rehearsing only concert material. Other directors who have not had the benefit of jazz pedagogy rehearse in the same fashion as concert or symphonic bands. While there is nothing wrong with rehearsing solely the charts for concert, or applying some concert band rehearsal techniques to the jazz ensemble setting, there are techniques for addressing a broader need that will allow the students to internalize concepts. The idea is to avoid having to re-teach a technique each time you perform a different chart. I have observed an inordinate amount of time spent on ensemble playing at the expense of addressing other matters that are really at the core of jazz. Improvisation!

As you address improvisation, you also must include the improviser's interactions with the rhythm section. This opens the door for a higher level of discussion and interaction between the rhythm section and the soloist. This is the point at which listening becomes crucial. This ventures into a more ambiguous area of music making. Here we are discussing music making at the highest level. It is easy to understand why many directors ignore this aspect of rehearsal. This is an area with which most directors are least comfortable. If the director is a wind player, he may not be as familiar with piano/guitar voicings, comping patterns, bass line construction, or the function of drums in variety of styles.

If a director is devoting the majority of his rehearsal time to ensemble figures while ignoring the rhythm section and soloist, this can only lead to a non-swinging band. This speaks to a larger concern of many music educators, particularly those who teach in the high school ranks, those who may not have had the benefit of jazz education experiences.

To their credit, they are doing the best they can by attending IAJE conferences, summer workshops, master classes, taking their students to live concerts, bringing in guest artists to perform with their ensembles, and a variety of other initiatives to improve their situation. Unfortunately, many still fall short of maximizing rehearsal by focusing only on charts without looking at the *big picture*. It is vital to realize that the notes on the page are only a road map; that music and art is a metaphor for life.

I have long been a subscriber to the phrased coined by the well-known ethnomusicologist Alan Lomax, who stated, "As we live, so do we sing." This is especially true in talking about performing America's classical music. It is very important that students have a balance between music theory and the cultural ramifications of how, where, and who were the innovators of this music. Forward-thinking teachers and students will do the research and find this out on their own. They will read liner notes from CDs, autobiographies of their favorite artists, and talk to jazz masters when the opportunities arise. Unfortunately, most will not, and rehearsal will be a time of simply trying to read what is on the page without having done the "real" homework.

• • •

In this chapter I want to share some of the techniques I have used over the years that helped develop ensembles that performed with passion and an understanding of how to communicate with each other and an audience.

My first two university teaching positions were at schools that did not have jazz majors. Many of my students were majoring in engineering, physics, political science, and other areas outside of music. Because many of the students in my ensembles were not music majors, I had to find ways to condense all material I injected jazz improvisation, jazz history, and jazz keyboard classes into weekly rehearsals. In a short period of time, these ensembles developed the ability to perform with a strong sense of jazz heritage and were able to demonstrate a broad knowledge of theoretical principles ranging from variations of blues and rhythm progressions, the Coltrane Matrix, and other harmonic and rhythmic concepts. The majority of these concepts were introduced within the context of the ensemble rehearsal. Although these techniques were applied at the college level, they are equally effective at any level. I have had opportunities to implement some of these techniques at the middle school and high school levels.

I would be remiss if I did not mention that many of the ideas that I employed were concepts learned while studying with my mentor and Distinguished Professor of Music, David Baker from Indiana University. I am one of thousands that have been touched, inspired by the teachings of Professor Baker.

Beginning the Rehearsal

I have discovered that how the rehearsal starts sets the tone for how much will be accomplished during rehearsal. Students today are not exposed to jazz music the way students were years ago. Jazz is not played on radio or television as much as other popular music. Therefore, the only real exposure students receive is in school. (Of course, there are exceptions. There are some parents and other relatives who value this music enough to play it in the home, thus giving the student an edge.) This exposure occurs while attempting to play charts without having heard professional examples of the music. To facilitate students' awareness and understanding of music at the most basic level, I like to start rehearsal by playing one track from a CD.

Rehearsal time is precious, so I suggest playing only one track. When finished, ask a series of open-ended questions, e.g., Describe the tone of the solo alto player. Was there vibrato? Did you hear the drummer play the bass drum on all four beats? What register was the solo trumpet player using the most? The intent is to ask questions that will prompt students to listen analytically. As their listening skills become more astute, begin asking more specific questions, e.g., In the third course of Bird's solo on the blues, what chord substitutions were used?

In some situations, I have used a listening sheet for students to complete. This is accompanied with a listening assignment comprised of a series of artists. Some students will require a more selective artist introduction. For example, Miles Davis' *Bitches Brew* is probably not a good choice for an introduction to jazz for developing students. The listening assignment can be a take-home exercise. This allows students to listen to examples repeatedly in the privacy of their homes. The point is to develop listening skills. There is a direct correlation between playing well and consistent listening habits. See the listening sheet below as a model for how to listen and what to listen.

The Listening Guide Sheet

This guide sheet is designed to aid the development of analytical, rather than passive listening skills. The intent is to isolate various aspects of the performance so that the student will develop an understanding for the subtle and not-so-subtle nuances of jazz performance.

Artist: ______________________________

Record label: __________________________

Leader: ______________________________

Side players: __________________________

Recording date: ________________________

Overall style: __________________________

Configuration of the Ensemble ______________
(big band, combo, vocal, strings, etc.)

PIANO: Describe the comping style of the pianist/guitarist.

____

Are the harmonies quartal, tertian, or a combination of

the two?

____

Are the roots of chords present at all times in the piano voicings?

____

How is the sustaining pedal used?

____

When there is both piano and guitar in the same ensemble, how do they work together?

____

How does the left hand interact with the right during the piano soloist?

____

Does the piano comp behind the guitar soloist?

____

If a standard tune, does the rhythm section re-harmonize the melody or use chord substitutions?

____

If so, where and how?

____

DRUMS: Describe the style of the drummer.

____

Is she primarily a time-keeper, or is there much rhythmic interplay?

____

Is the bass drum played on all four beats, or does she use the bass drum to punctuate accents?

____

How is the high hat used?

____

What role does the drum assume during horn, vocal, bass or piano solos pianos?

____

Is there additional percussion?

____

If so, what and how is it used?

BASS: Describe the style of the bass.

____

If the style is "straight ahead," are the bass lines legato, or more staccato?

____

In what register is the bass player during the tutti sections verses the solo sections?

____

FRONT LINE: What is the front line configuration?

____

Do the horns play in unison or harmony?

____

Which plays the melody? The harmony?

____

What is the usual order of solos?

____

Who plays last?

____

Is there trading of fours, eights, sixteens, or complete choruses?

____

Describe the make-up of the solo.

____

In what register did he play?

____

Were there double time ideas?

____

Was the solo more vertical, (arpeggios) or more linear?

____

Show and Tell: In-Class Solo Transcriptions

Show and Tell is best done at least twice during the course of the semester. It is a venue for students to show what they have done individually. Part of the magic of becoming an accomplished jazz musician happens when students discover nuggets of information on their own.

One of the most important tasks for any developing student is transcribing improvised solos by the masters and then performing the solo with the recording in class. Notating and playing everything artist played verbatim helps the student glean the vocabulary employed by the artist, allowing the student to see and hear how the soloist constructed his solo and how he interacted with the ensemble.

This builds a better understanding of the conversational aspect of improvisation, and is one of the most important tasks any developing jazz student can embrace. Not all students, however, will do this.

But there will be a few students who will surprise with the accuracy and complexity of their transcriptions. It is common for the positive benefits of this task to become infectious among students. With each show and tell exercise, transcriptions will improve.

How the Process Works

1. If a student is a novice, assist the student in selecting a transcription subject. Make sure that the transcription is within the student's technical ability. Recommended first transcriptions are early solos by Miles Davis, Paul Desmond, Chet Baker, and Dexter Gordon. These artists are generally more accessible to students who are still developing transcribing skills.

2. Blues, modal progressions (e.g., *So What* by Miles Davis) or rhythm changes are a good place to start. This helps students see how melody relates to harmony.

3. As my colleague, John Clayton suggests, have the student think in terms of *becoming* the selected artist, pretending to be Miles Davis, Clifford Brown, or Max Roach, for example. By doing so, they begin to embrace the articulations, inflections, and nuances of the chosen artist, as well as his melodic and harmonic tendencies. The goal is for students to become a composite of the selected artist, with the intent of discovering their own unique voice.

4. The last and perhaps least important component of this exercise is to notate what has been transcribed. This should not be attempted until the solo of choice can be sun verbatim. Include chord symbols. Make a copy of the transcription available to all students in the class.

5. Instruct students to enclose common chord progressions in parentheses, e.g.:

   ii–V^{7}–I
   iii–vi–ii–V^{7}–I
   I–vi–ii–V^{7}–I

   This encourages students to look for universals in tunes, allowing them to transfer what they've learned as they encounter new tunes.

6. Try learning the transcription in real time. Avoid software, such as Amazing Slower-Downer, that slow down the transcription. It is best to learn the solo in context. Avoid transcription books as well, unless they are used as a source for etudes. Books such as *Omni Book* are often good only for the person who wrote the book, as she is the one who did the work. A transcribed solo read from a book is often forgotten within minutes. Transcribe the solo yourself and the vocabulary will be yours for life!

The Benefits

Have each student in the ensemble transcribe eight to ten artists a year. (Motivated students will do more). The benefits and dividends will be evident in a short amount of time. Here are some benefits of transcription observed during my work with ensembles over the years:

1. A heightened sense of *time*.
2. Better harmonic and rhythmic vocabularies.
3. Improved technique.
4. Improved quality of improvised solos throughout the band.
5. The band will start to really swing!

Bebop Heads as Jazz Etudes

This is a class exercise I learned from David Baker: Take a bebop head (melody) and use it as a jazz etude. This teaches style and develops a true ensemble sound. Stress that many bebop tunes were born out of the composer's improvisation. Therefore, these "heads," or melodies, should be played in an improvisatory style.

In general, accent the first, highest, and last note of a phrase; ghost (play much more softly) the lowest note in the phrase. Play legato.

Example 1
Bebop line interpretation

Here is a short list of tunes that are work well with this exercise:

Donna Lee	*Anthropology*	*Sippin' at Bells*
Groovin' High	*Good Bait*	*Hot House*
Woodyn' and You	*Yard Bird Suite*	*Confirmation*
Scrapple from the Apple		

Have the ensemble learn one tune per week, memorizing the heads and doing the following as a class:

1. Play heads in unison, including bass, drums, and guitar. Repeat with the rhythm section comping.

   Benefits: Improved rhythmic accuracy.

   Improved reading of melodic lines for guitar and bass

   Drummers begin thinking in terms of melody.

   Guitar and bass are forced to move beyond the role of comping, functioning as a horn playing by playing the line.

2. Play only odd measures, and then play only even measures.

Example 2a
Hot House *(odd measures)*

Example 2b
Hot House *(even measures)*

Benefits: Players learn to feel silence, thus improving their concept for time.

3. Play the melodic pattern whenever the similar chord progression appears (e.g., play the first two measures of *Hot House*. Note that the first pattern occurs over Gm^{f5}–C^{7f9}. Each time the minor ii–V^{7} progression occurs, the ensemble plays (transposes) that pattern.

Example 3
Hot House *(chord progressions)*

Benefits: Students learn jazz vocabulary in a variety of keys.

4. Play the heads in a variety of keys.

   Benefits: The ensemble will become comfortable in a variety of keys.

5. Play the heads in a variety of meters (e.g., 3/4, 5/4, 7/4, etc.).

   Benefits: Students begin to get a feel for different meters and are able to internalize the tunes in a completely different manner.

6. Play the heads in a variety of styles (e.g., bossa nova, samba, rock, funk, hip-hop, waltz, etc.).

   Benefits: Students are able to discern a variety of styles and eighth note treament in each style.

7. Superimpose vocabulary from one head over another head (i.e., play measures three and four of *Groovin' High*, which happens over a ii–V7 progression. Play the same vocabulary over *Confirmation* wherever the ii–V7 progression occurs.

Example 4

Grovin' Hard *played over the bridge of* Confirmation

Benefits: Students will internalize vocabulary from other bebop heads.

Instant Arrangements

Guide Tones

Having players engage in instant arranging will help them to further internalize tunes. Begin with the tune *Hot House*. Have students play guide tones (the seventh of the ii chord—the tonic note—resolving down by half step to the third of the V^7 chord—the leading tone) throughout the tune whenever ii–V^7–I or ii^{f5}–V^7–I progressions occur.

For major chords, resolve the sixth scale degree down by whole step to the fifth of the major chord.

Example 5
Guide tones for Hot House

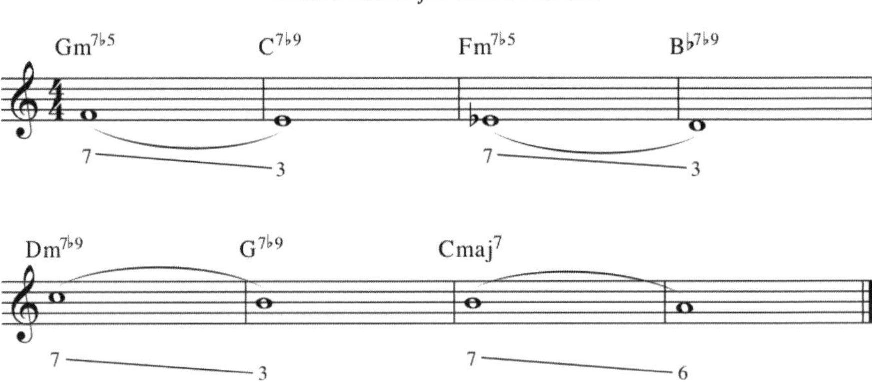

This concept is applicable to any ii–V^7–I progression. The bridges of *Confirmation* and *Cherokee* are perfect examples of what is possible with this guide tone concept.

Example 6

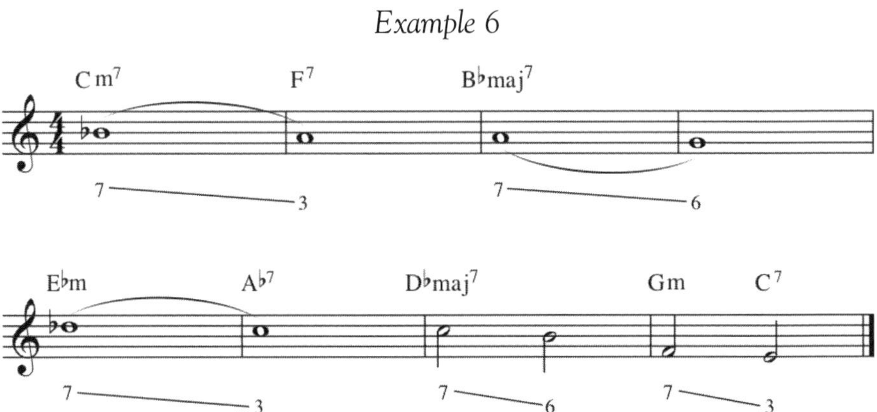

The instant arranging concept allows for rhythm alteration and/or pitch embellishment to make the lines more interesting.

Example 7
Bridge to Cherokee *with embellished guide tones*

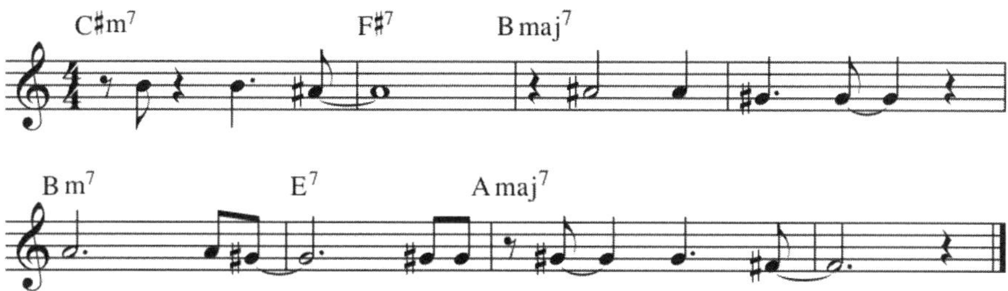

Voicing the Horns
Simple four and five note voicings allow the ensemble to listen more analytically. Assign voicings and rhythms for trumpets while trombones play guide tones and saxophones play the melody in unison or octaves.

Example 8
Groovin' High *head arrangement*

3 Am9 D7 E♭maj7

6 Gm7 C7♭9

9 F7 Fm7

This is not the most creative arrangement, but it allows students to get an idea what kind of thinking goes into crafting an arrangement. Parts may be switched so that trombones play the chords while trumpets play the melody and saxophones play guide tones. As the ensemble plays more arrangements, eventually players will begin to realize how their particular part fits into the total scheme of the arrangement. They will be able to listen, realizing that they have the melody or countermelody, or that they are playing pads (chords). Later they will begin to understand that they are playing the third, seventh, or ninth of a chord. This kind of understanding enables the band to function at a higher intellectual and artistic level.

Jazz Performance and Historical Relevance

Most directors at almost all levels neglect the historical relevance of jazz performance. They spend an inordinate amount of time working on getting the ensemble to play well together or have students spend many hours in the practice room working out patterns; but from where do these patterns, licks, growls, slurs, bends, and smears come?

My good friend and colleague, Justin DiCiccio, always says, "Music is about emotions and feelings." He is absolutely correct! In order to emote and feel there must be some imagery or something to draw from. This is why the knowledge of history and culture becomes crucial to the informed musician. Performing a composition by Ellington and not having a sense of Ellington's life and its historical context is tantamount to an opera singer performing Wagner's *Der Ring des Nibelugen* without any knowledge of the social and political ramifications of the work. In both cases the performer is simply playing or singing notes on the page without any regard to social, political and cultural ramifications. This can only lead to a lack-luster performance. Directors assume that students will somehow get this information on their own, or they fail to see the importance of students having this information while performing.

Imagine mimicking someone speaking a foreign language without knowing the meaning of any of the words. You might sound convincing for a while, but at some point your performance will lose some of its authenticity. As mentioned, most of today's students were not born when many of our jazz masters were in their prime. They have only audio and some video recordings on which to rely. Most students have no idea what was happening in the world historically during certain periods in jazz history. They may know names of some of the jazz masters, but often there is a disconnection between students and the historical and cultural context of the music they perform.

I return to the phrase coined by Alan Lomax: "As we live, so do we sing." This is very true as it relates to the development and evolution of jazz.

I am reminded of a conversation I had with Dr. Billy Taylor in 2000 during the term of my IAJE presidency. Those who know Dr. Taylor know he is always willing to share stories about jazz greats. The night of my conversation with him was no exception. He told a story about the great Art Tatum, who he served as a protégé. On one occasion, an English pianist approached them at Ivy Anderson's after-hours club in Los Angeles. He expressed to Art how much he admired his playing and told of how he had transcribed his piano solo in *Massenet`s Elegie* (one of the most virtuosic performances Art Tatum ever recorded). The man asked Art if he could play this transcription for him. Art reluctantly agreed. About two minutes into the performance Art got up and went over to the bar to order a drink, basically ignoring the efforts of the young man's performance. Puzzled, Dr. Taylor asked Art why he chose to ignore what the young man was doing, given the fact that the performance was technically masterful. "Didn't you hear that he was playing your solo verbatim?" Art's response was, "Yes, he played all the notes; but he doesn't know *why* I played those notes!"

This story forced me to contemplate the content we as jazz educators disseminate to those we teach. The question of why Art Tatum and so many other jazz innovators played and sang the way they did should be a topic of discussion in the classroom. We are missing a very important link in the chain when we fail to explain the social, economic, religious, political, cultural, and technological variables that influenced how jazz was performed, as well as the impact on human life, which also influenced the music. We should not focus solely on the technical aspects of performance while ignoring the humanity of the music.

To illustrate, it is very difficult to discuss the music of the Mississippi Delta without discussing the great migration of African Americans in 1915, Jim Crow, and the institution of sharecropping; it is nearly impossible to discuss the Cotton Club years of Duke Ellington (circa 1927–31) without mentioning the stock market crash of 1929. All of these variables had an impact on both performers and listeners.

The underlying message I received from Dr. Taylor`s story is the importance of moving beyond the written page. Yes, it is important to continue to teach theoretical principles, instill good practice habits within our students, and insist on high-quality performances. But what about the human beings who listen to and perform this music? As performers, are we only playing for ourselves? Or should we be concerned with ways to better connect with our audiences?

There is a reason *why* Billy Holiday`s *Strange Fruit* touched so many people. There is a reason *why My One and Only Love*, by Johnny Hartman and John Coltrane, is so emotionally stirring. The question is: Why? Was it simply the technical prowess of the artist (or the instrumental or vocal tone quality) that intrigued you? Perhaps. Or was there some intangible human quality that is difficult to explain that captured your attention?

This is the issue: the Why! So I suggest we pursue two things: a better understanding of the historical events that helped to shape the music, and an investigation into our souls as artists and educators, asking ourselves if we are doing all that we can to connect our students to the historical and cultural ramifications of the music.

A few years ago, I was performing one of the Ellington Suites with my college jazz band. We had finally gotten all of the notes, dynamics, tempos, inflections, and nuances together, but for some reason, the band and the music was not swinging. The "time," for the most part, was good, but something still was not right! I could not identify those intangible ingredients that prevented the band from swinging.

I decided to play for the class a DVD titled *On the Road with Ellington*. This particular DVD showed Duke Ellington performing and conducting his band. It also had many behind the scene moments will Billy Strayhorn, Jimmy Hamilton, Johnny Hodges, and many other sidemen interacting with Ellington. It showed him in Harlem at his apartment, and featured many other candid moments of Duke just being Duke. In short, it showed the human side of Duke. Before showing the DVD, I talked to my class about the Harlem Renaissance. I told them about W. E. B. Du Bois, Langston Hughes, Richard Wright, Zora Neal Hurston, and many other intellectuals during that time. I also mentioned to them about the dynamics of the Cotton Club and what was occurring in the Savoy Ballroom. I talkd about some of the other prominent bandleaders during that time. Then we watched the DVD.

I cannot completely explain what happened, but the next time we played *Rockin' in Rhythm*, my band was completely transformed. They got it! All of a sudden they were able to see and hear examples of the role of music in society during that period in history. They finally got the correlation between dancing and music! This time out from rehearsing took about twenty-five minutes, but it proved to be the best twenty-five minutes I could have spent. From that moment on we never had to revisit those concepts again. They were able to transfer that information to every subsequent chart we played in that style.

Here is an outline for a discussion of the historical context for *One O'clock Jump* by the Count Basie Orchestra. It can serve as a jumping off point as you develop your own.

Chart: *One O'clock Jump*

Composer: William "Count" Basie

Biographical information on the Composer

When and where was he born?

When did he pass away?

What was his instrument?

How did William Basie become the Count?

Who were some of the major side players from the Basie Band from 1941–46?

Who were some of the principle arrangers for the Basie Band?

What were some of Basie's more notable compositions?

Historical Information about Kansas City:

Who was Mayor Pendergast?

What was Prohibition?

What was the primary source of commerce in Kansas City during Prohibition?

What are Territorial Bands? Who were some of the major Territorial Band Leaders?

World Issues and Cultural Matters

What are the dates of WWII? Who were the primary countries involved?

What was Sharecropping?

What were Jim Crow Laws?

What was the primary mode of transportation regionally and nationally?

The concept of integrating history into the context of rehearsal can certainly be expanded. You can integrate this material into your rehearsals regardless of the level at which you teach. I have found that this is even more effective when you are able to communicate with your colleagues in other academic disciplines. For example, if students are studying American literature of the 1920s, more than likely students will read F. Scott Fitzgerald's *The Great Gasby*. A discussion in History class about women's suffrage, prohibition, and a host of other notable historical events can tie into jazz studies. This is a cooperative teaching approach that provides an opportunity for all academic subjects to relate to one another. This approach will do wonders to help students connect the historical and artistic dots. This is but one example of what is possible when teachers and students engage in a more holistic approach to teaching and learning.

Conclusions

The jazz ensemble director is faced with a multitude of challenges, particularly those who teach in the high school ranks where they are asked to serve as the director of bands. Usually this role includes directing marching and concert bands, helping students prepare for solo and ensemble competitions, raising funds, and a host of other tasks. Truly successful teachers manage their time to allow for effective teaching and learning. It takes time and planning to condense and synthesize material in such a way that students begin to get the connection between performing jazz and the historical context of the players and music.

The ideas presented here are not rocket science. They are illustrations of what might be done if separate classes were held in each of these areas. Unfortunately, most schools do not have the luxury of having an expanded curriculum in jazz studies. The job becomes getting information to students in the context of rehearsal. In many ways, this is truly the ideal time for teaching and learning new concepts. What better way than to learn a new concept and then immediately apply it within the context of the rehearsal?

Inspiring students is a vital part of what we do as teachers. Jamey Aebersold shared a story with me years ago that illustrates this.

Ayoung insurance agent had been on the job for over six months and had not sold a single life insurance policy. He was called into his boss' office to discuss the problem. The young salesman lamented about how he had done his prospecting and how he had spoken to well over a hundred potential clients, to no avail. He ended his rant by saying: "You can lead a horse to the water, but you can't make 'em drink."

The seasoned boss listened patiently until the young neophyte was finished. Finally, he told the young man: "Your job is not to make them drink; your job is to make them thirsty!"

In short, this is our job as educators. Our job is to make students thirsty for knowledge. I have discovered students tend to retain information if they understand the concepts and have an opportunity to immediately apply those concepts as opposed to learning by rote. When students are presented with a more holistic approach to teaching and learning they are more inclined to engage in self-discovery. When that occurs, we have exceeded our job as informative and inspirational educators.

CHAPTER 4

Rhythm Section: The Band Within the Band

Reginald Thomas

The rhythm section of the jazz band is one of the most unique sections in any ensemble setting. This is a group that must play together, as any unit must, but while performing separate functions. Each of the instruments within the section provides similar functions, but often in dissimilar ways. This is the only section of the jazz band that plays without rest for almost the entire chart. And it is the only section that improvises throughout. It is a section that can play melody and accompaniment, harmony and rhythm—*it is essentially a band unto itself within the big band.*

When working with a saxophone section, for example, it is important to be familiar with the peculiarities of the instrument to help students sound as one. Directors must be familiar with embouchure, breath support, fingering, etc., to get all players functioning as a unit. With the rhythm section, however, the techniques for playing each instrument are different, yet the players must still function as one. So, while the techniques required to play each instrument in the rhythm section are important, it is more important to focus on the role and functions of the rhythm section as a whole and separately.

Role Of The Rhythm Section

The basic role of the rhythm section within the jazz ensemble is to create an accompaniment to the melody that is being created. This is true when accompanying a soloist or playing a big band chart and must be the primary concern of each member of the section. While improvisation is integral to the music, the improvised solo is only a part of a larger picture. A bass player who can play a great solo but cannot perform the role of accompanist in the ensemble is of little use to the band. A drum fill can display all of the technical mastery in the world, but that is useless if a drummer cannot put four quarter notes in a row. Accompaniment must be in the mindset of the rhythm section player if the section is to have any musical success within the ensemble.

In order to create an appropriate accompaniment, awareness of style is crucial. For the purposes of this chapter, swing style will be the focus. The principles discussed are applicable to other styles as well; however, since swing is not often heard by students today, it is more difficult to master. Still, if students can achieve an understanding of swing music, with its more complex subdivisions and rhythms, it becomes much easier to hear the same principles applied in other music. In this chapter we will discuss these principles, not by instrument, but rather by function.

Functions of the Rhythm Section

There are several functions rhythm section players need to know in order to accomplish the role of accompaniment; yet, there are also many general myths about rhythm section *comping* that exist and make the task even more daunting. Let us try to dispel some of those myths:

It is the rhythm section's job to keep time for the band.
False. Though the rhythm section serves a time-keeping function, *it is everyone's responsibility to keep time.*

The guitar and piano create the harmonies for the soloist.
False. The soloist must know the harmonies in order to create a melody. *It is extremely difficult to comp for a solo that doesn't make sense.*

The pianist and guitarist should never play at the same time.
False. If the pianist and guitarist understand their respective functions, they can coexist very well.

The pianist and/or guitarist should always be comping.
False. Orchestration concepts will help the students determine when to play.

A good rhythm section can make the ensemble swing.
False. Just as it is everyone's responsibility to keep time, it is everyone's responsibility to swing.

A bad rhythm section can ruin an ensemble's swing feel.
True.

A good rhythm section can make the ensemble's job easier.
True!

Time/Feel

The most important function of the rhythm section is establishing a good time/feel. Again, this does not mean that the rhythm section is responsible for keeping time for the group, but the rhythm section does play constantly throughout the chart and the time/feel is apparent at all times. The section does provide the rhythmic backing for the ensemble, and if that backing doesn't feel good, then nothing feels good. The time/feel is determined by two elements: the *pulse* and the *subdivision* of that pulse. Keep in mind this simple formula: *pulse* ÷ *subdivision* = *time/feel.* Renowned drummer Ed Thigpin refers to these elements as *pulse* and *mini-pulses*. Jazz guitarist James Chirillo has phrased it this way: "Meter is the organization of the quarter note pulse; rhythm is what occurs between those pulses."

It is clear from these explanations that the first order of business is to establish a good quarter-note pulse. In order to do this, the time must first be established in the body—*playing time is physical.* Each student needs to physically display the time/feel in his body by keeping a consistent quarter-note pulse with the heel. Externalizing the subdivision (through singing;—see Example 1) will help each player lock that pulse with the rest section to create a quarter note that does not waiver. Each instrument then contributes to the quarter note pulse in its own unique way.

Example 1

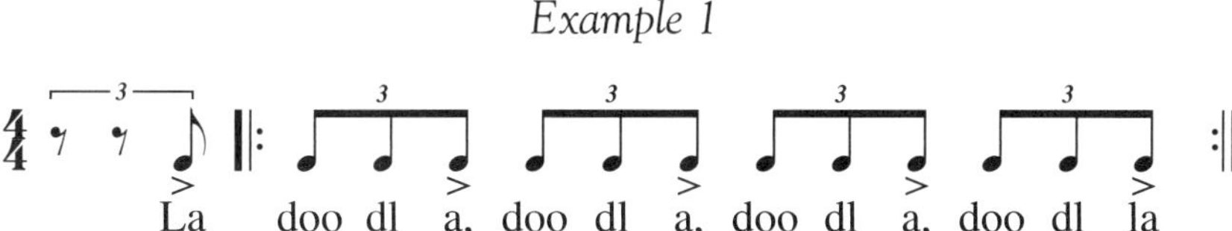

The guitar is the most important instrument in creating a good quarter-note pulse. This is simply because the attack is very crisp and precise. The desirable sound is made from the percussive sound of the stroke—the *chunk*. The sound of that chunk is actually more important than the sound of the chord. To establish the quarter note, all strokes are down; the upstroke (or *upchuck*) will disrupt the consistency of the pulse. *Each down stroke is equally important*. The emphasis on beats 2 and 4 will be created by the drummer's hi-hat; it is not necessary for the guitar to do this. A downstroke that is too slow will create a "spraying" effect, almost as though the chords are strummed. *It is important to remember that the sound must be percussive*. Trying to play all of the strings at once will create a very quick downstroke, thus giving a strong attack to the sound.

The next part of this process depends on the ability to mute the strings. The more the strings are muted, the better the percussive effect. However, the guitar is still providing a harmonic purpose; somehow, the guitar should still create the sound of the chord progression. By playing the voice leading, or third or seventh of the chords, the guitar will still display harmonic movement. The challenge in muting requires that the third or seventh sound on one string (generally on the fourth string; see Example 2), while the other strings are muted.

Example 2

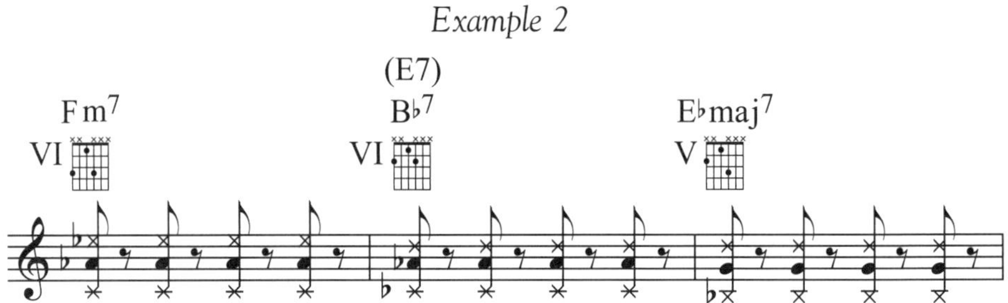

The roman numeral represents the fret; an x indicates a muted not or string.

This is not a long ring (the word *chunk* most accurately describes the length), but that string must vibrate while the others do not. It is possible to play an entire progression on one string while muting all others, even without a full chord shape in the hand. However, it is still important for students to learn the chord shapes for those occasions that warrant hearing the entire chord. The best example is Freddie Green of the Count Basie Orchestra. Encourage students to listen to recordings to emulate his sound.

The bass is next in importance in establishing a pulse. The bass is just as important for creating a good time/feel, but the envelope of the bass sound is different than that of the guitar. The word *doom* best reflects the sound of the bassist's quarter note. This sound reflects a strong attack that decays very quickly. Unlike the guitarist's quarter-note pulse, the bassist's pulse *does* ring; the length of each note most often lasts through to the beginning of the following note. This creates a legato feel with constant motion. This is why it is referred to as a *walking bass line*. While the guitarist is keeping one note throughout the duration of each chord sound, the bassist is changing notes to lead from one chord to the next.

Example 3

Harmonically, the bass is the most important instrument in the entire ensemble because it plays the fundamental pitch on which all chords are based and to which all instruments tune. If the bass is out of tune, so is the band; if the bass changes the fundamental pitch, then the chord is changed. It is important, therefore, the bassist not be in denial of his job—playing roots and fifths in the lower register the majority of the time *is his job*. Through diatonic (and sometimes chromatic) motion, the bass also helps lead from one chord to the next. This walking line, coupled with the third or seventh supplied by the guitar, creates the harmonic framework for the music.

The drummer in the jazz ensemble might be referred to as the cymbalist, in that most of the work in regard to time/feel is done on the cymbals. The *tang* of the ride cymbal is very similar to the *doom* of the bass. The attack is hard and bright, and the sound rings through to the beginning of the next attack. The drummer also contributes to the feel by creating the natural backbeat that is felt in jazz music on the hi-hat cymbal. The hi-hat should create a *chomp* sound that is crisp and full. This is accomplished more easily if the bottom hi-hat is angled slightly. The drummer may also *feather* the bass drum on all downbeats as well to help create a larger bass sound. This technique requires that the bass drum be *felt* as part of the bassist's sound, not heard individually. Think of the bass drum as an amplifier for the acoustic bass.

If the guitarist, bassist, and drummer can consistently lock the feel of their respective quarter notes, the rhythm section is well on its way to creating a good *pocket*. Still, the feel of the music must be created by the subdivision; a quarter note devoid of the subdivision will not groove.

In swing tradition, the quarter note is divided into eighth note triplets. This is the mini-pulse to which Ed Thigpin refers. This triplet subdivision allows each of the section members to consistently put the quarter note in the same place and gives the music its forward momentum and drive. While the bassist, guitarist, and drummer are all laying down the quarter-note foundation, the drums can also give the triplet subdivision by playing upbeats on the ride cymbal (most often on the second half of beats 2 and 4; see Example 4)—"spang, spang-a-lang," or "cheese, cut the cheese" on the hi-hat.

Example 4

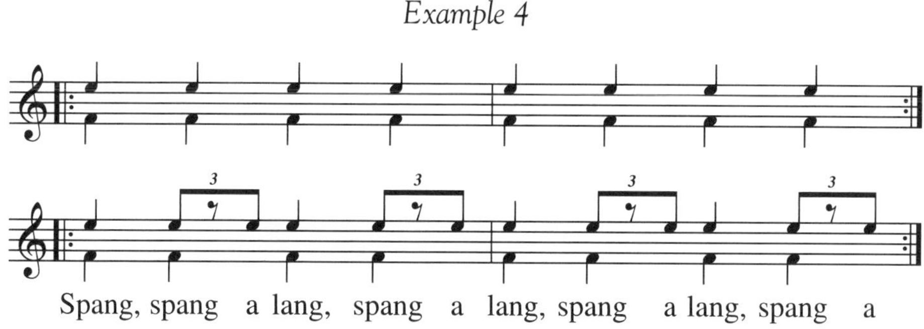

It is crucial that the drummer hears this as triplets, not sixteenths (a common misconception is a dotted eighth followed by a sixteenth). More advanced drummers learn to feather parts of the triplet with the left hand on the snare when developing comping patterns and fills.

The pianist's role in creating the time/feel differs in that she is not establishing the quarter-note pulse, as her companions are—at least not in most music today. However, the pianist is vital in helping establish the triplet subdivision. The sound of this subdivision can be vocalized by singing *doodl-a, doodl-a, doodl-a, doodl-a,* with the emphasis on *la.* This is where accents naturally occur in swing music. If the pianist, then, places chords on the third beat of the triplet, or the "la" syllable, the triplet feel is easily created and makes the pulse feel good. Though this rhythmic placement of the chord can happen on the *and* (or *la*) of any beat, it is the placement on the second half of beats 2 and 4 that gives the feel of forward momentum. It is important for the student to remember to anticipate the upcoming chord to achieve this effect—chords written on the downbeat *of 1* are placed on the second half of the previous beat 4; chords on the downbeat of 3 are placed on the second half of beat 2 (see Example 5). This rhythmic anticipation also helps the other section players to better feel the pulse.

Example 5

Harmonic Function

The rhythm section's harmonic function also contributes to the idea of a band within the band. By laying down a harmonic foundation, the rhythm section creates the sound of the music's form and the arrangement's framework. This foundation begins with the bass. The bassist supplies the fundamental pitch on top of which everything else in the band is built. It is worth saying again that if the *bass* is out of tune, the *band* is out of tune; if the bass changes the root of the chord, then the chord changes. It is critical for the bassist to understand and accept this role. Often students want to become so creative and avoid playing roots in order to be "hip," but a bassist in denial of her role is not helping the band. This is not to say that the bassist should play only the root of the chord, but rather that this is her *most important harmonic function.*

The next step is to lead to each upcoming chord through a walking motion. This is done by using diatonic motion, arpeggios, passing and leading tones—any type of motion that can lead to the next chord in the progression (see Example 6). Bassist Steve Kirby describes it as the bassist leading everyone into each room in a harmonic house; the room represents the chord, while the house represents the form.

Example 6

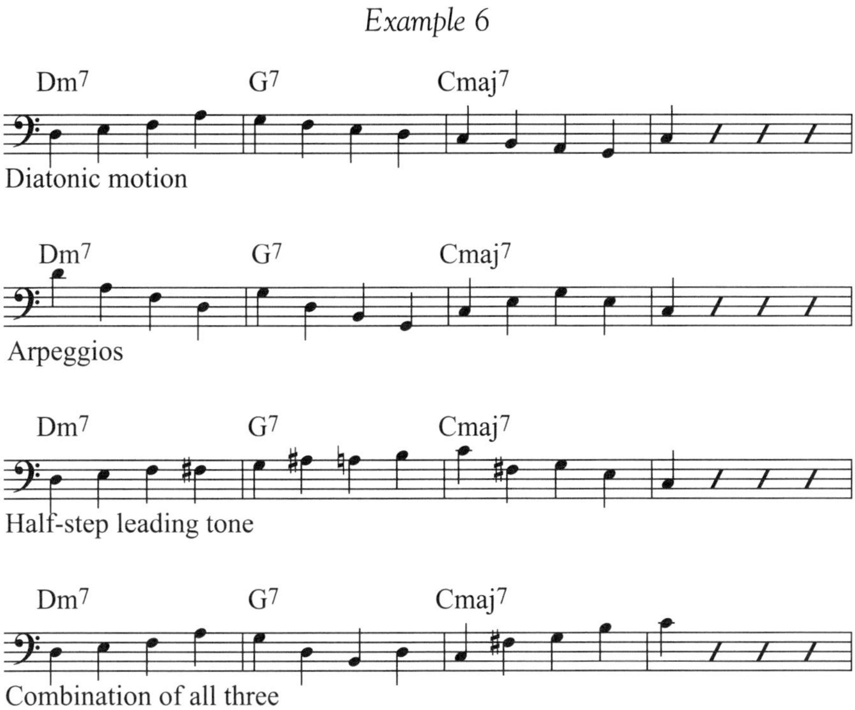

If the bassist leads to each chord, the piano and guitar help establish the sound (or quality) of each chord. To establish the quality, the sound of the third and seventh must be present. In this way, the guitar chunking can be seen as the tenor voice to the bass as discussed earlier in the chapter. The challenge for pianists is to create voicings that display the quality of the chords and are appropriate to the sound and style of the music. For example, triads do show chord quality but are *not the most appropriate* sounds in most jazz music. Though voicing concerns can differ slightly for different styles, here are some voicing tips that will get pianists in the right ballpark:

Start with the third and seventh in the left hand.

It is not necessary to play the root since the bass supplies the foundation. This simple two-note voicing in the left hand creates the sound of the chord;

Example 7

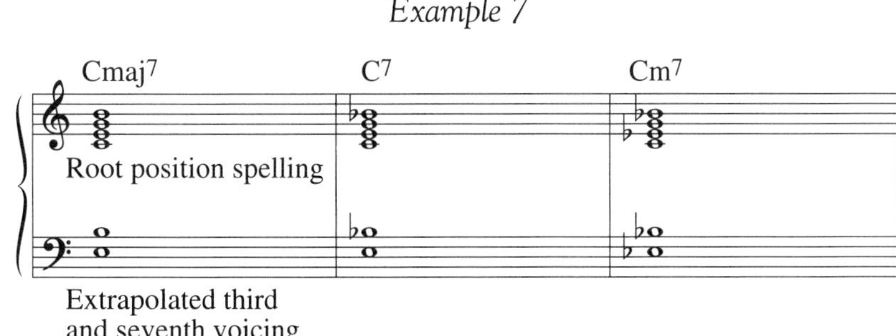

Let the voices lead.

When chords move by large intervals (a third or larger), the third of the chord resolves to the seventh of the next, and vice versa. When chords move by step, the third moves to the third and the seventh moves to the seventh.

Example 8

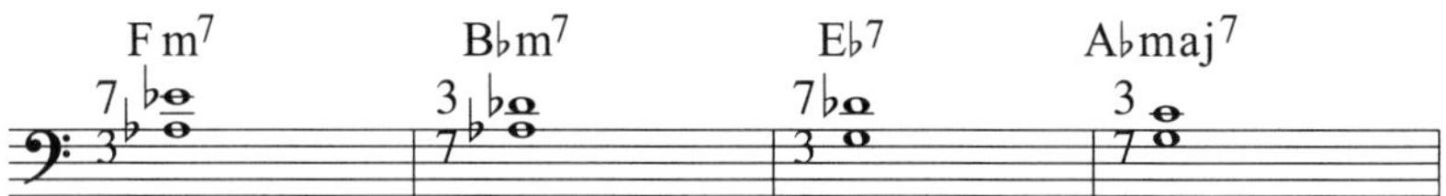

Add the chord tone above the highest note in the two-note voicing to create a three-note chord voicing.

This is easy to see if the next tone is added with the right hand; however, it can be done in the left hand alone. If the highest note is the third , then add the fifth (or the thirteenth for dominant chords); if the highest note is the seventh, then add the ninth .

Example 9

Fm7 B♭m7 E♭7 A♭maj7

9 7 3 | 5 3 7 | 9 7 3 | 5 3 7

Add the chord tone above the lowest note to the *top* of the three-note voicing to create a four-note voicing.

By playing two chord tones in each hand, the voice leading will be easier to see. In the right hand the fifth (or thirteenth) will resolve to the ninth of the next chord and vice versa.

Example 10

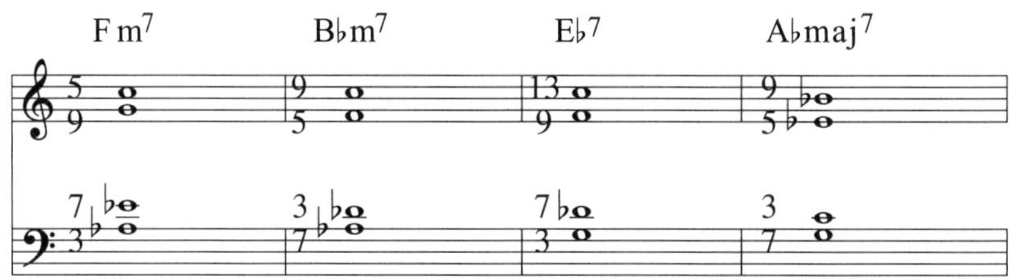

These four simple guidelines will allow students to create two-, three-, or four-note chord voicings that lead well through the chord progression. Coupled with the bass and guitar, the harmonic framework for the tune (or form) is created (see Example 11).

Example 11

(E7)
Fm7 B♭7
VI VI
Guitar
Piano
Fm7 B♭7
Bass
Drums
E♭maj7
V
E♭maj7

Direction And Motion

The rhythm section is well on its way to fulfilling its role when the harmonic and time/feel functions are coupled. Remember that the role of the rhythm section within the jazz ensemble is to *create an appropriate accompaniment*. The accompaniment has a great bearing on the overall direction of a chart. If there is no dynamic motion or textural changes in the accompaniment, there is none in the band's performance. Furthermore, the rhythm section does not follow the band's motion; rather, it leads the motion. In order to accomplish this the rhythm section must know what is going on in the rest of the ensemble: *Who has the melody? Is there a shout chorus? Where is the climax of the arrangement?* Answering these questions helps the rhythm section orchestrate the accompaniment.

All of the charts played by the band will be made up of tunes that are expanded into arrangements. Each tune has a specific form, and the rhythm section helps display that form. The form could be a 12-bar blues, AABA, or some other common song form. Though the form should be heard from the harmonic framework, there are other things the rhythm section can do to help display the form: a drum fill at the end of the form to indicate the top, or a change of texture to mark the beginning of a solo. Learning the form of the tune also makes learning the arrangement much easier once students realize that the form is repeated throughout the arrangement.

Once the students learn the form of a tune, the next step is to learn the form of the arrangement. They should know how many times the form is repeated, who has the melody, when backgrounds enter, where the climax is, and the general dynamics of the tune. In short, the rhythm section will find its job much easier by knowing the rest of the band's parts.

Dynamics in the rhythm section are created not only by changing volume but also by changing the orchestration. It is not necessary for the pianist to play all of the time. The drummer may change cymbals in order to give the illusion of changing volume. The bass may play with a two-feel rather than a walking four-feel to change the intensity. These types of changes in orchestration occur as the arrangement suggests, and the band has an easier job creating the dynamic motion when the rhythm section lays out that orchestration. Here are some common effects used by rhythm sections to help orchestrate the music:

Moving from a two-feel to a four-feel (walking) creates more intensity.

> This could be done by playing section A of a tune in two, then section B in four, or playing the first statement of the entire tune in two and the next in four. This does not have to occur at each section change, because it can become redundant.

Moving to a different cymbal will create different textures.

Moving the ride pattern from the hi-hat to the ride cymbal is often used to change intensity. Changes in texture can also be accomplished by changing from one cymbal to another; the drummer should be able to ride on any of the cymbals (expect specialty cymbals like a splash). Again, this should be done to contrast large sections and not be overdone.

Changing comping instruments can affect the texture.

Switching the comping from piano to guitar (or vice versa) will create a dynamic difference because of the change in timbre.

The drummer has a profound effect on the dynamics. In fact, the drummer often leads the dynamics of the ensemble. This is done through his set-ups. If the drummer thinks more of set-ups rather than fills, he has an easier job creating dynamic motion. In fact, a drum fill can be thought of simply as a longer set-up. By setting up an upcoming section or hit, the drummer can project to the ensemble the appropriate dynamic level. He has a lot of control over how loudly the band plays. Also, his simple set-up will cue the ensemble for its entrance. As a general rule, the drummer's set-up should end on the beat before the ensemble or section's entrance. If the band enters on beat 2, for example, then the drummer's set-up should end on beat 1. Finally, it is the drummer's job to end the piece. If the band is holding the last chord, the drummer should play on the cut-off. A simple ruff or crash, depending on the piece, is all it takes to make sure everyone in the band ends together.

Dialogue and Communication

The last facet of the rhythm section's role is to communicate with the ensemble or soloist. As mentioned above, knowing the band's parts makes this job easier when dialoguing with the big band. However, in small group settings this can be a bit more challenging because solos are not the same each time. The ability to listen and react quickly becomes crucial. Much, though not all, of this dialogue occurs with the piano (or guitar as a comping instrument) and drums (particularly the left hand on the snare). A common misconception about this dialogue is that the comping instrument should play back what the soloist plays. A good example of how to dialog musically comes from a comparison with speech. When we speak, we don't repeat what is being said; instead we answer, usually in short, succinct phrases relating to the subject. Likewise, comping instruments can answer what is being said musically. Students must listen at all times, because this dialogue can happen between several people. Some tips to keep in mind are:

It is not necessary to comp all of the time.

Space is many times a good option that will allow for a solo to build. Adding more as the solo progresses helps the soloist develop ideas.

Comping instruments should avoid playing in the same space.

A common problem is piano and guitar comping together. Using the Freddie Green approach or taking turns (for different soloists) can help eliminate this problem. Try not to conflict with drum comping; if the drummer plays fills at the end of sections, for example, try having the harmonic comping instrument at the beginning of the phrase.

Give each soloist his own space.

Make a general rule of bringing the volume and activity down at the beginning of each solo to allow the soloist to build in her own manner. Try to create contrast from solo to solo—change cymbals for a new textural pallet, change the comping sound (instrument, texture), etc. This not only gives each player her own space, but also creates more interest for the listener.

The use of riffs can work for comping.

Repeated riffs, just as in big band arrangements, can be effective; not all comping need be dialogue. Get into a groove as a section.

The best asset for an effective rhythm section is a group of players that keep their ears open. The rhythm section is the only section that improvises throughout the piece, and the ability to listen to each other, the ensemble, and the soloist is vital to making good musical decisions.

Setting Up The Section

The set-up of the rhythm section can be crucial to the feel of the ensemble and the section's ability to effectively communicate with one another and the rest of the ensemble. There is no one and only set-up for the group; however, things can be made easier for the group with a few tips to use as guidelines. To accomplish the goal of creating a time/feel together, the rhythm section should take three things into consideration about set-up:

Line of sight.

Make sure that everyone can see each other and can make eye contact for communication.

Proximity.

Section members need to be in close proximity to each other and to the rest of the ensemble.

Aural clarity.

Each rhythm section member should be able to hear himself, each other, *and* the rest of the ensemble.

Bass players often differ on where to stand in relation to the drums. One common approach is to set up the bass player on the left of the drums, next to the hi-hat. This allows for the bassist to really feel beats 2 and 4 of the hi-hat, and it puts the bass more in the center or heart of the big band. This is most common in big band settings, and allows for everyone in the ensemble to hear the bass clearly. Another approach is to set up the bassist on the right of the drums, next to the ride cymbal and between the drums and piano. Setting up on the ride side allows the bassist the visual and audible advantage of being near all of the quarter note pulses of the ride cymbal. Also, the piano can be heard more easily from that side. This is the most common set-up for trio and combo performance. Either set-up is fine. It is important to find what works for your players.

The piano often creates a common set-up problem. Too often it is placed as far to the right of the band as possible to allow everything else to be placed in front of the rhythm section (vibes, guitar, solo mic, etc.). Not only does this set-up cause the pianist to feel less a part of the ensemble, it is also makes it hard for other players to hear him. Try to get the piano as close to and tight with the rest of the section as possible. One concern might be getting drum bleed into the piano mic (if one is being used). There are several different micing techniques that can be employed. Just get the pianist into the section. Some directors use only electronic keyboards to remedy this set-up problem. However, unless the piano is so out of tune as to not be usable, an acoustic piano is always be the better choice—unless the music calls specifically for electric piano or synthesizer. Remember, jazz is primarily *acoustic* music that calls for *acoustic* instruments.

The most authentic sound for rhythm guitar is an acoustic arch-top guitar. The flattop, round-hole guitar can work, but usually lacks the volume and the midrange to cut through a big band. Electric arch-top guitars, which are usually plywood, can work with the help of an amplifier. The trick is to set the amp volume so that the guitar is *felt* but not necessarily *heard*. The optimum position of the amp is to the left of the guitarist, thereby putting the player's body between the amp and the back of the guitar. This also cuts down the possibility of feedback.

Solid-body guitars are more difficult to adjust for a good percussive rhythm sound, but guitarist Rick Haydon gives some tips to help get a decent sound from the solid-body. If the guitar has two pickups, the neck pickup works best for rhythm. These guitars are usually strung with light gauge strings and very low action, making it difficult to get a good *chunk*. It will be necessary to adjust the amp to a darker setting in order to make a solid-body guitar fit into to the band. Tone controls usually vary from one to ten. *Bass* (or *Low*) should be no more than four. Midrange can be as high as seven or eight. *Treble* (or *High*) works well at four or five. This would be a good *starting* EQ setting for guitar, but it is important for the guitarist to use her ear and be aware of the sound.

The placement of guitar and bass amps is often decided by the need to get them out of the way. Keep these things in mind, however:

1. Everyone needs to be able to hear the instrument.
2. The amp needs to be far enough away so that the player can hear herself balanced with the other musicians.
3. The amp needs to be close enough so that it can be reached for tweaking.

Often drummers are set up away from the ensemble so as not to blast the trombonist or saxophonist's ears off. *Remember that we are training musicians.* Part of training students to be musicians means teaching them about balance. We are not demanding that the drummer be a sensitive musician who uses musical taste by moving the drums away from the ensemble. Also, the closer proximity is needed to combat the challenge of physics. Sound travels at different rates; the closer the proximity, the better chance the students will have of playing together. Getting the drums as close to the ensemble as possible is always be the best choice.

The drummer also needs to have a good, ergonomic set-up of the drum kit; all parts of the kit should be within easy reach. Many student drummers come to the jazz ensemble from other types of music—rock, gospel, etc.—where the set-up may be different than the desired set-up for jazz. Having the cymbals set really high may look cool for a rock drummer, but will really wear on the drummer's shoulder after long periods of playing the ride cymbal. The drummer's set-up starts with good balance on the drum throne. The position of the seat should form a tripod between the throne and the drummer's feet. With this type of base, the player should be able to operate both feet without rocking or losing balance. The hi-hat and bass drum pedal should then be set according to this position, and the player should be able to rest on the ball of the foot or the heel. Every part of the kit should then be placed within easy reach without really having to extend the arms. Most important is the placement of the main ride cymbal, since this is the instrument that will be utilized the most. All other cymbals still need to be within easy reach, as the drummer should be able to ride on any cymbal. Renowned drummer Harold Jones recommends keeping the same set-up for big band and small-group playing with one exception: He likes to raise the cymbals slightly in the big band setting to create more distance to get a bigger crash when needed. After the drums are set the player still needs to make sure he can see the others in the section.

Rehearsal Strategies

Rehearsing the rhythm section in the sectional and big band setting will be different from every other section of the band. With the other sections of the band, the major concerns are concepts such as phrasing together, matching articulations, balancing, and following the lead player. Playing together as a rhythm section, as has been noted throughout this chapter, requires different concerns; therefore, rehearsing the rhythm section will require different strategies. Major concerns include:

- Creating a consistent quarter note pulse *together*.
- Creating the appropriate subdivision for the feel of the music.
- Creating a variety of textures and orchestrations for accompaniment.
- Understanding the overall direction of the arrangement.
- Dialoguing with the soloist and ensemble.

Often in the jazz ensemble rehearsal, much attention is given to the winds—fixing rhythms and articulations, and in general making sure parts are played correctly. The rhythm section can often be overlooked and may feel neglected. Though it is necessary to spend time with the winds to fix parts, the rhythm section should still be involved. Vocalizing to fix parts is not only valuable for the winds but also for the rhythm section. Whenever any section sings its part, the rhythm section (as well as the rest of the ensemble) should sing along with it. *All members of the section, regardless of whether playing the chart or not, should sing the parts*. It is important for the rhythm section to learn those parts in order to effectively play the chart, and singing is the best way to learn those parts. It is also helpful to have the drummer sing the set-up for the entrance to the section of music being played; this gets her in the habit of leading in the ensemble. As much as possible, have the rhythm section play along with any section that must rehearse a particular part of the piece (i.e. trumpets *and* rhythm section or saxes *and* rhythm section). This keeps the rhythm section involved and underscores the importance of the rhythmic feel at all times.

Sectional rehearsals for the rhythm section are distinctly different than sectionals for other parts of the band. It is more important for the rhythm section to just *play together*. Part of the rhythm section sectional should be spent playing just the solo section or some repeated part of the chart. This allows players to focus on creating a groove—pulse and subdivision. Though individuals in the section can play solos during this rehearsal, it is not always necessary; there is much value in just playing *time*. Here are a few ways to keep this interesting:

- Change the texture at the beginning of each new chorus—change cymbals, comping instruments, feels (two versus four)—all while maintaining a consistent groove.
- Play two at a time (bass/piano, drums/guitar, any combination), changing at the beginning of each new chorus while maintaining a consistent groove.
- Have *all* students in the section (i.e. *all* drummers, *all* bassists, etc.) participate in these exercises, regardless of whether they normally play the tune being rehearsed. *It is important for each member of the section to be able to play all charts in the rehearsal folder.*

When the rhythm section does need to rehearse a specific section of music, those not playing should sing wind parts. Vocalization should remain an integral part of the sectional rehearsal.

The jam session is extremely valuable for rhythm section players. We are often overly concerned about abusing rhythm section members in jam session situations, reasoning that rhythm section players should not have to endure soloists using them for practice. While it is true that we want young musicians be respectful of one another, it is also true that the rhythm section benefits just as much as the soloist from these jam situations. Playing in the rhythm section is physically demanding, and jam sessions allow students to build strength and endurance and the ability to sustain a groove for long periods of time.

Finally, listening to music should become a regular activity for rhythm section members. This should be done in sectionals, ensemble rehearsals, and together outside of rehearsal. Students should listen *recreationally* together, for there is a great deal of information that can be transferred through osmosis. This also allows each student to share his likes with other members of his section. Still, it is through *participatory* or *active* listening where student actually put in the time with the recordings. This means being involved with the music during the listening process, and listening for very specific things. Here are some suggestions for active listening:

- Students should have the chord changes in front of them while listening, following along to get the sound of the progression in the ears, hear the form, etc.
- Students should listen with their bodies. The time/feel is crucial to understanding jazz music. Get the foot or heel moving in time to the music. If there is a backbeat, students should clap or snap along and try to sing the subdivision of the music. *The bottom line is to dance or somehow get the body involved.*

- Students should listen specifically for whatever techniques or ideas they are working on. This means listening to a group's two-feel or a drummer's ride pattern or the bassist's walking line, etc.
- Students should listen for instruments besides their own. There is much to learn from all of the instruments on the recording, from listening to how the other rhythm players function to listening for the language of the soloist.
- *Most importantly, students should listen specifically to great rhythm sections.* They must listen to the way the rhythm section comps for soloists, how the soloists communicate with the section, and try to understand why something was played when it was. Students should listen for the way a great big band rhythm section guides the dynamic movement of the ensemble and sets up the order of events.

The rhythm section is not the place for every student in the ensemble. Successful rhythm section players are selfless and accept the role of being accompanists. Once players understand that role and how to function within a section to fulfill it, the stage is set for achieving swinging and satisfying musical experiences. Bassists will not be in denial of their harmonic function; drummers will understand the importance of the quarter-note pulse; guitarists will feel as though they are contributing rather than being in the way; and pianists will understand how to create rhythmic subdivision. Students will find joy in creating a groove, in driving the band, and helping the ensemble and soloists get their groove on!

CHAPTER 5

Promoting a Jazz Band

Ron Modell

I arrived in June of 1969 to assume my duties as associate professor of trumpet and to initiate a jazz band program at Northern Illinois University in DeKalb, Illinois. Once the band was formed, the next step was to have it heard. Being new to the university and the community, I had to find out where most of the students hung out, and at what time. I went to the head of our University Center (which not only had guest rooms, but a snack area and cafeteria), and asked when and where we could get our biggest audience. He told me 6:00 p.m. in the Pow-Wow Room, which was the cafeteria area.

Zane, with whom I had become acquainted in Dallas, was a real expert in the field of advertising and promotion, and had once told me that you can have the greatest product in the world, but if nobody knows about it, it will never sell. With that thought in mind, I had posters made and put all over campus announcing the first concert of the newly-formed NIU Jazz Ensemble. The poster gave the time, the place, and in the lower right side, thee words "X-rated." You can imagine the effect that had in the minds of young college students. We drew about 1,000 students and had a wonderful concert.

Of course, I had to do something to justify the X rating, so I once again called on the head of the University Center who helped me enlist the help of a very beautiful and talented junior student. During the course of the concert, she and I did an old burlesque routine and got a big laugh. We were off and running.

The real challenge was to promote the name of Northern Illinois University, and as three of the sitting presidents of NIU would later remark in the press, "The NIU Jazz Ensemble is our great public relations." How did we get there? My yearly budget from the music department was $200 per year; not nearly enough to buy four or five arrangements. A lot of the early funding came from the student government. DeKalb was famous for the creation of barbed wire and DeKalb Ag. I like to think our ensemble was added to the list of attractions after many years of reaching out to all of the communities within a hundred-mile radius of the school.

One of my first phone calls was to the publisher of *Downbeat* magazine, asking about the location of the finest high school jazz programs. District 214 was the answer; my next step was to bring the Jazz Ensemble to the schools in District 214 and let the students there know there was jazz at NIU. We would do a school-wide assembly, usually in the gym, and while I always played the music of Basie, Ellington, Kenton, and the other great jazz leaders of the day, I ended each performance with music to which the audience could relate, which meant, since it was the 1970s, music from groups such as Blood, Sweat, and Tears, Chicago, the Beatles, etc.

After doing several of these recruiting concerts, my next step was to help our own local and college communities realize what a treasure they had in the talented, young students of the NIU Jazz Ensemble. We played at major functions for the big companies in town and provided small combos from within the big band for organizations such as the Rotary Club, the Kiwanis Club, etc. The media was the main source of promotion. At my disposal was the DeKalb newspaper, *The Daily Chronicle*; the university paper, *The Northern Star*; local radio stations and the public access cable channel at the university, and *The Mid-Week*, a once-a-week paper that was distributed to many surrounding communities.

It took only a few years to attract some of the media from neighboring Chicago, and that occurred because of our yearly artist series, which always featured some jazz greats. Roy Leonard, of the flagship radio station WGN in Chicago became not only a real fan of the Jazz Ensemble, but a great friend personally. His audience numbered in the millions, and given his kind words and support of the Jazz Ensemble through on-air playing of our latest recordings, in addition to appearing on his show with world renowned jazz artists, he became the single most important factor in the promoting of our program.

In addition, the dean of jazz disc-jockeys, Dick Buckley on WBEZ-FM was also a great supporter, and again through on-air play and many interviews brought NIU to the forefront of jazz education in Illinois and the surrounding states.

I believe that involving all of our university presidents as well as city and state officials made it possible to produce a program of which they were proud to boast. Every official was invited to guest-conduct a special Lawrence Welk-type arrangement, and that made them very popular with their constituents. In twenty-eight years at NIU, the most important thing was to realize that exposure in many venues will win you a lot of friends.

• • •

In order to provide high school jazz band directors as well as prospective directors on how to promote a jazz program, I consulted with two of the most highly regarded educators in this field: Janis Stockhouse at Bloomington High School North in Bloomington, Indiana, and Mark Bettcher at Irving Crown High School in Carpentersville, Illinois. Here I have combined thoughts from both; hopefully this will give you some insight as to what needs to be done when promoting a jazz band.

Community appearances seem to top the list. They not only give students a chance to perform publicly, but they can also nurture the financial future of your program. By performing for no fee you may be developing future benefactors who will be very important down the road.

Festival appearances are very important in establishing a feeling of importance as well as just who the students are. Recording every other year can be a very significant experience. Imagine getting on a bus and going to a professional recording studio in Chicago or Indianapolis. Having a recording to use for promotional value can bring great rewards.

For junior high schools, touring is almost critical these days, as students have so many different choices to make. Hearing a live performance by your group can really be the deciding factor in a student's choice. With the advent of e-mail, letting the media, family, and friends know of your program's activities becomes a much easier task than it was twenty-five years ago. Students in the program need to become highly involved in ways such as hanging flyers and personally inviting the aforementioned family and friends.

Having the opportunity to work with a great soloist-clinician can be the highlight of the school year. It can also produce income if promoted properly, and the date of the performance is given serious consideration as to what else is going on in the community. Developing small combos is the most definitive way to introduce your students to improvisation. There will be many opportunities in the community and surrounding areas where taking a twenty-piece jazz band is not feasible, but a combo will always work.

Peace and Love,
Ron Modell
Professor Emeritus
Founder and Director
NIU Jazz Ensemble
1969-1997

PART II

THE BAND CONDUCTOR AS MUSIC TEACHER

Teacher Resource Guides

Developing Bands

Teacher Resource Guide

Afro Blue
Mongo Santamaria
(1922–2003)

arranged by Michael Sweeney
(b. 1952)

Unit 1: Composer/Arranger

Ramon "Mongo" Santamaria was born in 1922 in Havana, Cuba, and is most noted as a very influential Afro-Cuban/Latin jazz percussionist. Mongo, along with percussionist Chano Pozo, helped popularize the conga in the fusion of American jazz and Cuban rhythms. Initially it was mostly bongos and other percussion instruments that propelled Cuban music forward.

Mongo's first major hit was a 1959 recording of a tune entitled *Afro Blue* on the self-titled album *Mongo*. Many jazz musicians, including those of Cuban decent, have recorded variations of *Afro Blue*. Most noted are recordings by Dizzy Gillespie, Cal Tjader, and John Coltrane. Coltrane took a particular interest in the tune in the 1960s because it allowed complete rhythmic and harmonic freedom (a symbol for the socio-political struggle in the 1960s as well). This tune has become a standard in the jazz library, and many jazz musicians still perform it today.

Mongo moved to New York in 1950 and jump-started his professional career with musicians such as Mambo Perez Prado, Tito Puente, and Cal Tjader. He also worked with the great Dizzy Gillespie. These collaborations significantly aided the development of the Afro-Cuban jazz sound. Mongo made some of his legendary recordings in the late 1950s.

Mongo also made the most of his time in New York during the 1960s. He influenced the sixties boogaloo jazz sound, and recorded many records in the rhythm and blues and soul music genres. He also scored a hit by penning a cover of Herbie Hancock's *Watermelon Man* in 1963. Mongo continued to record and perform for more than four decades. He died at the age of eighty-five in Miami, Florida on February 1, 2003.

Michael Sweeney, arranger (b. 1952), is one of the premier writers/arrangers for concert and jazz bands today. He has made significant contributions, mostly within the areas of writing/arranging for younger concert and jazz ensembles. Sweeney completed degrees in music education and composition at Indiana University, and has taught elementary through high schools within the public school system.

He currently writes and composes works for the Hal Leonard Corporation in Milwaukee, Wisconsin, focusing on arrangements for concert and jazz bands. Sweeney won the ASCAP award for two of his compositions, *Ancient Voices* (1994) and *Imperium* (1992).

Mr. Sweeney continues to write, arrange, and serve as a clinician and conductor for schools and universities throughout the United States.

Unit 2: Composition and Arrangement

Mongo Santamaria originally recorded *Afro Blue* in May, 1959. Sweeney's arrangement was published in 2004, and maintains the same rhythmic emphasis of the 3/4 Afro-Cuban grooves that comprised the original piece. The bass line resembles the original recording as well.

The solo form of the original tune is a 24-bar minor blues; however, Sweeney arranges it in a 16-bar minor blues form that mostly addresses the tonic and subdominant parts of the minor blues form. The solo section challenges younger players, but is not overwhelming. The brass parts are orchestrated to complement the melody of the tune, which is carried by the saxophones. Other elements of call and response can be found within the part writing.

In the bridge section (the alternate melody section is referenced as the "bridge" because its make-up differs from George Gershwin's *I Got Rhythm* or Miles Davis's *So What*), lead trumpet and trombone carry the melody until the recapitulation within the saxophone section. An eight-measure interlude precedes the solo section (open to any player in the ensemble). The climax begins after the soli at rehearsal number 78; the shout section starts at rehearsal number 86; recap of the B section begins at rehearsal number 94, and an exciting build ends the piece.

Unit 3: Historical Perspective

During the late 1940s/early 1950s, Dizzy Gillespie led a movement to fuse American jazz and the rhythms of Cuba in what we now refer to as Afro-Cuban jazz. A more common term nowadays is Latin jazz. There are also influences of Latin/Caribbean rhythms in jazz as early as *Ragtime* with Jelly Roll Morton. Puerto Rican trombonist Juan Tizol also penned *Caravan* in 1937, a tune made famous by the Duke Ellington Orchestra. Critics also note this recording because of its significant impact on the fusion of Afro-Cuban jazz. Other compositions that have contributed to the Afro-Cuban jazz genre include *Cubano Be, Cubano Bop; Manteca; Woody N You;* and *Afro-Cubano Suite,* just to name a few. Influential percussion players' cultural roots sprouted from Cuba, Puerto Rico, Brazil, Africa, and Asia.

Mongo Santamaria, one of the most influential Cuban-style percussionists, not only influenced Afro-Cuban jazz, but also impacted rock, rhythm and blues, and funk genres. Santamaria's *Afro Blue,* considered a jazz standard, has been recorded by Dizzy Gillespie, Cal Tjader, and most notably John Coltrane. The tune was penned in May, 1959 and recorded uner the Fantasy Records label. Band members included Paul Horn (flute); Emil Richards *Caravan* (vibraphone); Al McKibbon (bass); Armando Peraza and Mongo Santamaria (conga, bongo, percussion); Francisco Aguabella, Modesto Duran, and Carlos Vidal (conga, percussion); Willie Bobo (timbales); Juan Cheda and Jerry Rivera (percussion, vocals); and Jose' Gamboa (percussion, vocals).

John Coltrane has provided the modern jazz world with the most definitive jazz recording (a swing waltz feel in 3/4) on *Live at Birdland.* Musicians on that recording are John Coltrane, soprano saxophone; McCoy Tyner, piano; Jimmy Garrison, bass; and Elvin Jones, drums.

Unit 4: Technical Considerations

This chart is rated as a Grade 2, and the recommended tempo marking is ♩ = 160. There is a 4-bar introduction, marked at ♩ = 80, but no additional tempo changes occur in the piece.

Sweeney scored his arrangement for full jazz ensemble with five saxophones, four trombones, four trumpets, and full rhythm section (guitar, piano, bass, drums, and percussion). However, it is playable with four saxes, three trombones, three trumpets, and small rhythm section (piano, bass, and drums).

Playing time is approximately two minutes, fifty-four seconds, but can be altered if taken at a slightly brighter tempo (about ♩ = 180, which is playable). The brighter tempo will not diminish the feeling or groove of the piece. In fact, Mongo Santamaria originally recorded the tune at a tempo quicker than suggested.

The tune has a straight eighth note Afro-Cuban groove throughout the piece, and the rhythm of the melody carries the piece. The rhythm helps dictate and suggest the syncopation in the melody.

The lead trumpet range goes up to G above the treble staff (g^1), but if a player is capable, she should aim for A as the highest note at the end of the tune. If the student cannot comfortably play A, E should be played, if possible. The lead trombone plays up to an F (f).

The harmony (in the solo section) moves from G minor seven to C minor seven concert (i and iv chords) of the minor blues. Instead of the original 24-bar blues form, this form is sixteen bars. Sweeney included harmony chord change sheets pitched in the keys of E♭, B♭, C, and bass clef. Each sheet contains a written solo and suggested scale reference, but students should be immediately encouraged to improvise. The ensemble director can obtain recordings that will allow students as well as the director to hear the arrangement. Listening is very important.

Unit 5: Stylistic Considerations

This arrangement is a medium tempo, straight-eighth based Afro-Cuban tune in 3/4 meter. The straight-eighth feel pays homage to the authentic Afro-Cuban style in the original recording (unlike John Coltrane's more swinging, open concept that became the standard for jazz players). The articulation should be characteristic of the 1950s and 60s big bands: Stan Kenton, Woody Herman, Dizzy Gillespie, Basie, and Thad Jones, etc. The band should phrase in more of a legato style (not slurred style) to ensure the smoothness, spirit, and drive of the modern big band sound. The band should also use fatter articulations such as "daht" (for more length, especially on notes marked with a *roof top* (^). Ghost notes and legato passages should be consistent to enable the piece to flow smoothly.

Improvising students should listen to authentic jazz players improvise on these types of Latin tunes. Listening allows students to get a sense of style, ideas, articulation, and phrasing (relying heavily on the influence of the rhythm). This composition can provide a stable foundation for any member of the ensemble to improvise over. Suggested soloists might include trumpet, trombone, and some type of rhythm instrument. This jazz standard arrangement illustrates an authentic Afro-Cuban groove (very accessible) in an odd meter, and at a medium tempo.

Unit 6: Musical Elements

MELODY:

The melody is not complicated and is very singable (singing is encouraged). The syncopation in the rhythm helps to dictate the melody. It is essential that the ensemble learn how to sing the rhythm as well as the melodic line. Everyone should study the melody, as this will help to open up an understanding of the call and response and harmonization in the melody line.

HARMONY:

The arrangement remains consistent with the tonic key center of G minor. It moves harmonically from i–iv–ii–V–I throughout the piece with the exception of the 8-bar phrase which moves from F7, E♭, F7 to G^{6}_{9}. The solos remain in the 16-bar form with eight bars of G minor, four bars of C minor, and four bars of G minor, never going to the standard turnaround in the minor blues format. Mr. Sweeney has provided chord sheets and has suggested scale-related studies to aid beginning improvisers.

RHYTHM:

The feel of the arrangement is a straight-eighth Afro-Cuban groove in 3/4 meter. Make sure that the rhythm section understands the difference between an authentic Afro-Cuban groove and a Brazilian samba or bossa nova. Sweeney has written a great drum chart that has the Cuban *cascara* pattern dictated in the ride cymbal (usually played on the bell or sometimes the side of the drum shell). If a conga player is available, the student should play the suggested (written) conga part, or if an alternate Afro-Cuban groove is preferred, the student can play that. The drummer may be able to work out a pattern that includes the toms (reminiscent of the conga pattern) inside of the *cascara* pattern if there is not a percussionist available. Rhythm section players should listen to authentic Afro-Cuban grooves when possible.

The ensemble should also practice singing the rhythm in the entire piece. It is important that the ensemble attacks the rhythms and gets a thorough understanding of the placement of the rhythm. Several moments in the piece require a quarter note on beat two. There are also several recurring measures of the dotted quarter note rhythm that gives the illusion of 2/4 time inside of the 3/4 time signature (or two against three). This rhythm occurs very frequently in jazz improvisation and composition.

Unit 7: Form and Structure

In the original composition (the standard way most jazz musicians play the tune), there is a 24-bar minor blues. However, in Sweeney's arrangement the soloist improvises over a 16-bar form.

The form suggested by the initial melody in Mike Sweeney's arrangement can be viewed as AB (8-bar vamp section), ABCB. If one abbreviates this it could be seen as AABA' (with a vamp between the first two As); a 40-bar form total.

Section	Measures	Event and Scoring
Intro (1):	1–4	Rubato section is marked at ♩ = 80. This tempo can be conducted or established without conducting. Make sure to emphasize the smoothness in the line (legato style). Also pay strict attention to dynamic build and contrast in this opening section.
Intro (2):	5–12 (vamp)	Firmly establish the tempo at ♩ = 160 or perhaps 180. It is essential that the rhythm section and conductor commit the tempo to memory to avoid having to count off the tune. The rhythm section can establish the time because the horns are playing long tones. As the rhythm section establishes the groove, the horns have a 4-bar *diminuendo* from *forte* to *piano*. Make sure the air remains consistent in the wind instruments releasing on beat one of measure nine.
Rehearsal 13	13–28	These sections are the melody being led by the saxophones. Make sure to listen for the blend and phrasing from the lead alto player.

Section	Measures	Event and Scoring
	13–27	This section is repeated, but the second time the backgrounds accompany the melody. The brass section provides emphasis and validation to the melody. There is also some call and response counter-melody going on. Make sure the ensemble keys in on the lead trumpet for overall phrasing, releases and articulation. The ensemble accents on beat two (in measure 13), and should be articulated as a "daht" to ensure a nice, fat, and lengthy quarter note. The two eighth notes followed by an eighth rest then another eighth note should have the articulation of "do-daht-daht." Also pay close attention to the two against three polyrhythm in those phrases. Pay attention to dynamic contrast as well.
Rehearsal 29	29–37)	8-bar vamp (interlude). If members of the rhythm section are strong and comfortable with it, they can lightly improvise during this 8-bar vamp section.
Rehearsal 38	38–45	This section can be viewed as the bridge, with measure 37 (also the second ending) providing the pick-up into measure 38. Here the trumpet and trombone take over the melody. The brass outlines with an accompaniment, as the saxophones play a response line. The baritone sax also accompanies the brass section. Saxophones should pay attention to shaping their lines in a legato manner, and the brass section should focus on making its accompaniment crisp and precise (always keying in and playing to the rhythm section).

SECTION	MEASURES	EVENT AND SCORING
Rehearsal 46	46–53	This section recaps the second or B part of the melody.
Rehearsal 54	54–61	This section is an 8-bar interlude that builds up to the solo section. Pay close attention to the dynamics and always keep the intensity in the long notes moving forward as the ensemble builds. Sweeney orchestrates great harmonic movement towards the solo section (which adds tension and release).
Rehearsal 62	62–77	This is an open solo section. It is great for any soloist/instrumentation in the band to improvise over. It is a 16-bar form built on the i and iv chords of a minor blues. On each soloist's last chorus have the backgrounds enter on cue (without dynamically getting in the way of the soloist. Notice the *crescendo* and *diminuendo* that occurs from measures 70–77 in the background figures.
Rehearsal 78	78–85	After the solos, the next section builds up to the shout section. The arranger orchestrates the distribution of the melody (in an abbreviated format) through the alto saxophones, trumpets, tenor saxes along with the trombones, and the tension finally climaxing through the lead trumpet and lead alto saxophone. The guitar picks up each of these melodic fragments. The remainder of the ensemble plays long notes, continuing to build up to the shout chorus. The drums set up the transition to the shout chorus. The drums have the only moving line while all other parts *crescendo* into measure 86.

SECTION	MEASURES	EVENT AND SCORING
Rehearsal 86	86–93	This should be a very exciting and climactic part of the piece. All sections (wind instruments) play the melody here in a harmonized orchestration.
Rehearsal 94	94–101	This is the recap of the initial B section of the melody again, but should maintain the intensity of shout chorus.
Rehearsal 102	102–end	This section is the outro. Intensity should remain consistent with the shout section as stated previously. There are accented (2-bar) ***fp*** passages beginning on beat one. These set up the *crescendo* four measures to the end. The last two measures should be long quarter notes played at *fortissimo* (***ff***), and should be long (releasing on beat two), with the articulation of "daht." The full ensemble ends this exciting piece together on the very last note.

Unit 8: Suggested Listening

John Coltrane Quartet, *Coltrane Live at Birdland*, MCA Impulse!, 1964.
Dizzy Gillespie Big Bands of 1962 and 1968, *The Big Bands*, LRC, 1993.
Mongo Santamaria Orchestra, *Mongo's Greatest Hits*, Fantasy Records, 1959.
Mongo Santamaria Orchestra, *Mongo*, Fantasy Records, 1959.

Unit 9: Additional References and Resources

Berendt, Joachim E., *The Jazz Book*, revised by Gunther Huesmann (Brooklyn: Lawrence Hill Books Publishing, 1992).

Charley, Gerard, *Music From Cuba: Mongo Santamaria, Chocolate Armenteros, and Cuban musicians in the United States* (Westport: Praeger Publishing, 2001).

"Mongo Santamaria," http://www.en.wikipedia.org.

"Mongo Santamaria," http://www.drummerworld.com.

Contributed by

Leon Anderson, Jr.
Director of Jazz Studies
Florida State University
Tallahassee, Florida

Teacher Resource Guide

Alamode
Curtis Fuller
(b. 1934)
arranged by Paul Murtha
(b. 1960)

Unit 1: Composer/Arranger

Curtis Fuller was born in Detroit, Michigan on December 15, 1934. Fuller is one of many jazz greats produced by Detroit, including Paul Chambers, Donald Byrd, Elvin Jones, Thad Jones, and Tommy Flanagan. These musicians and many others migrated to New York during the 1950s and became jazz legends.

Fuller first played professionally with an Army Band led by Cannonball Adderley in 1953. After serving his two years, Fuller moved back to Detroit and began working with Yusef Lateef. In the mid 1950s Fuller moved to New York, where his career took off. Within months of moving to New York, Fuller had already recorded numerous albums as a leader and sideman. In 1961 Fuller joined Art Blakey and the Jazz Messengers, making the group a sextet for the first time in its history. While with this group Fuller composed several tunes and left a legacy of recordings featuring the finest musicians of the hard bop era, including Freddie Hubbard, Wayne Shorter, and Cedar Walton.

Fuller has led a full life of playing and recording with nearly every major jazz musician. He has the honor of being the only trombone soloist to record with Bud Powell, Jimmy Smith, and most notably, John Coltrane on the album *Blue Train*. Fuller recorded as recently as 2005 and will always be the quintessential hard bop trombonist.

Unit 2: Composition

Curtis Fuller wrote *Alamode* (1961) during his residency with Art Blakey and The Jazz Messengers. The original arrangement is written for trumpet, tenor sax, trombone, piano, bass, and drums. As with many jazz tunes, the name of this composition is a clever pun referring to its modal qualities. In addition to being modal, *Alamode* embodies many elements from the hard bop era. This composition displays all of the characteristics of Art Blakey and The Jazz Messengers as a sextet including Curtis Fuller. The hard-driving quarter notes of the drums and bass provide momentum behind the melody of harmonized, simple, repetitive horn lines answered masterfully with hits from the rhythm section. The original recording of this composition can be found on the album *Art Blakey and the Jazz Messengers* under Blakey's name.

Unit 3: Historical Perspective

Throughout the 1950s and 1960s Art Blakey and The Jazz Messengers were one of the most important bands of jazz. From 1961–65 the horn section of Freddie Hubbard on trumpet, Wayne Shorter on tenor sax, and Curtis Fuller on trombone produced powerful compositions, arrangements, recordings, and performances. One of the most identifiable sextets in jazz history, this group showcased its virtuosity with a wide range of styles and sounds that reflected the metamorphosis of hard bop.

Since Miles Davis's classic 1959 album, *Kind of Blue*, jazz musicians have been experimenting with different modes of composition and improvisation. The 1961 recording of *Alamode* successfully demonstrates a perfect mixture of Davis's modal jazz and the hard bop characteristics of Art Blakey.

Unit 4: Technical Considerations

The chart is rated Grade 3 and the tempo is ♩ = 192 or faster. Playing time is approximately 4:30. The tempo of the original recording is ♩ = 246. Somewhere in between is recommended for a performance tempo.

The lead trumpet range goes to fifth line concert F (f^1), and the lead trombone goes to concert F above the bass clef (f). Range should not be an issue for most young ensembles. Solos are written out for tenor sax, trumpet, and trombone, but students are encouraged to transcribe solo ideas from the original recording.

The guitar part has chord symbols and a few rhythms, but there are mainly slash marks and no chord voices written out. The piano part is written out completely and has chord symbols. The chord voices notated for piano are overwritten at times with the root in the left hand, often doubling the bass. Both guitar and piano should transcribe comping rhythms and voices from the original recording. The bass part has chord symbols and a written walking bass

line. This is an excellent tune for young bass players to practice a walking bass line over one chord for an extended period of time.

Unit 5: Stylistic Considerations

This modal, hard bop composition is undeniably in the early 1960s style of Art Blakey and The Jazz Messengers. All ensembles should strive for the essence and intensity of the original recording in performance. The harmonized melody should not be overpowering from any one voice, and the rhythm section must always keep the groove intense, but never frantic. The drums should not always play the written pattern of . This pattern played repeatedly can become stiff and clumsy, hampering the overall swing feeling. By emphasizing the quarter notes on the ride cymbal, beats two and four on the hi-hat, and a rim shot on beat four, the time, rhythmic drive, and swing feeling remain constant. Although the above-mentioned modification should be made to the drum pattern, drummers must play all background drum hits as written (i.e., measure 11).

This composition is an up-tempo tune that works well in featuring multiple instrumentalists. The arrangement is playable for beginner ensembles, yet does not feel too diluted or oversimplified. It is important to listen to the original recording and transcribe articulations, solo ideas, and most importantly, the feel of the professional recording.

Unit 6: Musical Elements

MELODY:

The melody of this composition features the saxes in the A sections and the trombones on the bridge. All instruments, including the rhythm section, are responsible for melodic figures at some point in the tune.

HARMONY:

In this 64-bar AABA composition, the key signature of F minor is misleading in that the A sections are in F Dorian, not F Aeolian (minor). The A sections consist of eight bars of Fm^9, three bars of G♭maj^9, one bar of C7 and four more bars of Fm^9. This breaks the A sections into four 4-bar phrases, creating an AABA form within each A section. This makes *Alamode* a good tool for teaching beginning students to recognize chord changes.

When improvising over the Fm^9 chord, players can use an F Dorian scale to capture the modal feel of the tune. When the harmony changes to G♭maj^9, the F Dorian scale will no longer work; it is imperative, therefore, that students know and hear when the chords change. There are very few chord changes in this composition, making it ideal for students to explore one tonal center at a time.

RHYTHM:
The bass player and drummer are responsible for the rhythmic groove, but *everyone* is responsible for the time and feel of the tune. As in all music, everyone must feel the pulse. Rhythms often do not line up, due to different articulations within the ensemble. It is imperative to sing together (including the rhythm section) to help everyone articulate together.

Unit 7: Form and Structure

The basic form of the composition is AABA.

SECTION	MEASURE	EVENT AND SCORING
Intro	1–8	The tempo is ♩ = 192 or faster. The introduction features the melody in the trombones. Chords on the *second half of beat four* should be light and crisp, never long or muddy. Each 2-bar phrase can *crescendo*, and the introduction as a whole should be much louder by the end of bar eight.
9	9–25	The melody is in the saxes and should be learned vocally; this is guaranteed to sound clumsy and straight at a fast tempo. Not all the notes should be played with the same accent. The phrase markings do not mean slur the melody; all the accented notes must be tongued. The hits in the brass and rhythm section must be light and crisp, pushing through to the end of the measure. This section is repeated and can be louder the second time through.
26	26–41	The trombones have the melody on the bridge and are answered by the baritone sax, bass trombone, and rhythm section. the trumpets eventually join in, as do the saxes, causing the bridge to build to the next section. Make the most of the ***fp*** on the long notes, always building to the next phrase.

Section	Measure	Event and Scoring
42	42–57	A restatement of the melody occurs in the saxes; treat this section as in bars 9–25 with a bigger build and climax at the end of bar 57.
58	58–65	This is a send-off to the solo section. Trombones have the melody, as in bars 1–8. Build to bar 64. A 2-bar solo break in the trumpet should build to bar 66. Instruments playing the whole note with fall should sustain the note and fall as the lead trumpet does.
66	66–99	This solo section with written solos and changes for trumpet II, trombone II and tenor sax I is repeated to accommodate all soloists, but could be shortened or opened for various soloists within the ensemble. All soloists are strongly advised to listen to the original recording and transcribe phrases or entire solos.
100	100–116	A full band shout section. All full band sections should be sung together to guarantee the same articulations and inflections within the composition. Follow the lead trumpet for volume and style. This shout section repeats, and should be stronger the second time.
Coda	117–120	Saxes have the melody for two bars. In the final two bars, all instruments must speak together. The quarter note on beat three of bar 119 should not be short. Articulate this note with a "fat" articulation of "dot". *Crescendo* on the final note as the drummer fills behind it in the style of Art Blakey.

Unit 8: Suggested Listening

Blakey, Art, *Art Blakey and The Jazz Messengers*, GRP Records.
Art Blakey and The Jazz Messengers, *Caravan*, OJC.
Coltrane, John, *Blue Train*, Blue Note Records.

Unit 9: Additional References and Resources

Cuscuna, Michael, liner notes, *The Complete Blue Note/UA Curtis Fuller Sessions* (Mosaic 166, 1996).
Kernfeld, Barry, and Andrew Waggoner, *Fuller, Curtis*, *Grove Music Online*, ed. L. Macy, http://www.grovemusic.com.

Contributed by:
Adam Hucke
Director of Jazz Ensembles
McKendree College
Lebanon, Illinois

Teacher Resource Guide

All of Me

Seymour Simons
(1896–1949)

Gerald Marks
(1900–1997)

arranged by Roger Holmes
(b. 1957)

Unit 1: Composers/Arranger

Seymour Simons was born in Detroit in 1896. After World War I military service in the Army Air Force, Simons worked in the Detroit area as a pianist, orchestra leader, and composer. In the late 1920s and early 1930s Simons ran a booking agency, worked in radio production, and led his own radio orchestra. Simons wrote a number of popular tunes as well as special material for several performers; however, he is best remembered for *All of Me* (1931), his collaboration with Gerald Marks. Simons died in his native Detroit of a heart attack in 1949.

Gerald Marks was born in Saginaw, Michigan in 1900. Marks was a prolific writer, penning over 1000 songs. In addition to writing popular music Marks composed the music for a twenty-two song series of humorous musical lessons on safety, health, and friendship for school children that was translated into various languages for use in numerous countries. Marks is best remembered for *All of Me*, written with Seymour Simons, and the very successful *Is it True What They Say About Dixie?*, featured by artists such as Jimmy Dorsey and Al Jolson, and now a standard in the traditional jazz repertoire. Over his long career, Marks received many awards and honors from organizations and institutions including The

American Heritage Foundation, The Defense Department, and The University of Charleston, West Virginia. Gerald Marks died in 1997.

Roger Holmes was born in 1957 and grew up in Newport Beach, Orange County, California. Roger majored in music composition and woodwind performance at North Texas State University (now the University of North Texas). He toured with Woody Herman and the Thundering Herd before moving to Dallas as a freelance performer, writer, and producer. Holmes has performed with Ella Fitzgerald, Ray Charles, Doc Severinsen, and many others. He has written music for commercials, films, television, and school groups. Roger Holmes has been a staff arranger for Hal Leonard Publications since the 1980s.

Unit 2: Composition

All of Me (1931), the one important musical collaboration of Seymour Simons and Gerald Marks, is an excellent example of ABAC 32-bar song form, one of the most common alternatives to AABA 32-bar song form. Each compositional section is eight measures long, and the song is usually mapped with the B section as first ending and the C section as second ending. The harmonic structure makes frequent use of secondary dominants, creating a constant forward harmonic momentum while remaining relatively simple, making *All of Me* a longtime improvisational favorite with jazz artists. The melodic construction makes prominent use of chord tones, often outlining the underlying harmonic structure. The occasional use of non-chordal *blue notes*, such as ♭5 and ♭9, in the melody provides interest and contributes to the appeal that this composition has held for jazz musicians for almost eighty years.

Unit 3: Historical Perspective

All of Me was written in 1931, in the middle of the Great Depression in North America. The lyric is cast in the first person, telling the tale of a one-sided love affair. The singer implores the object of his infatuation to make the relationship complete and "take all of me." It is a story and sentiment that transcends generations and musical styles. *All of Me*, remaining popular for almost eighty years, has been performed by countless artists.

The first major recordings of *All of Me* were by Mildred Bailey with Paul Whiteman and His Orchestra and by Louis Armstrong. Both recordings topped the charts in 1932, the same year the composition was featured in the Fox Studios's comedy, *Careless Lady*. Billie Holiday recorded the tune in 1941, accompanied by Eddie Heywood and His Orchestra, featuring a tenor saxophone solo by Lester Young. Frank Sinatra recorded several versions, each different, the best known being his collaboration with Nelson Riddle for the *Frank Sinatra: Swing Easy* album in 1954.

Roger Holmes's arrangement is based on the style of jazz band writing pioneered by Don Redman and Fletcher Henderson in the 1920s and 1930s. The scoring is primarily homophonic with choirs of brass and saxophones used in antiphonal (call and response) patterns. The influence of Midwest swing bands, particularly Count Basie's, is heard in the implied triplet subdivision of the beat, in the overall timbre of the rhythm section, and in the interplay of the rhythm section, both among the four rhythm section parts and with the horn section.

Unit 4: Technical Considerations

This chart is of medium difficulty, suitable for junior high or middle school groups and for less advanced high school groups. Tempo, instrumental ranges, note values, rhythmic figures, overall length, and solo space are all appropriate for players who have between two and three years of playing experience.

The tempo is ♩ = 132, slower than the famous Count Basie/Billy Byers version (which is ♩ = 152), making the chart manageable by less experienced players. More advanced ensembles could increase the tempo up to the Basie standard, but should ghost some of the notes in the eighth note passages in order to maintain the swing feel at the faster tempo. The highest note in the lead trumpet part is written G at the top of the staff (g^1). The lead trombone plays up to F4 (f). The scoring is for four or five saxophones (second tenor is optional), three or four trumpets (the fourth optional), and three or four trombones (the fourth optional). The fourth trombone part includes optional *8va* notes when the range descends below F2 (F_1), making the part accessible to students who do not have a bass trombone or a tenor with an F-trigger.

The rhythm section parts are well notated. Piano voicings and comping rhythms, a written bass line, and a detailed drum part are provided. The guitar part consists of chord symbols and a few rhythmic figures; no voicings are provided.

Solos are brief with the second trumpet and first tenor saxophone sharing half a chorus. The trumpet solos on the A section and the tenor saxophone solos on the B section of the form. Well-constructed, written solos are provided, and once learned can serve as the basis for personal interpretation. The chart consists of an 8-bar introduction, two complete choruses, and a coda, a total of ninety measures. The playing time at the suggested tempo would be approximately 2:43.

Unit 5: Stylistic Considerations

Roger Holmes's arrangement of *All of Me* is a medium tempo swing chart. Eighth note figures are to be interpreted with a triplet subdivision in the style of the Count Basie Orchestra playing a medium tempo. Horn articulations should be crisp, and careful attention should be given to the difference between notes marked staccato and those with a short (hat) accent (^). Notes with no articulation mark and those with a sideways accent (>)should be played full value. Triplet figures should be played with equal emphasis on all three notes.

Pianists with little jazz experience will be aided by the written part that illustrates appropriate comping rhythms and chord voicings that can be used as a model while the player gains skill in playing this style. The pianist need not play everything that is notated, as it often doubles the horn parts. Some judicious editing of the piano part will help create the Basie swing style of this chart.

The guitarist should emulate the style of Count Basie's famous guitarist, Freddie Green, by playing four quarter notes, all down strokes, in each measure. The use of four-string voicings, a slight emphasis on beats two and four, and keeping the volume below that of the piano will help create the correct feel for this chart.

The swing style calls for the bassist to provide a walking line of long, connected quarter notes with a very slight emphasis on beats two and four. If the bassist is playing an electric bass, she should strive to create the timbre, attack, and decay of a string bass.

The drummer should maintain a standard swing pattern and not lapse into a 12/8 rock-and-roll feel.

Unit 6: Musical Elements

MELODY:

The melody, for the most part, outlines the harmonic progression. The melody is presented in an elaborated or ornamented version, in 8-bar antiphonal phrases between the brass and the saxophones. Learning the unornamented melody and the words will help the musicians remember and interpret the ornamented version. The ornamented melody makes use of offbeat eighth note entrances, syncopation, and eighth-note triplets, but avoids the quarter-note triplets found in the original. Accidentals are fairly common and some inside voices could challenge inexperienced players.

HARMONY:

The chart is written in the key of B♭ major, enabling easy key signatures and tessitura for all instruments. The harmonic progression is not difficult, but does deviate slightly from B♭ major through the use of secondary dominants. The basic chord structure of the composition is enhanced by the chromatic alteration of chord extensions and by the use of tritone substitutions which provide a smoother, more interesting bass line. The chord alterations and substitutions give the chart a more up-to-date sound than would be the case if the basic harmonization of the original melody were followed. The optional second tenor saxophone, fourth trumpet, fourth trombone, and guitar parts do not merely duplicate non-optional parts, but enhance the sound of the chart. If the optional parts are used, the pianist should play less to avoid duplication between the written piano and horn parts. The baritone saxophone and fourth trombone often outline the root progression, while the other voices in the horn section complete the chords.

RHYTHM:

The chart has a medium tempo swing feel. All ensemble members should feel the triplet subdivision of the beat as they play this chart. The placement of isolated eighth notes on offbeats may be problematic for inexperienced players. Practice these spots by having the rhythm section perform a series of eighth-note triplets as background to these entrances. Have the players count the subdivision during rests, "one triplet, two triplet, three triplet, etc." The rhythmic swing feel will be achieved when the tempo is steady and the ensemble adheres to the printed articulations. The best performance will be generated when all ensemble members audiate the same syllable for each type of articulation. Use "dot" for hat accents (^), "dit" for unaccented staccato notes, and sustain notes with a sideways accent (>) and notes without articulation marks for full value. A slight emphasis on offbeat eighth notes will help with the feel of any grouping of four or more eighth notes.

All of Me from the 1954 Nelson Riddle/Frank Sinatra album, *Frank Sinatra: Swing Easy* is a good model for the correct swing feel, as the tempo is the same (♩ = 132) as Roger Holmes's suggested tempo for this chart.

Unit 7: Form and Structure

SECTION	MEASURE	EVENT AND SCORING
Intro	1–8	The tempo is a medium swing, with ♩ = 132. Saxophones play a melodic riff answered by the brass. Strive for a smooth saxophone line contrasted with powerful brass hits. Drums should reinforce the brass. Observe the dynamics to build excitement going into the tune in measure 9.
A	9–16	The brass plays the harmonized melody with rhythmic interpretation. Balance unison trumpets in measures 12–16 with harmonized trumpets in measures 9–11. Saxophones have rhythmic hits; use "dit" for crisp articulation. Move air through the falloff in measure 12 and the glissando in measure 15. There should be no breath for saxophones in measures 15–17. There is a percussive Count Basie style piano hit in measure 16. Teach the form; this is section A.
B	17–24	A role reversal from section A. Saxophones have the melody; the brass answers with rhythmic hits. Learn accidentals at a slower tempo. Move air through the glissando in measure 19. Use "dot-dot" for quarter notes in measure 24. Connect dotted quarter notes to the following note. Tongue notes with a hat accent (^). The drums should reinforce notes with a hat accent (^).
A	25–32	The melody is in the brass. Saxophones have rhythmic hits. This is exact repeat of measures 9–16, other than the saxophone parts in measures 31–32.

SECTION	MEASURE	EVENT AND SCORING
C	33–40	Saxophones have the melody. Balance the volume of unison measures and harmonized measures. Play triplets with equal emphasis on all three notes. The drums/bass setup have concerted rhythms in measure 38. There should be silence on the downbeat of measure 39. A trumpet solo starts in measure 39.
A	41–48	A trumpet solo, supported by simple comping from the rhythm section. Inexperienced soloists should learn the written solo and then personalize it. The drummer should switch ride cymbals to provide contrast with ensemble sections.
B	49–56	A tenor saxophone solo with trombone and saxophone background. The background hits in measures 53–56 should build intensity into D.S. al Coda. Drop one dynamic level at the start of the *crescendo* in measure 56.
A	25–26	D.S. al Coda.
C	33–38	Jump to the coda after the first six measures of the C section.
Coda	57–76	Measures 57–58 are a solo fill for drums. Saxophones enter with strength on beat four of measure 58. Measures 59–66 are the C section of the form. Lyrical saxophone phrases are punctuated by brass hits. Measures 67–70 and 71–74 are repeats of the last four measures of the form. Melodic and rhythmic material is taken from measures 65–66. The final two measures have concerted ensemble hits with a fermata on the final chord in measure 76. Balance and tune the final E♭$^{13(\sharp 11)}$ chord. Balance and tune the root,

third, and B^7, voices followed by the ninth, sharp eleventh, and thirteenth voices (an F major triad), then combine all voices.

Unit 8: Suggested Listening

Count Basie Orchestra, *Compact Jazz: Count Basie*, Verve Records, 831 364–2.

Fitzgerald, Ella, *Ella Swings Gently With Nelson*, Polygram Records, Inc., 314 519 348–2.

Holiday, Billie, *Billie Holiday With Lester Young: Lady Day & Prez, 1937–1941*, Giants of Jazz, CD 53006.

Sinatra, Frank, *Frank Sinatra: Songs for Young Lovers & Swing Easy*, Capitol Records,. Inc., CDP 7 48470 2 DIDX 2489.

Washington, Dinah, *Compact Jazz: Dinah Washington*, Mercury Records, 830 700–2.

Young, Lester, *Jazz-Club Tenor Sax*, Polygram International, 840031–2.

Unit 9: Additional References and Resources

Aebersold, Jamey, *Volume 95: 500 Miles High* (New Albany: Jamey Aebersold Jazz, Inc., 2000). Book and CD.

Baker, David, *How to Learn Tunes: A Jazz Musician's Survival Guide* (New Albany: Jamey Aebersold Jazz Inc., 1997). Book and CD, Volume 76 of the Play-a-Long Series.

Berg, Shelly, Lou Fischer, Fred Hamilton, and Steve Houghton, *Rhythm Section Workshop for Jazz Directors* (Van Nuys: Alfred Publishing Co., Inc., 2005). Book and DVD.

Byers, Billy, *All of Me*, recorded by the Count Basie Orchestra (Milwaukee: Hal Leonard Corp, 1963).

Gillespie, Luke, *Stylistic II/V7/I Voicings for Keyboardists* (New Albany: Jamey Aebersold Jazz, Inc., 2000).

JazzStandards.com, http://jazzstandards.com.

McCarthy, Albert, *Big Band Jazz* (London: Barrie & Jenkins Limited, 1974).

Tirro, Frank, *Jazz: A History* (New York: W.W. Norton & Company, Inc., 1977).

Songwriters Hall of Fame, http://www.songwritershalloffame.org.

Steinel, Mike *Essential Elements for Jazz Ensemble: A Comprehensive Method for Jazz Style and Improvisation* (Milwaukee: Hal Leonard Corp., 2000).

Contributed by:

Thomas Dust
Associate Professor
Secondary Music Education
University of Alberta
Edmonton, Alberta, Canada

Teacher Resource Guide

Autumn Leaves
Joseph Kosma
(1905–1969)

arranged by Peter Blair
(a.k.a. Blair Bielawski)
(b. 1958)

Unit 1: Composer/Arranger

Joseph Kosma (a.k.a. Jozsef Kozma) was born October 22, 1905 in Budapest, Hungary. He was related on his mother's side to celebrated painter/photographer Laszlo Moholy-Nagy. His formal education included courses at the Academy of Music in Budapest and Academy Liszt, where he studied privately with Béla Bartók. After earning diplomas in composition and conducting, he secured a grant for study in Berlin where he met and later married fellow musician Lilli Apcl. The couple emigrated to Paris in 1933, where Kosma's association with lyricist Jacques Prevert and director Jean Renoir led to an active career of soundtrack writing for French language motion pictures. During World War II, Nazi occupation forces placed Kosma under house arrest and officially banned him from composing. But he continued to write under various pseudonyms in tacit cooperation with fellow musicians, most often using the names of his colleagues. Some of his best-known works graced stylish cinema classics like *La Grande Illusion* and *The Rules of the Game*.

Following a 1944 explosion that nearly took his life, Kosma composed the song for which he is best known, *Autumn Leaves*, and lived out the rest of his life in Paris, where he died in 1969.

Arranger and Milwaukee, Wisconsin native Peter Blair (a.k.a. Blair Bielawski) was born in 1958. He has devoted much of his career to educational publications (Heritage Music Press, Hal Leonard, The Lorenz Corporation), and has worked professionally with Natalie Cole, Manhattan Transfer, Johnny Mathis, Aretha Franklin, the Temptations, Lionel Hampton, and the Milwaukee Symphony Orchestra. He has also served on the board of directors for the Retail Print Music Dealers, and the Wisconsin Music Education Association.

Unit 2: Composition

In 1945, Kosma composed *Autumn Leaves* under the title *Les feuilles mortes* (*The Dead Leaves*) in collaboration with lyricist Jacques Prevert as part of a 1946 Marcel Carne film *Les Portes de la Nuit*. Over the years it became a favored melody for vocalists and (mostly) jazz instrumentalists. This was due in part to its easily recognizable form and straightforward II–V–I progressions in the tonic and relative minor. The song's minor key, along with its seasonal metaphor, made it an obvious choice for musically describing introspection and regret.

Unit 3: Historical Perspective

Kosma originally composed *Les Feuilles Mortes* (*Autumn Leaves*) in 1945 as ballet music for Roland Petit's *Le Rendezvous*. Moved by the music and dance, French film director Marcel Carne requested the melody be included in his 1946 drama *Les Portes de la Nuit*, written by poet/lyricist Jacques Prevert. *Les Feuilles Mortes* was performed on screen by singer/actor Yves Montand and became an immediate hit with French audiences. After 1949, the renamed *Autumn Leaves* became one of the most covered songs in music history, based in part to a less melancholy rewrite by lyricist Johnny Mercer. Beginning in 1950, the song was recorded by a plethora of vocalists, including Frank Sinatra, Nat King Cole, Bing Crosby, Placido Domingo, and Barbara Streisand.

In 1955, pianist Roger Williams discovered the song's exclusive melodic potential when his own version became the only piano instrumental to achieve a number one ranking on *Billboard* magazine's popular music charts. Still, it is with jazz musicians that *Autumn Leaves* has retained its most obvious charm, with historic renditions performed and recorded by Miles Davis, John Coltrane, Cannonball Adderly, Bill Evans, and Duke Ellington.

Unit 4: Technical Considerations

This arrangement of *Autumn Leaves* is rated Grade 2–3, and the recommended tempo is ♩ = 144–152. However, it functions adequately at a slower tempo, and is easily adapted to solo instruments, including vocal, with simple editing in the saxophone section, guitar, auxiliary percussion (vibes), and/or trumpet I parts.

Brass ranges peak comfortably at concert G (top of staff [g^1]) for lead trumpet, and third octave concert F (f) for lead trombone. Saxophone solos are written predictably with the baritone saxophone often imitating lead alto parts an octave lower. Articulation and dynamic considerations remain consistent and uniform. No doubles are required and the rhythm section parts are entirely written out with chord changes included. No improvisation sections are written, but are easily included with minor editing.

Unit 5: Stylistic Considerations

This Peter Blair arrangement is brighter than other jazz-based interpretations, bearing little resemblance to Miles Davis's slow paced hipness or the dirge-like introspection of the Duke Ellington version. In fact the introduction takes on the temporary feeling of an early Oliver Nelson work, with tersely articulated mid-register saxophones doubling in tandem with trombones, while reinforced with pedal point in the baritone saxophone and fourth trombone parts.

Despite its occasional dense timbre, the arrangement profits from a softer than marked volume with greater attention paid to precise section articulation. Although written for full big band, performers should treat it with the compactness of a supplemented combo. An example of this feeling is best represented in the recording *Autumn Leaves/The Great Jazz Trio* (441 Records/2002), featuring pianist Hank Jones.

Blair's obvious leanings towards a younger, lesser experienced ensemble should not deter its qualifications as a mature, well written adaptation. Many important lessons can be taught here, including stylistic uniformity and attention to intonation in the solo voices, drum set terminologies including but not limited to a 2-beat feel and ride cymbal patterns, tasteful yet practical keyboard substitutions, and the aforementioned articulation and dynamic concerns.

No improvised sections are included, but can be written in by repeating the song's form anywhere before measure 42, with alto saxophone, guitar, vibes, and/or piano meshing best with the preexisting timbre. A transcribed piano (optional vibes) solo begins at measure 62, with chord changes provided for possible further exploration. It is also commonplace for pianists to tack on a solo rubato section in front of the arrangement, and treat it as framework for an improvised piano feature in the style of Bill Evans or Keith Jarrett.

This arrangement also converts easily to feature a vocalist by omitting melodic lines in the lead alto, lead trumpet, guitar and vibes while leaving the saxophone soli at measure 42 intact, and reentering at the D.S.

Unit 6: Musical Elements

MELODY:

The simple, recognizable melody should be played in an understated manner with little or no vibrato and exacting articulations, similar to those performed by 1950s West Coast Style jazz musicians. Chord progressions are logical, with proper substitutions transcribed in the rhythm section.

HARMONY:

The Blair arrangement, written in D minor, lays well for all instruments. There is no modulation present, as the chart remains true to its original design. *Autumn Leaves* is also an excellent vehicle for younger ensembles to explore the creativity associated with overlapping key centers and their wide range of harmonic improvisational possibilities.

RHYTHM:

Feel and momentum dictate that the entire band should react uniformly to brass outlines present in the drum part. Many young bands tend to ignore drum outlines at the expense of implied articulation, added clarity, and reinforced power, which can often sidestep hazards associated with unnecessary brass exertion. Precision outlining (especially in the responsorial trombone/internal saxophone sections) can mimic the allusion of additional musicians and enhance performance excitement while retaining proper musicality. Moreover, correct outlining is a benchmark of great big band drummers past and present, including Jo Jones, Buddy Rich, and Jeff Hamilton.

Requiring a band to vocalize stylistic and rhythmic articulations beforehand is very important to the successful performance of any swing composition and is strongly encouraged.

Unit 7: Form and Structure

The basic form of the composition is A (8-bars) B (8-bars).

Section	Measure	Event and Scoring
Introduction		Measures 1–8, the tempo is ♩ = 144–152. Play at a slower tempo until the swing and style are established. A pedal point is established in baritone sax, trombone IV, piano, and bass. Many bands with electric bass tend to overplay this section at the expense of baritone saxophone and trombone IV, when actually the reverse should be true. The third note should also be separated and lightly accented. Remaining saxophone and trombone parts should follow suit. This includes the extended dotted quarter notes in measure 2. It is recommended that notes marked staccato be played very short, using the syllable "dit," while marcato markings (–) utilize the syllable "bot."
Introduction of melody	8–14	Melodic lines should be played at a very light ***mf*** volume, with adherence paid to uniform articulation. Little or no vibrato should be utilized, and no one solo voice should predominate. Saxophone, trombone parts, and bass and ride cymbal should be separated and performed at a very light ***mf***. Measures 15–16 consist of an exacting *crescendo* in which the drums are allowed to open up a bit before returning *immediately* to the original lighter ***mf*** volume at measure 17. An implied 2-beat feel is then established in the drum and bass parts (written out). Measure 17 also establishes the first of several drum-outlining scenarios with trombones and saxophones. It is suggested that these sections practice with the drummer separately from the full ensemble.

Section	Measure	Event and Scoring
B Section	25–39	At measures 25 and 29, the second and fourth of the four eighth notes in the brass should be rehearsed separately, as should the ascending/descending call and response patterns in the piano/brass sections at measures 27–28. The drums at measure 35 should be played exactly as written, while the dotted quarter/eighth patterns in the baritone saxophone, bass, and piano can be played long, but not exceeding the written volume. The saxophone and trombone sections have a tendency to incorrectly react to the subordinate patterns by playing loudly. This deemphasizes an important *crescendo* at measure 39.
Saxophone soli	42–61	Saxophones enter at measure 42, with alto I and baritone sax ideally heard at identical volume. The second and fourth of the four eighth notes must be lightly accented and uniform. The soli is then played in legato style except when marked otherwise. The brass pattern beginning on the second half of beat three in measures 46–47 should be rehearsed separately, with the drums establishing the outline routine that continues through measure 61. It is appropriate for the brass drop at measure 47 to extend into beat two, but no longer. Additionally, drums can also lightly outline the offbeat saxophone soli pattern at measure 47 with ride cymbal. Piano is best served throughout this section by observing stylistic similarity and/or articulation with the trombone section.

SECTION	MEASURE	EVENT AND SCORING
Piano/Vibes solo	62–71	A written solo for either piano or vibes begins at measure 62, reinforced by light, articulated saxophone accompaniment. If the written solo is performed in lieu of improvisation, it should be played legato with few if any accents. It is the tendency of young rhythm sections to drag tempo when moving to softer volumes. This should be observed closely by the director, and is assisted by having drums observe the momentum associated with the rim knocks at measures 63–64. Trumpets enter at measure 71, and should play tight in the stands (1–3 inches away).
D. S. al Coda	78–84	An important drum fill occurs on beats three and four of measure 78. This sets up the saxophone melody at the B section D.S. at measure 25. The coda transition occurs at the end of measure 38, with measures 79–84 of the coda played stylistically identically to the introduction. A written drum solo is played at measure 85 before drums outline the uniform ***fp*** ensemble section on the second half of beat four.

Unit 8: Suggested Listening

Adderley, Cannonball, *Somethin' Else*, Blue Note Records.
Ammons, Gene, and Stitt, Sonny, *We'll Be Together Again*, Prestige, 7606.
Carter, Benny, *Autumn Leaves*, Movietone, 72020.
Cole, Nat King, *Nat King Cole at the Movies*, Capitol, CD 99373.
Coltrane, John, *The Complete Graz Concert*, Charly.
Davis, Miles, *The Best of Miles Davis*, Blue Note Records.
Dorham, Kenny, *This is the Moment!*, Riverside, 275.
Ellington, Duke, *Ellington Indigos*, Columbia Records.
Bill Evans Trio, *Portrait in Jazz*, Riverside, 1162.
Farmer, Art, and Golson, Benny, *Jazztet, Real Time*, Contemporary, 14034.
Gillespie, Dizzy, *Birks's Works*, Verve, MGV–8222.

Golson, Benny, *Gone with Golson*, New Jazz, 8235.
Great Jazz Trio, *Autumn Leaves*, 441 Records, 2002.
Hall, Jim, and Carter, Ron, *Alone Together*, Milestone, 9045.
Hodges, Johnny, *Johnny Hodges at Sportpalast, Berlin*, Pablo, 2620–102.
Holman, Bill, *Mucho Calor!*, Andex, A3002.
Jarrett, Keith, *At the Blue Note: The Complete Recordings*, ECM, POCJ1305.
Pepper, Art, *The Way It Was!*, Contemporary, 7630.

Unit 9: Additional References and Resources

Davis, Miles, arrangedy by Peter Blaire, *Milestones* in *Easy Jazz Ensemble Series* (Milwaukee: Hal Leonard Corp).

Contributed by:

Tom Smith
Senior Fulbright Professor
Fulbright Professional Specialist Program

Teacher Resource Guide

Baytrail Shuffle
Maria Schneider
(b. 1960)

Unit 1: Composer

Composer/arranger Maria Schneider is one of the freshest voices to emerge since the nonpareil orchestrator Gil Evans. Schneider's expansive compositions for big band tell personal stories in sound which unfold in arrangements that are the antithesis of the traditional theme and variations approach. Twice featured on the cover of *Jazz Times*, she is in demand around the world as a guest conductor, most notably with the finest European jazz radio orchestras.

Born November 27, 1960, in Windom, Minnesota, Schneider began studying piano at age five. She earned degrees in music theory and composition from the University of Minnesota and the Eastman School of Music. After moving to New York in 1985, she landed a three-year assistantship with her idol and mentor, Gil Evans. Initially charged with a variety of re-orchestration projects, she graduated to work closely with Evans on the film score for *The Color of Money* and has been referred to by many as his heir apparent.

Writing for other bands, including aggregations led by Mel Lewis and Woody Herman, only fueled her desire to hear her compositions exactly as she sonically envisioned them, played by an ensemble of handpicked musicians. In 1993 she formed the Maria Schneider Jazz Orchestra, which for many years was a mainstay on Monday nights at the Greenwich Village Club Visiones.

Evanescence, the band's debut recording, was released in 1994, followed by *Coming About* in 1996, and then her most critically acclaimed CD, *Allegresse* in 2000. All three earned Grammy nominations and in 2006 the *DownBeat* Critics' Poll listed Maria Schneider at the very top of both the best arranger and best composer categories.

Unit 2: Composition

Commissioned by the Penfield Music Commission Project in 1990 and premiered by the Baytrail Middle School Jazz Ensemble, *Baytrail Shuffle* is a medium-groove shuffle tune that is playable by bands looking for medium-easy music. It features a shuffle-march soli section that showcases the precision and dynamics of any group.

If you try to order *Baytrail Shuffle*, your music dealer may state that it is out of print. Ask them to order it from the Kendor Archives.

Unit 3: Historical Perspective

Shuffles have been a popular branch on the tree of jazz throughout the various eras. What a coup to have a cutting-edge composer such as Maria Schneider adding a quality original composition to the developing jazz ensemble repertoire.

Unit 4: Technical Considerations

This composition is rated Grade 3, and the recommended tempo is ♩ = 124 with a duration of 3:30. The rhythm section parts are thoroughly written out, including a good shuffle beat pattern for the drummer and actual written voicings for the guitarist. The piano and bass parts are also fully written, with chords cued above the staff for both instruments.

The lead trumpet and trombone parts are manageable in range going up to high F concert in their respective clefs (trumpet: f^1; trombone: f). All of the horn players have soli sections and every single part looks enjoyable and fun to play. Cup mutes are called for in the trumpet section.

This charts is from the *Kendor Convertibles* series so it works well with a full jazz ensemble (5–4–4 plus rhythm) or can be played by as few as three saxophones (two altos and tenor), two trumpets, and one trombone plus rhythm. There are written solos for piano and lead alto, however in a quasi-F blues composition such as this, any instrument could be featured. If you have a full ensemble, you might want to put your bass trombonist on first and your lead player on second trombone.

Unit 5: Stylistic Considerations

Shuffle tunes are always a nice change of pace, and this piece would make an outstanding opener at festivals or concerts. Schneider has clearly marked in all of the articulations and they are consistent with the shuffle style of more advanced charts. The march-style section from measures 26–40 is simple, both rhythmically and note-wise, so the ensemble can use this as a good opportunity to concentrate on articulations and dynamics. This section will also serve as an exercise in playing quarter notes evenly without rushing or dragging the time.

Unit 6: Musical Elements

MELODY:
The initial saxophone melody is very singable, as is the brass response eight measures later. Falls at the end of phrases are natural and present an excellent teaching opportunity. Schneider offers up enough new melodic material throughout the piece, which keeps it interesting for both players and listeners.

HARMONY:
Although the chords do not follow a 12-bar blues formula, the harmonic progression is very blues-like in concept. Young improvisers can sound confident on this chart by using the F blues scale. The piece sounds advanced, as Schneider's vocabulary (clearly notated for the rhythm section) features thirteenth and altered chords (♭9, ♯9) along with a tasteful chromatic turnaround.

RHYTHM:
This medium shuffle chart has real rhythmic propulsion, as most of its phrases begin with pick-up notes. The trumpet section has the most rhythmically challenging soli (measures 18–40) and would benefit from a separate sectional in the early learning stage.

The shout chorus beginning at measure 74 has many repeated rhythms or similar rhythmic phrases. Students will find this easier to play if they are aware of these consistencies. Of course, vocalizing the various sections of this chart before trying to play it will certainly lead to better style and the appropriate articulation.

Unit 7: Form and Structure

The basic form of the composition is a 16-bar blues-like progression.

SECTION	MEASURES	EVENT AND SCORING
Intro	1–5	The drummer kicks off this chart as the horns answer back and forth with a three-note motif before a surprise *subito* ***p*** in measure four.

Section	Measures	Event and Scoring
A	6–13	The saxophone section plays the opening melody in unison with falls, accents, and the signature Thad Jones figure (♫ 𝄾 ♩).
B	14–25	The brass, answers in unison with a new melody as the saxophones stay involved with a counter line. This phrase has a 4-bar extension with a challenging octave rip for the trumpet section.
C	26–41	This is the march section. Very careful attention must be paid to not rush the short quarter notes. The dynamics play a crucial role in pulling off this section, as does the hip, cup-muted trumpet melody.
D	42–57	Piano solo. A written one is provided, as are chord changes. This is the same 16-bar, blues-like progression that is used throughout the piece. Any instrument could solo here, as there are no backgrounds.
E	58–73	The band comes in strongly after the piano solo to give a 4-bar kick-off to the next soloist, which is written for the lead alto. This section has the same chord changes, and a few backgrounds near the end help to build up to the shout chorus.
F	74–89	This shout chorus has dense and complex harmonies making it sound much harder than it really is! Again, very careful attention should be paid to the accents; students will benefit by singing their lines so that they use the proper idiomatic style on all eighth-note lines. The drummer has many great opportunities here for fills, and especially for learning to set up the horn players for their strong entrances on beat two.

G	90–109	This recap is a repeat of the A and B sections with an unexpected and tasty $E^{7(\sharp 9)}$ chord to end the tune.

Unit 8: Suggested Listening

Jones, Thad, and the Mel Lewis Jazz Orchestra, *Central Park North*, Blue Note Records. *Big Dipper* on this recording is an ideal example of shuffle style.
Maria Schneider Jazz Orchestra, *Allegresse*, ENJA Records.
Evanescence, ENJA Records.

Unit 9: Additional References and Resources

Dunscomb, Richard, and Willie L. Hill, Jr., *Jazz Pedagogy: The Jazz Educator's Handbook and Resource Guide* (Miami: Warner Brothers, 2004).
Enstice, Wayne, and Janis Stockhouse, *JAZZWOMEN: Conversations with 21 Musicians* (Bloomington: Indiana University Press, 2004).

Contributed by:

Janis Stockhouse
Director of Bands
Bloomington High School North
Bloomington, Indiana

Teacher Resource Guide

Blue Note Special

Mike Tomaro

(b. 1958)

Unit 1: Composer

Born in Connellsville, Pennsylvania on October 9, 1958, Mike Tomaro has been the director of jazz studies at Duquesne University in Pittsburgh, Pennsylvania since 1997. Prior to his appointment at Duquesne, he served for seventeen years as a member of the Army Blues Jazz Ensemble based in Washington D.C. As a saxophonist, flutist, clarinetist, composer, and arranger, he has been an active recording artist, with four nationally released recordings under his own name. In addition, he has performed with artists as diverse as Nancy Wilson, Louis Bellson, the Pittsburgh Symphony, Linda Ronstadt, the Pittsburgh Ballet, and the Woody Herman Orchestra.

Mike's compositions have been performed by nationally known artists such as Randy Brecker and the New York Voices, and by high schools, colleges, and universities all around the world. Doug Beach Music, Hal Leonard Publications, and Walrus Music publish over eighty of his compositions and arrangements.

Mike is a member of the resource team of the International Association for Jazz Education in the area of arranging and composition. He is also affiliated with the American Society of Composers, Authors and Publishers, where, for four consecutive years, he received an ASCAP Plus award. He is also an active gust soloist, clinician and adjudicator. Mike is a Yamaha Performing Artist who exclusively endorses Vandoren reeds, mouthpieces, and ligatures.

Unit 2: Composition

Published in 1998 as part of the Doug Beach Music's *Threshold Series* (Kendor Music), *Blue Note Special* alternates between shuffle and swing styles, providing a opportunity for a developing band to learn the differences between the two and to smoothly switch between them without altering the time or intensity. The form is AA'BA, but it not strictly strophic; the form in its entirety occurs only once. There is no introductory section.

Unit 3: Historical Perspective

This chart is written for educational purposes and fits into the category of music that is designed to meet a learning objective. In this instance, it provides a vehicle by which students learn to alternate between two similar, but distinct, styles: shuffle and swing.

Unit 4: Technical Considerations

Blue Note Special is rated Medium Easy (Grade 2), and the recommended tempo is ♩ = 152. The composer strongly feels that the band should adhere to this tempo, as the feel should be driving but not rushed. The duration of the piece is 3:30.

The lead trumpet range is a concert G (g^1), with an optional concert B♭ ($b\flat^1$). The lead trombone goes up to a concert F (f), with concert G (g) appearing in the written-out solo. The bass part is written out, with chord changes present should the bassist choose to use themeasure The measures that need to be played verbatim are clearly marked "Play as written."

The guitar and piano parts have the voicings written out, with "Comp Rhythms" over the notated half notes, which will encourage the players to develop their own comping style.

The drum part is well written, designed to help the drummer (and non-drumming directors) distinguish between the shuffle and swing styles. Solo fills are also written out.

The featured soloists are tenor sax I and trombone I. Solos are written out with the chord changes included. Both get solo space; later in the chart they trade four's and two's before soloing together for seven measures just before the ending.

Unit 5: Stylistic Considerations

This piece certainly fits into the mold of the Art Blakey band. Not only is a driving shuffle characteristic of the hard-bop era, but there are also a number of Blakey recordings that alternate between shuffle and swing feels.

Note the different styles of writing in the two sections. In the pickup measure, beat four has 𝅘𝅥𝅮 𝄿 𝅘𝅥𝅯. This is to strongly emphasize the "bitten-off" aspect of the short notes in a shuffle. The short note should be stopped with the tongue ("dit"), as clipped as possible, albeit without rushing. You will never see this rhythm written in the swing sections of this piece, as even the short notes should have a slightly longer vowel (e.g., "daht").

Phrase marks abound. Following the dictum that slurring too often is better than tonguing too often, a band could sound passable by treating the phrase markings as slurs and using breath accents when accents are notated. However, the sooner the director starts to judiciously add articulations, the better. Each accent need not be tongued, but the director and the band should decide which accents should be more strongly emphasized.

Unit 6: Musical Elements

MELODY:

The entire ensemble should be able to sing the opening melody with proper inflections. Short notes should be exaggerated, and a metronome should be set to beats two and four to inhibit rushing. After the band is comfortable with both style and pulse, try having them sing with the click occurring only on beat four.

The swing section at Letter E is a perfect spot to get the horns swinging as one. The eighth-notes stylings of the bass should match the horns.

HARMONY:

The A and A' sections are modal, in the fashion of *Killer Joe* (I to ♭VII), but the B section descends through the entire chromatic scale. Fortunately for the developing soloists, the solo sections use the changes for the A sections, not the B section.

RHYTHM:

The rhythms are not overly complex, which suits the hard-bop style. Rhythmic unisons are the rule within sections, with the exception being the typical use of the baritone sax as both a member of the sax section and the trombone section. There are occasional examples of Basie-style unisons across the three horn sections (e.g., at letters E and I).

Unit 7: Form and Structure

The basic form of *Blue Note Special* is AA'BA, although this form only occurs in its entirety at the start of the piece.

SECTION	MEASURE	EVENT AND SCORING
A	1-8	The tempo is ♩ = 152, and the key is concert B♭ major. The alto and tenor saxes start in unison and are answered by the bari sax, trombones, and rhythm section. The solid swinging of the answer should offset the clipped style of the saxes. The dynamic is only ***mf***; don't start too loudly. The rhythm section comping starts in measure 5 with a driving shuffle feel.
B	9-16	Trumpets take over the melody at the subdominant tonality, answered by the trombones. The trumpet style should match the initial saxophone statement of the theme. In measure 13 the sax melody returns, with trumpets, trombones, bari sax, and rhythm punctuating the end of the A-A' section. The drummer does a roll, ending it with a snap on beat four along with the second note of the trombone pickups to section B.
C (bridge)	17-24	The rhythm section should switch to a swing feel. In addition to the change in the playing style of the drummer, the comping by the guitarist and pianist should be slightly less percussive. The trombones play a unison melody for four measures. Make sure that the release in measure 20 is clean. Saxes should release at the same time. Trumpets finish the melody of the bridge, and the entire band should cut off together at the end of measure 23. This bridge can be tricky, so take care that the piano and guitar voicings do not conflict.

Section	Measure	Event and Scoring
D	25-35	The closing section of the form has a 2-bar extension followed by a drum fill that leads into the first ***ff*** of the piece.
E	36-40	Switch to a driving swing feel. This rhythmically unison section should build to the trombone solo.
	41-44	At this point there is a trombone solo with *Killer Joe*-type changes and a shuffle feel.
F	45-52	Backgrounds should not overwhelm the soloist, but should still be played with intensity.
G/H	53-68	A tenor sax solo begins here. Backgrounds build toward letter H, but the volume should come down as letter I approaches.
I/J	69-84	Horns start in rhythmic unison at an ***mf*** level. At J trumpets and altos need to come out a bit more, as the weight of the lower parts has been taken away.
K	85-92	The last big swinging shout chorus; let them loose!
L	93-102	This is the return of section A, in a shuffle feel. No dynamic is indicated, but it would be proper to come up one dynamic to an ***f***.
	103-106	The rhythm section should switch back to a swing feel. The composer suggests a cross-stick.
M	107-114	The trombone and tenor trade fours. This 8-bar section can be opened up, if desired. The director should cue letter N.

SECTION	MEASURE	EVENT AND SCORING
N/O	115-122	The trombone and tenor trade twos while backgrounds are added and three saxes play the opening riff as a counter-melody.
	123-130	Trombone and tenor solo together as backgrounds continue to build. It is imperative that each soloist has a microphone so that backgrounds can build in an exciting manner.
P (bridge)	131-139	Interestingly, section B returns for the first time since letter C, and is used to close out the piece. The trombone melody at letter P should be a strong *forte*, but the trumpet answer in measure 135 needs to be ***ff***, as it leads to the ending. The drum fill in measure 138 needs to be very solid, as it sets up the final three notes of the piece.

Unit 8: Suggested Listening

Art Blakey and the Jazz Messengers, *The Big Beat*, Blue Note.
Art Blakey and the Jazz Messengers, *Paris 1958*, Bluebird.
Farmer, Art, and Golson, Benny, *Meet the Jazztet*, MCA/Chess.
Beach, Doug, *Jazz Charts: Volume 19*, Kendor.
Jones, Quincy, *Walking in Space*, A&M.

Unit 9: Additional References and Resources

Aebersold, Jamey, *Killer Joe: Jazz Play-A-Long Volume 70* (New Albany: Jamey Aebersold Jazz, Inc., 1996).

Dunscomb, Richard, and Willie L. Hill, Jr., *Jazz Pedagogy: The Jazz Educator's Handbook and Resource Guide* (Miami: Warner Brothers, 2004).

Jarvis, Jeff, and Doug Beach, *The Jazz Educator's Handbook* (Delevan: Kendor Music, Inc., 2002).

Riley, John, *The Art of Bop Drumming* (Miami: Manhattan Music, 1994).

Contributed by:

Joe Lill
Director of Bands
North Park University
Chicago, Illinois

Teacher Resource Guide

Bye, Bye Blackbird

Ray Henderson

(1896-1970)

Mort Dixon

(1892-1956)

arranged by Dave Rivello

(b. 1962)

Unit 1: Composers/Arranger

Ray Henderson was born in Buffalo, New York, December 1, 1892. He studied piano and composition at the Chicago Conservatory, and later moved to New York City to work in Tin Pan Alley, where he frequently teamed with other composers to write popular songs. Some of his most recognizable works include *Five Foot Two, Eyes of Blue*, *Varsity Drag*, and *I'm Sitting on Top of the World*. In addition to composition, Henderson also worked as an accompanist in vaudeville productions.

Lyricist Mort Dixon was born in New York City and, like many musicians at the time, began his career in Vaudeville. Although he did write for musicals and film, the majority of his work consisted of popular songs. He has several credits to his name, including *I'm Looking Over a Four Leaf Clover* and the well-known standard *You're My Everything*.

Arranger Dave Rivello is currently on faculty in the jazz studies and contemporary media programs at the Eastman School of Music. He also leads the Dave Rivello Ensemble, a twelve-piece group dedicated to performing his music. Among his many commissions are works written for Randy Brecker, Jiggs Whigham, the Smithsonian Institute, and Billy Hart.

Unit 2: Composition

The tune is a 32-bar, modified AABA song form in the key of F major. While the harmony does not strictly conform to the traditional practice for this version of song form, the melody does generally follow the standard outline. A slight variation occurs in measure 9 (the first restatement of section A), where the melody is played up a diatonic step, as well as in measure 29 (the second half of the last A section), where the final four bars are written to bring closure to the tune.

Bye, Bye Blackbird was published in 1926 and first recorded by American singer/songwriter Gene Austin that same year. A notable success at the time of its original release, the tune has remained a favorite among jazz musicians and aficionados alike. It has appeared in no less than seven movies and been memorably recorded by musicians such as Sarah Vaughn, Frank Sinatra, Keith Jarrett, John Coltrane, and Miles Davis, whose version on his album *'Round About Midnight* (1956) was the impetus for this arrangement.

Unit 3: Historical Perspective

This arrangement should be considered from different perspectives for two reasons: first, the original tune was not a jazz composition, but rather a hugely popular Tin Pan Alley hit of the 1920s. This was a period in American history also known as the Jazz Age, often characterized as carefree and riddled with vice, when jazz was beginning to establish itself in the American psyche as the music of choice in speak-easies across the country.

The second point to consider is that this arrangement is based on the 1955 recording by the first of Davis's famous quintets which was released six years after recording *Birth of the Cool*, and four years before the landmark album *Kind of Blue*. The 1950s was a period of significant change in jazz, demonstrated by Miles's cool collaborations with Gil Evans, his quintet's two-day/four-album recording spree for Prestige records, and his excursion into modal improvisation in the aforementioned *Kind of Blue*.

Two elements of Davis's evolving style during the 1950s clearly demonstrated in this recording include his patience with phrases and his liberal use of space. This track is an excellent display of the gradual transition of melodic playing over the more rigid harmonic structures of hard bop and cool to the increasingly flexible and less predictable sounds of modal jazz.

Unit 4: Technical Considerations

This chart is rated Grade 3 and the recommended tempo is ♩ = 120 with a duration of 3:44. The tune could be played at a slightly faster tempo, but will likely not work well any slower. The arranger encourages close adherence to the suggested tempo.

The lead trumpet range goes to concert G on top of the staff (g^1)and the lead trombone range goes to concert F-sharp above middle C (f). This tune features trumpet II with a harmon mute without stem. The melody is played as a solo and is immediately followed by an improvised solo. A written solo is provided as an option. The chords are relatively advanced, frequently using extensions and alterations, but could easily be simplified if necessary.

The guitar player will need to be experienced, as the part is a combination of written notes, rhythmic notation and slash notation. The piano part is fully notated throughout and includes chord symbols, which will work well for intermediate players new to jazz. The bass part is fully notated throughout and includes chord symbols. The drum part includes written notes and rhythmic notation, but is primarily slash notation with ensemble figures cued above the staff. This part appears more advanced; but with some guidance the drummer should be fine, as there is a substantial amount of helpful information included.

Unit 5: Stylistic Considerations

Because this arrangement is a variation based on Miles Davis's performance of the tune on his album *'Round About Midnight* (1956), it is highly recommended that the ensemble use that recording as a guide to the appropriate performance style. In his treatment of the tune, arranger Dave Rivello wanted to recreate the feel of the original recording in a manner that would be both interesting and engaging for younger musicians.

Stylistic interpretation of swing eighth notes should produce a relaxed feel reminiscent of the cooler sound of Miles in the 1950s, with marcato and staccato notes being played, in general, longer, as opposed to the heavier accents and shorter note lengths typically associated with big bands of the swing era.

Central to the success of this tune is the classic harmon mute sound of Miles Davis which can be accomplished by completely removing the stem from the end of the mute and playing with the mute as close to a microphone as possible. The soloist is advised to transcribe the solo from the album to better understand the articulation, phrasing, and other musical elements of Davis's playing.

Unit 6: Musical Elements

MELODY:

Though the melody is probably simple enough to sight-read, it is a good idea for the entire ensemble to learn it by ear, first singing together and then playing. Use a lead sheet for this exercise, not the written arrangement, as the arranger has applied a rhythmic treatment to the melody. This will be of tremendous help when teaching style as well as help to establish the appropriate context for articulation and phrasing throughout the entire ensemble. The structure of the melody is 8-bar phrases through the A sections and 4-bar phrases through the B section. All sections have clearly defined beginnings and ends.

HARMONY:

Bye Bye Blackbird is relatively straightforward in its harmonic construction. The first A section is primarily a series of ii^7–V^7–I progressions in the key of F major. In the second A section, the melody is repeated exactly but played a diatonic step up. Here the harmony begins with a common progression with the same minor triad used in successive measures. The extensions change from measure to measure, however, creating a descending chromatic line within the harmony and a sense of motion, though the root remains constant. Section B is comprised of two ii^7–V^7–I progressions, the first in G minor, the second leading back to F major. The final A section is a slight harmonic variation of the first.

RHYTHM:

The band should sing triplets together in a legato style (as taught by Ron Carter of Northern Illinois University) using the phrase "doo-dle-la" with the emphasis on "la," the entire phrase representing an eighth-note triplet.

Sing this pattern together, tap heels (not toes) on the quarter-note pulse. This will greatly help establish both a common pulse and its subdivision, which is a triplet in the case of swing. The translation to standard eighth notes is such that the first two notes of the quarter note triplet ("doo-dle") equal the first of two eighth notes and the final note of the triplet ("la") equals the second eighth note. This is important because with swing eighth notes, the first note is longer than the second.

Additionally, the band should spend time in guided listening exercises with recordings of the Count Basie Orchestra, the Duke Ellington Orchestra, and the Miles Davis album *'Round About Midnight* to begin to identify the

different styles of swing. Hopefully the students will then be able to emphasize those distinguishing qualities in the appropriate style of performance for this particular chart.

Unit 7: Form and Structure

The basic form of the composition is AABA.

SECTION	MEASURE	EVENT AND SCORING
Intro	1–7	The tempo is ♩ = 120. This is probably slow enough for the band to sight read at tempo. This section features the brass and saxophone sections playing against each other before a unison rhythmic hit to set up the solo trumpet melody. It is important to reinforce the rhythmic figures found in the rhythm section parts in measures 2, 4, and 6 in the drums. The drummer may also wish to reinforce the brass lines in measures 1, 3, and 5, which are not notated in the drum part. The texture will change frequently in the up-coming melody, and the band must be very careful with balance, as the melody will be passed from a muted soloist to different sections playing in unison with the use of backgrounds and counter-melodies.
Melody 1A	8–15	The melody begins with solo trumpet accompanied by the rhythm section and should be approached as if performing in a quartet.
Melody 2A	16–23	Trombones and baritone saxophone enter with backgrounds behind the solo trumpet melody. Tenor saxophones have an interesting counter-melody that should be performed with subtlety, as it will have no trouble projecting. Overall, be careful not to overpower the sound of the muted trumpet. It is still the primary melody.

Section	Measure	Event and Scoring
Bridge	24–31	The melody is passed to the brass section. Trumpets play the first four measures in unison; trombones play the last four in unison. Saxophones have backgrounds throughout.
Last A	32–37	The melody returns to the muted trumpet soloist and saxophones continue with backgrounds. The entire ensemble plays the final two measures of the melody as a send-off to the trumpet solo.
Trumpet Solo	38–71	Measures 35–36 are a solo break and should be silent except for the soloist and the drum set-up into measure 40. If the soloist has trouble maintaining a steady pulse through the break, encourage the drummer to keep the hi-hat going on beats two and four to reinforce time. Saxophones begin right away in measure 40 with backgrounds. The entire horn section has backgrounds from measures 48–64. Again, be very careful not to overpower the soloist. Saxophones continue with backgrounds from measures 64–69. Measure 71 is the set-up to the shout chorus and the drummer should be aggressive with the figures there.
Shout Chorus	72–87	The shout chorus begins with block writing. The drummer should pay close attention to the ensemble figures at this point, which should be reinforced in measures 72–76 with a combination of cymbal crashes and kicks instead of simple snare figures. If there is confusion as to how this might be done, listen to a shout chorus as played by another big band recording. An excellent example is the shout chorus in *Corner Pocket* as played by the Count Basie Orchestra from the suggested listening in Unit 8. Measures 77–87 feature the saxophone and brass sections playing against each other.

Section	Measure	Event and Scoring
Melody-out	88-end	The shout chorus ends with an immediate transition to the muted trumpet playing the melody in a quartet format, as with the initial statement of the melody. This transition could be tricky and should be rehearsed with the idea of eliminating a potential seam in the music. A strong entrance by the solo trumpet and significant dynamic change in the rhythm section will help. The saxophone section returns with backgrounds at measure 92. The brass section finishes the tune by tagging the melody, beginning in measure 100. The chart concludes with a strong, two-measure statement in traditional big band, block fashion. Muted trumpet, however, has the last word, unaccompanied, in measures 106–107, and the band answers with a subdued fermata on beat three of measure 107. If the soloist has trouble playing this passage in time without the rhythm section, the same technique involving the hi-hat may be applied in measures 106–107, as was suggested for the solo break.

Unit 8: Suggested Listening

Basie, Count, *Live at the Sands–Before Frank*, Reprise.
Davis, Miles, *'Round About Midnight*, Columbia/Legacy.
Porgy and Bess, Columbia.
Ellington, Duke, *Three Suites*, Columbia.

Unit 9: Additional References and Resources

Dunscomb, Richard, and Willie L. Hill, Jr., *Jazz Pedagogy: The Jazz Educator's Handbook and Resource Guide* (Miami: Warner Brothers, 2004).

Houghton, Steve, *A Guide for the Modern Jazz Rhythm Section* (Oskaloosa: C.L. Barnhouse Company, 1982).

Lawn, Richard, *The Jazz Ensemble Director's Manual* (Oskaloosa: C.L. Barnhouse Company, 1981).

Contributed by:

Aaron Moe
Jazz Director
Normandale Community College
Bloomington, Minnesota

Teacher Resource Guide

Cherry Point
Neal Hefti
(b. 1922)

arranged by Ray Phillipe
(b. 1957)

Unit 1: Composer

Born in Hastings, Nebraska, October 29, 1922, Neal Hefti was one of the great jazz composers and arrangers during the 1950s and 1960s. He is probably best known for his work with the Count Basie Orchestra and for his film and television scoring.

Neal began playing trumpet at the age of eleven, and during his high school years he performed with local bands in the Omaha area. He credits Harry "Sweets" Edison and Buck Clayton from Count Basie's band and Dizzy Gillespie (whom he heard with Cab Calloway) as early influences. In addition to his playing he wrote arrangements for area bands; some of his charts ended up in the library of Earl Hines's big band. In the early 1940s Neal spent time in New York where he followed the development of the bebop style; he played with several bands, including Charlie Barnett's and Charlie Spivek's big bands. He joined Woody Herman's ensemble (known at the time as Herman's Herd) in 1944 and stayed for two years. His writing for Herman reflected his (and the group's) interest in incorporating the bebop musical language, and his most important contribution to the ensemble may have been his writing. While with Herman's Herd, Neal met and married Frances Wayne, the group's vocalist. The two left Herman in late 1946 so that Neal could pursue a full-time career as a writer.

In 1950 Neal began his association with Count Basie. Basie's band was undergoing some reorganization, resulting in a style and repertory less dependant on the "head arrangements" of Basie's Kansas City years. Neal's writing fit in well with the band's new direction, which is occasionally termed Basie's "New Testament" period. One album that exemplifies Neal's work with the band was originally titled *Basie* with the subtitle *E* = MC[2] = *Count Basie Orchestra + Neal Hefti Arrangements*. The recording is now commonly referred to as the "Atomic Basie" recording. It contained eleven songs (the CD re-release has sixteen) composed by Neal, including *L'il Darlin'* and *Splanky*. This was followed by *Basie Plays Hefti*, which included *Cute*.

Neal Hefti led his own big band in the 1950s as well, although it did not attain the level of success enjoyed by some of the leaders for whom he wrote. Miles Davis once noted the importance of Neal's contribution to the Basie band, but also observed that Neal's arrangements did not sound as good performed by someone other than Count Basie. In the later 1950s and 1960s most of Neal's energy became increasingly focused on film and television work. Among his many well-known movie scores are *How to Murder Your Wife* and *Barefoot in the Park*, and his television themes include the themes from *Batman* and *The Odd Couple*. He also arranged and conducted the music for Frank Sinatra's 1961 recording *Swingin' Brass*.

Unit 2: Composition

Neal Hefti originally wrote *Cherry Point* for a performance by an all-star big band at the Marine base in Cherry Point, North Carolina. He later rearranged it for the Count Basie Orchestra, which recorded the piece in December 1953; he also recorded it with his own ensemble on an album called *Pardon My Doo-Wah* in 1958. *Cherry Point* is a 12-bar blues that calls to mind the Kansas City Swing style; it makes extensive use of riffs—small repetitive musical units—and of the call and response technique so prominent in jazz of the Swing era. The song has been recorded by several artists in addition to Basie's and Hefti's orchestras, including Herbie Mann, Jimmy McGriff, and Stanley Turrentine.

Unit 3: Historical Perspective

In the 1920s and early 1930s, the music that came to be known as Swing—though still considered by many an ethnic or race-oriented music—was becoming increasingly popular throughout the United States through the medium of radio. In the Midwest, "territory" or regional bands played in a distinctive style based not on written sheet music but on parts learned from memory. The blues was an important (but by no means the only) influence on the music performed by these bands, and their head arrangements often incorporated the call and response technique as well as the use of riffs. Improvised solos played a more significant role in the performance of Kansas City bands than in the more overtly structured swing tunes played by bands from other areas. This attracted many musicians to Kansas City, the artistic center of this music. The style came to be known as Kansas City Swing, and most jazz scholars and enthusiasts consider the best of the bands in this style to be Count Basie and his Barons of Rhythm. Radio broadcasts of Basie's band from Kansas City's Reno Club led to a recording contract with Decca, a relocation of the band to New York, and fame. Some of the significant recordings from the band, renamed the Count Basie Orchestra, include *One O'clock Jump* (1937), *Jumpin' at the Woodside* (1938), and *Taxi War Dance* (1939). Some of Basie's personnel of this period included drummer Jo Jones, guitarist Freddie Green, bassist Walter Page, tenor saxophonist Lester Young, trumpeters Buck Clayton and Harry "Sweets" Edison, trombonist Dickie Wells, and vocalists Jimmy Rushing, Billie Holiday, and Joe Williams. (Each of these musicians deserves listening study as a means of understanding the style).

Economic hardships in the early 1950s forced Basie to reduce the size of his ensemble, but he reformed his full big band in 1952. Basie's new ensemble sought to preserve the essence of the well-known Basie style while making greater use of arrangers such as Neal Hefti and, later, Sammy Nestico and Quincy Jones.

Unit 4: Technical Considerations

Roy Phillipe's arrangement of this Neal Hefti standard is geared toward young ensembles. The recommended tempo is ♩ = 105, and the chart should be performed close to that tempo—no faster than ♩ = 115.

The highest note in the first trumpet is a written F on the top line of the staff (f^1), and the top first trombone pitch is the D♭ above middle C (d♭). The lowest note for the baritone saxophone is a written D below the staff (d). The rhythm section parts are completely written out except for the optional guitar part, which uses slash and rhythmic notation with chord symbols. Chord symbols are also provided in the piano and bass parts. The arranger notes that the following parts are optional: second tenor and baritone saxophones, third trumpet, second and third trombones, and guitar. Optional alternate parts are provided for flute (which doubles the first alto saxophone or first trumpet), tuba, and French horn and baritone treble clef (each of which doubles the first trombone).

Plunger mutes are indicated for the brass for a passage of about eight measures. Solo opportunities are given for piano, first tenor saxophone, and first trumpet; solos are written out and chord changes are also provided if the players wish to improvise.

Unit 5: Stylistic Considerations

Cherry Point is a 12-bar blues in the key of B♭. The piece is described in the score as a "greasy blues"; it is important for the ensemble to not confuse "greasy" with "sloppy." Listening to a recording of this piece, in particular Count Basie's version on *King of Swing*, will be helpful in getting the proper feeling for this arrangement. The ensemble should agree on the length of the notes articulated with a marcato—these should be detached but "fat," in the Count Basie style. The unison ensemble soli should not be completely slurred; legato tongue should be added to the most important pitches in the phrases, which are typically the high notes, the longer notes, and the last notes.

Unit 6: Musical Elements

MELODY:

The first two phrases of the piece's AAB blues form utilize a three-note riff. When it occurs, the last of the three notes is the most important and should be treated as an arrival point. This can be accomplished by making each of the pitches a bit louder than the previous one. It would help to have the whole ensemble play or sing the riff together. Then, divide the group in half and have one group echo the other in call and response fashion. Younger ensembles may experience some difficulty starting the riff in the correct place rhythmically; the first note should be felt as a reaction to beats one or three. The four-note pattern in the tenth and eleventh bars of the melody should be treated in a similar fashion.

HARMONY:

The chord progression is essentially a 12-bar blues in the key of B♭. One distinctive change is that—in all the choruses except two—the typical dominant seventh chords are replaced by a minor seventh chord over two beats moving to the dominant seventh lasting two beats. The effect is that of a "ii^7–V^7" progression found in many jazz tunes.

RHYTHM:

A successful performance of *Cherry Point* depends on the band realizing the laid back feeling for which the Count Basie bands were famous. The piece must not feel rushed. As previously noted, putting the three-note riff in the proper place rhythmically may require some special attention. Similarly, the four-note idea in the tenth measure of the melody begins on beat three, but its reoccurrence in the eleventh bar begins on the second beat.

Unit 7: Form and Structure

The basic form of the composition is AAB: the 12-bar blues.

Section	Measure	Event and Scoring
Intro	1–8	The full ensemble plays material from section B of the melody. The ensemble must agree on the length of the marcato notes, so it will be beneficial to play them in isolation. Also, the instances of the accented notes on the second half of beat four, even though detached, should be felt as tied melodically to the next note on the second half of beat one.
Melody (1)	9–20	The first time through, the melody features a call in the piano with a response in the brass for the first two A sections. The full ensemble plays section B, which contains the same material as the introduction.
Melody (2)	21–32	The second time through, the melody resembles the first except that saxophones join the piano in the call.
Ensemble soli	33–44	Horns play a unison soli with stop time in the rhythm section. The phrasing should be smooth, in the bebop style, with legato tonguing on the high notes and final notes of the phrases. The lead trumpet player is ultimately responsible for setting the phrasing. It will be helpful to have the section leaders play the soli together to unify the style, and then add the rest of the horns.

SECTION	MEASURE	EVENT AND SCORING
Soli	45–56	The score indicates that the solo section should be played three times with backgrounds on cue. Soli are written out for piano, trumpet, and tenor saxophone. As with most jazz tunes, this could be altered to shorten or lengthen the performance, or to allow others to solo. The offbeat dotted quarter notes in the saxophones and trombones should be felt as reactions to the beat.
Shout Chorus	57–68	Again utilizing call and response, the brass section plays a short-long figure which is echoed in the saxophones. It begins soft and gradually builds to a *forte* by the end of the chorus. The ensemble should make the increase in volume gradual and steady. Plunger mutes for the brass are indicated in the score.
Melody/End	69–88	The return to the melody divides the call and response between lower saxophones and trombones and upper saxophones and trumpets. The final B section of the melody is repeated two additional times. The last note should be nice and "fat."

Unit 8: Suggested Listening

Count Basie Orchestra, *King of Swing*, UMVD Labels.
Count Basie Orchestra, *The Complete Atomic Basie*, Blue Note Records.
Hefti, Neal, *Pardon My Doo-Wah/Hefti, Hot 'n Hearty*, Collectibles.

Unit 9: Additional References and Resources

Basie, Count and Albert Murray, *Good Morning Blues, the Autobiography of Count Basie* (New York: Donald Fine Inc., 1985).
Gitler, Ira, *Swing to Bop* (New York: Oxford University Press, 1985).

Contributed by:

Larry Nelson
Assistant Professor of Jazz Studies, Saxophone, and Musicology
Eastern Kentucky University
Richmond, Kentucky

Teacher Resource Guide

Do Nothin' till You Hear from Me

Duke Ellington

(1899–1975)

arranged by Dave Wolpe

(b. 1936)

Unit 1: Composer/Arranger

Edward Kennedy (Duke) Ellington was born in Washington, D. C., and there he pursued his early music career. At the age of seven he started playing the piano and learned his art by listening to local ragtime performers. He first had planned to study commercial art, but changed his mind in his teens and decided to study music. Many of his compositions allude to colors from his early interest in art. He started a successful dance band in Washington and soon began to play many commercial engagements. In 1923, he moved to New York and his band performed shows and dance sets at the Kentucky Club. By 1927 the band had moved to the Cotton Club in Harlem, where they remained the house band until 1931. It was during this engagement that the band began to gain international recognition. Ellington also composed many of his early masterpieces during this time. These pieces were written for floorshows at the club and this era has been referred to as his Jungle period.

1938–1941 is generally considered the period in which he produced many of his great masterpieces. These included many popular songs, instrumental works, jazz standards and one of the first extended works for jazz ensemble *Black, Brown and Beige*. Written in 1940 and revised in 1943, *Do Nothin' Till You Hear From Me* is also from this period. Ellington continued to compose through the 50s, 60s, and 70s, producing many masterful extended works and the film score for *Anatomy of a Murder*.

Ellington is now considered one of the great composers of the twentieth century. His works for jazz ensembles have become the models for many younger generations of jazz composers. He also was the first jazz composer to write extended works for the jazz ensemble.

Ellington's compositional style focused on the personal sounds of individual musicians to create his particular ensemble sound. He had musicians experiment with sounds such as growls, mutes, bends, and other different approaches to their instruments, incorporating them into new compositions. He also tried many different pairings of instruments across sections and/or using them in different roles to create new colors in the ensemble. The soloist's idiomatic performance and ensemble became inextricably linked to create a colorful and interesting composition.

Dave Wolpe was born in San Bernardino, California on July 16, 1936. After high school, at the age of seventeen, he enlisted in the U.S. Air Force. During his service career (1954–1976), he was a member of the famous NORAD Band as trombonist and arranger for the "Commanders" dance orchestra. He was later assigned to the U.S. Army Field Band and continued to play and arrange for the Studio Band (now called The Jazz Ambassadors). He was the leader of the Studio Band from 1974 until he retired from the military in 1977. Wolpe has been publishing compositions and arrangements since 1965. To date he has arranged over 600 pieces for various publishers, including Kendor Music, Creative Jazz Composers, Hanson Publications, Hal Leonard Publishing Corp., and Columbia Pictures Publications (which became CPP/Belwin and later Warner Bros. Publications, now owned by Alfred Publishing Co.). Wolpe scored dozens of arrangements for the Glenn Miller Orchestra and is co-arranger on the platinum CD "In The Christmas Mood." He has arranged music for Walt Disney World and Disneyland Paris for groups ranging from small theme park bands to symphony orchestras. He has also arranged for the bands of Ray Anthony, Les Brown, and many others. In the late 70s and early 80s he played lead trombone with Ray Anthony and later with Les Brown and His Band of Renown. Dave Wolpe lives in Orlando, Florida.

Unit 2: Composition

Do Nothin' Till You Here From Me is derived from Ellington's earlier work *Concerto for Cootie*, written in 1940 to feature the many diverse trumpet styles of Cootie Williams. To create this work, Ellington listened to William's unique approach to the trumpet, which was founded in a bluesy New Orleans style. Williams showed Ellington his mastery of many different techniques and the mutes that manipulated the pitch and timbre of the trumpet. Ellington then created a compositional masterpiece that featured Williams. In 1943, Ellington borrowed the first AABA form and melody from *Concerto for*

Cootie, reworked it and added lyrics by Bob Russell to create the popular song *Do Nothin' Till You Hear From Me*. It was originally recorded in November, 1943 in New York with Al Hibbler on vocal on Circle CLP-101. Since that time this song has become a standard, and has been recorded over 420 times by a wide range of artists. This arrangement stays true to the original.

Unit 3: Historical Perspective

This popular song was written during World War II in what is considered to be Ellington's second creative period with the Blanton/Webster band at the height of the big band era. This was a very productive time for Duke Ellington and his orchestra. Many of his compositions from this era are now jazz standards, and the orchestra's performances of them are great examples of Ellington's realization of composition combined with unique individual improvisation.

Unit 4: Technical Considerations

This arrangement of the great Ellington popular standard is a vocal feature for low female or high male voice in the key of C. There is also a substitute tenor saxophone solo if no vocalist is available. This arrangement is not rated, but is approximately at the Grade 3 level. The recommended tempo is ♩ = 92.

The lead trumpet range goes to concert B♭ ($b\flat^1$), and the lead trombone range goes to concert F (f). The vocal range is from F (F) to B♭ (b♭). There are complex harmonies throughout in the guitar and piano parts, with chord voicings provided for both instruments. The chord changes for the saxophone soloist are not difficult, staying close to the key of concert C. The arrangement has no doubles for the saxophones and no mutes for the brass.

Unit 5: Stylistic Considerations

This arrangement is written in swing style. The ensemble should play with this triplet feel throughout. All eighth notes are written even, but should be played with a light swing triplet interpretation. This also applies to the pyramid effect starting at measure 22, and again at measure 54. Listening to the original *Concerto for Cootie* and some of the listed versions of *Do Nothin Till You Hear From Me* is a good way to learn the style of this composition.

Wolpe states:

> One very important thing to point out is the last eighth note in measure 5. This note is still a concert D♯. Anyone playing the melody, including the vocalist, should be aware of this every time this figure occurs. There is a strong tendency to

> play a D♮. Even the experienced musicians who recorded the demo of this chart missed it every time.
>
> The molto rit. at the end of the piece can actually begin with the vocalist slowing down a bit in measure 71.

Saxophones need to use a scoop into the responsorial background to the vocal. This can be accomplished by dropping the jaw and using half fingerings, creating the effect of sliding into the note from below.

Unit 6: Musical Elements

MELODY:
The melody is simple and repetitive but well constructed and memorable. The first phrase in each A section is repeated three times. On the third statement the motive varies, and then is followed by a new closing motive. The bridge melody starts with a new motive repeated twice and then ends with a closing phrase.

HARMONY:
The A section of the song is in C, moving briefly to F. The Bridge modulates to A♭, then works back to C. The chord sequence has been modified with passing chords to create harmonic interest. Chords are sevenths, ninths, and thirteenths, with the occasional altered dominant (♯5 and ♭9) and passing diminished.

RHYTHM:
Rhythms are in swing feel throughout the composition, and are either derivative of the melody, responsorial to the melody, or backgrounds supporting the vocal or the soloist.

Unit 7: Form and Structure

The basic form of the composition is AABA.

The arrangement is two choruses of the song with a 6-bar full band introduction, followed by a short tag ending. The vocal is featured in the first chorus (AABA), with a tenor sax solo for next two A sections. The vocal returns for last B and A sections plus the tag.

SECTION	MEASURE	EVENT AND SCORING
Introduction	1–6	Full ensemble introduction ending on the dominant chord. Vocal pick-ups in measure 5.

Section	Measure	Event and Scoring
A	6–14	Vocal with saxophone backgrounds in a call response manner.
A	14–22	Vocal with brass and saxophone backgrounds.
B	22–30	Bridge in A♭. Saxes and brass backgrounds. Measures 22, 24, and 26 feature trombone and saxophone pyramids.
A	30–38	Sax backgrounds. There is a full ensemble hit at measure 36.
A	38–46	Tenor solo with band backgrounds.
A	46–54	Tenor solo continues with backgrounds.
B	54–62	Vocal with backgrounds. Measures 54, 56, and 58 feature trombone and saxophone pyramids.
A	62–73	Vocal and tag ending. In measure 70 there is a full band hit followed by a soft ending.

Unit 8: Suggested Listening

Basie, Count, *Count Plays Duke*, Mama Records, 1998, MMF 1024.

Bennett, Tony, *Hot & Cool (Bennett Sings Ellington)*, Sony Records, 1999.

Clooney, Rosemary, *Many a Wonderful Moment*, Bear Family Records, 2000, BCD 15927 HK.

Connick Jr., Harry, *20*, Columbia, 1988.

Ellington, Duke, *Duke Ellington Centennial Edition: Complete RCA Victor Recordings: 1927–1973*, RCA/BMG, 1973.

Ellington Duke, *Concerto for Cootie*, Smithsonian Collection of Classic Jazz, Norton, 1988.

Fitzgerald, Ella, *Ella Fitzgerald Sings the Duke Ellington Songbook*, Verve, 2000, CD Reissue 830533–2.

Holliday, Billie, *Billie Holiday: Portrait*, International Music, 1948.

Krall, Diana, *Diana Krall Ellingtonia: Justin Time Toasts Duke*, Justin Time, 1999.

Unit 9: Additional References and Resources

Suggested Reading:

Dance, Stanley, *The World of Duke Ellington* (Cambridge: Da Capo Press, 1988).

Ellington, Mercer and Stanley Dance, *Ellington In Person* (Cambridge: Da Capo Press, 1988).

Hasse, John Edward and Wynton Marsalis, *Beyond Category: The Life and Genius of Duke Ellington* (Cambridge: Da Capo Press, 1995).

Tucker, Mark, *Ellington: The Early Years* (Champaign: University of Illinois Press, 1995).

Jazz Vocal Series (Van Nuys: Alfred Publishing, 1999).

Contributed by:

Gordon Towell
Professor of Music
Jazz Studies/Music Education
Morehead State University
Morehead, Kentucky

Teacher Resource Guide

Keys to the Heart

Larry Neeck

(b. 1954)

Unit 1: Composer

C.L. Barnhouse, Larry Neeck's publisher, provides the following biographical information:

> Larry Neeck has over fifty works for concert band and jazz ensemble published internationally by C.L. Barnhouse Company. Many works have been commissioned for concert band, jazz ensemble, orchestra, and theatre. He has written for the internationally acclaimed jazz violinist Regina Carter, and for jazz saxophonist James Carter. For the past four years, he has participated in The Commission Project's Composer-in-Residence program, a nationally recognized program that places composers in schools. His music has been recorded by Walking Frog Records, and has been heard on PBS television. He has received four ASCAP awards for his compositions.
>
> Mr. Neeck holds a B.A. in music from the University of Pittsburgh, and an M.M. in music education from the Eastman School of Music. He is a member of the American Society of Composers, Authors, and Publishers (ASCAP), Music Educators National Conference (MENC), New York State School Music Association (NYSSMA), International Association of Jazz Educators (IAJE), and the New York State Band Directors Association (NYSBDA).
>
> In addition to composing, Mr. Neeck teaches instrumental music in the Webster (NY) Central School District. He directs concert bands,

jazz ensembles, and is co-founder and director of the Willink Middle School Student/Parent Band. He resides in Pittsford, NY with his wife and daughter, and his two miniature wirehaired dachshunds.

Unit 2: Composition

Keys To The Heart is a beautiful chart, featuring piano in a light rock ballad style. Written to be playable with as few as six horns (two altos, tenor, two trumpets and trombone), this composition is an excellent and effective introduction to the rock ballad. The solo piano part is scored throughout the piece, and although no space is left for improvisation, many good models of voicing and register are given the player for future improvisation opportunities. The background parts (except guitar) are easy and effective due to the scoring and melodic style. Interesting modifications to the basic AABA form help to keep the listener engaged throughout the piece.

Unit 3: Historical Perspective

The birth of jazz involved a conglomeration of music styles (including slave songs, field hollers, blues, French military music and ragtime), and diverse musical forces have continued to influence jazz throughout its history. From the 1930s on came a parade of styles that were absorbed and adapted into the jazz world, styles such as Cuban, Brazilian, Afro-Cuban, Western classical "third stream," salsa, and rock fusion. Stylistically, *Keys To The Heart* belongs to an area of the fusion movement known as light rock, which was first popular in the late sixties.

Unit 4: Technical Considerations

This chart is rated Medium Easy (Grade 3), and the recommended tempo is ♩ = 88–92 with a duration of 3:35. The chart will lose stylistic clarity if performed much slower or faster. It is important to pay close attention to the accuracy of the syncopations. Be sure everyone understands they are based on straight eighths, and the location of the beats during and after the syncopations. To clear up any problems, have the sections play the passages slowly, playing all the subdivisions (two eighths to a quarter, three eighths to a dotted quarter) to hear where the whole measure lies. There is a tendency to rush the slurred sixteenth note run in measures 48 and 70.

The solo piano part is well written and suitable for any well-trained middle school player. The piano part is completely written out. It will sound best on a tuned grand, but if that is not available, it will work very well on a good electronic piano. An upright should be avoided, if possible, because much of the pianistic writing will not cut through the backgrounds without over-playing. Use the best microphones you can on the acoustic instruments.

Brass and saxophone range is not an issue in *Keys To The Heart.* Although all parts stay in the staff, be aware that the reduced instrumentation scheme places the second trombone part above the first when using the full instrumentation.

Ballad playing has a tendency to highlight faulty intonation, and there are several tuning issues in this piece. Unison lines (trumpets in measures 2–3, 29–30, 37–40, 48–52, and 72–73, tenors in measures 33–38, trombones in measures 33–38, and all winds in measures 70, and especially the full wind G harmonic minor scale in measure 24) are best tuned by having the lead player dominate, the others softer so they can hone in on the correct pitch. Unison playing is problematic for balance as well, since unisons are inherently louder than harmonies, so the above strategy is also beneficial here. Other tuning problems arise with the complex chords, especially those that include occasional unisons within a section. Be sure to spend some time playing the chordal pads as long notes, out of rhythm, holding them long enough for the pitch to settle. If necessary, tune chord roots first, then fifths, then thirds, then sevenths, and finally any additional notes. Remember that major thirds and minor sevenths need to be brought down considerably.

One last issue is the guitar part. The complexity of the chords required here (which include C^9, $B\flat maj^9$, $D^{7(\flat 9)}$, $D^{7(\flat 5)}$, and $Aaug^7/F$) will likely require some individual help or simplification.

Unit 5: Stylistic Considerations

The basic style here is light rock, featuring moderate range and dynamics, a lightly syncopated rhythmic feel based on straight eighth notes, a fairly lush chordal language, and tunes that are "more pretty than gritty."

Articulation is a major factor in playing light rock. The articulations in this piece are simple and marked well in this piece; they should be followed explicitly. When encountering a series of accented off-the-beat quarter notes (or two tied eighths) in this style, it is wise to put a light separation between them, even if they are under a phrase or slur marking.

The dynamics are appropriate, but need to be played under the solo sections. Feel free to bring out the *forte* sections. *Keys To The Heart* demands more difference between ***mf*** and ***f*** than between ***mp*** and ***mf***.

The bass and drum parts are completely written out, but players should be encouraged to stretch their parts out a bit with occasional and tasteful fills, but nothing that calls attention away from the piano.

Unit 6: Musical Elements

MELODY:

The melodies in this piece are beautiful and simple. They are almost completely diatonic with a frequently repeated two-bar motive and two secondary motives providing contrast. There is an almost constant melodic tonal implication of F major, although the harmonic underpinning in the background is more complex.

HARMONY:

The changes are considerably fairly sophisticated for this level, exhibiting a root movement that is typically jazz, rather than rock in nature. However, most cadences use ii^7/V in place of the dominant, and there are some whole step root movements more typical of rock style. The harmonies are much more chromatic than the melody. The harmonic rhythm of this composition speeds up around cadences from approximately one to two chords per measure.

RHYTHM:

The straight eighth light rock style is most evident in the melody, bass and drums. The rhythms in background parts are mostly long tones, except for the bridge. The importance of the written articulations is worth repeating here.

Unit 7: Form and Structure

The well-integrated form of *Keys To The Heart* exhibits a sophisticated simplicity and is one of the piece's great strengths. The four-measure intro, based on material from section A later serves as the last section of the first chorus and then again as the coda.

The form of the composition is a modified AABA.

SECTION	MEASURE	EVENT AND SCORING
Intro	1–4	The tempo is ♩ = 88–92; the style is rock ballad. A unison trumpet section carries the melody based on section A. There is a full band unison rhythm in measure 3.
A	5–12	The piano has the section A melody over the rhythm section alone.
A	13–20	The piano has the section A melody over the rhythm section plus saxophones, followed by saxophone and trombone pads.

SECTION	MEASURE	EVENT AND SCORING
Bridge	21–28	The bridge. The piano has the section B melody over the full band. Horns have fills in unison rhythm, returning to pads at measure 25.
	29–32	Four-bar return of the intro. A unison trumpet section carries the melody based on section A. The full band has unison rhythm in measure 31.
A	33–40	Trombones and tenors have the section A melody over the rhythm section. unison trumpets conclude the melody over saxophone and trombone pads.
A	41–48	The piano has the section A melody over the rhythm section plus saxophone, and then saxophone and trombone pads. There is a *crescendo* at the end with a unison trumpet run into measure 49.
Bridge	49–56	The bridge. This is the climax of piece. Here is the first sustained *forte*. Trumpets have the section B melody in octaves over the full band. Horns return to pads at measure 55.
A	57–64	The piano has the section A melody over pads in the full band. Horns repeat measure 57 at measure 64 with a *crescendo* to measure 65.
	65–71	Transition to coda with full band. The trumpet section has the melody in unison. There is new material at *forte*. The dynamic level drops and builds back to the coda.
Coda	72–79	The coda with full band. There is a return of the intro. Trumpets have section A material in unison. Horns have whole notes for the last five measures. There is a rallentando, a drop in dynamic level to *piano*. The last measure is at ***mp***, followed by a *crescendo*.

Unit 8: Suggested Listening

Excerpts from *Keys To The Heart* can be beard on the C. L. Barnhouse website: http://www.barnhouse.com/product.php?id=032–3324–00.

Hazell, Chris, *Mr. Jums* on *The Lighter Side*. Philip Jones Brass Ensemble. Decca Records.

Unit 9: Additional References and Resources

Dunscomb, Richard, and Willie L. Hill, Jr., *Jazz Pedagogy: The Jazz Educator's Handbook and Resource Guide* (Miami: Warner Brothers, 2004).

Contributed by:

Jay Hildebrandt
Professor of Music
University of Delaware
Newark, Delaware

Teacher Resource Guide

Leap Frog
Joe Garland
(1903–1977)
arranged by Paul Lavender

Unit 1: Composer/Arranger

Joe Garland was an African American composer and saxophonist. Born in 1903 in Norfolk Virginia, he played saxophones at school in Oxford, North Carolina in concert bands, studied music at the Aeolian Conservatory in Baltimore under Alfred Jack Thomas, and later at Shaw University in Raleigh North Carolina.

In 1924 Garland played his first jazz gigs with Graham Jackson's Seminole Syncopators before moving to New York in 1925 for an engagement with Elmer Snowden's band at the Bamville Club. Later he worked with Lucky Millinder (1932–36), Duke Ellington (1933), Edgar Hayes (1937), Don Redman (1938) and then, from 1939 to 1947 with Louis Armstrong's big band. In the latter part of his stint with Armstrong he became the band's musical director. Armstrong is said to have described Joe Garland as "one of the greatest musicians I ever worked with."

During the remainder of his full-time playing career, Garland also played with Claude Hopkins and was musical director for Earl Hines (1948). Garland retired from full time music in the 1950s.

As a performer Joe Garland tended to specialize in the lower saxophones: tenor, baritone and bass. He is perhaps best known, however, for his compositions *In the Mood*, the wartime hit for the Glenn Miller band, and *Leap Frog*, which became the theme tune of the Les Brown band.

Unit 2: Composition

Leap Frog was written in 1941 while Joe Garland was with Louis Armstrong and recorded by Armstrong's band in the same year. It was later a major hit for Les Brown *and His Band of Renown* when he recorded it in 1945, becoming that band's theme tune.

It is a riff tune, drawing in part on the tradition of the Kansas City big band style, exemplified by the early Count Basie band. It is essentially a dance tune, swinging gently all the way but with virtually no space for improvised solos.

Paul Lavender's arrangement sticks very closely to the original in structure and content, but is a third lower to make it more accessible to young players. Even the cameo tenor sax solos from the Les Brown (1945) version are transcribed as optional written solos.

Unit 3: Historical Perspective

Leap Frog was a popular hit in the later part of the classic big band era, the late 1940s. In 1947 Les Brown stopped touring with his band replacing, Desi Arnez as the house band for Bob Hope, an engagement that continued for some forty years.

The Les Brown style, exemplified by *Leap Frog,* tended to emphasize tight ensemble playing without necessarily showcasing any virtuoso soloists. This was music aimed squarely at dancers and with strong commercial appeal.

Unit 4: Technical Considerations

This arrangement is rated as Grade 3 with a suggested tempo of ♩ = 166–172, a little slower than the well-known Les Brown 1945 recording. It could be played faster once the band is comfortable with it, but not too much if it is to be used for dancers.

Lead trumpet goes to concert high G (g) (or F [f] if using the optional alternative notes) and the lead trombone range extends to middle F (f). Saxophones face no real technical difficulties, although some of the syncopations may require work to play them correctly.

The bass part is fully notated without any chord symbols and moves into higher positions only briefly. Piano is notated with chord symbols. The guitar part has chord symbols and slashes with only a few bars of notation. The chords are not overly complex, but require a knowledge of movable chord shapes.

The only solo is in the first tenor part. The changes are relatively simple, and a written solo, based on the 1945 recording by the Les Brown band, is provided.

No doubles are required.

Unit 5: Stylistic Considerations

This chart is similar in style to the music of the Glenn Miller and Benny Goodman bands, but drawing on a Kansas City riff style, somewhat "hotter" than other commercial music of the 1940s. Articulations in an early Basie style are appropriate. Accents should be attacked quite strongly, and the insistent forward motion should be maintained, though without speeding up. For an authentic performance, bebop inflections should be avoided. Some vibrato is appropriate in the saxophones on longer notes.

The guitar should play a steady quarter note pattern—a Freddie Green-style pattern. The bass drum can be feathered almost throughout.

The Les Brown band used this chart as an opener, and this arrangement is well suited to this. If not playing for dancers, sections could be opened up for additional solos.

Unit 6: Musical Elements

MELODY:

The melody in this piece consists mostly of a series of riffs. Each one can be isolated and learned by singing it with correct articulation. If the whole band learns all the key riffs they will be better understand how all the parts fit together.

The riffs taken together form the main idea, with each section of the ensemble generally having only one part of a longer phrase that is passed from section to section.

HARMONY:

The harmony is quite straightforward and logical, well suited to younger bands. Chords are scored solidly in close voicings and with little chromaticism. In the block chord sections, encourage strong playing in the bass and middle parts for a pyramid balance. Back off in the frequent unison passages.

The chords in section A of the melody are a simple turnaround. The only brief moment of chromaticism comes at the start of the bridge (measure 15, for example), with the concert $D\flat^7$ acting as a tritone substitute for the II^7 chord. The arrangement does not modulate.

RHYTHM:

Leap Frog should be played with a swing feel, each beat having an underlying triplet subdivision. It can be useful to practice parts of the piece slowly, with the drummer playing triplets so that everyone can feel how their lines should fit into the swing feel.

If the band is relatively new to this style they will probably need to learn many of the rhythms and articulations by singing them first. As a general rule, all notes marked with an accent should start with the tongue.

The hat accent (^) should start and finish with the tongue and be articulated as "daht," giving a detached yet "fat" sound. The basic accent (>) should only start with the tongue and then fade. It should be articulated as "dah." When a phrase ends with two eighth notes, they should be articulated as "doo dot."

The whole band needs to feel every quarter note beat and how syncopated rhythms bounce off that pulse.

Unit 7: Form and Structure

Section	Measure	Event and Scoring
Intro	1–4	Saxes, trombones and rhythm section are in unison at the octave, establishing one of the thematic riffs in this composition. This should be played strongly with attention given to the indicated accents and a clean cut-off on four. The quarter note on one should be quite "fat."
Theme	5–10	Trumpets enter, introducing the main melodic theme. The short-long articulation on the last two eighth notes in the pickup is important. Drill this until they get it right! The two eighth notes at the end of the trumpet line in measure 5 should be articulated as "doo dot."
		Saxes and trombones work together here with the saxes starting the riff and the completing it. Again, the cut-off on four is important for the saxes. The fall in the trombones every second measure should be short.
	11–14	Young players may want to rush the offbeat rhythm at the end of the section. Practicing it vocally will help, articulating the rhythm.

Section	Measure	Event and Scoring
Bridge	15–22	Saxes take the melody through the bridge, accompanied by sustained chords in the trombones. The chords descend chromatically to the dominant to set up the return of the main theme.
	19–22	A brief stop-time interlude with call and response between sections.
Theme	23–30	A repeat of the original theme, with a slightly different "finished" ending.
	31–38	In the first of several contrasting sections, the trombones play an accompanying riff with plunger mutes while the saxophone section is divided into two groups, alto saxophones taking the melody with answering phrases played by the tenor and baritone saxophones. In measures 36–38 the line is repeated three times in quick succession, played first by the altos and then imitated by the lower saxophones and then by the trombones.
		It would be worthwhile singing this line to help band members agree on the exact articulation. As each new section enters, the line should flow smoothly so it all sounds like part of the one idea. Each section should play its entry strongly, and then play softer as each new section comes in.
		The rhythm section should play *mezzo forte*, as indicated, or less—but without losing any intensity.
	38	The rhythm section needs to set up the loud ensemble entry at measure 39.

Section	Measure	Event and Scoring
Tenor Solo	39–48	The ensemble plays a loud launch figure, in a typical scoring of saxophones versus brass. The solo tenor saxophone takes the second half of the phrase, either improvised or using the transcribed solo provided.
Shout I	49–56	Harmonically this is the same as the bridge section in measures 15–22, with the section taking the melody. Saxes and trombones should shape their long notes as an ***fp*** followed by a *crescendo* to the end of the note. The drummer should play a strong backbeat on the snare on beats two and four. The written part here will work well. All sections should play strongly and clearly in measures 53–56.
	57–64	The chords from the bridge are repeated behind another brief tenor saxophone solo. In a reversal of the previous solo, the tenor plays first and the ensemble plays a response.
	61–64	If everyone learns the trumpet line here by singing it, they will better understand how all the parts fit together.
	65–71	An exact repeat of the previous launch figure to set up the final cameo tenor saxophone solo.
	72	Straight eighth notes in all the horns and the drums. They should be crisply played, short and tongued. Cut off on beat four.
	73–76	A brief improvised drum solo to set up the return to the main theme at measure 5. Observe the *decrescendo*.

Section	Measure	Event and Scoring
Coda	77–78	As indicated, this two-measure drum fill should be big, as it sets up the shout chorus. The quarter note at measure 77 should be played "fat."
Shout II	79–85	This should be very strong. The lower voices should be a bit louder than the higher ones, ensuring a good balance and support for the lead trumpet. The swing will be enhanced if the drummer plays quite simply. Kicking the dotted quarter note figure at the start of measures 79, 81 and 83 is good, though simple time with a strong backbeat would also be effective.
	86–88	The saxophone line is important here, as it keeps momentum going from the preceding shout chorus. Everyone should blow through to a clean cutoff on beat three of the last measure. Adding a slight shape to the note will add polish.

Unit 8: Suggested Listening

Louis Armstrong and his Orchestra, *1940–1942*, Classics.
Basie, Count, *The Complete Decca Recordings*, MCA/GRP.
Count Basie Orchestra, *The essential Count Basie, Vol.1–3*, CBS.
Les Brown and His Band of Renown, *Best of The Capitol Years*, Capitol.
Goodman, Benny, *On the Air 1937–1938*, Sony.

Unit 9: Additional References and Resources

Carr, Ian, Digby Fairweather, and Brian Priestly, *Jazz, the Rough Guide: The Essential Companion to Artists and Albums* (London: Rough Guides, 1995).

Lansing, Autumn, *Solid!: The Encyclopedia of Big Band, Lounge, Classic Jazz and Space-age Sounds*, http://www.parabrisas.com/d_brownl.php.

Lawn, Richard, *The Jazz Ensemble Director's Manual: A Handbook of Practical Methods and Materials for the Educator* (Oskaloosa: C.L. Barnhouse, 1995).

Les Brown Band of Renown, http://www.lesbrownsbandofrenown.com.

Russell, Ross, *Jazz Style in Kansas City and the Southwest* (New York: Da Capo Press, 1997).

Schuller, Gunther, *The Swing Era: The Development of Jazz 1930–1945* (New York: Oxford University Press, 1989), 194–195, 386–389, 420–422, 674–675.

Spink, George, *Les Brown and his Band of Renown*, www.tuxjunction.net/lesbrown.htm.

Contributed by:

Saul Richardson
Director of Jazz
North Sydney Boys' High School
Crows Nest, New South Wales
Australia

Teacher Resource Guide

Limbo Jazz

Duke Ellington

(1899–1974)

arranged by David Berger

(b. 1948)

Unit 1: Composer/Arranger

Duke Ellington was born Edward Kennedy Ellington in Washington, D. C., on April 29, 1899. He began piano instruction at age eight, but did not pursue it seriously until later in his youth. His interest in art led him to study to become a commercial artist at the Armstrong Manual Training School. During this period of his life he would periodically go to listen to local ragtime pianists. However, it was on a vacation trip to the Jersey shore that he encountered a very talented pianist named Harvey Brooks. Mr. Brooks explained to him some techniques for learning how to play jazz piano, and from then on, Ellington invested his energies in his music. He later studied with Oliver "Doc" Perry and Louis Brown and began working in Washington area clubs.

In 1917, he formed his first band, the Serenaders. He moved to New York in 1923 and renamed his band the Washingtonians. The band recorded that year and his popularity grew rapidly, due in part to radio broadcasts and his work in clubs in New York during the Prohibition Era, most notably the Cotton Club. The steady work for his band provided a platform for Ellington to develop his unique sound. By the time of his death in 1974, he had given over 20,000 performances around the world and established himself as an icon of American music. His compositions, many of which were collaborations with Billy Strayhorn, include such well-known standards as *Do Nothin' Till You Hear From Me*, *Don't Get Around Much Anymore*, *Cottontail*, *Take the A Train*, and many more.

The arranger of this composition, David Berger, has become synonymous with revived interest in Ellington's music afforded by the growing popularity of neo classic jazz. Berger is a renowned composer, arranger, bandleader, educator, and trumpeter residing in New York City. He is recognized as one of the leading authorities on the music of Duke Ellington and served as the conductor of the Lincoln Center Jazz Orchestra from its inception in 1988 until 1994. His works include transcriptions of classic recorded jazz performances, including more than 350 works by Duke Ellington and Billy Strayhorn. Many of his arrangements and transcriptions are utilized as repertoire for the Essentially Ellington Festival hosted by the Lincoln Center, which attracts young jazz groups from schools nationwide and introduces them to Ellington's wonderful legacy.

Mr. Berger's works also have been performed on television, the Broadway stage, and by many well known jazz artists, including the Thad Jones/Mel Lewis Orchestra, Buddy Rich, the Lincoln Center Jazz Orchestra, Clark Terry and many more.

Unit 2: Composition

Limbo Jazz is a selection from a 1962 Impulse! album with Coleman Hawkins entitled *Duke Ellington Meets Coleman Hawkins*. It also appears as part of Ellington's *Virgin Island Suite* recorded in 1965 on an album entitled, *Concert in the Virgin Islands* and the reissue of his Reprise recordings on the Mosaic label. It is based on the harmonic structure found in *Panama Rag*, itself an embellished chord progression to *Happy Birthday*, and is set in a traditional calypso style.

Unit 3: Historical Perspective

Prior to the 1950s, big bands were common outlets for America's popular music. Big band leaders became the pop icons of that period with many artists achieving the notoriety once reserved for movie stars. Songwriters and publishing companies of the day depended on the better-known big bands to promote their works. In some cases there was a symbiotic relationship. Many leaders were eager to find material likely to generate a hit and drive their own popularity higher. By the 1960s, pop music had experienced a major shift, with Rock and Roll music supplanting jazz in popularity. Many factors contributed to this: the philosophy of modernism in jazz and the divergent developing jazz sub-styles; cultural shifts in post-war America, including the emerging Civil Rights movement; the emergence of the "Baby Boom" generation; and other factors.

The net result was that some of the few remaining big bands, and even small jazz groups, found themselves playing arrangements of familiar rock and pop songs and Broadway show tunes as part of their repertoire in order to reach a younger audience. In addition, record companies were eager to find anything that might generate large sales, especially if it was already from the catalog of their own publishing company. Duke Ellington was not immune to this pressure, and his work during the 1960s included selections made famous by Frank Sinatra, the Beatles, and from popular movies like *Mary Poppins*. The album, *Duke Ellington meets Coleman Hawkins*, on the Impulse! label, has Duke bucking the trend in a coupling with the great tenor saxophonist Coleman Hawkins and features original compositions rather than pop tunes. The group was an octet, and the arrangements were light fair for what one might expect from Duke, but the important elements, the interaction of these players and the smooth relaxed delivery by the ensemble were pure Duke and part of what shines in all his work. *Limbo Jazz* is similar in conception to tunes such as *C-Jam Blues* and *Perdido*: a simple melody over a 12-, 16-, or 32-bar (in this case, 16) chord progression intended as a vehicle for improvisation.

Unit 4: Technical Considerations

This arrangement is part of a collection of works for *Jazz at Lincoln Center "Jazz for Young People Series!"* and is geared towards a beginner band with a rating of Grade 2. The tempo marking is ♩ = 160 with a straight eighth feel in the rhythm section and a slight swing feel in the horns. Duration is approximately 3:50. Solos are written out for alto sax, trumpet, trombone and tenor sax. The trumpet range is to written A♭ above the staff ($a\flat^{1}$)and the trombone range is to F above middle C (f). There are alternate and optional parts included for C flute, tuba, horn in F (doubling the first trombone part) and two parts for treble clef baritone which double the first and second trombone parts. Brass players will need mutes, specifically hats in the trumpets and plungers in the trombones. Piano and bass parts are completely written out. A guitar chord guide is included. David Berger's performance notes accompany the score and include much helpful information.

Unit 5: Stylistic Considerations

The style of this piece is similar to that of an older, more traditional calypso style. This tune juxtaposes a straight eighth feel in the drums with the rest of the ensemble playing in a slightly swinging manner, a combination similar to the tune, *Tequila*. The rhythm parts are relatively simple, and the same feel runs throughout the piece. The rhythm section should work on keeping time in a steady but relaxed manner. This chart provides a suitable stylistic contrast to either a swing-oriented program or one with a more pop-based emphasis.

Unit 6: Musical Elements

MELODY:
The melody is simple and almost riff-like, and could be learned as a head chart quite easily. Having the entire band sing and or play the melody line by ear as part of the learning process will help them in developing their aural skills and unify the ensemble in their stylistic concept.

HARMONY:
The chord progression to this piece is based on *Panama Rag*, a slightly embellished version of *Happy Birthday* utilizing chord voicings that include the ninth and occasionally, the thirteenth. The horn voicings include Ellington style dissonances or "rubs" to add a bluesy flavor to it—a technique he used with many of his other larger ensemble pieces.

Rhythm:
There is a great deal of syncopation in this piece, but it is used repetitively, and so should not prove too difficult for younger players. The recording that accompanies the score will help the students hear how a swing feel works over a calypso feel. The ensemble figures, including the written recorded solos, are played with just as much swing as a regular swing chart.

Unit 7: Basic Form and Structure

SECTION	MEASURE	EVENT AND SCORING
Intro	1–4	The chart begins at a tempo of ♩ = 160 and remains there throughout; the rhythm section establishes the groove with brass hits for ornamentation; saxes play melody pick-up in measure 4.
Melodic Statement	5–20	Saxes play melody with rhythm section; the brass is tacit. Have the band both sing and learn this melody on their instruments by ear to help unify the stylistic concept and familiarize itself with the form, as well as give it a framework for a theme and variations based improvisation should the chart be opened up for more solos.

SECTION	MEASURE	EVENT AND SCORING
Repeated Melodic Statement	5–20 (2nd time)	Brass joins in with background figures using mutes. The brass should sing figures to help with style concept. The piano part has some quarter note triplet figures that may require some extra attention.
Solo Section(s)	21–52 (1st time)	Written solos are well done, and follow the practice of the original Impulse! recording with soloists leaving some space during the first eight bars, and then moving into a solo over the figures in the second eight bars of each solo; trumpet two solos for the first sixteen bars (bars 21–36) while saxes have the background figure for the first sixteen. Saxes should sing their figures as part of learning them. Second alto takes the next solo (bars 37–52) with the brass playing backgrounds. As with all of these background figures, the sections should sing them.
Solo Section	2nd time	Saxes continue with background figure on the first eight bars behind a first trombone solo; brass background joins in as well. Care should be taken with dynamics, as these added layers can become too loud behind the soloist. A tenor solo begins at measure 37, and saxes add a background figure to the brass figure. Pointing out the use of layered backgrounds to build excitement into the shout chorus will help players understand how arrangers use density of orchestration to build energy and excitement as the band heads for the shout chorus.

Section	Measure	Event and Scoring
Shout Chorus	53–68	The shout utilizes full horn section figures (brass and saxes) playing in homophonic rhythm on a riff type figure. The rhythm section continues to groove with piano right hand adding a counter riff in between the horn figures. Horns should sing and play the figures to help unify articulations and conception of the motive. The dynamic marking is *forte*, and should not be so heavy or loud as to overshadow the piano part.
D. S.	5–20	The melody is restated and the repeat is to be taken on this D.S. A jump to the coda is to be taken at measure 18.
Coda	69–70	A tutti ensemble figure with a clean cutoff.

Unit 8: Suggested Listening

Ellington, Duke, *Duke Ellington Meets Coleman Hawkins*, Impulse! Records.
Demonstration disk for Warner Bros. Publications *Jazz for Young People Series* included with the arrangement (PP6044).

Unit 9: Additional References and Resources

Dunscomb, Richard, and Willie L. Hill, Jr., *Jazz Pedagogy: The Jazz Educator's Handbook and Resource Guide* (Miami: Warner Brothers, 2004).

Contributed by:

Larry Panella
Director of Jazz Studies
The University of Southern Mississippi
Hattiesburg, Mississippi

Teacher Resource Guide

Maiden Voyage
Herbie Hancock
(b. 1940)

arranged by Mark Taylor
(b. 1948)

Unit 1: Composer/Arranger

Herbie Hancock was born on April 12, 1940 in Chicago, Illinois. He performed Mozart's D Major Piano Concerto with the Chicago Symphony at the age eleven after only fours years of study. Although he was very familiar with classical styles, his emphasis was mostly jazz throughout his career.

At Grinnell College in Iowa, Herbie studied electrical engineering and graduated with a degree in music composition in 1960. He played with local jazz talent and well-known artists that traveled through Iowa before moving to New York, where he played and recorded with Donald Bryd. He released his first solo album, *Taking Off*, which led to his compositional skills being recognized with the selection *Watermelon Man*. It was later recorded by Mongo Santamaria and became a top ten single in the pop charts.

He was one of the most sought-after pianists in the 1960s. His piano playing and compositions made significant contributions to modern jazz phases such as hard-bop and the jazz rock/jazz funk genres of the 1970s and 1980s. He played for the Miles Davis Quintet from 1963–1968.

His style of playing piano (solo and comping) reflect a politeness and sensitivity that is a departure from others. The bluesy, rhythmic figures in Hancock's playing were borrowed from pianists Horace Silver and Wynton Kelly. His voicings and harmonic sensibilities were derived from the music of Claire Fischer. His most significant influence was Bill Evans, with the use of ringing chord voicings and mode based harmonic structure, which relies more on feel, sound, and color than standard harmonic progressions to create tension and release in the music. Twentieth-century classical composers Maurice Ravel, Claude Debussy, and Paul Hindemith also influenced Hancock.

Herbie Hancock's recordings after his years with Miles Davis and leading his own groups are considered to be his most prolific as a composer. Tunes such as *Dolphin Dance* and *Maiden Voyage* are considered standard repertoire for all jazz players.

Mark Taylor is known for his arrangements with the Stan Kenton Orchestra. His contributions to the jazz ensemble idiom are apparent with his many arrangements and compositions, which span all levels of abilities and styles. His recent project released in 2006 with the Taylor/Fidyk Big Band highlight the diversity of his compositions and arrangements.

Unit 2: Composition

Maiden Voyage is an arrangement of the title selection from Herbie Hancock's 1965 album and reflects his modal period of composition. This arrangement offers the same spirit of improvisation based on limited harmonic changes. The floating feeling that exists in the original small group version can be achieved with the rhythm section (piano, bass, drums, vibraphone, and guitar) exploring a variety of sounds and textures. The AABA form is maintained with sections A and B each utilizing two chord changes: D^{7sus} and F^{9sus} for section A, and E$\flat^{sus}$ suspension and D$\flat^{sus}$ for section B. The initial melody is presented by first trumpet, first tenor saxophone, and guitar. Although the tenor saxophone is the designated soloist, the arrangement can be opened for additional soloists if desired. There is a brief shout section followed by a D.S. to section B, followed by a coda.

Unit 3: Historical Perspective

The piece *Maiden Voyage* depicts four different modes (four chord changes) which create the feeling of being on an ocean for the first time[1]. During the mid-1960s, there was a movement away from the standard harmonic progressions associated with the jazz quintet. There was a need to incorporate additional musical styles. From a rhythm section standpoint, this approach allowed for greater expression and improvisation among the rhythm section than had been heard before. Herbie Hancock ushered the jazz community into a fusion of different styles for a wider audience and acceptance.

Unit 4: Technical Considerations

This chart is rated Grade 3, and the recommended tempo is ♩ = 120 in a medium Latin style. However, this chart works well in a slower tempo if the stated tempo does not lend itself to the floating feeling needed for the arrangement.

The lead trumpet range goes to concert A (a^1), and all trumpet players will need a harmon and cup mute. The lead trombone range goes to concert F♯ (f♯), and all trombone players will need a cup mute. It is important for the lead trombonist to have good control of the upper register. The saxophone section uses standard instrumentation with no doublings. The baritone saxophone part has an optional high part for those not able to execute the written lower register. Bass line parts are written out with chord changes. The guitar part has a written-out melodic line when needed, and the vibraphone part is completely written out and requires some four-mallet technique.

The harmonic chords are indicated in the guitar and piano parts, with chord symbols provided for both. The piano part has written voicings for all chords. There is a solo changes part provided for the open section in all keys with suggested scales. The changes for the soloist(s) are simple, but they require some creative rhythmic ideas to give the solo(s) direction and forward motion. This is an excellent chart for a beginning/intermediate improviser in the modal style.

Unit 5: Stylistic Considerations

This composition reflects the fusion style of the 1960s that has both a Latin feeling (even eighth note rhythm) and a floating feeling that still reflects a swing orientation. The Miles Davis rhythm section of Herbie Hancock, Tony Williams (drums), and Ron Carter (bass) were famous for creating this dream-like effect and for changing moods and textures instantly.

This selection is ideal for helping all sections of the ensemble develop improvisational skills in the modal context, but is written for tenor saxophone. (The piece was originally written for Freddie Hubbard on trumpet and George Coleman on tenor saxophone). *Maiden Voyage* is a great tune to allow the younger improvisers to gain some experience while the rhythm section has an opportunity to stretch the Latin/swing feeling in various sections. There are many repeated notes in unison with and against different sections in the arrangement. The challenge will be balancing these notes at the various dynamic levels while maintaining a controlled sound.

Unit 6: Musical Elements

MELODY:

The simple melody should be learned by all sections in order to balance when background figures occur. The phrasing of the melodic line will need to be addressed since some of these parts are in unison. The modal/harmonic shifts are very clear and are well defined by the melody and the open solo section. The melodic rhythm is eighth-note oriented with a floating feeling that is supported by the rhythm section.

HARMONY:

The 32-bar form (AABA) with indicated transitional material is used to allow the four chords throughout the piece space to breathe and develop. The use of the suspended chord allows the harmony from being defined in the major or minor context. The suggested use of the Mixolydian scale minus the third degree helps create this vagueness while at the same time providing the improviser with possibilities.

RHYTHM:

The Latin/eighth-note feel requires that the entire band internalize the time. The rhythm section should have the freedom to establish this feeling without worrying about losing time with a slow or fast entrance. There are some areas where the saxophone backgrounds are independent of the melodic idea. The articulation of staccato and accented notes in the harmonized parts is important for establishing the foundation for the harmonic rhythm throughout the arrangement. It will be important for the rhythm section to work on comping behind the soloist(s) so they can listen and tune into the tendencies of each. Recording these sessions could prove rewarding in the discovery process.

Unit 7: Form and Structure

The basic form of the composition is AABA with a D.S. and a Coda.

Section	Measure	Event and Scoring
Introduction	1–8	The tempo is ♩ = 120. Work at a much slower tempo until the Latin/floating style is established. The alto saxophone section and the trombones minus the lead players outline the harmonic rhythm that can be heard on the original recording of the tune with the rhythm section. It is important that the articulation of notes marked staccato and/or accented is clear and in balance with the feel from the rhythm section. If appropriate, these measures can be repeated in the rehearsal setting to work through ideas for establishing the correct feel.
A	9–17	The trio of first tenor saxophone, second trumpet, and guitar introduce the melody in unison with a pickup into measure 9. It is important for the rhythm section to balance with this reduced instrumentation while maintaining the established feel. Listening to the original recording will help with melodic phrasing and rhythm section feel.
A (repeat)	9–17	The trio from above is joined by the first trumpet with a harmon mute, first trombone, and optional vibraphone in unison. This texture changes adds a bell-like tone to the melody that needs to balance accordingly.

Section	Measure	Event and Scoring
B	18–25	First alto saxophone joins the melody, and the vibraphone assumes some of the harmonic duties. The texture thickens with a two-measure harmonized background figure in the saxophone, trumpet and trombone sections. The rhythm section supports these figures. It is important not to lose the feeling with the *forte* dynamic and the additional forces. This section is the tension in the tune.
(D.S. begins at measure 18.)		
A (return)	26–33	The arrangement returns to the texture used in the introduction with the original trio joined by first trombone and vibraphone on the melody. There is a two-bar unison rhythmic figure (measures 32–33) that propels the piece into the solo section. It is important for the backgrounds to play underneath the melody, so the dynamic of *forte* will need to be adjusted due to the thicker instrumentation.
(On the repeat, take the coda after measure 33.)		
A	34–41	Beginning of the open solo section. The rhythm section needs to focus on establishing the mood so the soloist will feel free to create over the first A section. The rhythm section will have to adjust dynamics according to the soloist. In the designated first tenor saxophone solo, the arranger has a written-out solo as well as suggested scales for each chord change.

SECTION	MEASURE	EVENT AND SCORING
A	42–49	The rhythm section continues to support the soloist, but must balance with the cup mute entrances of the trumpets and trombones in unison rhythm every two bars starting in measure 42. The saxophones minus the first tenor solo have a held ***fp*** on the second half of beat three in measures 42 and 46. The *crescendo* on this note must not occur until the trill in the last bar of each phrase, and must stay underneath the texture established by the rhythm section as well as the soloist.
B	50–57	There is a two-bar harmonized background played by trumpets, trombones and baritone saxophones. The dynamic of *forte* must be adjusted based upon the soloist as well as the rhythm section. Articulation of notes marked marcato, staccato, and accented notes will need to be addressed for phrasing purposes. The remaining saxophones have two four-measure phrases that end with rising quarter note triplets in unison. It is important that this figure not be rushed or clipped so the feel and time are maintained underneath the soloist.
A (return)	58–65	The material in this section is similar to measures 42–49. At the end of this section, the soloist returns to measure 34. The backgrounds from measures 34 through measure 65 could be reserved for each soloist's last chorus. This allows the rhythm section an opportunity to develop their small group comping skills behind different soloists.

Section	Measure	Event and Scoring
		66–73 This section features a brief drum solo in measures 66–69 that brings down the build-up that should have occurred from the last soloist. In measure 70 there is a pyramiding rhythmic pedal that starts in the trombones and tenor saxophones and is supported by the rhythm section. There is some dovetailing of the rhythm idea that occurs with the addition of the alto saxophones in measures 70 and the trumpets in measures 71. The section comes to an end with unison *fortissimo* quarter notes in measure 72 on beat four and in measure 73 on beats one and two. This leads to brief shout section.
Shout	74–82	The trumpets enter in unison on the section A melody while upper saxophones play a unison counter line with the baritone saxophone and trombones mimic the harmonic rhythm established by the piano and bass parts in the introduction. There is a D.S. to measure 18 (section B) and a jump after measure 33 to the coda in measure 83.
Coda	83–92	The arrangement returns to the three-horn unison melody (first tenor, second trumpet, and first trombone) with an expanded rhythm section from measures 83–90. The lead alto joins this instrumentation in unison on beat one of measure 91 with the familiar interval from the original (Perfect fourth). The rest of the ensemble is led by the drummer into a ***mp*** played into the stand on beat four of measure 91 with a D^{9SUS} chord. It is important not to overplay the dynamic and let the piece come to rest.

Unit 8: Suggested Listening

Herbie Hancock, *Maiden Voyage*, Blue Note.
The Taylor/Fidyk Big Band, *Live at Blues Alley*, Blue Note.

Unit 9: Additional References and Resources

Copeland, Keith, *Creative Coordination for the Performing Drummer, 4th edition* (New York: Carl Fischer, 1986).

Dunscomb, Richard, and Willie L. Hill, Jr., *Jazz Pedagogy: The Jazz Educator's Handbook and Resource Guide*, (Miami: Warner Brothers, 2004).

Gridley, Mark C., *Jazz Styles: History and Analysis, 9 edition* (Upper Saddle River: Pearson/Prentice Hall, 2006).

Office of Communications, *NEA Jazz Masters Program Booklet for 2006* (Washington, D. C: National Endowment for the Arts, 2006).

Soph, Ed, *Essential Techniques for Drum Set, Book I* (Galesville: Meredith Music Publishers, 1993).

Vernick, Gordon and Geoffrey Haydon, *Jazz History Overview* (Dubuque: Kendal/Hunt Publishing Company, 2002).

Contributed by:

Don N. Parker
Assistant Professor of Music (Percussion/Jazz)
Fayetteville State University
Fayetteville, North Carolina

1 Vernick, Gordon and Geoffrey Haydon, *Jazz History Overview* (Dubuque: Kendal/Hunt Publishing Company, 2002), 191.

Teacher Resource Guide

Maximum Velocity

Russ Michaels

(b. 1958)

Unit 1: Composer

An accomplished composer and arranger, Russ Michaels (Blair Bielawski) has over seventy compositions and arrangements in print, as well as many commissions for college, high school and middle school groups throughout the United States. ASCAP recently recognized him for his compositions for young jazz ensembles and vocal jazz choir.

As a performer, Bielawski has worked with many artists, including Natalie Cole, Manhattan Transfer, Johnny Mathis, Aretha Franklin, the Temptations, Lionel Hampton, and the Milwaukee Symphony Orchestra. As a clinician, he has presented numerous workshops at various state music educators conferences, has been the featured speaker for sessions in London, Toronto, and Vancouver, and has appeared as a clinician at jazz festivals with Bob Mintzer, Frank Mantooth and Doug Beach.

Bielawski is currently the creative instrumental director for Heritage Music Press. Before joining the Lorenz team, he was a member of the Hal Leonard editorial, arranging, and sales staff for seventeen years, working on all aspects of the instrumental catalog. He also served on the board of directors for the Wisconsin Music Education Association and the Retail Print Music Dealers Association.

Unit 2: Composition

Maximum Velocity was published in 2001. This composition displays the all the features of the current funk style: solid groove from a unified intention in the rhythm section, a blues-based harmonic foundation, punctuating tutti horn shots, and abundant syncopation in the melody. The solo section is expandable and interesting harmonically. A soloist just gaining improvising skills can still sound convincing by limiting note choices while using or paraphrasing rhythms employed elsewhere in the chart.

Unit 3: Historical Perspective

The music of artists such as James Brown and Sly and the Family Stone brought the sound of a punctuating horn section to mainstream listening in the sixties. The concept was extrapolated by groups such as Blood, Sweat and Tears, Chicago, Tower of Power, and Earth, Wind and Fire in the seventies and eighties and continues in popular practice by groups performing in the soul, funk, and rhythm and blues genres.

Unit 4: Technical Considerations

This chart is rated Grade 1.5, and the recommended tempo is 𝅗𝅥 = 88–94 with a duration of 2:38 when using only one soloist. This chart works well through the entire tempo range and a little faster as long as the style is not rushed. It is written in half time in order for younger musicians to perform rhythms using quarters and eighths sound like the sixteenth note syncopations characteristic of rhythm and blues horn band sections such as Tower of Power or Seawind.

Both first trumpet and first trombone encompass the range of a minor tenth. The highest pitch for each is concert D♭ (d♭ for trombone; $d♭^1$ for trumpet).

Complex chords are voiced well for pianists requiring the realization of extended harmonies. The guitar part requires three contrasting utilities: melodic unison with saxophones, doubling the bass line at the octave, and a harmonic accompaniment limited to the two chords of $B♭m^7$ and $E♭m^7$. The most effective drumming will support the brass accent in the introduction (beat 4 of measures 2 and 6) and well-conceived fills during measures 26–27, repeated at measures 63–64 and measure 55, which is repeated at measure 94.

The solo section is expandable and features brass backgrounds that may be used in at least three combinations; trumpets only, trombones only, or all brass at once. The harmonic structures allow a wide variety of improvisation approaches. Recommended written solos provide an excellent point of departure, as do the composers ideas included for limiting beginning improvisation choices to two notes to promote rhythmical experimentation during soloing. Practice tracks on the accompanying CD are a very useful tool for extra practice at home or during improvisation instruction without the rhythm section. These tracks also provide a professional realization of the rhythm section instrument responsibilities within this contemporary style.

Unit 5: Stylistic Considerations

Wind parts require clean and crisp unison articulations, including attention to releases of long notes. Observation to the common practice of ***fp*** followed by a *crescendo* on long notes enhances the 8-bar introduction section that reappears with regularity throughout the chart. The contrasting, descending legato phrases at measures 23–25, repeated in measures 60–62 and paraphrased as a countermelody in section C, should be well balanced to ensure moving lines continue unobstructed throughout the full duration of the cascading passage. The *decrescendo* and regard to the release of the whole note will add finesse to the end of this phrase.

The guitarist should be aware of which section is doubled to ensure the matching of articulations. The guitar/piano roles are carefully orchestrated to minimize duplication of accompaniment assignments. Bands with musically mature pianists could enhance the overall rhythm section affect by including rhythmic interest during block chords or harmonic sideslips with discretion. Drum fills should allow for some open space by mixing a variety of note and rest values when creating rhythm choices. This approach helps give integrity to the funkier style of the composition. Caution should also be given not to over-syncopate the basic drum groove so that the drummer regards the rhythmic unison of the bass line.

Unit 6: Musical Elements

MELODY:

Three melodies are employed; each is riff based. The introductory 2-bar fragment allows articulations to be attended initially for maximum return throughout the chart. The brass/saxophone call and response in the second section requires consideration to an octave jump. Section three employs a counterpoint requiring legato alto and trumpet lines and tutti tenor/baritone/trombone unison melodies that necessitates a unified approach to articulation for greatest consistency with stylist practices and effective performance.

HARMONY:

The 8-bar introduction/interlude pivots through a variety of key centers before settling onto the dominant of B♭ minor, creating forward motion to the next section. The second section firmly establishes the B♭ minor key center, held modally for the full length of the section. Section three is a 24-bar blues in B♭ minor (which sounds like twelve due to the half-time writing approach). The solo section is a variation on minor blues extending the form to sixteen bars. A unison for the full ensemble supports the composition's strong final statement during the last three measures.

RHYTHM:

Rhythm section musicians must support the push of an "anticipated" downbeat, which is written on beat 4 of measure 2, which feels like the second half of beat four due to the half-time writing. The melodic riffs tie into rhythmic ostinati as well as call and response: the syncopation of measure 2, which sounds like ; measure 12, which sounds like on beat 4, but is written ; and measure 15, where four eighth notes tied to beat three ( ) tend to sound like like the "one-ee-and-**ah**" of many funk horn lines. The descending legato culmination of the phrase lasts three measures, enhancing the asymmetry, interest, and underlying impression of a 2/4 bar in the perceived rhythm.

Unison "hammer-strokes" in measure 54, repeated again at the end of measure 93, must remain clear and should not be rushed in order for the piece to retain its funk groove and resistance. This idea also applies to the last measure of the piece. Much of the success of this composition is drawn from the performers' ability to keep a solid, steady, metronome-like tempo, avoiding the tendency to "rush to get there first."

Unit 7: Form and Structure

The basic form of the composition is ABACDABC'.

SECTION	MEASURE	EVENT AND SCORING
Intro: A	1–8	The introduction riff stated by alto and tenor saxophones is supported harmonically by the brass and rhythm section, creating mounting tension. The riff is repeated through three rising keys, concluding on an altered dominant harmony to propel the piece past the introduction.

SECTION	MEASURE	EVENT AND SCORING
B	9–27	Stagnant harmonic motion firmly establishes B♭ minor (Dorian). The call from the brass is a repeated riff based on an octave jump up followed by a step down (to ♭7) that bounces back to the tonic. Saxophones respond to the riffs with syncopated melodic interjections in unison. The section concludes with a three-measure inverted harmonic pyramid, smoothly cascading down to form a B♭m^{7SUS} (sometimes called B♭m^{11}). This flourish creates a non-symmetrical phrase length that creates an urgency stated by the two-measure drum fill to continue on to a new section.
A	28–35	This section is an exact repetition of the introduction. Now used as an interlude, a false sense that the composition will return to another B section is created. The composer adds interest to the piece by not reinforcing this logical predication.
C	36–64	Low brass and woodwinds take over a new riff-based melody. Altos and trumpets paraphrase the descending, legato, inverted pyramid motif in comment on the statement of the unison melody in the tenor range. Harmonies beneath follow a strict blues progression. The complete blues format culminates and an additional section, previously heard as an elision at the end of section B, is now presented as a transitional-yet-familiar addition to facilitate motion towards the next section.

SECTION	MEASURE	EVENT AND SCORING
D	65–80	This is a solo section that can be opened to allow for multiple soloists. If desired, brass players may be accommodated as soloists by withdrawing background figures or choosing to limit backgrounds, i.e., trombone figures only to support a trumpet soloist, or trumpet figures only to support a trombone soloist. If multiple soloists are employed, backgrounds should not be utilized for every repeat. Harmonically, the form for this section is a 16-bar blues: traditional blues for the first eight measures, followed by the augmentation of the harmonic rhythm for the final bars. (I I I I IV IV I I ii ii V V I–I–I–I). Do not rush the tutti punctuation the dominant chord in measures 75–76. These bars foreshadow the coda.
A	81–88	This interlude, again, a repeat of the introduction, now reinforces the previously unfulfilled expectation by returning the listener to a B section.
B (D.S.)	9–27	A literal repeat of the previous section B. Measure 27 sends musicians to the coda.
C' (*Coda*)	89–97	This section is a truncation of section C as previously described. It begins exactly as the initial section C, however, but then jumps to the dominant chord in the the fifth measure of the section instead of following the complete blues form. The punctuated tutti hammer strokes are once again used to thrust energy toward the tonic. In this final statement, horns declare the melody in a strong unison proclamation.

Unit 8: Suggested Listening

Blood, Sweat and Tears, *Blood, Sweat and Tears III*, track 5, Mobile Fidelity Inc., 1970.
Lucretia MacEvil.
Chase, *Chase*, track 5, Sony/Epic, 1971.
Get It On.
Chicago, *Chicago III*, track 1, Rhino, 1971.
Sing a Mean Tune Kid.
Sly and the Family Stone, *Stand*, track 8 (You Can Make It If You Try), Sony Music, Inc. 1969.
Tower of Power, *Souled Out*, track 8 (Diggin' On James Brown), Warner Bros. Records, Inc., 1995.

Unit 9: Additional References and Resources

Baker, David, *Jazz Improvisation: A Comprehensive Guide for All Musicians, 2nd Edition* (Los Angeles: Alfred Publishing Company, 1988).
Houghton, Steve, and Tom Warrington, *Essential Styles for the Drummer and Bassist* (Los Angeles: Alfred Publishing Company, 1990).
Lawn, Richard J. and Jeffrey L. Hellmer, *Jazz Theory and Practice* (Los Angeles: Alfred Publishing Company, 1996).
Mantooth, Frank, *Voicing for the Jazz Keyboard* (Winona: Hal Leonard Publishing Company, 1986).
Martinez, Maria. *Instant Guide to Drum Grooves: The Essential Reference for the Working Drummer* (Milwaukee: Hal Leonard Publishing Company, 2002).
Sorenson, D. and Bruce Pearson, *Standard of Excellence Advanced Jazz Ensemble Method for Group or Individual Instruction* (San Diego: Neil A. Kjos Music Company, 2004).
Steinel, Mike, *Essential Elements for Jazz Ensemble: A Comprehensive Method for Jazz Style and Improvisation* (Milwaukee: Hal Leonard Corporation, 2000).

Contributed by:

Murray F.A. Smith
PhD Candidate, Secondary Education
University of Alberta
Edmonton, Alberta, Canada

Teacher Resource Guide

May's Way

Jeff Jarvis

(b. 1952)

Unit 1: Composer

Jeff Jarvis has had a multi-faceted career. He is a trumpeter, composer, jazz educator, author, and music publisher.

As a trumpeter, he has worked as a studio player on more than a hundred albums for artists that include Lou Rawls, Melba Moore, and the O'Jays. In live performances he has performed with numerous artists, including Dizzy Gillespie, Joe Lovano, Jimmy Heath, Henry Mancini, Eddie Daniels, and Doc Severinsen.

Jarvis's composition credits are many. He has been commissioned to write for a wide variety of groups, including high schools, universities, military, and professional groups. As part owner of Kendor Music, Jarvis has also contributed many pieces to the educational jazz repertoire.

Jeff Jarvis is the director of jazz studies at California State University Long Beach. He is a frequent conductor of all-state and honors groups throughout the country. He is also widely recognized as an effective clinician and lecturer. Jeff has also written several important jazz education textbooks.

Unit 2: Composition

Jarvis wrote *May's Way* (2002) as a tribute to the legendary big band writer Billy May. Many of Billy May's trademarks are evident in the writing, including saxophone scoops, economical, swinging melodic lines, and the rhythmic use of brass punches. The blues form is the foundation of the piece. The open solo section provides flexibility for solo assignments.

Unit 3: Historical Perspective

From the 1940s through the 90s, Billy May was one of the most respected of all big band writers. His early work as a writer for Glenn Miller's orchestra gave way to several legendary recordings as a leader. His writing always swings, and yet has a sense of humor about it as well. He was regarded as one of the best arrangers for vocalists in the business, contributing several charts to the library of Frank Sinatra. Few were ever published, and are not accessible to most student groups. Jeff Jarvis has created the opportunity for young players to study this style with *May's Way*.

Unit 4: Technical Considerations

This chart is rated Grade 3; the recommended tempo is ♩ = 138 with a duration of 3:20. The length of the performance will vary based upon the number of solos. The style is swing.

The lead trumpet range goes to concert G (g^1), and the lead trombone range goes to concert F♯ (f♯). The saxophone soli provide a good stylistic challenge, but are not difficult from a technical point of view. All bass lines are written out, and the piano part provides sample voicings. Chord changes for soloists are basic blues changes.

Unit 5: Stylistic Considerations

The music of Billy May always swings. Listening to recordings of some of May's great arrangements will be time well spent in learning this chart. Saxophones will need to work to execute scoops together. Brass articulations that answer the saxophones should be crisp. The importance of playing in good time should be stressed, since so much of the success of the chart relies on rhythms locking together.

Unit 6: Musical Elements

MELODY:

The melody and the scoops that are so important to it are most easily learned by singing them. Sing with proper inflections, then have students sing back. Playing the melody should fall in line once this is done. Make sure it is sung and played with a strong swing feel.

HARMONY:

The changes are a very straightforward blues in B♭ major. There is a modulation at measure 78 to C major. This makes the harmony accessible to young players.

RHYTHM:
The swing feel requires that the entire band feel the four downbeats as well as the triplet sub-division on each downbeat. Singing the rhythms is strongly encouraged. When doing so, having the drummer beat time on a closed high-hat may prove helpful.

Unit 7: Form and Structure

SECTION	MEASURE	EVENT AND SCORING
Intro	1–14	A solid drum kick leads to the ensemble entrance. Strong accents on all up beats establish the swing feel. Drums kick the brass; saxes must have good air flow through the linear phrases. Crisp articulations in measure 14 are important.
Choruses 1 and 2	15–27	Altos and tenors play melody; the inflections are crucial. Keep the line flowing. Brass punches on the repeat with crisp articulations; work for brass section balance on these punches.
Chorus 3	28–40	Brass takes over the primary part. Make sure *tenuto* quarter notes are stretched out here. Saxophones answer in melodic fashion. The ensemble should build into the solo section.
Chorus 4	40–51	A solo section; open as desired. All backgrounds should be played with crisp articulations. Encourage the use of dominant or bebop scales throughout.
Chorus 5	52–63	Rhythm section is out. Make sure horns work at the time. Saxophone soli must be played with good balance. Bebop style phrasing will help the lines.
Chorus 6	64–77	Much like chorus two. Measures 76–77 are an extension that set up a modulation. Build into measure 78.

Section	Measure	Event and Scoring
Chorus 7	78–93	Full shout chorus. Brass should be strong here, but should not dominate the melody in the saxophones. Tag and extension in measures 88–93. The chart should go out strong.

Unit 8: Suggested Listening

Billy May, *Sorta May*, Capitol Records, T562.
Big Band Bash, Capitol Records, T349.
Frank Sinatra, *Come Fly With Me*, Capitol Records.

Unit 9: Additional References and Resources

Jarvis, Jeff and Doug Beach. *The Jazz Educators Handbook* (Delevan: Kendor Music, 2002).

Contributed by:

Doug Beach
Director of Jazz Studies
Elmhurst College
Elmhurst, Illinois

Teacher Resource Guide

Milestones
Miles Davis
(1926–1991)

arranged by Peter Blair
(b. 1958)

Unit 1: Composer/Arranger

Miles (Dewey) Davis was born May 26, 1926 in Alton, Illinois to an upper middle-class family. Miles's father was a dental surgeon with strong political ties to the community. Miles also lived with his mother, older sister and younger brother. Miles was a very talented teen who became the protégé of trumpeter Clark Terry, who eventually helped him get a job in Billy Eckstein's band. Miles's father financed his move to New York, intending for him to study at Julliard. However, Miles's intention was to "hang" with Charlie Parker and learn to play bebop. Though it was a great challenge, Miles eventually became the replacement for Dizzy Gillespie in Charlie Parker's band, the most important jazz band of that time.

Though Miles thrived as trumpeter in Parker's band, he also began to invent a way to perform music that was more accommodating to his lyrical and dynamically refined ideal of playing. The first of many ways of playing that Miles invented was called the "Birth of the Cool." Cool jazz was subtle, impressionistic, and used non-traditional instrumentation, such as tuba and French horn.

By the late 1950s, Miles had gone further into subtlety and created "modal" jazz. In this style, songs were organized around one or two particular scales as opposed to a complex battery of chord changes. In the early 1960s Miles redefined jazz quintet performance with his group consisting of Herbie

Hancock, Wayne Shorter, Ron Carter, and sixteen-year-old sensation Tony Williams. By the late 1960s, he was inspired to create jazz-rock fusion after watching a performance of *Sly and the Family Stone* in the Monterey Jazz Festival.

Miles Davis is regarded as a monolithic icon in jazz because he invented many new and challenging performance styles over the years to accommodate his changing aesthetic values. His career spanned an unprecedented fifty years as the leading influence in jazz.

Unit 2: Composition

Milestones is a 48-bar AABA tune with a 16-bar bridge. There are only three chords in the song. Conventional melody and chord progression relationships are abandoned in favor of melodic and harmonic material built around a scale or mode. This sparse harmonic structure gives the soloist greater freedom to improvise and explore.

Section A is a repeated 8-bar phrase, organized as six measures of G Dorian minor resolving to two measures of Fmaj^{7}. The bridge is a 16-bar pedal on A minor. Although the bridge melody is similar to the melody in section A, the pedaling rhythm and broader, more sustained texture create a very satisfying contrast. At first, the static bridge is a natural resolution to the forward motion of section A. This soon changes, however, as the consistent pedaling over one unresolved minor chord becomes a source of tension that is resolved by the return of quarter note movement in the last A section.

Unit 3: Historical Perspective

An earlier version of *Milestones* was written in 1949 when Miles first struck out into the world as a leader. That version (now called *Old Milestones*) is a noteworthy bebop tune. The version here is the "new" *Milestones*, written in 1958. Jazz, then as now, was in search of new sounds. Art Blakey and the Jazz Messengers were creating the Hard Bop sensation. Duke Ellington was enjoying a revival, and Ornette Coleman was recording *Something Else*, his first record date as a leader.

For his 1958 *Milestones* recording, Miles put together a quintet consisting of both John Coltrane and Cannonball Adderly. Bill Evans was the pianist, along with Jimmy Cobb on drums and Paul Chambers on bass. The title track was Miles's first modal composition and a bellwether for things to come from him. After of the success of *Milestones*, Miles went on to record a whole album of his modal compositions, now considered the most important recording in the history of jazz titled *Kind of Blue*.

Unit 4: Technical Considerations

This chart is rated at the Grade 1–2 level. This arrangement is a confidence builder for young bands: it offers easy road maps, no harmonic challenges, and an easy-to-play melody.

All instrumental ranges are reasonable. The trumpet range is on the staff and the highest note is E (e^1). The trombones may often go to F above the staff (f) with an occasional E♭ above middle C (e♭). The guitar part is optional, as are parts for second tenor and third trumpet. Bass lines are completely written throughout.

The tempo is moderately bright at ♩ = 172. There are few eighth notes, so the tempo will be quite comfortable. Encourage the band to play a slightly brighter tempo after playing this chart for a while. The faster this arrangement can be comfortably played, the better it sounds.

Unit 5: Stylistic Considerations

The band that recorded *Milestones* in 1958 was an eclectic mix of opposite performers: John Coltrane, Cannonball Adderley, Bill Evans, Jimmy Cobb, Paul Chambers, and of course Miles himself. The success of this band illustrates the fact that modal music structures are like empty picture frames that can handle a broad stylistic range.

This arrangement of *Milestones* is an ideal chart for encouraging reluctant students to take a solo. It is also good for a more advanced player. It is likely best for the bass and the drums to hold down the fort and not solo, because they are in charge of rhythm and form. Note that, for soloing, the style is closer to bebop than swing, which calls for more even eighth notes and a slight accent on every other quarter note.

Unit 6: Musical Elements

MELODY:

Milestones is a playful three-note jazz nursery rhyme that lends itself to a compelling swing groove. The melody will not be a challenge to the beginner or intermediate band. There is just enough melody to move into the sparse chord changes.

To be truly appreciated, however, this melody must be felt. One way to accomplish this is to have students nod the head to quarter notes and tap the foot on beats 2 and 4 while clapping on the beat 4 of each measure. Once that pattern is established, sing the melody as well. Do this with section of the band at a time, gradually bringing the whole band together.

HARMONY:

There are three basic chords to the entire 48-bar piece. Section A consists of G minor resolving to F major. The bridge is a 16-bar floating pedal on A minor. All of these chords occur normally within the F major scale. The challenge is deciding what to do with so much freedom and space. The arrangement comes with sample melodic solo ideas for the beginner to try.

Notice that the A minor mode of section B includes a B♮ (the ninth), which does not occur in the F major mode of section A. Including the B♮ in a solo will distinguish the bridge from section A.

Consider limiting beginning to intermediate soloists to a five-note scale to offer a more focused, organized and melodic approach to soloing. For section A, try a G Dorian scale minus the fourth and seventh notes. In section B, try the A minor scale minus the sixth and seventh notes for contrast. If practiced, these ideas will empower a new improviser with a sense of accomplishment and newfound ability.

RHYTHM:

The rhythm is straight-ahead, medium, up-tempo, bebop quarter notes. They are more even than swing quarters, with a very slight accent on every other beat. The drummer does a rim-shot on the fourth beat in the A sections. Section B is a more static pedal, which at first appears to be a release from hard driving section A. The displaced whole note pedal in turn begins to build tension in anticipation of a return to motion, with the forward-moving quarter notes of the final A section. The impression is one of driving down the street in the A sections but waiting at a red light in section B. The full structure works as a sequence of tension-and-release events.

Unit 7: Form and Structure

Milestones is an AABA tune. In this arrangement, it appears first with full band, next as a backdrop to individual soli, and then as band soli before a return to the opening. A brief intro and coda open and close the piece.

SECTION	MEASURE	EVENT AND SCORING
Intro	1–4	The intro is a short 4-bar unified effort that includes the entire band in unisons, simple harmonies, and easy-to-read rhythms.

Section	Measure	Event and Scoring
AA	17–23	The melody is stated by alto sax and fourth trombone, giving the piece a big, broad, and bold sound. Trumpets are conspicuously absent, letting saxes take the first lead. At measure 11, trumpets enter with a unison pedal to accent the rhythm of the lead melody in the saxophones.
B	21–30	The band performs the section B melody in a choral style with lower brass and rhythm section pedaling. First trombone balances between melody in the upper brass and saxes and the pedal of the lower brass, giving a Doppler effect to the melody. The first ending features the lower brass re-energizing the pedal effect. The second ending functions as a transition to the forward motion of the last A section.
A	31–38	Trumpets take over the melody with support from the lower brass. Saxophones take over the duties of pedaling the accent.
Solo	39–62	This section can range in difficulty at the director's discretion. If your soloists are inexperienced, allow them to experiment by extending the G minor section (bars 39–46). Everyone can have a go at a solo with very little risk of failure. Cue the B section of the melody (measure 47), which can work either as section B proper or a background to another soloist. The last A section (measures 55–62) introduces the first eighth-note reading, beginning gradually. This works as a solo background, but could also be a band soli. For additional soli, a repeat to measure 39 is possible.

Section	Measure	Event and Scoring
Band soli	63–94	The band soli begins with eighth-note riffing in unison throughout the band and melodic repetition. Measure 71 reiterates backgrounds from measures 55–62, giving the band director an opportunity to build intensity toward measure 76, which is a release into more unison band riffing. From measure 79 on, the band unison riffing becomes more syncopated and chromatic, adding to the intensity, and finally climaxing to a band fall-off and hand-off to a 2-bar drum fill at measure 85. This syncopated drive for intensity continues at measure 87 and leads to measures 93–94, which are essentially the turnaround and pick-up to measure 5, the return of the melody played in its entirety to the coda marking at measure 38.
Coda	95–98	Long tones in the band bring this machine to a halt in as many bars as it took to start it. Baritone sax and rhythm section play quasi-pedal figures in unison to slow the momentum. A sharp and snappy unison eighth-note figure performed by the entire band gives an abrupt cut-off to finish the piece.

Unit 8: Suggested Listening

Miles Davis, *Kind of Blue*, original release, Sony Records, 1959.
Miles Davis, *Milestones*, original release, Sony Records, 1958.

Unit 9: Additional References and Resources

Chambers, Jack, and J. K. Chamber, *Milestones: The Music and Times of Miles Davis* (Cambridge: Da Capo Press, 1998).

Chilton, John, *Who's Who of Jazz*, fourth edition (Cambridge: Da Capo Press, 1985).

Dibb, Mike, *The Miles Davis Story* (Channel 4 Television Ltd. DVD, 2001).

Ward, Geoffrey C., and Ken Burns, *Jazz: A History of America's Music* (New York: Knopf, 2000).

Contributed by:

Steve Kirby
Director of Jazz Studies
Faculty of Music
University of Manitoba
Winnipeg, Manitoba

Teacher Resource Guide

One More for the Count

Mike Lewis

(b. 1938)

Unit 1: Composer

Since graduation from the University of Miami in 1965, Mike Lewis has been in constant demand as an arranger, orchestrator, producer, and conductor. He has worked with such notables as Jackie Gleason, KC & The Sunshine Band, Tanya Tucker, Dr. Hook, Rod Stewart, Julio Iglesias, John Cougar Mellencamp, and others far too numerous to name. Lewis also toured with the Charlie Spivak and Jimmy Dorsey orchestras in the sixties, and more recently has produced fifty shows for many of the major cruise line companies.

Unit 2: Composition

Dedicated to the late Count Basie, *One More For The Count* captures the hard swinging style of the great Count Basie Orchestra. This is an easy swing composition with simple but effective melodic ideas and riff-oriented repetition, typical of the Count Basie style. Brass is often in buckets or alternatively plays into the stand for a warm and relaxed sound. Shout sections are limited in length and range to keep the overall character of the composition relaxed and comfortable. The solo is written in the first trombone part but could easily be moved to any other wind player.

Unit 3: Historical Perspective

In the early years of the Count Basie Orchestra and other pioneer big bands, many compositions were riff charts. Often in blues forms, certain melodic ideas, or riffs, are repeated over the changing harmony of the blues form. Players in the ensemble harmonize the riffs by ear while others improvise

counter lines that eventually become part of the composition. Scores and parts are not usually written, but rather memorized, and thus need to be simple and memorable. The resulting arrangements are melodically simple, repetitive, and hard driving. In later years, big band music reached higher levels of sophistication with more complex harmonies, longer and more developed melodies and counter lines. *One More For The Count*, while not quite a true riff chart, is reminiscent of the early days of the Count Basie Orchestra.

Unit 4: Technical Considerations

The difficulty rating of *One More For The Count* is medium easy. The tempo is ♩ = 104 with a duration of 4:10. This chart is easily played by a smaller-than-standard big band instrumentation, and can be effective with as few as three saxophones, two trumpets, one trombone, piano, bass, and drums. Lead trumpet plays briefly to a written G above the staff (g^1) and lead trombone plays to an E above the staff (e). Rhythm section parts are moderate and well notated. The drum part is easy to follow and contains good suggestions for cymbal choices, possible set-ups, and fills. The bass part contains both chord symbols and a written line that is easily executed by young players. The guitar part is easy to read and an excellent guitar chord chart is provided to assist young players with negotiating all chord types encountered in the chart, including extended chords and altered chords. The piano part contains both chord symbols and suggested voicings, and has both written figures and space available for free comping.

Unit 5: Stylistic Considerations

One More For The Count is the perfect vehicle for accessing the sound and style of the Count Basie Orchestra and other historic big bands. It is important that students spend a substantial amount of time listening to recordings of music in the same style before or as they are learning this music.

Each rhythm section player should observe style and technique particular to her instrument. The guitar player should imitate Count Basie's guitar player, Freddie Green, playing all quarter note down strokes with a slight release of pressure on the strings between strums so that there is a slight gap between notes. Tone controls should be on a medium setting to produce a warm and nearly acoustic sound. In this style of music, the guitar is a major factor in providing pulse. The bass should focus on steadiness of tempo and achieving a bass/drum "lock," the feeling of groove and forward motion that occurs when bass and drums agree on placement of notes within the pulse. The drums, while often expected to set-up and kick ensemble figures, should remember that pulse and groove is primary, and should never play anything that would disrupt or weaken the pulse and groove. To keep with the simple character of the chart, drums should lean towards playing simply instead of complexly.

Saxophones and brass are challenged not by the technical difficulty of the chart, but rather by making it swing. At this slower swing tempo, it is imperative that ensemble players keep the swinging triplet sub-division in mind at all times so that upbeats are not rushed. Wind players should be reminded that the chart is marked with phrase marks that should not be confused with slurs. To achieve the correct accent points and contour of line, players are encouraged to first sing through their parts using jazz syllables, (e.g., "doo," "daht," "dah," etc.) until all players are in agreement.

Unit 6: Musical Elements:

MELODY:

The main melody consists of two melodic fragments that are repeated and sequenced. It should be sung first to find the accent points and goal notes, then should be played with the same amount of accent within the line. The second melody is smoother, but should still have a feeling of slight accent on the longer notes.

HARMONY:

The harmony consists of many dominant seventh chords extended to 9ths to give it a quasi-jazz blues sound. The harmonies are not purely diatonic or functional, and a significant amount of half-step planning is utilized throughout the chart. Melody notes are sometimes extensions or alterations within the chord, and require careful listening for intonation adjustments.

RHYTHM:

The rhythm is medium swing and requires that all players are interpreting the eighth-note swing in the same way. The drummer should experiment with varying the swing feel on the ride cymbal to find the perfect eighth-note swing and set the groove for the rest of the band. The entire ensemble can practice rhythms by slowing the tempo down and speaking "dood-n-dah" for each beat of the measure while clapping rhythms, or speaking rhythms while walking in time to the rhythm section pulse.

Unit 7: Form and Structure

The basic form of the composition is AABA.

SECTION	MEASURE	EVENT AND SCORING
Intro	1–2	This material is borrowed from the last two measures of section A. It is simple and sets the mood for the music to follow.
3 (1)	3–12	The full ensemble plays the harmonized melody. First trumpet has melody notes with first trombone reinforcing an octave lower, making it easy to project the melody through the harmony. The piano has some written splashes in the gaps between melodic phrases.
3 (2)	3–12	A repeat of the previous section with a transition into section B (the bridge).
13	13–20	Section B. Young players will tend to rush the two-measure *fortissimo* section at the end. Practice figures with triplet sub-division for rhythmic accuracy.
21	21–28	Final A section of the first chorus. Make sure the dynamic level drops back to ***mp*** and that there is no tempo shift at the transition.
29	29–60	A full chorus of trombone solo, but the solo is broken up by ensemble figures throughout. The solo part provides both chord symbols for improvisation and a written solo for non-improvisers.
61	61–68	A simple shout chorus written over the first A section of the form. Saxophones are encouraged to make their glisses as chromatic as possible.
69	69–76	A repeat of the previous section with a transition into section B.
77	77–84	A repeat of section B.

SECTION	MEASURE	EVENT AND SCORING
85	85–92	A repeat of section A.
93	Ending	The tag ending. Two measures are repeated twice, signaling the ending of the chart. The signature Count Basie ending in the piano part must be played accurately.

Unit 8: Suggested Listening

Count Basie Orchestra, *Prime Time*, Pablo Records.
Count Basie Orchestra, *Straight Ahead*, MCA Records.
Frank Capp, *In A Hefti Bag*, Concord Records.
Frank Capp Juggernaut, *Play It Again Sam*, Concord Records.

Unit 9: Additional References and Resources

Count Basie Orchestra, *Diane Schuur & The Count Basie Orchestra*, Image Entertainment DVD, 1987, GRP Records CD, 1990.

Jarvis, Jeff, and Doug Beach, *The Jazz Educator's Handbook* (Delevan: Kendor Music, Inc., 2002).

Contributed by:

Susie Jones
Jazz Studies
Mt. Hood Community College
Gresham, Oregon

Teacher Resource Guide

Samantha

Samuel "Sammy" Lewis Nestico
(b. 1924)

Unit 1: Composer

Sammy Nestico is a well-known, prolific composer and arranger of big band music. He began his life in Pittsburg, Pennsylvania, on February 1924 as Sammy Nistico, and later changed it to Nestico. His Italian father taught him patriotism and gratitude, and perhaps that influenced his decision to work and perform in military bands for a major part of his career.

By the time Sammy was seventeen he was the staff arranger for ABC radio station in Pittsburgh. He received his BS degree in music education from Duquesne University, and has been honored three times by the school with an honorary doctorate in music, the Distinguished Alumni Award, and in 1994, he was inducted into the Century Club. North Texas State also presented him with special music awards in 1978, 1979, and 1980. In 2005 he received an honorary doctorate in music from Virginia's Shenandoah University. He then joined the United States Air Force Band in Washington, D. C. as staff arranger and became the leader of the famous Airmen of Note. After his fifteen-year tenure with the Air Force, he enlisted with the U. S. Marines and served as chief arranger and director of the White House orchestra that performed during the Kennedy and Johnson administrations. Sammy was the composer/arranger for the Count Basie Orchestra from 1970–84, recording ten albums of original music, four of which won Grammy awards. During that time he also worked for Capital Records as arranger/orchestrator for the equivalent of sixty-three albums.

A versatile composer/arranger, Nestico has collaborated with Steve Allen, Stan Freberg, Bobby Troupe, and Johnny Mercer in the songwriting field, and has orchestrated for such major film studios as 20th Century Fox, Universal, Paramount, Warner Brothers, MGM, and Columbia. He has also arranged and/or conducted albums for recording artists Phil Collins, Barbra Streisand,

Natalie Cole, Frank Sinatra, Bing Crosby, Sarah Vaughan, Toni Tennille, Patti Austin, Nancy Wilson, Pia Zadora, Paul Anka, Pat Boone, Ronnie Milsap, Daniel Rodriguez, and others. Sammy has also written commercials for Anheuser Busch, Zenith, Ford Motor Company, Mattel Toys, Pittsburgh Paints, National Guard, Dodge, Remington Bank Americard, and more. The United States Air Force Band sponsors the Sammy Nestico Arranging Award annually.

Nestico is the author of *The Complete Arranger*, published in 1993, currently marketed throughout the world in four languages. His arrangements have been played by leading symphonies and recorded by the Boston Pops and Andre Kostelanetz Orchestras; he is most proud of the nearly 600 numbers published in the education field and played in the schools of America.

Unit 2: Composition

Sammy Nestico wrote and published this arrangement of *Samantha* in 1972. Kendor Music publishes the arrangement. This beautiful contemporary ballad features tenor sax in front of some nice ensemble work. This is an excellent vehicle for the saxophonist to develop motivic, melodic, and stylistic techniques such as bending notes, playing behind, and stretching time, and, in general, being a soloist out in front of the band. Sammy wrote a more advanced level of this chart for Count Basie, yet this Kendor arrangement is versatile enough to be performed by any level of band, from junior high to professional ensembles.

Unit 3: Historical Perspective

When the name Nestico appears on a chart, it is natural for many to assume it is a Basie style swing chart. In this arrangement, however, Nestico surprises the listener with a beautiful ballad. *Samantha* was originally written for and played by Bud Shank as a showpiece for alto saxophone. This Kendor arrangement is technically more simplistic and features tenor saxophone instead of the original alto.

Unit 4: Technical Considerations

This chart is quite playable by most high school bands and advanced junior high bands. The recommended tempo is ♩ = 66 with a duration of 3:12. The chart can work well at a slightly faster tempo, however. The solo part is written out and requires no demand to improvise, but it is recommended that the soloist add his own creative stylistic and melodic touches, especially on the closing cadenza.

Brass and wind parts are written in a comfortable range. The lead trumpet range goes to concert E on the staff (e^1); the lead trombone range goes to concert E♭ above the staff (e♭). The piano, bass line, and drum parts are written out, so improvisation is not required. Improvisers with limited reading skills may benefit from the simple rhythmic figures included.

The slow tempo can pose a challenge to the rhythm section, particularly the drummer, since there is a tendency to rush a slow tempo such as this. The chart provides a perfect opportunity, however, to allow the rhythm section to focus on time and feel.

Unit 5: Stylistic Considerations

This contemporary ballad is reminiscent of the style of Michel LeGrand, Henry Mancini, and 70s TV show theme style, and is played in a legato style. Nestico wrote many TV show themes throughout his career. As an arranger, he has written for television specials by Julie Andrews, George Burns, Gene Kelly, Merv Griffin, Mary Tyler Moore, Goldie Hawn, The Grammy Awards, *The Tonight Show*, Perry Como, Toni Tennille, Liza Minnelli, Bob Hope, and many more. As an orchestrator, he has worked on *Mission Impossible*, *The Tony Randall Show*, *Medical Center*, *The Mary Tyler Moore Show*, *Hawaii Five-O*, *The Bob Newhart Show*, *Gomer Pyle*, *The Streets of San Francisco*, *Mannix*, *Mayberry RFD*, *The MOD Squad*, *The Bionic Woman*, *Cannon*, *Emergency*, *Columbo*, *Charlie's Angels*, *The Lou Grant Show*, *M.A.S.H.*, and many others.

This selection is ideal for featuring either tenor saxophone or trumpet. It could also be played with a trendy funk backbeat, if desired, to obtain a more contemporary feel. Accurate intonation, blend and balance are called for throughout the piece.

Unit 6: Musical Elements

MELODY:

The simple, pretty melody is featured in the tenor sax solo and consists of a 4-bar motif from measures 5–32, and should be interpreted in a lyrical style. The melody is repeated and developed until the modulation at measure 32, where call and response of the melody occurs between saxophones and trumpets until measure 38. At measure 39, trumpets have the melody with supporting backgrounds from saxophones, piano, and guitar.

HARMONY:
The chart is moderately easy to read, yet sophisticated and intelligent-sounding. Thick chords and complex harmonies often use pedal tones, which require players to listen to one another in the section as well as in other sections of the band. The saxophone soloist may play what is written or improvise a cadenza.

RHYTHM:
Samantha is a straight-eighth-note pop ballad with drums playing mostly eighth notes on the hi hat and dotted quarter/eighth figures in the bass drum.

Unit 7: Form and Structure

The form of *Samantha* is AAB, then AB—first and second. The bridge is eight measures with a two-measure extension for a modulation back to section A in a new key, up a fourth. The introduction from measures 1–5 is a call and response between trumpets and alto and tenor saxophones. Baritone saxophone doubles the bass. The intro is four measures with a pick-up measure into the first A section. After the intro, the chart settles into the F Major and modulates at measure 32 into G minor, ending on B♭maj^7. This is a well-written, attainable chart.

Unit 8: Suggested Listening

Nestico, Sammy, *This is the Moment*, Fenwood Music, Inc.
The Quincy Jones-Sammy Nestico Orchestra, *Basie and Beyond*, Qwest/Warner Brothers.
Count Basie library.
Sammy Nestico library.

Unit 9: Additional References and Resources

Nestico, Sammy, *The Complete Arranger* (Kendor Music, Inc., 1993).
Compositions and arrangements are available from Kendor, Hal Leonard, and Warner Brothers and at www.sammynesticomusic.com..

Contributed by:

Mary Jo Papich
Fine Arts Department Chair
Highland Park High School
Highland Park, Illinois

Teacher Resource Guide

Second Line (Joe Avery's Blues)
Traditional

arranged by Victor Goines
(b. 1961)

Unit 1: Composer/Arranger

Percy Humphrey, trumpet player and leader of the Eureka Brass Band in 1964, cites Joe Avery as his inspiration. Joe Avery played trombone in New Orleans in the early part of the twentieth century. Humphrey tells the story of how the band would line up on the street for a New Orleans parade and Joe Avery would say, "Let's satisfy the second line." When Avery was asked, "What are we going to satisfy them with?" Avery would start playing the melody to *Second Line* and that's all it took to get the second line jumping. It was with this spirit in mind that clarinetist and saxophonist Victor Goines created this arrangement of the great New Orleans standard, *Second Line*.

Victor Goines was born New Orleans in 1961. At the age of eight he began to play the clarinet and continued his studies with Carl Blouin, Sr. at St. Augustine High School. It was Blouin who introduced him to the saxophone. In 1980 he entered Loyola University in New Orleans where he studied clarinet and saxophone, earning a bachelor of music education degree in 1984.

As Mr. Goines's interest in jazz grew, he contacted Ellis Marsalis for private lessons. Mr. Goines left New Orleans in 1987 to pursue graduate studies at Virginia Commonwealth University in Richmond, Virginia and received his master of music degree in 1990.

Since that time, Mr. Goines has performed on Broadway, on television, and for motion pictures. He has also toured and performed nationally and internationally with some of the world's great jazz artists, among them Dizzy Gillespie, Freddie Hubbard, Lionel Hampton, Branford Marsalis, Wynton Marsalis, and a host of others. In 2000 he was appointed the first director of jazz studies at the famed Juilliard School in New York. He is currently a member of the Lincoln Center Jazz Orchestra and performs with his own quartet. Mr. Goines is deeply committed to jazz education and is in constant demand as a clinician.

Unit 2: Composition

Second Line has been a standard for many years, and falls under the "traditional" or "New Orleans" category. Goines's arrangement was created in 2005 for the Jazz for Young People Series sponsored by Jazz at Lincoln Center. It was intended to fit with the Jazz for Young People Curriculum that can be found at www.jazzforyoungpeople.org or www.jalc.org. This tune correlates with "Lesson 1: New Orleans" of the curriculum. Among the many jazz devices this tune uses are the following:

Blues form. Structurally, this is the 12-bar blues chord progression. It is used as a repeating harmonic structure for composition and improvisation.

Call and response. The performance of musical phrases in alteration by different voices or distinct groups, used in opposition in such a way as to suggest that they answer one another. The term has its origins in descriptions of the singing of Afro-American work songs, in which a leader and chorus respectively sing a verse and a refrain or successive verses in alteration.

Riff. A short, melodic ostinato which may be repeated intact or varied to accommodate an underlying harmonic pattern.

Shout chorus. Often the loudest part of a jazz composition, which usually contains the climax of the piece.

Standard. A composition that becomes an established item in the repertory; by extension, therefore, a song that a professional musician may be expected to know.

Unit 3: Historical Perspective

Second Line is emblematic of the celebratory music of early twentieth century New Orleans brass bands. The bands were most often associated with funeral processions, performing slow hymns or dirges on the way to the cemetery and hot jazz or lively marches on the return journey. On this return from the cemetery, those following the band, known as the "second line," marched and danced on the streets. These same bands also played for parades, picnics, dances, and many other social occasions. They were a key element of the social fabric of New Orleans.

Unit 4: Technical Considerations

This chart is rated a Grade 3; the recommended tempo is ♩ = 180. It may be performed more slowly, as long as the characteristic, 2-beat groove remains intact. The chart is written for five saxophones, eight brass, and four rhythm section parts, as well as optional parts for flute, tuba, horn in F, and treble clef baritone.

The lead trumpet range goes up to a fourth line concert D♭ ($d♭^1$). The lead trombone must be able to negotiate a G above the staff (g). Saxophone parts present no great difficulty; tenor saxophones however, repeatedly play a low concert B♭ (B♭) as the bottom note of their melodic statement.

Written soli are transcriptions of the soli heard on the demonstration CD included with the arrangement. Range becomes more extreme in the written trumpet solo (concert G above the staff [g^1]), and saxophones have more technical/rhythmical demands placed on them. Saxophone soli also extend to a written E above the staff (e^2). All soloists are encouraged to memorize the written soli and then transcribe soli from original recordings and further create their own improvised soli. Riffs written as backgrounds to soloi must not be played too loudly.

Rhythm section parts are all completely written out with voicings and chord changes included.

Unit 5: Stylistic Considerations

This joyous New Orleans brass band standard features some of the basic devices of jazz: call and response, riffs and the shout chorus. It is primarily written in a two-beat groove, which had its roots in ragtime. The groove alters at the beginning of the shout chorus at measure 114 with the addition of a walking bass line. Balance between the call and response sections (saxophones, trombones and trumpets) is essential throughout. The band must not play too loudly in the shout chorus. Play ***mp*** and ***f*** dynamic levels as written.

Winds should be careful to articulate cleanly and with separation where indicated. Marcato accents (^) should be played as if saying the word "daht": air must continue beyond the note for proper phrasing. There is a clear beginning and end to the note. Pay special attention to notes at phrase endings, making them short if marked with a staccato mark as if saying the word "ut." This syllable will put a back end on the note and end the phrase cleanly. Accents, phrasing, and shading (best learned from listening) are the key to an authentic performance of this piece.

Rhythm players should begin work on this piece by listening to the subtleties of the players on the demo recording. This exercise will help players tune in to the accents and phrasing of the written parts. This process is accelerated if the tempo is slowed, parts are memorized, and focus on the triplet subdivision and getting the proper feel is the goal. You are off to a great start if the drummer can match the groove of the bass drum on the recording. Build the rhythm section on this foundation.

The guitar player has a unique challenge, as she must emulate the percussive quality of a banjo. Listen to Freddie Green of the Count Basie Orchestra to get the crisp quarter note feel with slight accents on beats 2 and 4. The guitar part should not be too loud and should have an acoustic quality to it. The guitar is the "engine" of the rhythm section. The pianist should subdivide the triplet feel and accent longer notes in such places as measure 6. The bass player should phrase as if he was playing a tuba and work with the bass drum.

The rhythm section can take its performance to a higher level by listening to the *Eureka Brass Band* or *Preservation Hall Jazz Band* recordings of this tune. Rhythm section students should focus on two-measure phrasing, the subdivision, the two-beat groove (beginning with bass drum) and ways of varying written patterns written that match the professional recordings.

To better understand the *riff* style of playing, listen to any of the early Count Basie recordings from Kansas City.

Unit 6: Musical Elements

MELODY:

This simple, major triad-oriented melody outlines the chord changes to a concert B♭ blues. Singing the melody in time and thinking in subdivided beat, using the syllables "*daht-daht-daht, daht-do-daht, day-do-day-daht-daht-daht,*" etc., will be beneficial. Singing "*d*" to begin articulations helps students use the tongue properly, and using the exact same syllables/words for singing cleans up ensemble articulation. The melody is repetitive enough to be easily memorized. It will greatly enhance performance to internalize parts. At the same time, have the rhythm section play, focusing on the triplet sub-division of the beat (*do-od-la*), giving the "*la*" a slight accent. It is best to start slowly and gradually speed up as comfort with these techniques is gained.

HARMONY:

Second Line is primarily a B♭ blues. Students should listen to the demonstration recording or one of the original recordings and indicate they hear chord changes by clapping as they the changes. Focusing on the bass helps when beginning to listen for chord changes.

Next, winds may play chord roots to better recognize the blues progression while the rhythm section plays. Since the melody is an arpeggiation of the melody in root position, it lends itself to aiding the memorization of the chord tones of a 12-bar blues.

RHYTHM:

Rhythm should be learned simultaneously with the melody. Focusing on the subdivided beat is very important for both winds and rhythm section. It is beneficial to have students step side to side on beats one and three and clap on beats two and four. Once this is mastered, have students speak the "*do-od-la*" subdivision of the beat while stepping and clapping. Eventually students should sing their parts while stomping and clapping. Some may still speak the subdivision while others sing their parts, checking each other to be sure that it feels correct. Students can also perform this exercise while listening to the original recording to focus on the professional's interpretation of the feel and subdivision.

Unit 7: Form and Structure

The basic form of the composition is the traditional 12-bar B♭ blues with a brief, rubato introduction and a short coda.

SECTION	MEASURE	EVENT AND SCORING
Introduction	1–4	Rubato call-and-response between trumpets and ensemble.
First statement of melody	5–17	Melody begins unison in the winds with brief harmony at measure 13. The section repeats for a second statement of the melody.
Break	18–21	A harmonized break for the entire band.
Return to melody	22–29	A return to the melody as previously scored.
Break	30–33	A harmonized break.

Section	Measure	Event and Scoring
Trumpet solo/soli	34–65	A written solo that may be performed by a trumpet soloist or the entire section. This may be improvised if not performed by the section. This solo begins on the fifth measure of the blues form (on the IV chord).
Riff background	54–65	Trombones are added as a riff-oriented background. Volume must be softer than the soloist.
Saxophone solo/ soli	66–89	A written solo that may be performed by a saxophone soloist or the entire section.
Riff background	78–89	Trumpets are added as a riff-oriented background. Volume must be softer than the soloist.
Trombone solo/ soli	90–113	A written solo that may be performed by a trombone soloist or the entire section. This may be improvised if not performed by the section.
Riff background	102–113	Saxophones are added as a riff-oriented background. Volume must be softer than the soloist.
Shout chorus	114–137	Begins at an ***mf*** dynamic level for first twelve measures and is in the call and response style. All parts must be balanced. The bass changes to a walking bass line. This section builds to the D.S.
D.S.	5–31	A return to the original statement of the melody.
Coda	158–159	Trumpets state this short coda melody punctuated by the rest of the winds and rhythm section.

Unit 8: Suggested Listening

Count Basie Orchestra, *The Best of Early Basie*, Decca Records.
Eureka Brass Band, *Jazz at Preservation Hall, Volumes 1 & 2*, Atlantic Records.
Preservation Hall Jazz Band, *Sweet Emma and Her Preservation Hall Jazz Band*, Preservation Hall.

Unit 9: Additional References and Resources

Dietrich, Kurt, *Jazz 'Bones* (Rottenburg: Advance Music, 2005).
Kernfeld, Barry, ed., *The New Grove Dictionary of Jazz* (New York: St. Martin's Press, 1995).
Mantooth, Frank, *Voicings for the Jazz Keyboard* (Milwaukee: Hal Leonard, 1986).
Schuller, Gunther, *Early Jazz* (New York: Oxford University Press, 1986).
Ward, Geoffrey and Ken Burns, *Jazz: A History of America's Music* (New York: Knopf, 2000).

Contributed by:

Steve Sveum
Director of Bands and Jazz
Sun Prairie High School
Sun Prairie, Wisconsin

Teacher Resource Guide

Soft Winds

Fletcher Henderson

(1897–1952)

arranged by Michael Sweeney

(b. 1952)

Unit 1: Composer/Arranger

Pianist, composer, and arranger Fletcher Henderson was very important in the 1920s as the leader of a great jazz big band that lead us into the "swing era." He moved to New York City for a career in chemistry, but he rapidly found employment as a pianist, joining W. C. Handy as a song plugger. This jump-started his career in the music business.

Some top jazz musicians played for Henderson, including alto saxophonist Benny Carter, tenor saxophonists Coleman Hawkins, Ben Webster, and Lester Young, trumpeters Louis Armstrong, Rex Stewart, and Roy Eldridge, and trombonist J. C. Higginbottom.

Fletcher became an important arranger in the 1930s, his arrangements for the Benny Goodman band becoming big hits. At the height of the swing era his own band was little known. Henderson's peak years directing his band were from 1923 to 1939. *Christopher Columbus* was his theme song.

Michael Sweeney (b. 1952) is a graduate of Indiana University where he studied music education and composition. Since 1982, he has worked full time for the Hal Leonard Corporation in Milwaukee, Wisconsin. He is currently director of band publications. Michael is particularly known for his composing and arranging for young jazz bands.

Unit 2: Composition

Fletcher Henderson wrote *Soft Winds* in 1940 at the end of his peak big band years, but never recorded the tune. Some people give credit to Benny Goodman for this piece, but the Goodman version is in a 16-bar blues form. Sweeney's arrangement is a 12-bar blues form and was influenced by Art Blakey's Jazz Messengers recording of *At the Café Bohemia, Vol. 1*. This composition is in the riff style of writing. The opening two measures form the melodic content of the piece. It is in "swing triplet" feeling at a medium tempo.

Unit 3: Historical Perspective

When jazz became popular in the 1920s and demand grew for larger dance bands, it became necessary for ensemble music to be notated, particularly when a group included more than three or four horns.

It was Fletcher Henderson and Don Redman who took the freewheeling New Orleans jazz sound of clarinet, trumpet and trombone front line and incorporated it into ensemble playing by making each instrument the lead of its own section. Clarinet players started doubling on saxophone. Together with the backing of a four-person rhythm section (piano, banjo, tuba, and drum set), this format carried forward the drive and syncopation of the original New Orleans jazz bands and eventually culminated in the swing style of Benny Goodman and others. This block concept of arranging by Don Redman (saxophone and brass sections) developed into the format still used today. Swing was largely invented when Louis Armstrong joined Fletcher Henderson's orchestra in 1924, and Don Redman began writing arrangements for the band that echoed the cornetist's relaxed phrases.

The swing era was officially underway in 1935 when Benny Goodman's orchestra caught on with the public. Swing was a major force in American popular music until the big-band era largely ended in 1946. Swing differs from New Orleans jazz and Traditional in that the ensemble sections (even for small groups) are simpler and generally filled with repetitious riffs, while soli are more sophisticated. Individual improvisations still pay close attention to the melody but, due to advanced musicianship, solo flights are more adventurous.

The instrumentation of Henderson's band changed from 1923 to the following by 1933.

1923 Instrumentation	1933 Instrumentation
1 alto sax/clarinet	2 alto sax/clarinet
1 tenor sax/clarinet	2 tenor sax/clarinet
1 bass sax	
2 trumpets	3 trumpets
1 trombone	2 trombones
1 piano	1 piano
1 banjo	1 guitar
1 tuba	1 string bass
1 drum set	1 drum set

Unit 4: Technical Considerations

This chart is rated Grade 2–3; the recommended tempo is ♩ = 120 with a duration of 3:51. A faster tempo also works well.

The lead trumpet range goes to a concert E fourth space (e^1); the lead trombone range goes to a concert E above middle C (e).

The soli are for alto and tenor saxes, trumpet, and piano, and are written out as a guide.

Suggested rhythm section parts are written out for comping on piano, the bass line, and the drum part with ensemble hits. The guitar part has chord symbols and written ensemble parts. A vibes part is also included, as is a full performance recording.

Unit 5: Stylistic Considerations

This 1940s chart is an example of Henderson's later period. It is a good example of the evolution from the Dixie 2-beat style to the swing style of four beats per measure. It is important not to rush when moving from the 2-beat to the 4-beat section and to not drag when moving from the 4-beat back to the 2-beat section.

The articulations are based on the triplet swing style developed by Louis Armstrong and the Henderson band.

Henderson's band was a dance band, so a nice, easy dance groove must be established.

Unit 6: Musical Elements

MELODY:

First learn the riff-style melody vocally. Establish the triplet groove so that it fits the 2-beat feel of the bass and drums. The melody is a good example of an easy swing-style tune.

HARMONY:

The form of the tune is a modified 12-bar blues progression in B♭. The chord changes are:

Measures 1–6:	B♭^{7}–E♭^{7}–B♭^{7}–B♭^{7}–E♭^{7}–E♭^{7}–Edim (the standard blues progression)
Measures 7–8:	B♭^{7}–A^7–A♭^{7}–G^7 (moving down chromatically)
Measures 9–10:	Cm^7–F^7 (the ii^7–V^7 progression)
Measures 11–12:	B♭^{7}–G^7–C^7–F^7 (a turnaround)

This is a very playable chart, useful for teaching triplet swing phrasing and also a new blues progression. Soloing can be taught from the chord progression and also with a major blues scale.

RHYTHM:

This chart requires two swing feelings: the 2-beat and 4-beat feels. The triplet pulse ("doo-oo-la") on each beat must be felt by everyone in the band and not just the rhythm section.

Singing stylistic and rhythmic articulations are very important in any swing composition. Have students sing rhythmic examples from the composition.

Unit 7: Form and Structure

The basic form of the composition is a 12-bar blues form.

SECTION	MEASURE	EVENT AND SCORING
A	1–12	Bass starts the piece. A front line of alto sax, trumpet and piano in thirds joins with the bass and drums in a 2-beat feel.
A2	1–13	The full ensemble now has the tune voiced in four-part harmony.
B1	14–25	Tenor sax solo with rhythm section background.

SECTION	MEASURE	EVENT AND SCORING
B2	14–25	Trumpet solo with trombone section and rhythm section background.
B3	26–37	Alto sax solo with trumpet and trombone ensemble background.
B4	26–38	Piano solo with rhythm section background.
(B)	14–38	A solo section that can be opened up for more than twelve bars for each soloi. Backgrounds may be used at the director's choice.
C	39–50	Full ensemble with sax counter lines. This shout chorus (the peak hit of the chart). Accents must be articulated correctly. Use "dah" with full duration for accents; use "daht" with a full sound but shorter for the roof tops (^).
D	51–62	Same as section A1.
E	63–74	Same as section A2.
F	75–80	A tag ending which includes a Basie-style piano solo. The last chord must be played softly with a balanced sound.

Unit 8: Suggested Listening

Basie, Count, *Giants of the Big Band Era*, Madacy Entertainment Group.
Burns, Ken, *Jazz, the Story of America's Music*, Verve Music Group.
Ellington, Duke, *Giants of the Big Band Era*, Madacy Entertainment Group.
Goodman, Benny, *Giants of the Big Band Era*, Madacy Entertainment Group.
Henderson, Fletcher, *The Definitive Fletcher Henderson*, Ken Burns Jazz, Columbia/Legacy.

Unit 9: Addition References and Resources

Lee, William F., *American Big Bands* (Milwaukee: Hal Leonard Corp., 2006).

Marsalis, Wynton, *Jazz for Young People Curriculum* (Van Nuys: Alfred Publishing Company, 2002).

Yanow, Scott, *Swing* (Third Ear Productions/Miller Freeman Books, 2000).

www.allmusic.com (jazz).

www.nfo.net (Big Bands Database Plus).

Contributed by:

Robert Waggoner
Director of the Community Music School Jazz Lab Ensemble
Adjunct Instructor of Jazz Education
Webster University
St. Louis, Missouri

Teacher Resource Guide

Sugar

Stanley Turrentine

(1934–2000)

arranged by Mark Taylor

(b. 1948)

Unit 1: Composer/Arranger

Stanley Turrentine was born in Pittsburgh, Pennsylvania on April 5, 1934 into a musical family. The whole family played instruments, and music was always a topic of conversation. Stanley's father, Thomas Turrentine, Sr., was a successful part-time jazz musician who gave his children all the advantages he could to help them carry on the family's musical tradition. He taught each of his five children private lessons, took them to hear live jazz performances, and would often quiz them at home. Every night after dinner the family would sit around the radio and listen to the jazz bands of Count Basie, Duke Ellington, Tommy Dorsey, and other greats. Thomas, Sr. would give the children little tests, such as asking them to identify exactly who was playing each solo. Since every player has a unique way of playing something, he was using this as an ear-training opportunity to teach his kids to really listen to the musician's sound, style, and other individual traits.

The Turrentine children were raised on blues, gospel, and jazz, all of which were received with equal importance. Stanley said, "It is my belief that gospel and blues are the roots of this music that we play, all of this popular music we hear today. I play the blues in everything I play—fast, slow, ballad, whatever. The blues is in there, just like with that spaghetti sauce commercial—it's in there."[1]

Stanley's first instrument was cello, but at age eleven he switched to tenor sax after his dad took him to hear Coleman Hawkins. Stanley's father made him stand facing the wall while playing long tones for hours, concentrating on producing a warm, rich sound. Stanley's sound on the tenor sax soon became characteristically his own. Like him, his sound was large, deep, and earthy, which are some of the unique traits that make his sound so distinct and recognizable. Bassist Ron Carter says, "Stanley was one of the few sax players who came around with Sonny Rollins, Ornette Coleman, and John Coltrane who had his own unique sound. He didn't sound like anybody else, and that's not an easy thing to do."[2]

Stanley Turrentine was actively performing from the 1950s through the 1990s. He is best known for his performances in the styles of soul-jazz, hard bop, and fusion. His 1970 soul-jazz hit *Sugar* established him in the popular mainstream and influenced many musicians in all styles of music.

Stanley Turrentine was nominated for four Grammy Awards. During his career he collaborated with Freddie Hubbard, Ron Carter, Herbie Hancock, Max Roach, Tadd Dameron, McCoy Tyner, Horace Silver, Jimmy Smith, Ray Charles, George Benson, and Joe Sample, among others. He also performed with organist Shirley Scott, to whom he was married from 1961 to 1971. Turrentine recorded over thirty-five albums throughout his career.

Following a stroke on September 10, 2000, Stanley Turrentine died in New York City on September 12, 2000 at the age of sixty-six.

Unit 2: Composition

Stanley Turrentine composed *Sugar* in 1970 and recorded it for the CTI record label. This composition is based on a fairly simple 16-bar melody, which is constructed in AB form using one long diatonic sequence on the minor pentatonic scale. In this arrangement by Mark Taylor, the melody is first stated by a quintet including lead alto, lead tenor, baritone sax, second trumpet, and lead trombone accompanied only by the rhythm section. The next statement is made by the same quintet with the addition of rhythmic punctuations and simple backgrounds in the winds. An open solo section follows next with sample solo sheets provided in B♭, E♭, C, and bass clef. An easy, but effective 16-bar solo then leads to a D.S. returning to the opening statement at measure 9. The composition concludes with a ten-measure coda during which the original quintet winds down the arrangement with a repetitive figure from the final motive of the main melody with appropriate backgrounds in the horns and rhythm section. Piano and bass parts are fully written out, as are the drum and optional vibraphone parts. The guitar part is notated with chord changes and rhythmic figures.

Unit 3: Historical Perspective

Stanley Turrentine first went on the road with the Lowell Fulson Band in 1950–51. That band featured a pianist/vocalist by the name of Ray Charles. While on the bus, Ray spent most of his time listening to gospel music on his transistor radio, and Turrentine would sit close enough to hear the music through Ray's headphones. During his two years with the Fulson Band, Turrentine and Charles shared their love of gospel music regularly. Turrentine left the Fulson Band and joined the Tadd Dameron Big Band in 1952 and continued to develop his skills and refine his art. In 1953 he was recruited to fill the tenor sax chair previously held by John Coltrane (on Trane's recommendation) in the Earl Bostic Big Band. Stanley then spent three years (1956–1958) in the United States 158th Army Band. Upon his discharge in the late 1950s, he joined the bebop movement when he accepted the tenor sax spot in Max Roach's band.

Stanley decided to go solo in the 1960s. Between 1960 and 1969 he recorded a series of albums for Blue Note that cemented his reputation in the soul-jazz idiom. Soul-jazz is considered a sub-style of hard bop, which is based on the swing rhythm as opposed to the duple subdivisions found in funk, rock, and fusion. His blues-influenced riffs brought him a fair amount of commercial success with albums such as *Stan "The Man" Turrentine* and *Up at Minton's*. He is probably best known for his ability to blend jazz with pop, soul, and gospel music.

Turrentine was a truly unique artist, and therefore does not fit neatly into established jazz categories. What makes his music great is his love of and commitment to the roots of jazz: gospel and the blues. In 1970, he released the album *Sugar*, the title track becoming a huge hit. That album also helped further the careers of several young jazz musicians, including Ron Carter, Freddie Hubbard, and George Benson.

Unit 4: Technical Considerations

This chart is rated Grade 2.5–3; the suggested tempo is ♩ = 120. The tune would definitely lose its groove if taken too quickly, so the given tempo or a little slower would be most stylistically appropriate.

The brass ranges are very reasonable for young bands. The lead trumpet part remains in the staff for the entire arrangement with the exception of one G (concert F) (g^1) in measure 68. The lead trombone goes up to the concert F two ledger lines above the staff (f) on a regular basis. The bass trombone part has notes down to the concert F just below the staff (F) with optional notes throughout the arrangement going as low as concert C two ledger lines below the staff (C_1).

Saxophone ranges require the lead alto to go up to a C (concert E-flat) two ledger lines above the staff (c^2) and the lead tenor must go up to a D (concert C) two ledger lines above the staff (d^2). The baritone sax part requires the widest range, from low A (concert C) two ledger lines below the staff (A) up to C (concert E-flat) two ledger lines above the staff (c^2).

The rhythm section parts are fully written out throughout the arrangement with the exception of the guitar part, which has chord changes and rhythmic accompaniment figures. Many of the chord changes have extensions (often with alterations) such as ♭5, ♯9, ♯11, and 13. Though the changes may be a little complex, they are repetitive. There is an optional vibraphone part, which plays along with the background winds for most of the chart and requires just a bit of four mallet playing in the coda.

The open solo section includes sample solo sheets in each key. This is a well-arranged chart that will be relatively easy to prepare and can make your band really sound fantastic due to the catchy melody with nice accompaniment figures and terrific scoring by Mark Taylor.

Unit 5: Stylistic Considerations

Sugar is composed in the soul-jazz style, which is considered a sub-style of hard bop. Soul-jazz, while requiring sort of a "funky" groove, is based on swing as opposed to straight eighth notes. The style and articulations are basically the same as in any swing tune, and they are marked well in the score and parts. The ensemble will learn the style much more quickly by listening to the recordings referenced in Unit 8 below. There is also a sample recording of this arrangement available from the publisher.

Unit 6: Musical Elements

MELODY:

Turrentine's melody is simple yet catchy. It is a diatonic sequence composed using only the notes from the concert C minor pentatonic scale (scale degrees 1, 3, 4, 5, and 7 from the minor scale). The melody will be easy to learn (even by ear) due to the simple scalar sequence of notes and the repetitive rhythmic figure on which the melody is based.

HARMONY:

The chart is in C minor throughout with no modulations or key changes. Taylor does, however, incorporate some very rich harmonies through the use of chord extensions and dominant chord alterations. There is also a good deal of chromaticism in the chord progressions including the introduction of tritone substitutions.

RHYTHM:
The rhythmic figures, while being relatively simple and repetitive, are effective in conveying the soul-jazz style. The moderate tempo will require all the members of the ensemble to feel the triplet subdivision to avoid rushing (especially after rests). Students should learn to not only sing the subdivisions of the triplet figures, but also the correct syllables for each of the articulation markings.

Triplet subdivision	doo-od-la
Legato eighths	doo
Staccato eighths	dit
Standard accents	dah
Marcato accents (^)	dot

Unit 7: Form and Structure

The composition is a 16-bar AB song form in C minor.

SECTION	MEASURE	EVENT AND SCORING
Introduction	1–7	The marked tempo is ♩ = 120. This is a good tempo for the style and should be observed. The introduction highlights a punctuated, rhythmic interplay pitting the baritone sax and rhythm section against the rest of the ensemble to create a sense of energy right from the start.
Theme	8–23	The first statement of the melody is made by a quintet consisting of lead alto sax, lead tenor sax, baritone sax, second trumpet, and lead trombone. The quintet is accompanied very lightly by only the rhythm section during this statement.
Theme	24–39	The original quintet plays an exact repetition of the melody from measures 8–23. This statement does, however, increase in intensity as the rest of the wind section adds punctuated backgrounds with nice dynamic contrasts to create more energy and drive during the long notes in the melodic line.

Section	Measure	Event and Scoring
Transition to the soli section	40	The full band plays a strong four-note figure which defines the end of the first section of the arrangement and the start of the soli.
Open soli	41–56	The open soli section remains in the same 16-bar AB form; however, the first six bars are more harmonically static than the melodic statements of this arrangement. This makes it a little more comfortable for young musicians to solo. The arrangement also includes sample solo sheets in all keys and clefs.
Soli	57–71	An easy but effective full band soli. Pay special attention to matching all articulations and note lengths during this section. Also, be sure to shape the phrases, which are marked well in the chart. The optional vibraphone part plays the soli along with the winds. The bass part participates in the soli line for the first four measures while the rest of the rhythm section continues to accompany. The piano part lays out most of the soli and only adds in some simple octave solo work to fill in the gaps.
Theme	9–23	A D.S. takes the ensemble back to an exact repetition of the first statement of the melody.
Theme	24–38	The chart continues with the exact repetition of the second statement of the melody before going to a short coda.

Section	Measure	Event and Scoring
Coda	73–82	The original quintet winds down the arrangement by repeating the final two measures of the melody four more times with a molto rit. marked on the final statement. The rest of the ensemble plays a simple two-measure accompaniment figure to fill in the long notes and the rests in the melody. The arrangement ends on a *pianissimo* Cm^{13} chord with a fermata.

Unit 8: Suggested Listening

Benson, George, *The Essential George Benson*, Legacy Recordings.
Ferguson, Maynard, *These Cats Can Swing!*, Concord Jazz.
Freeman, George, *Jazz For the Two of You*, Highnote Records, Inc.
Hendricks, Jon, *Freddie Freeloader*, Denon Records.
Count Basie Orchestra, *Live at Orchestra Hall, Detroit*, Telarc.
Sanborn, David, *Timeagain*, Verve.
Turrentine, Stanley, *Best of Mr. T.*, Fantasy Records.
Turrentine, Stanley, *Sugar*, Legacy Recordings.

Unit 9: Additional References and Resources

Davis, Natalie, *Music Monthly Archives: Stanley Turrentine*, http://www.musicmonthly.com/archives/archive.cgi?id=11.

Jones, Njemile Carol, National Public Radio's *Jazz Profiles: Stanley Turrentine*, 2006, http://www.npr.org.programs.jazzprofiles/archive/turrentine.html.

Kernfeld, Barry, *What to Listen for in Jazz* (New Haven: Yale University, 1995).

McRae, Barry, *The Jazz Handbook* (Boston: G.K. Hall & Company, 1989).

Nowlin, Rick, *Hill District-born Jazz Great Turrentine Dies*, Post-Gazette.com News, September 13, 2000. http://post-gazette.com/magazine/20000913turrentine1.asp.

Nowlin, Rick, *Stanley Turrentine*, http://en.wikipedia.org/wiki/Stanley_Turrentine.

Polatnick, Gordon, *Fuller Up: The Dead Musician Directory, Stanley Turrentine*, September 13, 2000. Eric Schumacher-Rasmussen, editor, http://elvispelvis.com/stanleyturrentine.htm.

Rosenthal, David, *The Hard Bop Home Page: Stanley Turrentine*, http://hard-bop.tripod.com/stanley.html.

Schoenberg, Loren, *The NPR Curious Listener's Guide to Jazz* (New York: Berkley Publishing Group, 2002).

Wynn, Ron, editor, *All Music Guide to Jazz* (San Francisco: Miller Freeman Books, 1994).

Contributed by:

Curtis Essig
Director of Jazz Studies
Associate Director of Bands
Youth Performing Arts School
Louisville, Kentucky

---

1 Davis, Natalie, *Music Monthly Archives. Stanley Turrentine.* http://www.musicmonthly.com/archives/archive.cgi?id=11,

2 Polatnick, Gordan, *Fuller Up: The Dead Musician Directory, Stanley Turrentine*Eric Schumacher-Rasmussen, editor, http://elvispelvis.com/stanleyturrentine.htm.

Teacher Resource Guide

Una Mas

Kenny Dorham

(1924–1972)

arranged by Paul Murtha

(b. 1960)

Unit 1: Composer/Arranger

McKinley Howard Dorham, commonly known to jazz aficionados as Kenny Dorham, was born on August 30, 1924, near Fairfield, Texas, a small town about forty-five miles southeast of Dallas. Growing up learning piano in a musical family, he began playing trumpet at Anderson High School in Austin, Texas. Later enrolling at Wiley College in Marshall, Texas, (interestingly, the first Black college west of the Mississippi), he studied chemistry, boxed on the school's boxing team, and became interested in jazz arranging.

After a brief stint in the army in 1942, notably boxing for the army boxing team, he commenced his music career in Houston in the band of trumpeter, Russell Jacquet, the brother of Illinois Jacquet. Over the next several years he honed his trumpet skills in a number of organizations, including the big bands of Dizzy Gillespie, Billy Eckstein, Lionel Hampton, and Mercer Ellington.

1948 found Dorham working in New York City and studying music at the Gotham School of Music. He was finding work and income at this time using his arranging and composing skills.

Realizing a long-held aspiration, he replaced Miles Davis in the Charlie Parker Quintet at the end of 1948. For almost a year, he gained increasing exposure playing with Parker on numerous club dates as well as a trip abroad to Europe.

A unique and innovative voice on bebop trumpet, many authorities nonetheless view him as an underrated player, overshadowed at various times in his career by the likes of Dizzy Gillespie, Fats Navarro, Miles Davis, Clifford Brown, Lee Morgan, and Freddie Hubbard. He notably followed Clifford Brown in Art Blakey's Jazz Messengers in the mid-50s and then in 1956 with Max Roach after the untimely death of Brown.

While other prominent jazz trumpet players went in different directions musically in the early 1960s, Kenny Dorham persisted in the hard bop idiom and produced a number of significant recordings for Blue Note Records, championing young, promising musicians of the day. His *Una Mas* recording, produced in 1963, featured young lions Joe Williams on tenor sax, Herbie Hancock on piano, seventeen year-old Tony Williams on drums, and Butch Warren on bass.

After the mid-1960s, Dorham's playing and recording output lessened, primarily due to economic considerations necessitating his employment as a postal worker. He remained active in the jazz music scene though, occasionally writing DownBeat reviews blasting the avant-garde and also studying at the New York University School of Music.

Kidney disease began to take its toll in the early 1970s; Dorham passed away on December 5, 1972.

Unit 2: Composition

Una Mas (One More Time) was written and recorded, on an album of the same name in 1963, and along with *Blue Bossa* became one of Kenny Dorham's signature compositions. Tapping into the increasingly popular Latin music movement, it combined elements of bebop, rock and Latin influences and became a jazz representation of the 1960s music called boogaloo.

Beginning with a *montuno*-like piano riff, trumpet and tenor sax enter with a syncopated punctuation for the first eight bars of the melody before a stop time sets up pickup notes into the next eight measures. Cycling through four measures of a II–V progression, the final four measures cadence rhythmically and harmonically back to B♭ minor.

On the original 1963 recording, the rhythm section of Herbie Hancock, Butch Warren, and Tony Williams stick exactly to the rhythmic and harmonic constraints of the head, allowing the listener to focus on the form as Kenny Dorham and Joe Henderson improvise.

Unit 3: Historical Perspective

The early 1960s were a time of explosion in popular music. With the influence of groups such as the Beatles, electronics in performance, and advances in recording technology, bebop and hard bop were decidedly taking more of a back seat in popular culture. The boundaries of what to that time had been called jazz began to be blurred with the melding of Latin (among other ethnic influences), rock, Motown, soul, funk, electronic amplification, and synthesizer technology. The political temper of the times fueled by the escalation of the war in Vietnam also contributed greatly to the turmoil and angst heard in all genres of music.

Blue Note Records was one of the primary companies that gave voice to the jazz music of the 1960s, promoting such artists as Joe Henderson, Horace Silver, Kenny Dorham, Ramsey Lewis, Cannonball Adderley, Eddie Harris, and Stanley Turrentine. The term "crossover" came into jazz vernacular, and was applied to artists and music that stylistically stood with feet in both the jazz and pop music worlds. One of the best known of the crossover boogaloo tunes that exhibited a similar style to *Una Mas* was Ramsey Lewis's *The In Crowd.*

Unit 4: Technical Considerations

The arrangement of *Una Mas* by Paul Murtha is a solid Grade 2 setting in the Hall Leonard Easy Jazz Ensemble Series. Holding true to the series, this arrangement is playable with a reduced instrumentation (optional second tenor sax, fourth trumpet, fourth trombone, and guitar).

Brass ranges are quite reasonable, with the lead trumpet not playing above the staff. All sax parts are standard big band instrumentation (alto, tenor and bari sax with no doubles). There is an optional auxiliary percussion part included for congas and claves.

Piano, bass, and drum parts are all notated with chord changes indicated. With the simplicity and repetition of the tune, however, it is entirely feasible and recommended that the rhythm section memorize the form and changes as quickly as possible, adopting the style and phrasing of the original recording (it is even in the same key.) The piano part is overwritten—a common practice in writing out piano parts.

Unit 5: Stylistic Considerations

The straight eighth-note feel of this particular style of music can best be assimilated by active listening to the original recording and other similar Blue Note recordings of the period. Distinctive from other eighth-note styles, this boogaloo feel has a crisp yet laid back feel, combining rock, Latin, and soul elements.

Unit 6: Musical Considerations

MELODY:

The repeating rhythmic element in section A (𝄽 ♩ 𝄾♪ 𝄽) actually becomes the melody for the first eight measures. The staccato pickups into section B set up a nice, lyrical 4-bar line, changing back to a staccato melodic turnaround back to the repeat of section A.

HARMONY:

Relatively simple harmonies make this a very recognizable tune even when played without the melody. A simple V^7–I^7 progression occurs in section A, with tonality shifting in the second four measures to set up the ii–V cycle in the first four measures of section B. The harmonic rhythm in the last four measure of section B coincides with both the melodic and rhythmic elements to set up a return to the repeat of section A.

RHYTHM:

To maintain a style true to the original spirit of the composition, the rhythm section, as well as the rest of the band, should generally stick to the "well notated" parts in the first rehearsals but quickly assimilate the feel and spirit as heard on the original recording. In this writer's opinion, the Latin Rock style marking inadequately describes the rhythmic style of the chart.

Unit 7: Form and Structure

The form of this arrangement is the same as the 1963 original: ABAB.

SECTION	MEASURE	EVENT AND SCORING
Introduction	1–4	Drums and auxiliary percussion set up the style and tempo of ♩ = 120.
A	5–12	Rhythm section, trumpets, and trombones enter. The entire band stops in measure 12, with trumpets playing staccato pickups into section B.
B	13–20	Brass and rhythm section enter again, playing up to the first ending in measure 17. There is stop time in the first ending with saxes, trombones, and rhythm section playing counter rhythms to trumpets. The repeat goes back to measure 5.

SECTION	MEASURE	EVENT AND SCORING
A (repeat)	5–12	A unison legato sax line is added to the first exposition.
B (repeat of first half)	13–16	Saxes are added.
B (repeat of second half)	21–24	The end of the repeat of section B with a 1-bar break for the soloist.
Open soli	25–40	Open soli over the form of the tune. Written soli and chord changes appear in first alto sax, second trumpet, and second trombone. Backgrounds in all parts may be used at the director's discretion.
B	41–45	A 4-bar drum break sets up a composed shout chorus.
Shout chorus	46–53	Tutti shout chorus for the entire band.
B	54–61	Alto saxes and trumpets play a stylized montuno, with trombones playing a descending legato line corresponding to the rhythm section. The first ending (measures 60–61) goes back to measure 46.
Shout chorus (repeat)	46–59	A repeat of the shout chorus, jumping to the second ending in measure 59.
D. C.	62–66	The second ending leads to a 4-bar drum intro going to a D.S.
D. S.	5–16	D.S. to measure 5; at measure 16, jump to the coda without taking the first ending. Saxes play on the D.S.
Coda	67–74	The coda repeats melodic material from section A and ends on an $E\flat^{13(\sharp 11)}$ chord held on beat 2 of the last measure.

Unit 8: Suggested Listening

Kenny Dorham, *Una Mas*, Blue Note, CDP 7 46515–2.

Unit 9: Additional References and Resources

Gioia, Ted, *The History of Jazz* (New York: Oxford University Press, Inc., 1997).

Yanow, Scott, *Trumpet Kings* (San Francisco: Backbeat Books., 2001).

Yurochko, Bob, *A Short History of Jazz* (Chicago: Nelson Hall Publishers, 1993).

Russell, Ross, *Bird Lives* (New York: Charterhouse, 1973).

Other arrangements in the Hal Leonard Easy Jazz Ensemble series, published and distributed by the Hal Leonard Corporation:

Title	Arranger	Product Number
Afro Blue	Michael Sweeney	07010985
All Blues	Michael Sweeney	07010656
Bésame Mucho	Rick Stitzel	07010844
Blue Bossa	Michael Sweeney	07010567
Cousin Mary	Paul Murtha	07010662
God Bless' The Child	Rick Stitzel	07010240
Let's Dance	Peter Blair	07010614
Milestones	Peter Blair	08050101
Sidewinder	Paul Murtha	07010660
Song For My Father	Paul Murtha	07011089
Stompin' At The Savoy	Michael Sweeney	00805660
Yardbird Suite	Michael Sweeney	00805877

Contributed by:

Ben L. Huntoon
Director, Otterbein College Jazz Ensemble
Jazz Education Consultant, Stanton's Sheet Music
President, Ohio IAJE
Columbus, Ohio

Teacher Resource Guide

The Woogie
Wycliffe Gordon
(b. 1967)

Unit 1: Composer

Wycliffe Gordon's accomplishments as a soloist, bandleader, and composer are perhaps even more striking when hearing his solo and co-leader work on CDs, plus numerous recordings with The Wynton Marsalis Septet. The 2000–01 LCJO concert season featured premieres of his compositions for a variety of ensembles, including jazz bands, symphonic bands, and concert and gospel choirs in Russia and the United States.

The Jazz Journalists Association honored Gordon in 2000 with the Critics' Choice Award for Best Trombone, named him Trombonist of the Year in 2001 and 2002, and nominated him for the 2003 Jazzpar Award. Currently serving on the faculty of the Jazz Studies Program at The Juilliard School, his work with young musicians and audiences from elementary schools to universities all over the world is extensive.

Gordon was born on May 29, 1967 in Waynesboro, Georgia, where his late father, Lucius Gordon, a classical pianist and teacher, first introduced him to music. His interest in the trombone was sparked at age twelve by his elder brother, who played the instrument in his junior high school band. Gordon's relentless pleading to his parents led to his first trombone. A year later, an aunt bequeathed Gordon her jazz record collection; and so began his passion for jazz.[1]

Unit 2: Composition

Wycliffe Gordon in the arrangement's included program notes, writes:

> The Woogie is an original composition arranged for the big band to be performed in the boogie-woogie shuffle style. Originally composed for the Lincoln Center Jazz Orchestra, The Woogie was performed with swing dancers in mind. This piece also functions as a musical dance between two members of each section (trombone, trumpets, and saxophones), a sort of 'head cutting' session. The solo sections are written at two choruses each, but may be opened up for the "katts" and/or "kittens" to strut their musical ideas in grand conversation style.

Unit 3: Historical Perspective

The title of this tune is *The Woogie*, as in boogie-woogie.

Clarence "Pinetop" Smith first used the term boogie-woogie in 1928 in the title of his recording *Pinetop's Boogie-Woogie*. The earliest manifestation of the style, however, traces back at least to the turn of the century.

The boogie-woogie piano style features improvisations over ostinato or quasi-ostinato bass patterns. These patterns included four-to-the-bar or eight-to-the-bar walking bass figures, broken octaves, arpeggiations of triads, sixth or seventh chords, and/or chordal bass accompaniments. Boogie-woogie improvisations often feature rolls, trills, rapidly repeated notes, extemporized runs, and sharply punctuated chords (Stewart 1998).[2]

Unit 4: Technical Considerations

This chart is rated Grade 3; the recommended tempo is ♩ = 160–180 with a duration of 5:10.

The lead trumpet range goes to high concert B♭ (b♭^{1}), although it may be taken down an octave; the lead trombone range goes to high concert G (g). Gordon states that measures 1–14 of the fourth trombone part may challenging, and may be omitted, since it is in unison with the rest of the trombone section. There are optional parts for C flute, horn in F and baritone treble clef (both of which double first trombone), second baritone treble clef (which doubles second trombone), third baritone treble clef (which doubles third trombone), and tuba (which doubles the bass).

Each section (saxophone, trumpet, and trombone) has a 12-bar soli, and the final chorus consists of three-part counterpoint with the three wind sections ultimately converging to end the piece in unison.

Bass and piano parts are written throughout the piece with chord symbols indicated over written parts most of the time. The guitar part has written melodic lines as well as passages with only chord symbols to be played Freddie Green style during the solo and soli sections. Gordon says "The drum part has mostly cues for the drummer which should be played throughout the piece, except where breaks are indicated. The cadenza at the end is designed to give the drummer the opportunity to express his or her 'closing the concert' musical comments."

Written blues soli with chord symbols are provided for piano, first and second trumpets, first and second trombones, first tenor sax, and baritone sax.

Unit 5: Stylistic Considerations

Gordon's program notes and notes to the conductor indicate that "The style is swing, as the boogie 'Woogie' indicates, but may also be played in a boogaloo-rock and roll straight eighth-note style. This may be easier for the younger musician to grasp, but it is encouraged to tackle the swing groove first."

The eighth notes in this piece should be played in a swing-shuffle rhythm. It is possible to play straight eighths, but this will change the interpretation and articulation of the eighth note through the entire piece, which will also change the way the dancers "bust a move."

The trombone parts at measure 32 should be played as straight eighths, regardless of the style the band decides to play.

The guitarist should refer to the Freddie Green style of accompanying (block chords on the beat, four to a measure) through most of the piece, except where indicated.

Measure 106 functions as the shout chorus and should be played as such, indicated by the written dynamics.

Unit 6: Musical Elements

MELODY:

This is a riff tune in Count Basie's Kansas City style. The opening 2-bar motif is repeated (with slight variation) four times before changing for the last four bars of the 12-bar chorus. The melody is reminiscent of *Vine Street Rumble* from Benny Carter's *Kansas City Suite*.

HARMONY:

The Woogie is a 12-bar blues beginning in E♭ and modulating to F, B♭, and finally back to E♭ for the final chorus. The chord progression begins using simple blues changes (I, IV, and V). Within the framework of the 12-bar blues, various substitutions and ii–V–I progressions are added to provide interest. The most complex harmonies are used during the trumpet soli when Gordon employs "Bird Blues" changes.

RHYTHM:
The rhythms are not complex, although there are a few places where saxophones, trumpets, and trombones have independent parts. The shout chorus is contrapuntal, with each section playing a line that intertwines with other parts. Students should rehearse this chorus in sectionals to save time in full ensemble rehearsal.

Unit 7: Form and Structure

The form of the composition is 12-bar blues. Rehearsal numbers are not always in multiples of twelve due to many first and second endings. For instance, measures 1–14 actually include a total of twenty-four bars.

SECTON	MEASURE	EVENT AND SCORING
Melody	1–14	The first two choruses consist of a chromatic blues riff played by trombones, guitar, and piano. Drums play in a swing/boogie-woogie shuffle style, while the bass plays a written boogie-woogie-influenced walking line. Saxophones and trumpets play backgrounds as well as some melodic material.
Piano solo	15–38	Stop-time piano solo with backgrounds quoting rhythms from *Don't Get Around Much Anymore*. The written solo has a boogie-woogie flavor to it.
Trombone soli	27–40	The trombone section takes over on the repeat back to measure 27. The trombone parts in measure 32 should be played as straight eighth notes.
First trombone solo	41–52	E♭ blues solo for first trombone. The written solo is slightly simplified from the demo recording. Saxophones have backgrounds.
Second trombone solo	41–53	E♭ blues solo for trombone two. The written solo is slightly simplified from the demo recording. Saxophones have backgrounds.

SECTON	MEASURE	EVENT AND SCORING
Trumpet soli	54–65	The piece modulates to F blues for the trumpet soli which begins with four measures of stop-time. Saxophones and trombones have backgrounds.
First trumpet solo	66–77	First trumpet solo over "Bird Blues" in F. The written solo is from the demo recording. Saxophones have backgrounds.
Second trumpet solo	66–79	Second trumpet solo over "Bird Blues" in F. The written solo is slightly simplified from the demo recording. Saxophones have backgrounds.
Saxophone soli	80–91	The piece modulates to B♭ blues for the saxophone soli.
First Tenor solo	92–103	First tenor solo over a modified "Bird Blues." The written solo is from the demo recording.
Baritone sax solo	92–105	Baritone saxophone solo over a modified "Bird Blues." The written solo is from the demo recording.
Shout chorus	106–117	The final chorus begins without the rhythm section while the saxophones, trumpets, and trombones perform in counterpoint. All parts (including piano, bass, and guitar) eventually come together to play the melody in unison. An open drum *cadenza* is featured before the final chord.

Unit 8: Suggested Listening

Count Basie Orchestra, *Blues and Boogie Woogie 1937–1947*, EPM Musique.
Count Basie Orchestra, *Kansas City Suite*, Roulette.
Count Basie Orchestra, *Stages*, Fuel, 2000.
Various artists, including Albert Ammons, Pete Johnson, and Pinetop Smith, *Boogie Woogie Giants*, Jazz Hour.

Unit 9: Additional References and Resources

Garcia, Antonio J., "Wycliffe Gordon: A Voice for the Trombone." *International Trombone Association Journal 34* (July 2006).

Stewart, Earl L., *African American Music: An Introduction* (New York: Schirmer Books, 1998).

Contributed by:

Pete Madsen
Coordinator of Jazz Studies
University of Nebraska at Omaha
Omaha, Nebraska

1 Antonio J. Garcia, "Wycliffe Gordon: A Voice for the Trombone," *International Trombone Association Journal 34* (July 2006): 44–49.

2 Earl L. Stewart, *African American Music: An Introduction* (New York: Schirmer Books, 1998).

Teacher Resource Guide

Work Song
Nat Adderley
(1931–2000)

arranged by Geoff Keezer
(b. 1970)

Unit 1: Composer/Arranger

Nathaniel Adderley was born in Tampa, Florida on November 11, 1931. Brother of renowned saxophonist and bandleader Julian "Cannonball" Adderley, Nat started out his musical journey as a vocalist and trumpeter, but became particularly attached to his favorite instrument, the cornet. After a tour of military duty in Korea with the 36th Army Band in the early 1950s, he toured with such luminaries as Lionel Hampton, J. J. Johnson, Woody Herman, and his brother, Cannonball Adderley, and recorded or concertized with such artists as Sonny Rollins, Tony Bennett, Philly Joe Jones, Sonny Fortune, Johnny Griffin, and Ron Carter.

Work Song was a big hit, and can be found on numerous recordings, such as Nat's own album, *Work Song*, Cannonball Adderley's *Capitol Years* and *Greatest Hits*, *Them Dirty Blues*, *Phenix*, *Japanese Concerts*, and *Ray Brown with the All-Star Big Band.*

Nat can be heard on at least thirty-seven recordings as a leader or side player. Heavily influenced by Miles Davis, he has been classified as a hard bop player with bebop influences and lyrical lines. He spent much of his career as a complimentary instrumental voice to his beloved brother, contributing a number of compositions to Cannonball's highly acclaimed group. He eventually returned to his native Florida in 1990, and taught at Florida Southern University for ten years. He passed away in Lakeland, Florida on January 2, 2000.

Unit 2: Composition

Work Song is a minor key tune built on two 8- bar phrases with an extended tonic formula and a distinctive blues flavor. It can also be considered an AA'BC form, similar to a through-composed work. The heart of the melody references what is often referred to as a form of the minor pentatonic scale. It was written in 1960 when Nat rejoined his brother's quintet—a group with which he remained until Cannonball's death in 1975.

Even though other compositions by Nat Adderley, such as *Jive Samba*, *Sermonette*, and *Old Country* received considerable attention over the years, *Work Song* is his best-known and most popular work. This piece was originally written for a small ensemble, but this arrangement by pianist Geoff Keezer offers a uniquely attractive orchestration. It still embodies the essence of the original composition even with the addition of effective timbres, thick harmonic textures and clever tempo and meter changes.

Unit 3: Historical Perspective

In the 1960s, small jazz groups were arguably more popular than big bands. Hard bop, soul or funk jazz, and cool/modal jazz styles were present, along with the harmelodicism and free jazz pioneered primarily by Ornette Coleman and Cecil Taylor. ("Harmolodics" is a term coined by Coleman to indicate a style of playing in which harmony and melody are of equal value, with an emphasis on freedom from tonal, rhythmic and harmonic limitations.) Ray Charles's recording of *Georgia On My Mind*, a significant hit song of the era, along with the wave of popular music that such groups as the Beatles ushered in from England, are indicative of the larger musical scope.

Historically, the Civil Rights movement in the United States was in full swing, and approximately seventy million children from the post World War II baby boom era became teenagers or young adults and started to move away from the conservatism of the 1950s. Change and revolutionary ideas were in vogue for many in the United States, and this was reflected in some of the music of the times.

Unit 4: Technical Considerations

This arrangement is rated Grade 3–4; the recommended tempo is ♩ = 120 with a duration of approximately 5:30.

The lead trumpet range goes up to a concert C above the staff (c^2); the lead trombone range goes up to a concert A♭ above the staff (a♭).

The trombone and bass soli section is both technically and stylistically challenging. Harmonies are fairly complex, and there are solo opportunities for lead alto saxophone and piano.

Unit 5: Stylistic Considerations

This medium swing arrangement begins very mysteriously, with low, open-fifth drone chords in the rhythm section, and builds into a big-band adaptation of a hard-driving combo piece. The arranger's recommended tempo is ♩ = 120, although a slightly slower speed will not diminish the excitement of this chart.

The horn section should address both specific and inferred articulations as well as extreme dynamic contrasts in order to capture the spirit and animation of lines and phrases. Attention to nuances and embellishments such as "doits," fall-offs, lifts, and trills are critical to a successful performance. Staccato markings, commonly performed with a "dit" articulation, may achieve greater impact when played as "daht" articulations (capped notes). Tongue releases should help horn players define some phrase endings.

Unit 6: Musical Elements

MELODY:

The melody is divided between horn and rhythm sections in a call and response. It is very vocal and soulful, and needs to project through the dense orchestration.

HARMONY:

This arrangement follows the harmonic outline of Nat Adderley's original composition with a few additional harmonic flavors. Soloists need to address the minor turnaround formula.

RHYTHM:

Figures in the rhythm section are carefully marked. Occasional meter and tempo changes give an attractive twist to the 16-bar minor blues progression.

Unit 7: Form and Structure

The basic form of the composition is a modified minor blues.

SECTION	MEASURE	EVENT AND SCORING
Intro	1–16	A chordal drone opening with a centered time feel. Haunting, mysterious chords build on a repetitive rhythmic figure with simple piano fills interspersed. Cup mutes on trumpets mixed with flugelhorn parts add a distinctive timbre.

Section	Measure	Event and Scoring
First chorus	17–32	The melody is thickly harmonized in a strong horn tutti countered with open chords and drum responses in the rhythm section. Dynamics need to taper before the next 7-bar phrase.
First interlude	33–40	Similar to the introductory material. with a strong pickup into the next section.
Second chorus	41–56	This section functions as a theme with chorus variations. The hard-charging horn tutti leads to a quote from *Miles's Mood*, played by the entire horn section and guitar. This section ends with a 2/4 bar leading to a recapitulation of the introduction.
Second interlude	57–64	A truncated version of the introduction.
Solo choruses	65–80	A piano solo with rhythm section accompaniment. This could easily be expanded for multiple solo opportunities via the written repeat.
Solo	81–96	The piano solo continues with saxophone section chorus background lines and horn section pops in the brasses.
Trombone/Bass tutti solo	97–111	A unison bebop-oriented written-out section for four trombones and bass, with high-hat accompaniment.
Recap	112–126	A *pianissimo* trumpet/flugelhorn melody with punctuated horn pads in the saxophone, trombone, and rhythm sections. Measures 123–125 build and release to the next section.
Solo choruses	127–142	A lead alto saxophone solo with rhythm section comping. A repeat of this section is indicated in the score, providing an opportunity for additional solo features if desired.

Section	Measure	Event and Scoring
Solo choruses	143–158	The lead alto solo continues, with rhythm section accompaniment joined by call and response figures in all brasses and the remaining saxophones.
Shout chorus	159–177	Energetic horn tutti figures are countered by sustained chord drones in the low trombones and rhythm section, climaxed by meter changes from 4/4 to 3/4 in measures 176–177.
Interlude	178–185	A rhythm section drone augmented with trombones and baritone saxophone and sustained notes with vigorous alto and tenor saxophone trills.
Recap	186–201	Similar to the first chorus (measures 17–32).
Final interlude	202–209	A restatement of original material, including piano fills leading to a full-band fermata in measure 209.
Coda	210–214	A conducted chorale ending with a ritard to the final fermata. The piano restates a portion of the *Miles's Mood* quote heard in the second chorus (measures 41–56). All instruments need to phrase together and pay careful attention to the concluding *diminuendo* so the piano solo can be heard. Required techniques include cup mute playing for first and second trumpets, and arco bass in the coda.

Unit Eight: Suggested Listening

Adderley, Nate, *Work Song*, Riverside.
Adderley, Nate, *Work Song Live*, Peter Pan.
Adderley, Cannonball, *Cannonball Adderley Collection, Volume 7: Cannonball in Europe*, Landmark.
Adderley, Cannonball, *Greatest Hits*, Riverside (9416).
Adderley, Cannonball, *Japanese Concerts*, Milestone (47029).
Adderley, Cannonball, *Live*, Capitol (2399).
Adderley, Cannonball, *Lugano*, TCB.
Adderley, Cannonball, *Phenix*, Fantasy (F-79004).
Adderley, Cannonball, *Ray Brown with the All-Star Big Band*, Verve (6–8444).
Adderley, Cannonball, *The Best of Cannonball Adderley*, Capitol (SKAO2939).
Adderley, Cannonball, *The Best of Cannonball Adderley: The Capitol Years*, Blue Note.
Adderley, Cannonball, *Them Dirty Blues*, Riverside (322).
Keezer, Geoff, *Work Song*, Sierra Music Publications (CD 104).

Unit Nine: Additional References and Resources

Aebersold, Jamey, *Cannonball Adderley's Greatest Hits*, Jazz play-along Volume 13 (New Albany: 1978).
Dunscomb, Richard, and Willie L. Hill, Jr., *Jazz Pedagogy: The Jazz Educator's Handbook and Resource Guide* (Miami: Warner Brothers, 2004).
Wright, Ray, *Inside the Score* (Delevan: Kendor Music, 1982).

Contributed by:

Chris Vadala
Director of Jazz Studies
Professor of Saxophone
University of Maryland
School of Music
College Park, Maryland

Teacher Resource Guide

Yardbird Suite

Charlie Parker
(1920–1955)

arranged by Michael Sweeney
(b. 1952)

Unit 1: Composer/Arranger

Jazz saxophonist and composer Charlie Parker was born to Charles Parker, Sr. and the former Addie Boyley on August 29, 1920 in Kansas City, Kansas. Charles Parker, Sr. was a nomadic cabaret performer from Memphis who, in 1927, settled his family in Kansas City, Missouri, which was considered by many the jazz capital of the United States. The nearness of such a musical environment fostered Parker's interest and career choice in entertainment. Parker developed his general love of music, rhythm, and the saxophone at age thirteen while a student at Lincoln High School, where he developed a strict practice regime.

Parker left school in 1935 to become a full-time musician. Over the course of the next four years, he found work with several groups, including the Count Basie Orchestra. Later, in 1937, Parker began working with Tommy Douglas, a saxophonist who taught him many things about music. Parker's first big opportunity came when popular bandleader George E. Lee hired him for a four-month show at a resort in the Ozarks. Upon returning from this gig, Parker began working with different bands, eventually getting the opportunity to play as a soloist with Jay McShann, who had formed a bigger traveling band. While a member of McShann's band in the early forties, Parker acquired his nickname, "Yardbird," or "Bird."

As the McShann band became well known, Parker's name began appearing in the music press. Parker soon settled in New York, the capital of the jazz scene, where he met trumpeter Dizzy Gillespie. Parker and Gillespie began collaborating and recording music together after discovering their common approach to music. They eventually became popular on the jazz scene in New York, and Parker established himself as one of the most influential and compelling jazz musicians of any era.

Because Parker's heroine addiction often prevented him from working alongside Gillespie, Gillespie formed his own band in New York, allowing Parker to work at night clubs and record in Los Angeles. Parker became the leader for the independent record label Dial in March of 1946, where he produced the classic *Yardbird Suite*. While creating memorable music, Parker's eccentric behavior and lack of self-discipline created many difficult situations for him and caused turmoil in his personal life.

By 1950, Parker was recognized as the architect of modern jazz and the bebop movement. Parker died on March 12, 1955, but his legacy continues today.

Arranger Michael Sweeney graduated from Indiana University, where he studied music education and composition. While there, Sweeney contributed compositions and arrangements to jazz ensembles and the marching band. Sweeney's credentials include five years in the public school systems of Ohio and Indiana, where he worked with successful concert, jazz, and marching programs ranging from elementary to high school. Sweeney has also worked for Hal Leonard Corporation since 1982, and is presently the Instrumental Product Manager. Sweeney, an ASCAP award-winning composer, is known for his contributions as a composer and arranger, submitting over 500 publications over his lifetime, including those in the best-selling *Teaching Music through Performance in Band* series.

Unit 2: Composition

This composition differs from many pieces of music of the time in that it is not solely based on the harmonic changes of a standard. The chord changes, in comparison, are closely related to the Earl Hines composition *Rosetta*. *Yardbird Suite* is a 32-bar piece in an AABA format that incorporates simple ii–V–I changes. Parker utilizes a descending chromatic element in the third and fourth measures of the first eight and plays higher notes of the changes in the first four measures of the bridge, creating a nice tension and relief before returning to section A. In terms of rhythm and harmony, Parker's composition is not as frantic as typical bebop standards; rather, it seems calm and fresh.

Unit 3: Historical Perspective

Burdened by the economic condition and rationing of World War II, Americans moved toward the jazz age of bebop in the 1940s. Bebop was truly a revolution in jazz, both aurally and economically. A significant factor that impacted the bebop movement was a ban on recording in 1942. The American Federation of Musicians insisted that record labels distribute royalties to musicians not only for record sales, but also for spins played by profitable radio stations. The ban applied only to instrumental music, which put a devastating strain on surviving big bands. Big bands were not very cost-effective, due to the number of musicians, and they were difficult to manage. As a result, musicians gravitated to smaller combos, thus opening the door for a new, innovative style of music. Charlie Parker, along with such jazz musicians as Dizzy Gillespie, Thelonius Monk, Bud Powell, Charlie Christian, Kenny Clarke, Max Roach, Miles Davis, and Ray Brown, helped to institute this radical movement of modern jazz. Bebop melodies and solos are generally longer and more complicated than earlier forms of jazz. Parker added complexity to the musical tradition by using creative and complex rhythms along with extended harmonies, having a profound effect on American music even today.

Unit 4: Technical Considerations

Though Sweeney's arrangement of *Yardbird Suite* was termed a Grade 2 chart when it was written in the 80s, some consider the composition to be a Grade 3 piece today. The recommended tempo is ♩ = 138–144; the duration is 3:15 at the slower tempo. This recommended tempo is slower than would be heard in a combo or jam session setting. The natural tendency is for the song to be played faster than suggested, which is appropriate for this style of music. The slower suggested tempo grooves very well in this big band arrangement.

The lead trumpet range extends to first ledger A (a^1) and the trombone range goes to an F (f). The alto saxophone range does not exceed an upper octave B♭(b♭^{1}), and tenor and baritone saxophone ranges are comfortably written. Piano rhythms directly parallel saxophone and trombone background hits, and are written in open and closed voicings. Changes are written for guitar, and the bass line is written in a walking style that occasionally reflects the tutti rhythms on impact points. Drums rhythms directly parallel horn rhythms throughout the arrangement and serve as a detailed roadmap, emphasizing horn cues. The personality of the drum chart reflects a sense of buoyancy and vigor, uniting the drumming styles of bebop and big band.

The melody is introduced as a unison duet for alto saxophone and trumpet. The unison melody is introduced in measure 5 and recurs in measure 93. The majority of the duet is unison with the exception of a parallel ascending harmonic variation in measure 106. Instruments should align stylistically and vertically throughout the duet. Suggested soli are tastefully written out for inexperienced improvisers in trumpet and tenor parts.

Overall rhythms of the arrangement are well written and may technically challenge younger musicians in measures 75 and 103. Students must have a decent understanding of beat sub-division in a swing style along with beat placement. The variety of rhythmic expressions makes this arrangement interesting for both musician and listener.

Unit 5: Stylistic Considerations

Yardbird Suite preserves characteristics found in many bebop songs. The scalar melody should be played with a smooth nonabrasive approach, while maintaining a firm sense of direction. Articulations should be sharp and lively, with equal emphasis given to the beginning and endings of notes. Tonguing and wind flow must be controlled to avoid harsh and choppy articulations. Encourage wind instruments to use a "doo" tonguing syllable when articulating swinging eighth notes. Insist that articulations be consistent and precise throughout the arrangement.

Dynamic contrast ranges from *piano* to *fortissimo*, with no variation in tempo or pulse. Young musicians tend to slow down during softer passages and accelerate when volume increases. Careful attention must be given to tempo to maintain the effervescent feel of the song.

While preparing this work for performance, focus on sectional practice when possible. Students must be able to sing and recognize sections A and B.

The chords of section B may sound unfamiliar to students. This will effect intonation and band stability. Exposure to recordings of the song will help students have a better understanding of chord functions. The rhythm section must have a firm grasp of chords so that winds perform with a firm sense of confidence and direction. Directors may want to take the music away from the drummer, forcing her to memorize important impact points and turnarounds. The drummer's role is very important for overall security of entrances and kicks throughout the song.

Sweeney's clever melodic and rhythmic manipulations can be better understood by having students collectively sing their parts. Directors can hear if students are interpreting articulations and rhythms precisely. If they cannot vocalize the rhythms collectively, then there may be discrepancies in performing rhythms. Encourage soloists to memorize the melody. This forces the soloist to listen carefully, leading to better choice of notes.

Unit 6: Musical Elements

MELODY:
Parker's melody consists of a 32-bar AABA composition. The melody is true to its form without alterations in phrase lengths. The theme is relatively simple and consistent but varies during the shout chorus and ending sections.

HARMONY:
Sweeney did an outstanding job of writing chord changes for young musicians, giving the band a firm harmonic basis while not stretching students too far. The chord structure is very consistent and does not address difficult alternate substitutions. Sweeney judiciously provides only one to two chords per measure, benefiting young guitarists and pianists. The rhythm section may require several sectional rehearsals to synchronize and match chords. The arranger does an excellent job choosing chord extensions, serving to broaden young musicians' chord vocabularies while not overwhelming them.

RHYTHM:
The meter of *Yardbird Suite* is 4/4 throughout; the basic rhythms are whole, half, dotted-half, quarter, dotted-quarter, eighth, and eighth-note triplets, along with corresponding rests. Students must possess a keen internal pulse and have a strong comprehension of beat subdivision. The ensemble's challenge will be to maintain steady subdivision and consistent tempo without either speeding up or slowing down. The song has a few syncopations that are demanding for young developing musicians, such as measures 77–78 and 103–105. Rhythms are accented on the anacrusis, causing uncertainty of the beat. Careful attention must be given to articulation in order for notes to vertically align. To solidify these measures, practice rhythms with a bass drum playing steady quarter notes. Insist on phrasing dotted half and whole notes with full value to help avoid obscurity of the bar line. Proper phrasing will help students in detecting beat 1 should the band experience pulse ambiguity.

Unit 7: Form and Structure

SECTION	MEASURE	EVENT AND SCORING
Intro	1–4	Full band with trumpet melody.
1A	5–12	The ain melody with trumpet and alto saxophone.
2A	13–20	A continuation of the melody.
B	21–28	Alto and tenor saxophone melody; baritone saxophone and trombone background chords.

SECTION	MEASURE	EVENT AND SCORING
2A	29–36	Saxophone, trumpet, and trombone have harmonized melody; 2-bar turnaround with this chord progression: I, $\flat III^{\flat 5}$, ii–$V{+}^{7}$, I.
1A	37–44	Trumpet solo.
2A	45–52	Saxophone harmony and countermelody.
B	53–60	Unison trumpet soli; saxophone and trombone harmony.
2A	61–68	Trumpet solo; 2-bar drum turnaround.
1A	69–76	Shout chorus for full band with harmonized melody.
2A	77–84	Brass melody, tutti rhythms, saxophone countermelody, and a 2-bar Basie-style piano turnaround.
B	85–92	Tenor saxophone solo.
2A	93–98	Trumpet and alto saxophone duet recapitulation.
Intro restatement	99–102	Full band; trumpet melody.
Tag/ending	103–111	Full band syncopated variation; chords at last four measures of section 2A; trumpet and alto saxophone duet; $B\flat^{7(\sharp 11)}$; first and second trumpets have the eleventh.

Unit 8: Suggested Listening

Count Basie Orchestra:

April in Paris
Corner Pocket
In A Mellow Tone
Jumpin at the Woodside
One O'Clock Jump

Earl Hines Orchestra:
Rosetta
Charlie Parker:
All the Things You Are
Groovin High
Ornithology
Scrapple from the Apple
Yardbird Suite
Michael Sweeney:
How High The Moon
Imperium
Satin Doll
Stompin' at the Savoy
The Forge of Vulcan
Yardbird Suite

Unit 9: Additional References and Resources

Atkins, Ronald, *All That Jazz: The Illustrated Story of Jazz Music* (Dubai: Carlton Books Limited, 1996).
"Charlie Parker," http://vnweb.hwwilsonweb.com/hww/shared/shared_main.jhtml?_requestid=131305.
Coker, Jerry, *Improvising Jazz* (New York: Simon and Schuster, Inc., 1964).
Koch, Lawrence O., *Yardbird Suite: A Compendium of the Music and Life of Charlie Parker* (Bowling Green: Bowling Green State University Popular Press, 1988).

Contributed by:

Randall Key
Director of Bands
Hartselle High School Band
Hartselle, Alabama

Intermediate Bands

Teacher Resource Guide

Afro Blue

Mongo Santamaria

(1922–2003)

arranged by Michael Philip Mossman

(b. 1959)

Unit 1: Composer/Arranger

Bandleader and conga drum artist Ramon "Mongo" Santamaria was born into a rich, musical environment in Havana, Cuba on April 7th, 1922. As a young man he studied violin, but soon was drawn to the drums and percussion. He quickly rose to become a top working drummer in Havana while holding down a job as a postman by day. His day job prevented him from playing with any band for very long, but this enabled him to have a wide playing experience. This may account in part for his life-long musical eclecticism as a bandleader.

After briefly moving to Mexico in the late 1940s (where he worked with Perez Prado), Mongo moved to New York in 1950. There he would soon achieve notoriety as a brilliant conga drum soloist with the popular Tito Puente band. In 1957 he became well known in jazz circles through his work with vibraphonist Cal Tjader. During his time with Puente and Tjader, Mongo began to record under his own name. Some of these early recordings include excellent examples of traditional Afro-Cuban music, including the religious music of *Santaria* (see Suggested Listening). While with Tjader, Mongo recorded his own composition, *Afro Blue,* which became a frequently recorded jazz standard.

By 1962 Santamaria was leading his own bands in New York and was incorporating jazz into the sound of his music. That year he briefly employed young pianist Herbie Hancock introduced him to his composition *Watermelon Man*. Mongo recorded that song in 1963 and it became a top-ten hit, thus giving Mongo name recognition for the rest of his career. Mongo remained an active bandleader into the 1990s, and his infectious blending of jazz, Afro-Cuban, and rhythm and blues music gave him a broad and lasting appeal to international audiences.

Unit 2: Composition

Afro Blue was written in the period just before Mongo attained popular success with *Watermelon Man*. In the recordings from this time we hear much music reflective of traditional Afro-Cuban religious and dance music. The original recording of *Afro Blue* was in a traditional (6/8) (*guiro* or *naningo*) feel. Since that time, the song has been performed numerous times by various artists who have played it, in some cases, in the original feel, but more often as a jazz waltz or a mix of the two (as John Coltrane has done; see Suggested Listening).

Unit 3: Historical Perspective

Since the tune was first recorded in 1959, it has been an oft-performed jazz standard, recorded by Cal Tjader, Dizzy Gillespie, John Coltrane and many others. Coltrane in particular was fond of the song and performed it frequently in the early 1960s.

Mongo Santamaria's contribution to jazz is an extension of the pioneering efforts of artists like Maurio Bauza, Dizzy Gillespie, and Chano Pozo, all of whom, in the 1930s and 40s, were among the first to fuse elements of Cuban music with jazz. In his own work, Mongo followed them to become one of the key figures in the Cuban jazz movement and to bring the conga drum to the forefront as an ensemble and solo instrument. Largely through Mongo's efforts, the conga drum is commonly used in many forms of popular music including jazz, rock, salsa, and fusion blends. In recent decades the Afro-Cuban influence in jazz has been enormous, thanks to artists like Ray Barretto, Pancho Sanchez, Arturo Sandoval, Eddie and Charlie Palmieri, and many others.

Unit 4: Technical Considerations

This arrangement by Michael Philip Mossman is Grade 4, which is of medium difficulty for high school bands (published by Hal Leonard). The tempo marking is ♩ = 196. The required range (lead trumpet goes to a frequent high B [b^1]) and technical requirements should not be out of reach for most high school bands. Brass players need to have built a fair amount of endurance to execute the repeated rhythmic phrasing presented in this chart. The harmonies are relatively simple excepting some brief transition sections with dense harmonic rhythm and uncommon root motion. The "blowing changes" are in a comfortable G minor 24-bar blues ("double blues") format with a preponderance of minor seventh chords. Suggested scales for improvisation (mostly pentatonic) are written above the changes.

Unit 5: Stylistic Considerations

This chart is indicated as having a traditional *guiro* feel, so it is important for students to recognize that this music can (and should) be felt in both 3/4 or 6/8 (though it is written in 3/4). This hemiola affect is common in much Afro-Cuban music and is a reflection of its roots in traditional African music. Horn players must avoid laying back and swinging the eighth note phrases as would be done in a jazz waltz and emphasize the triplet-based 6/8 feel. Rhythm section players must maintain the strength of their parts throughout and be aware that each rhythm is part of a combined rhythmic fabric. The piano player participates in creating this fabric essentially as a percussionist, rather than as a "comper." Horn players must also recognize that they function equally as percussionists in much of what they play, particularly rhythmic background parts.

Unit 6: Musical Elements

MELODY:
The melody of *Afro Blue* is simple but memorable. The smooth contour of the melody provides an effective contrast to the percussive nature of the rhythm and horn backgrounds. Students should learn to sing the melody and memorize it. As is common practice in Afro-Cuban music, the melody is only stated once in the beginning and then only referred to throughout the rest of the chart.

HARMONY:
The arrangement stays in G minor throughout, often using the simple cadential sequences heard on earlier recordings by Mongo and others. There are some areas of dense harmonic rhythm (measures 39–47, 75–86, 130–137). The piano and guitar players may have to spend extra time working out those passages to attain mastery of them. The harmony for the solos is in a 24-bar minor blues format.

RHYTHM:
As mentioned previously, this piece is to be performed in a traditional *guiro* 6/8 feel. The arrangement is notated in 3/4, which is easier for younger musicians to read, but a strong 6/8 feel should always be present. The rhythm section should provide for the strong 6/8 feel because the notated rhythms in the percussion parts emphasize the dotted quarter note, the primary pulse of 6/8. Horn players, however, must avoid the temptation to play phrases as is done in a jazz waltz or to swing their phrases. It is essential for students (and

the director) to listen carefully to recordings of music by Mongo Santamaria and other Afro-Cuban artists (see Suggested Listening).

Unit 7: Form and Structure

The melody is a series of 4-bar phrases that create the following form: AA BB' CC BB'. Combining the 4-bar phrases into 8-bar phrases and calling the form ABCB can simplify this. These larger phrases are referred to as motive A, motive B, etc, throughout. This form is interspersed by short transitional sections and by solo sections that are twenty-four bars of minor blues.

SECTION	MEASURE	EVENT AND SCORING
Intro	1–7	The intro starts first with the full percussion section, which for this chart requires drum set, congas, bongos, and shekere. In the measure three, piano, guitar, and bass are added. The tempo is marked as ♩ = 196 with a *guiro* (6/8) feel (also called *naningo* or simply, "6/8 clave"). As the rhythm parts are comprised largely of interlocking ostinato patterns, it is essential that these parts be played with absolute precision. As well, the musicians must learn to feel the 6/8 meter while reading in 3/4. The conductor can facilitate this by singing parts while clapping to the 6/8 primary pulse (dotted quarter notes).
Melody	7–38	The trumpets state motive A of the melody, followed by the saxes which state motive B. In contrast to the percussion, the melody should be smooth and the phrases connected. It is relatively unaccented except where marked. By measure 23 the trumpets trade phrases of motive C with the saxes. Be sure that one section connects its phrase to next (as with a call and response). At measure 31 the trombones begin to double portions of the piano/guitar parts, and they should feel that together in a percussive way. Practice these rhythms against a 6/8 (dotted quarter) beat.

Section	Measure	Event and Scoring
Transition	39–50	This is a transition section leading up to the solo section. It starts with a repeated rhythmic figure taken from the previous section. This is played first by the percussion with the brass layering the same rhythm on top of that. The feel is definitely 6/8 here, with the bass (later adding the baritone sax) underpinning the band with dotted quarter notes. In feeling these rhythms in 6/8, the accent should be placed on the first and third notes of the three-note figures. The kick-off to the solo section culminates with the entire band playing the same rhythm (6/8 clave) all at once.
Solo Section	51–74	The solo (tenor sax) section is a minor blues, but should be felt in the Afro-Cuban context. It would be useful for students to listen to some of the great jazz soloists who have recorded with Mongo Santamaria and other Afro-Cuban bands to get an idea of how to incorporate jazz elements into this style of music (see Suggested Listening). The background horn figures are essentially percussive and should not to be played in a swung or laid back fashion.
Transition	75–86	This section is a transitional and leads to a second (trumpet) solo. It is very similar to the section leading up to the previous (tenor) solo, but with more horns added. The start of this section should not be too loud, allowing the band to build up to the *fortissimo* at measure 87.

Section	Measure	Event and Scoring
Coda	91–137	The coda is a full-ensemble section similar to a shout section in jazz. Elements of the melody are interspersed throughout the reeds and brass. Melodic fragments of motive A are frequent throughout and should be played in a connected or legato fashion. There are some eighth-note lines in the saxes and trumpets in this section, and they should also be played more legato, except where marked otherwise. By measure 98 all the horns briefly lock together with the piano and bass. Trombones continue by doubling with the piano/guitar as before, and they should practice this together (from measure 98 to 106) until the rhythms are unified. At measure 107 elements of motive C are played by saxes, then trumpets, and then by the full band. This percussive 6/8 segment leads to a nicely contrasting legato 3/4 segment at measure 115 which uses material from motive B. At this point all the horns should be playing boldly with a broad legato sweep. Horns should reduce their dynamic briefly at measure 121 in order to effectively build up to measure 123. Then there is percussion only, with the piano/guitar initiating the same three-note rhythm played in the previous transition sections. The brass section then follows in at measure 127, doubling the same rhythm. The band should sustain great intensity from here on out, but should also be aware that it is building up to the final three bars of the chart. At measure 131 the saxophones add a series of contrasting half notes followed by five eighth notes, which should *crescendo* very boldly into the exciting full-band concluding statement of the 6/8 clave. This final statement should be percussive, loud, and fat.

Unit 8: Suggested Listening

Coltrane, John, *Afro-Blue Impressions*, Pablo, 2620–101.
Gillespie, Dizzy, *Summertime*, Pablo Live, 2308–229.
Santamaria, Mongo, *Afro Blue: The Picante Collection*, Concord Picante, 4781.
Santamaria, Mongo, *Greatest Hits*, Fantasy, MPF–4529.
Santamaria, Mongo, *Skin on Skin: The Mongo Santamaria Anthology 1958–1995*, Fantasy, 8058.
Tjader, Cal, *Concert by the Sea*, Fantasy, 8038.

Unit 9: Additional References and Resources

Fernandez, Raul A., *From Afro-Cuban Rhythms to Latin Jazz* (Berkeley: University of California Press, 2006).
Uribe, Ed, *The Essence of Afro-Cuban Percussion and Drum Set* (Van Nuys: Alfred Publishing, 2001). Includes two CDs.
Yanow, Scott, *Afro-Cuban Jazz: The Essential Listening Companion* (San Francisco: Miller Freeman Inc, 2000).
http//www.descarga.com.

Contributed by:

Art Davis
Assistant Professor of Jazz Studies
Northern Illinois University
DeKalb, Illinois

Teacher Resource Guide

All of Me

Gerald Marks

(1900–1997)

Seymour Simons

(1896–1949)

arranged by Billy Byers

(1927–1996)

Unit 1: Composers/Arranger

Gerald Marks and Seymour Simons were born in Michigan, although their paths did not cross until later in life. Marks began his musical career at the age of eleven and wrote over 1,000 songs, from popular music to children's tunes. He had a number of songwriting partners throughout his career and enjoyed some success composing for Shirley temple and Al Jolson. In the late 1930s Marks joined the traveling Vaudeville show "Songwriters On Parade," one of the last of its kind celebrating the music of hit songwriters.

Seymour Simons began his music career when he moved back to Detroit after serving in the Air Force during World War I. He was a bandleader and pianist, and worked in radio production from 1928 to 1932. Although neither Marks nor Simons achieved the fame of songwriters such as Cole Porter or Harold Arlen, they were just as active and did enjoy the success of their one important collaboration, *All Of Me*.

Billy Byers was born on May 1, 1927 in Los Angeles and was forced by arthritis to stop playing piano at the age of fourteen. He switched to the trombone and soon began gigging with Karl Kiffe, for whom he also wrote arrangements. He contributed charts to Buddy Rich and Benny Goodman's libraries in 1949, followed by several years of work in radio and television.

Byers joined Quincy Jones's band and acted as his assistant from 1960 to 1965. During this time, Byers arranged the music for Count Basie albums and recorded several Duke Ellington tunes under his own name.

Unit 2: Composition

With its combination of memorable lyrics and inventive melodic development over a standard ABAC form, *All Of Me* became an instant hit when it appeared in 1931. The tune was first performed by Belle Baker, a vaudeville entertainer active on Broadway and in Hollywood. It has since been recorded numerous times, including well-known performances by Frank Sinatra, Willie Nelson, Billie Holiday, and Count Basie.

This straight-ahead swing arrangement of *All Of Me* was written as a feature for Count Basie. After being recorded four times by Frank Sinatra, who had been performing and recording with the Count Basie Orchestra, Basie included it on the album *Frankly Basie.* Byers contributed several arrangements to the Basie catalog, and *All Of Me* became a staple of the band's repertoire. They recorded it at least twice more, excising the four-measure introduction both times and strengthening the ensemble's *fortissimo* entrance at measure 19.

Unit 3: Historical Perspective

All Of Me was written during the Great Depression, a time when songwriters were endlessly churning out tunes for recordings, radio, shows, and sheet music. Most tunes of the period that have become a part of the "standard" jazz repertoire are thirty-two measures in length, and many are either AABA or ABAC forms. Although *All Of Me* was not composed for a Broadway show, it was performed in vaudeville acts and appeared in several films in the early 1930s and soon became part of the American consciousness.

Basie first recorded this arrangement of *All Of Me* in 1963. It includes all the hallmarks of his style: uncomplicated form, swinging rhythms, plenty of space for the soloist, and tight ensemble passages. During this period the Count Basie Orchestra was the preeminent backing band for Ella Fitzgerald and Frank Sinatra, but the group recorded several instrumental albums as well. Although the Count Basie Orchestra continued to perform for twenty more years, it never again reached the level of public success achieved during the 1960s.

Unit 4: Technical Considerations

No tempo marking appears in the score of *All Of Me*, but it is consistently performed at a medium swing tempo of ♩ = ca. 120. Take care not to drag, which can happen by overemphasizing the underlying triplet feel and exaggerating the swing.

Range is a potential issue in the upper brass parts, with several trombone passages in the third octave (up to a B [b]) and a few high D's (d^2) in the lead trumpet part. These phrases are always supported by the rest of the ensemble, a fact that should help make them less of a challenge.

Unit 5: Stylistic Considerations

As a tune written in the Count Basie tradition, the most important consideration is that it swings. Swing feel will begin in the rhythm section, and each member plays an important role in achieving a good time feel. The guitarist, although playing only quarter notes, should strum percussively and leave a triplet eighth note rest at the end of each beat. The drums and bass must not be intrusive, but should lock in time to create a solid foundation for the soloist. The high-hat on beats 2 and 4 is very important, and the drummer should setup the band hits rather than play the rhythms with the ensemble.

The success of this piece hinges on the piano soloist, who should play in the typical, sparse Count Basie style. Occasional rhythmic chords in the left hand should accompany eighth note-based solo lines in the right hand.

Although the ensemble plays a supporting role throughout the arrangement, tight and precise playing is crucial. This can be developed by singing through the parts, from call and response exercises between the director and ensemble to sections or individuals singing through each short phrase.

Unit 6: Musical Elements

MELODY:

All Of Me is a well-known tune that welcomes a balance between exact melodic statements and embellished lines. Count Basie's playing exemplifies this, and listening to recordings will provide the most help. The piano melody is already embellished in the written part, which should only serve as a suggestion for the pianist. One interesting aspect of the composition is how the opening three-note motive weaves through the chord changes in various ways, and this is one avenue the soloist can take in developing the melody.

During the ensemble chorus between sections E and I, the pianist must act in conversation with the band, knowing when to leave space for responses, just as the ensemble parts leave room for the soloist.

HARMONY:

The chord changes in this arrangement do not stray far from the original chord changes, nor are there any key changes. During the second chorus there are chord substitutions and embellishments in the rhythm section that enrich the harmony without affecting the form of the arrangement. Outside of the first four and last six measures, the ABAC form is presented two and a half times.

For the soloist, finding chord tones that did not appear in the previous chord will help to outline the harmonies effectively. For instance, the G in the C major chord can lead to a G♯ in the subsequent E^7 chord. Guide tone lines (connecting thirds and sevenths) will also be helpful, especially since root movement is mostly by fourths.

RHYTHM:

Like every other Count Basie tune, the key ingredient to this arrangement is that it swings. In fact, it is said that Basie would discard any arrangement that did not swing on the band's first reading. While there are not many technical concerns in this piece, there are ensemble passages that must be tight. This will happen when everyone feels the same pulse and sings rhythms together. The arrangement is at a tempo slow enough that an underlying triplet feel should pervade the swung eighth notes. It is also important to swing the rests, which makes the use of silence a part of the musical phrase and keeps the performer actively participating in the music. This means that each musician needs to stay focused and continue to feel the pulse when not playing.

The written rhythms on the page look more complicated than they sound, particularly with the lack of written accents and articulations. In most cases, standard rules of swing will apply: eighth note lines should be legato, quarter notes are short (unless they are part of a legato phrase, as in the first four bars of section F), and eighth notes at the ends of phrases should be accented (though not rushed). The use of dotted-eighth and sixteenth note rhythms in sections E and F seems to indicate ghosting the sixteenth note. Note lengths and accents must be agreed upon from section to section; this can also be reinforced through singing each part.

Unit 7: Form and Structure

The basic form of the composition is ABAC.

SECTION	MEASURE	EVENT AND SCORING
Intro	1–4	The full ensemble plays block chords in unison rhythms that suggest a triple meter. Although a dynamic is not indicated, the introduction should be played *fortissimo*. The downbeat, as well as each dotted quarter note, should be long. The first eighth note is legato, while the second is short and accented, as in "doo-daht." A sforzando can be added to the last eighth note in measure 3.
A/B/C	5–28	The rhythm section presents the first twenty-four measures of the form. The piano solo should not stray too far from the melody and should emphasize embellished rhythms. The wind entrance before section C should be *fortissimo* with a slight sforzando.
D	29–36	Saxophones enter, supporting the last eight measures of the piano melody. Although the line is marked *pianissimo*, it should still have direction and can be personalized in the tradition of Marshall Royal's lead alto saxophone playing.
E	37–44	The second chorus begins with soft ensemble passages in 2-bar phrases. Even at *mezzo piano*, these phrases should be supported and energized. The piano should remain tasteful during the fills and does not need to play every on eighth note.

Section	Measure	Event and Scoring
F	45–52	Ensure that the ascending lines *crescendo* slightly in addition to leaving no space between notes. Brass is open (out of the stand) and at a much stronger dynamic three measures before section G, where the music recalls the introduction.
G/H	53–68	The dynamic should be *forte* or *fortissimo* here. The Count Basie Orchestra effectively plays slightly behind the beat on a few of these phrases, particularly in the third bar of section G. The drummer can provide interest in this section by setting up horn entrances. There is a brief saxophone soli before section I, and vibrato can be used to great effect on the two dotted quarter notes.
I/J	69–82	The texture is much more sparse and drops to a *pianissimo* dynamic, which is softer than the dynamic level at section E. The piano returns to the embellished melody, and saxophones play a background almost identical to section D.
K	83–88	The introduction material returns and should be played the as before, including the sforzando in the third measure of this section. Steady time in the piano break is important, and the last note should be in time. It can also be setup by the drummer.

Unit 8: Suggested Listening

Count Basie, *Frankly Basie: Count Basie Plays the Hits of Frank Sinatra*, Polygram.

Count Basie, *The Golden Years*, Pablo.

Unit 9: Additional References and Resources

Flanagan, David, "Billy Byers" in *The New Grove Dictionary of Jazz*, Barry Kernfeld, ed. (New York: St. Martin's Press, 1994).

Gammond, Peter, "Belle Baker" in *The Oxford Companion To Popular* Music (New York: Oxford University Press, 1991).

Contributed by:

Joren Cain
Assistant Professor of Music
Valdosta State University
Valdosta, Georgia

Teacher Resource Guide

Always and Forever
Pat Metheny
(b. 1954)

arranged by Bob Curnow
(b. 1941)

Unit 1: Composer

Pat Metheny, born August 12, 1954 in Lee's Summit, Missouri, emerged as one of the leading jazz guitarists of the late twentieth century and remains an innovative and influential figure on the early twenty-first century jazz scene. Metheny began music studies on the trumpet at age eight and switched to the guitar at age twelve.[1] By 1969, at the age of fifteen, he was gigging regularly on the Kansas City jazz scene, receiving invaluable experience by performing with top-name artists. At eighteen Metheny became the youngest person to date to teach at the University of Miami, and the following year, likewise, distinguished himself by teaching at the Berklee College of Music at the age of nineteen.

Metheny first appeared on the international jazz stage when he joined forces with Berklee colleague and world-renown jazz artist and vibraphone innovator, Gary Burton, for a three-year period beginning in 1974. In that year, Metheny made his recording debut on *Jaco*, with infamous jazz bassist Jaco Pastorius and Paul Bley.[2] In 1974, he also collaborated with Burton on the Gary Burton Quintet disc *Ring*, which included Burton, guitarist Mick Goodrick, bassists Steve Swallow and Eberhard Weber, and drummer Bob Moses. In 1975 Metheny released his first album, *Bright Size Life*, with a trio that included Pastorius and Moses. *Bright Size Life* demonstrated the diversity of Metheny's musicianship, as it included compositions by Ornette Coleman, the legendary and great free jazz artist.

During that time period, Metheny met and formed an important association with keyboardist Lyle Mays that has spanned their careers up to the time of this writing. Much as Josef Zawinul and Wayne Shorter formed the creative foundation of Weather Report, Metheny and Mays are the creative impetus for the Pat Metheny Group (PMG).

The first recorded collaboration of Metheny and Mays can be found on the 1977 ECM disc *Watercolors*, which includes Eberhard Weber and drummer Dan Gottlieb. In many respects *Watercolors* is a precursor to the direction that Metheny and PMG would follow for the next decade. This fusion-influenced music, full of color and new sounds, including a wide range of electronically synthesized effects, created a sonic identity that served as the signature of the PMG during the late 1970s and well into the 1980s. Metheny, Mays and Gottlieb were joined by bassist Mark Egan for the 1979 debut album of the ensemble, entitled *Pat Metheny Group*, which was followed by numerous recordings spanning a twenty-six-year time period. While Metheny and Mays have since been joined by various bassists, drummers and other instrumentalists throughout the history of the PMG, both remain constant as the creative nucleus of the ensemble.

Beginning with the 1980 recording *80/81*, Metheny began to reestablish his diversity as an artist who was grounded in the deeply rooted traditions of jazz. Featuring an ensemble that included Charlie Haden, Jack Dejohnette, Dewey Redman, and Michael Brecker, Metheny demonstrated that his musicianship and interests reached beyond the confines of fusion. Since this post-bop style recording Metheny has continued to engage in wide-ranging collaborative projects with a variety of artists that include, among others, Burton, Haden, Dejohnette, Brecker, Dave Holland, Ornette Coleman (*Song X*: 1985), Dewey Redman, Billy Higgins, Chick Corea, Herbie Hancock, Milton Nascimento, and Toninho Horta. He has also collaborated with minimalist composer Steve Reich (*Electric Counterpoint*: 1987) and composed film music (*The Falcon and the Snowman*, and *Toys*).

Many of Metheny's more than two hundred original compositions exhibit the influence of Brazilian music, both the bossa nova and the polyrhythmic Afro-Brazilian sounds of northeastern Brazil, a country in which he has lived.[3] Metheny's compositions include works for solo guitar, small ensembles, electric and acoustic instruments, large orchestras, ballet and film scores. His guitar sound, that of a hollow body guitar modified by synthesizer combined with the use of the wide end of a guitar pick, has inspired two generations of jazz guitarists since it was first unveiled on *Bright Size Life* in 1975. He is considered to be a pioneer in the application of new technologies to jazz guitar and has further contributed to the instrument's voice by the development of the twelve-string electric guitar, forty-two-string Pikasso guitar and his extensive use of guitar synthesizers.

Pat Metheny has received seventeen Grammy Awards including Best Contemporary Jazz Recording, Best Rock Instrumental, Best Jazz Instrumental Solo, and Best Instrumental Composition, and the PMG received an unprecedented seven consecutive Grammies for seven consecutive albums. The PMG has three gold records for *(Still Life) Talking*, *Letter from Home*, and *Secret Story*. Metheny, who was honored by the Berklee College of Music with an honorary doctoral degree in 1996, continues to demonstrate an intense passion for jazz education, having presented workshops at various venues throughout the world, including the Dutch Royal Conservatory, the Thelonius Monk Institute of Jazz and in Asia and South America.

Unit 2: Composition

Originally recorded on Metheny's *Secret Story* disc in New Brunswick, New Jersey in the autumn and winter of 1991 and released by Geffen in 1992, *Always and Forever* is a hauntingly beautiful ballad in a straight-eighth-note style.

Trombonist and bandleader Bob Curnow's version of *Always and Forever* is part of a series of twelve different arrangements of compositions by Pat Metheny and/or Lyle Mays that were originally recorded by the Pat Metheny Group. Curnow, a former member of the Stan Kenton Orchestra and past president of International Association of Jazz Educators, offers a rendition of the original tune that is richly scored, reminiscent of Kenton's orchestration techniques. Recordings of all twelve arrangements are available on the Bob Curnow L.A. Big Band disc: *The Music of Pat Metheny and Lyle Mays* (MMF 1009), released on January 1, 1994 through the Mama Jazz Foundation. The disc is available at www.artistdirect.com. Curnow's recording of *Always and Forever* features Bobby Shew performing the lead line on flugelhorn, offering students the opportunity to listen to an improvisational approach to jazz melodic styling and embellishments that is of exceedingly high quality. Curnow's big band arrangement of *Always and Forever* is available through Sierra Music Publications.

Unit 3: Historical Perspective

Jazz historians typically credit Miles Davis and his recording entitled *Bitches Brew* (1968) as the landmark for the beginnings of jazz fusion. This blending of the elements of jazz and rock led to the formation of numerous groups and solo artist/band leaders, including Weather Report, Chick Corea and Return to Forever, John McLaughlin and the Mahavishnu Orchestra, Herbie Hancock,

George Duke, Stanley Clarke, the Pat Metheny Group, and numerous others that flourished within this genre, particularly during the 1970s and early 1980s. Other influences began taking shape during the 1970s, including the blending of elements of world music and jazz, giving rise to groups including John McLaughlin and Shakti, and Ralph Towner and Oregon. The atmosphere of experimentation that produced the combination of jazz with other genres, helped to shape the wide variety of music that falls under the aegis of jazz today.

Unit 4: Technical Considerations

Always and Forever is graded as an intermediate ballad. The solo part is written for guitar, alto saxophone, or flugelhorn, with the choice of soloist being left to the director. Whatever the choice, the soloist should possess a strong sense of musical line and the ability to interpret the solo effectively. Curnow's transcribes Metheny's rendition of both the melodic line and the improvisational section (measures 31–56). This is very helpful for performers who are less advanced. Directors should encourage student soloists to develop a sense of rhythmic freedom with the solo line by having them listen to both the Metheny and Curnow versions of the tune, and work with the soloist to develop different manners of embellishing this line, including the use of modal and chromatic runs and appropriate jazz style turns. Directors should also assist student soloists with their understanding of the chord changes, thereby allowing the student to improvise during the solo section rather than performing the Metheny transcription. The transcription, a highly effective learning tool, can serve as a point of departure for the improvisation as necessary.

The instrumentation calls for two alto saxophones, two tenor saxophones, baritone saxophone, four trumpets (all doubling on flugelhorn), four trombones, piano, bass, guitar and drums. Curnow has included optional fifth trumpet and fifth trombone parts and leaves directions for which parts should be excluded, dependent upon the director's choice of soloist. Range considerations include trumpet to high C (c^2), with an optional high E (e^2), and trombone to high G (g).

The score includes written parts for both piano and bass, and the guitarist is given chord changes. The written part for piano includes simplistic, three-note right-hand voicing, with the left hand doubling the bass part in unison. The bass is given the roots with basic motion in quarter or half notes. The use of these parts will restrict the freedom of the rhythm section that is essential for both the groove, and the harmonic color and texture of ballad style. While the written parts may prove helpful to beginning pianists and bassists, more advanced players should be strongly encouraged to use the chord changes and work to create greater interest in the underlying harmonic motion. The written drum part is typical, in that it does not offer any suggestions for groove except for

straight quarter notes in most measures, with a few written out ensemble figures and suspended cymbal rolls. All rhythm section players should be encouraged to listen to both the original Metheny recording and the recording of the Curnow band as they develop a more mature concept of their functions within the section and appropriate ways to contribute to ballad style.

Unit 5: Stylistic Considerations

Curnow encourages directors to use the original Metheny recording as the reference for tempo, style and other interpretive elements as they develop their interpretation of this ballad.[4] As is always the case with ballad style, attention must be paid to the creation of nuance and linear shape through the careful use of articulation and dynamics. Curnow includes written *crescendo/diminuendo* figures that are essentially intuitive; to assist with internal phrase shapes and these should be given careful attention. Directors may consider the use of breath accents on offbeat eighth-note figures, during running eighth-note passages (e.g., tenor saxophone in measures 1 and 2), in order to create a more correct stylistic approach to the piece. Articulations should be smooth and legato, and students should be encouraged to use "doo" and "dah" articulations and not "too" or "tah" to ensure proper style.

As is always the case with straight-eighth ballads, directors should take great care to keep this piece in jazz style and not allow students, especially rhythm section players, to interpret the piece with rock style. The drummer should use mallets and brushes within the piece, with the brushes used in a stirring motion on the snare drum, in quarter or eighth notes, with accents and the hi-hat placed on beats 2 and 4. The drummer should not be allowed to play a straight eight-note pattern on the ride cymbal at any time during the piece. Work with the drummer to use both open and closed hi-hat sounds in order to enhance her contribution to the color of the piece. The drummer may use either sticks or mallets during the ensemble climax between measures 57–64, and is responsible for changing the mood by assisting with the *crescendo* (Kenton style, suspended cymbal roll) in measures 55–56. The drummer should return to brushes in measure 65 when the arrangement returns to its original dynamic and style.

Measure 55–64 should be interpreted by the full ensemble in the Kenton style, particularly with the use of dynamic changes. Students should be encouraged to play with both a full sound at the *forte* and *fortissimo* dynamic levels, and with sensitive tone and subtlety at the *piano* dynamic. Careful attention should be given to the balance of the ensemble during this section as the saxophones must be heard and not dominated by the brass sections. The climax of the piece occurs between measures 63–64. The saxophones and brasses should blow through the release point in measure 64.

Unit 6: Musical Elements

MELODY:

The simplistic melody is essentially minor and melancholy. It is an ABA (head-bridge-head) melody with a phrase structure of 8+8+10. Soloists should be encouraged to learn the melody vocally as well as instrumentally, as they develop their sense of phrasing and linear direction with this tune.

HARMONY:

The chord changes include major and minor seventh chords ($Fm^{\sharp 7}$ is also included) with few extensions or alterations (with the exception of passing motions created by the use of an occasional 7(♭9) chord). The root motion is often chromatic (F/G, E^7/G♯, Am^7, A♭, $Cmaj^7$/G, Am^7/F♯, $Fmaj^7$) or by step, with the exception of the turnaround at the end of each chorus that uses a $iim^{7(\flat 5)}$–V^{7*} motion. Harmonic players should be encouraged to add a ♭9 to the latter chord structure to create common tones between the ♭5 of ii and the ♭9 of V, with a resulting half step resolution to scale degree five of the minor i chord.

RHYTHM:

There are few rhythmic challenges in this arrangement as most of the piece contains eighth and quarter note figures only, with the majority of the rhythmic motion left to the soloist. Directors should, however, exercise great care with the sixteenth notes versus triplet rhythms and the offbeat sixteenth-note figures that set up the double time feel in measures 37–38.

Unit 7: Form and Structure

SECTION	MEASURE	EVENT AND SCORING
Introduction	1–4	Full ensemble.
A	5–30	Head performed by soloist with ensemble accompaniment.
B	31–56	Solo improvisation section. Double time feel in measures 39–46.
C	57–64	Full ensemble. Kenton style climax.
A	65–75	Soloist performs head. Return to original mood of piece.

* "$m^{7(\flat 5)}$," or "minor seventh with a flatted fifth," designates a half-diminished seventh chord. This nomenclature is used because the symbols designating fully diminished and half-diminished chords is ambiguous. "$m^{7(\flat 5)}$" makes clear the precise make-up of the chord.

Unit 8: Suggested Listening

Curnow, Bob, Bob Curnow's L.A. Big Band, *Always and Forever on The Music of Pat Metheny and Lyle Mays*, Mama Jazz Foundation, MMF 1009,

Metheny, Pat, *Always and Forever* on *Secret Story*, Geffen, 1992.

Pat Metheny:

Bright Size Life
Pat Metheny Group
(Still Life) Talking
Letter from Home

The Stan Kenton Orchestra:

Send in the Clowns
Early Autumn

Unit 9: Additional References and Resources

Jazz, Jude, http://www.judejazz.co.uk, for a complete discography of Pat Metheny recordings.

Metheny, Pat, http://www.patmethenygroup.com, http://www.en.wikipedia.org/wiki/Pat_Metheny.

Contributed by:

Robert Meunier
Director of Bands
Drake University
Des Moines, Iowa

---

1 http://www.patmethenygroup.com
2 http://en.wikipedia.org/wiki/Pat_Metheny
3 ibid
4 Bob Curnow. *Always and Forever* (Lake Liberty, Washington: Sierra Music Publications).

Teacher Resource Guide

April in Paris
Vernon Duke
(1903–1969)
E.Y. Harburg
(1896–1981)

arranged by Jeff Hest
(b. 1943)

Unit 1: Composers

April in Paris was composed in 1932 by Vernon Duke for the Broadway revue score *Walk a Little Faster.* Born Vladimir Dukelsky in Russia on October 10, 1903,Vernon received classical musical training at the Kiev Conservatory. During his life he was celebrated most for his popular songs, though he wrote a number of symphonies and other works in more traditional genres. The New York Philharmonic and the Boston Symphony performed some of his works. George Gershwin encouraged his interest in popular music.

E. Y. Harburg was born in New York City on April 8, 1898, and studied journalism at the City College of New York. After working at a variety of odd jobs, Harburg became acquainted with Gershwin. His friendship with Gershwin proved to be extremely beneficial, as Gershwin introduced him to many promising songwriters.

Unit 2: Composition

April in Paris was penned in 1932 by the joint efforts of E. Y. Harburg and Vernon Duke, and Ella Fitzgerald first recorded it in 1956. This famous arrangement performed by the Basie Orchestra was done by William "Wild Bill" Davis. The original key of the song is C major.

Unit 3: Historical Perspective

The 1950s saw an evolution in the music scene throughout the United States. The rock and roll bebop music craze had taken its toll on big bands throughout the country. Many great bands of the thirties and forties suffered from lack of work and disbanded; even Count Basie was forced to tour with a reduced instrumentation during the 1940s. *April in Paris* was the revival in the recording life of the Count Basie Orchestra.

Unit 4: Technical Consideration

The recommended tempo is ♩ = 130, with a duration of 3:30; however, the chart flows well at ♩ = 120 and ♩ = 124 as well. The lead trumpet range goes to concert D (d^1), and the lead trombone range goes to concert B (b). Woodwind writing is relatively simple, especially in the area of technical facility. It will take a concerted effort, however, from each section to match the vibrato that is characteristic of this piece. There are also five measures in which the composer calls for clarinet doubling in the first and second alto saxophone parts. This is, or could be, an excellent opportunity for the students to practice doubling skills. Alternatively, the conductor could transpose the parts for alto saxophone. The transcribed soli for lead trombone and fourth trumpet give students an excellent opportunity to study the improvisational skills of the great soloists of the Count Basie Orchestra. Chord symbols are provided for piano and guitar. Players should listen to the original recording for voicing ideas. The bass line is written out for the entire chart.

Unit 5: Stylistic Consideration

The simple, homophonic rhythms of this composition are typical of the Basie band. While the rhythms are not technically challenging, ensemble articulation and Basie swing style are paramount concepts in this composition. Proper note length and inflection is a concern for the ensemble members. Improvisational soli are less of an issue in this composition as the major soli have been written out.

The selection would be an excellent program opener or closer because of the familiar melody and historic importance. It is also a good chart to introduce students to the great band of Count Basie.

Unit 6: Musical Elements

MELODY:

Typical of most vocal melodies, the melody in this composition is very accessible for the instrumentalists, as the largest interval is only a major seventh. The triplet figure should be laid back so that the composition doesn't rush. Having the entire ensemble sing the melody could prove to be valuable when learning the piece. The rhythmic pattern of the melody in measure 35 changes to a straight swing feel. The triplet quarter notes are replaced with a quarter note and dotted eighth/sixteenth note figure. This section of the melody is tutti.

HARMONY:

The primary tonal center of the composition is C major. The opening pedal G in the bass and fourth trombone parts firmly establishes the dominant of C major. However, the use of substitution chords gives the listener a sonic diversion from the traditional chord progression.

RHYTHM:

The Count Basie Orchestra is lauded for its distinct swing feel and rhythmic accuracy. Hence, a successful performance of this chart requires special attention to these musical elements. The dotted eighth/sixteenth note figure should be played with a triplet feel. The triplet quarter notes should be played with intent to insure a relaxed feel. Listening to the Count Basie Orchestra play this composition is imperative to creating a solid performance. The students and director must be true to the Basie style. Singing rhythms and phrases is also an effective method for developing the rhythmic style of this composition.

Unit 7: Form and Structure

The form of this composition is Intro—A—Solo Break—A—Solo—B—Coda.

SECTION	MEASURE	EVENT AND SCORING
Intro	1–8	The introduction of the chart is a homophonic swing rhythm with the melodic material in the lead trumpet part. The ensemble should play the *mezzo pianos* even softer than written. Accents in the bass part are important when building tension to the downbeat of measure 9. Each section should strive for balance and blend among parts.
A	9–24	The melody is introduced in the lead alto accompanied by the saxophone section. While the melody is clearly in the lead alto part, other saxophone parts should be played boldly. The trombone section plays in unison, with a *diminuendo* phrase in measures 18 and 20. It should be played with confidence and gusto.
Solo break	26–32	It seems apparent that this was originally an improvised solo; however, it has become synonymous with this composition, and learning it is a good exercise for any young jazz trombonist. The saxophone section should be sensitive to the trombonist, but aggressive on the accented sixteenth notes.
A2	33–40	The melody is introduced by trombones and answered in a slightly altered form by saxophones. It is played in its new form by the entire horn section. The eighth note figures in measures 39–40 should be very light and comical.

SECTION	MEASURE	EVENT AND SCORING
Solo break	41–56	This solo is also a transcription of a very famous solo played by one of Basie's finest solo trumpeters. Chord changes are provided for the soloist; however, the student should learn this written solo and base his improv on this original.
B	57–64	This section of the composition could also be called the bridge, as it introduces completely different material from the A sections. The chromaticism found in measures 55–56 also suggests a change of tonal center. Saxophones introduce the main melody is introduced in measure 57. Players should strive for a smooth and connected phrase. They should not take a breath after the quarter notes on beat 1 of measures 57 and 59. Trombones and trumpets enter in measure 60. Balance and intonation are important, particularly on the unison parts.
Coda	66–86	The coda is repeated twice with some minor dialogue. The drummer is crucial to ensemble accuracy on the repeats. It is important for him to play a strong triplet pickup and a solid downbeat in measure 65. The lead trumpet may experience some fatigue, as the range is quite demanding in this section. The lead trumpeter can layout in measures 65–69, because these measures are in unison with the second trumpet. This will give her much needed rest to prepare for the second and third endings.

Unit 8: Suggested Listening

Count Basie Orchestra, *April in Paris*, Verve Records.
Count Basie Orchestra, *The Complete Atomic Basie*, Blue Note Records.
Ray Charles + The Count Basie Orchestra = Genius, Concord Records.
Ray Sings, Basie Swings, Concord Records.

Unit 9: Additional References and Resources

Bash, Lee, "Getting Beyond the Notes in Jazz Performance," *Jazz Educators Journal*, February/March 1983, 59–60.

Dunscomb, Richard, and Willie L. Hill, Jr., *Jazz Pedagogy: The Jazz Educator's Handbook and Resource Guide* (Miami: Warner Brothers, 2004).

Kuzmich, John, Jr. and Lee Bash, *Complete Guide to Improvisation Instruction: Techniques for Developing a Successful School Jazz Program* (Miami: Warner Bros., 1992).

Web sites:
http://www.theguitarguy.com
http://www.swingmusic.net
http://de.essortmentcom/biographywillia_rgyr.htm
http://www.songwritershalloffame.org/exhibit_bio.asp

Contributed by:

Ricky L. Fleming
Director of Bands
Buffalo State College
Buffalo, New York

Teacher Resource Guide

Atlantis

McCoy Tyner
(b. 1938)

arranged by Bob Washut
(b. 1951)

Unit 1: Composer/Arranger

McCoy Tyner began his early piano and theoretical training in the fertile jazz scene of his hometown, Philadelphia, Pennsylvania. In 1960, after a stint with the Benny Golson-Art Farmer Jazztet, Tyner embarked upon a five-year musical relationship with the legendary tenor and soprano saxophonist John Coltrane. Along with drummer Elvin Jones and bassist Jimmy Garrison, the John Coltrane Quartet created some of the most profound, complex and imaginative music in jazz history.

In Tyner, John Coltrane found a gifted and empathetic collaborator. His overarching harmonic approach at this time was one of a quartally voiced right hand (fourths) juxtaposed over an open fifth left hand. This powerful yet open and ambiguous voicing afforded Coltrane and the ensemble the sonic space to explore densely constructed modal improvisations. Similarly, Tyner's unbridled rhythmic energy suited the ensemble's sustained intensity. His improvisational style was one that often centered on both "inside" and "outside" pentatonic playing.

After leaving Coltrane in 1965, Tyner recorded a number of influential albums on the Blue Note, Impulse, Milestone, and Telarc record labels. Many of these recordings incorporate his interest in the sounds and rhythms of other cultures, particularly African (see *Sahara*, Milestone Records). Recently, McCoy Tyner has divided his energy between both small ensemble and big band writing and performing. With nearly eighty recordings as a leader, innumerable recordings as a side player, four Grammy awards, an NEA Jazz Master award, and generations of musical disciples, McCoy Tyner continues to be an innovator who has earned a place in the pantheon of jazz giants.

Arranger, Dr. Robert Washut is professor of music at the University of Northern Iowa, where he served as director of jazz studies from 1980–2002. An accomplished jazz composer and arranger, Washut has received numerous commissions from collegiate jazz ensembles, professional jazz artists, and symphony orchestras. Many of his works are published by the UNC Jazz Press (Greeley, CO), Walrus Music Publishing (Pismo Beach, California), C.L. Barnhouse (Oskaloosa, Iowa), and Heritage JazzWorks (The Lorenz Corporation, Dayton, Ohio).

During his twenty-two years as director of the award-winning UNI Jazz Band One, Washut recorded eleven CDs (two of which earned five-star ratings from *DownBeat* magazine), toured Europe three times, consistently received "Outstanding Band" recognition at collegiate jazz festivals throughout the Midwest, and was awarded three "Outstanding Performance" citations in *DownBeat's* annual student music awards.

He is in demand as a clinician and adjudicator throughout the country and is an active jazz pianist. He founded the Latin jazz band Orquesta Alto Maiz. He recorded and released a jazz trio CD entitled *Songbook* (Sea Breeze Jazz: SB-3036) in 1999. Washut was inducted into the Iowa IAJE Hall of Fame in 2003 and was selected as Outstanding Teacher at UNI in 1996. He holds degrees from Arizona State University and the University of Northern Colorado.

Unit 2: Composition

Bob Washut's arrangement captures both the rhythmic energy and modal sonorities of the original McCoy Tyner recording. The 32-bar formal structure (AA'BC) is preceded by both a rubato introduction and an open vamp. Formally, the big band version adheres to the overall structure of the original recording with one minor exception (section C is expanded to nine measures on the tune only). The opening orchestration deftly captures the essence of the rubato dialog between McCoy and his ensemble on the original recording. Similarly, the unyielding rhythmic drive, inventive background figures, and requisite quartal voicings pay further homage to the original while adding a new dimension to the tune. Background pyramids reinforce the open solo section while the coda develops the bass ostinato motive into a rousing conclusion.

Unit 3: Historical Perspective

Atlantis is the title track from McCoy Tyner's 1974 live album of the same name. It was recorded on August 31 and September 1, 1974 at Keystone Korner in San Francisco. The album also featured Azar Lawrence on tenor and soprano saxophones, Joony Booth on bass, Wilby Fletcher on drums, and Guilerme Franco on percussion. In an era when many pianists were experimenting with electric keyboards and synthesizers, Tyner remained unabashedly acoustic. His volcanic energy, quartal harmonies, "in/out pentatonicism," and Cecil Taylor-like flourishes are all evident on this recording.

Bob Washut's arrangement of *Atlantis* was written in 1977 and was recorded on *Alive II* by the University of Northern Colorado Jazz Lab Band. In 1981, *Atlantis* won the prestigious "Outstanding Performance" award for best jazz arrangement from *Downbeat* Magazine. It is published by UNC Jazz Press.

Unit 4: Technical Considerations

Although this chart is listed as Grade 3 in the UNC Jazz Press catalog, due to doubling, expanded instrumentation, brass ranges, and rhythm section demands, it is definitely a difficult Grade 3. Although there is no tempo listed, the chart works well anywhere between ♩ = 132–172. The instrumentation is as follows:

Saxophones
- Alto 1/Soprano
- Alto 2
- Tenor 1/Flute
- Tenor 2
- Baritone

Trumpets
- Trumpet 1
- Trumpet 2
- Trumpet 3
- Trumpet 4/Flugelhorn
- Trumpet5/Flugelhorn

Trombones
- Trombone 1
- Trombone 2
- Trombone 3
- Trombone 4
- Tuba

Rhythm Section
- Piano/Electric piano
- Guitar
- Bass
- Drums
- Percussion 1 (Bells, Vibes, Cowbell)
- Percussion 2 (Gong, Triangle, Timbales, Suspended Cymbal, Congas)

A mature rhythm section is needed to impart the rhythmic energy and style of this chart. The lead trumpet plays to concert D above the staff (d^2); the lead trombone plays to concert A♯ above the staff (a♯). This composition is the perfect vehicle to develop modal concepts both in improvisation and harmonic constructs.

Unit 5: Stylistic Considerations

The opening introduction is well marked and wonderfully orchestrated. It is important to build from measure 1 through to the vamp in measure 14. Similarly, it is crucial that all of the five-note motivic entrances in measures 11–13 speak equally and are articulated identically by trumpets and trombones.

The open vamp sets up the important bass ostinato as well as the omnipresent eighth-note-based groove. Dynamically, the vamp should begin *fortissimo* and subside slightly with the statement of the melody.

Several alterations may be considered when performing this composition:

1. Change the half-time funk groove in section C to a double-time samba feel. This updates the chart stylistically and aligns it closer to the original McCoy recording.

2. As the chart progresses, allow your bass player the freedom to improvise an alternate ostinato figure.

3. Begin each solo section in a "free and spacey" manner. The time should float over bass pedal points. Gradually morph into a groove by the second chorus.

4. The percussion solo at the end of the chart can be interpreted in any manner. *Be creative.*

Unit 6: Musical Elements

MELODY:
There are two main themes in *Atlantis*: The first is the 2-bar bass ostinato pattern that anchors the compositio; the second is the simple imitative melody that modulates in section A' and morphs in section B. The arranger employs the ostinato pattern to great effect by extracting the first five notes and constructing a motivic cell. This cell manifests itself most prominently in the introduction and the coda.

HARMONY:
As stated, this chart captures the essence of its Tyner as composer. It is a modal composition that relies predominantly on quartal harmony. The basic harmonic structure is:

A	Eight measures of Dm^{11}
A'	Eight measures of Cm^{11}
B	Eight measures of Fm/B♭ to B♭maj^7, one measure each
C	Eight measures of E♭m^{11}

RHYTHM:
Rhythmically this composition migrates through several distinct feels. The introduction is rubato and freely conducted, while the predominant feel of the tune is that of a straight eighth-note Latin or rock groove. Section C is notated with a half- time funk feel, but as stated in Unit 5, the groove can be changed to a double-time samba. Similarly, the first chorus of every solo can begin freely with pedal points and floating rhythms before developing back into the straight eighth-note feel.

Unit 7: Form and Structure

SECTION	MEASURE	EVENT AND SCORING
Introduction	1–13	This section should be phrased and interpreted as a complete unit but rehearsed in two parts. Measures 1–7 should be freely conducted while measures 8–13 set a tempo in or around ♩ = 72. Dynamically, the introduction should grow throughout. The pivotal measures occur in measures 8–10, where eighth notes in the saxophone and the descending bass voices transition the mysterioso opening into a tumultuous fanfare. Articulations and dynamics need to be unified in the statements of the motivic cell in bars 11–13.

SECTION	MEASURE	EVENT AND SCORING
Vamp	14–15	The bass and left hand piano establish the ostinato pattern in D minor while the drums setup the groove. The pianist should utilize the aforementioned quartal harmonic voicings. This establishes the unmistakable McCoy Tyner sound.
A	16–23 (A)	The melody is stated in the soprano, flute, flugelhorns, and guitar. This is punctuated by crisp backgrounds in the remaining saxophones and trombones.
A1	24–31 (A9)	Transposed melody and backgrounds continue in C minor.
B	32–39 (B)	Dotted quarters predominate as the tune evolves into a full ensemble tutti. There will be a tendency to be roaring at this point, be sure to start softer at (B) in order to grow into (B^9). The sixteenth-note saxophone runs are very important and need to be heard in bars 25, 27, and 29.
C	40–48 (B9)	This is a nine-measure phrase that stylistically is listed as funky in the score. An appropriate alteration in this section would be to change the half-time funk groove to a double-time samba. As stated, this updates the chart and aligns it closer to the original recording. All attacks and releases in bars 40–46 should be extremely aggressive. The ascending line in bars 46–48 should start softly and grow dynamically into the transitional vamp at (B18).
Vamp	49–52 (B18)	This is a transitional vamp that re-establishes the bass ostinato and brings the dynamic level down for the beginning of the solo section.

Section	Measure	Event and Scoring
Solo Section	53–84 (C)	Solo changes are written in the soprano, flugelhorn, and piano parts; however, the solo section can be opened up for as many soloists as desired. Begin each solo in a "free and spacey" manner. The time should float over bass pedal points and quartal harmonies. Gradually morph into a groove by the second chorus. The band reinforces the second solo chorus with background pyramids, harmonic pads and melodic fragments. During the final solo chorus in measures 81–84, the entire ensemble plays a four-measure dotted quarter hemiola (three against four). This figure should begin soft and expand dynamically to the downbeat of (D).
Percussion	85–86 (D)	This is an open percussion solo. The drummer and percussionists can trade, solo independently, both, or solo over the ostinato pattern. *Be creative*. The D.S. return to (A) is on cue.
Coda	87–93	The coda begins quietly as the ensemble, minus the trumpets and guitar, move chromatically through quartal voiced harmonies to the ***fff*** fermata in measure 93. At the same time, trumpets and guitar ingeniously state the ostinato figure three times. Each iteration of the melody appropriately begins a fourth higher than the previous statement. The piece concludes with a gong strike following the fermata cutoff.

Unit 8: Suggested Listening

Tyner, McCoy, *Atlantis*, Milestone Records.
University of Northern Colorado Jazz Lab Band, *Alive II*, UNC Jazz Press.

Unit 9: Additional References and Resources

Berg, Shelly and Lou Fischer, et al., *Rhythm Section Workshop for Jazz Directors* (Van Nuys: Alfred, 2005).

Dunscomb, Richard and Willie L. Hill, Jr., *Jazz Pedagogy: The Jazz Educator's Handbook and Resource Guide* (Miami: Warner Brothers, 2004).

Contributed by:

Brian Coyle
Director of Jazz Studies
Hope College
Holland, Michigan

Teacher Resource Guide

Autumn

Bob Florence
(b. 1932)

Unit 1: Composer

Bob Florence was born on May 20, 1932 in Los Angeles and took his first piano lesson when he was four years old. He began preparing for a career as a concert pianist, but changed his plans after studying arranging and orchestration at Los Angeles City College. Armed with a strong technical background and love of jazz, he joined the school's jazz band and honed his skills as a writer.

Florence started a rehearsal band in his early twenties and wrote a number of arrangements for Harry James and Si Zentner. His 1961 arrangement of *Up A Lazy River*, recorded by Zentner, became a hit and led to his associations with Stan Kenton, Dean Martin, Doc Severinsen, and Red Skelton. Two of Florence's notable and long-lasting musical relationships have been with Vikki Carr and Julie Andrews, for whom he has written numerous arrangements. It is from this breadth of experience that Florence is equally at home in jazz or commercial settings.

In the late 1970s, Florence returned to the rehearsal band format and recorded the first Bob Florence Big Band album for Discovery/Trend records in 1979. He has been writing, recording, and performing ever since. In addition to an active schedule as a clinician, Florence has received fifteen Grammy nominations (including a win in 2000 for his album *Serendipity 18*) and two Emmy awards.

Unit 2: Composition

Autumn was written for the 1981 album *Westlake* as a solo vehicle for tenor saxophonist Pete Christlieb. The scoring of *Autumn* is similar to the Stan Kenton model, which includes a large brass section (five trumpets/flugelhorns

and four trombones) and six saxophones (a strong tenor saxophone soloist and five doublers). Each saxophone player (two altos, one tenor, and two baritones) doubles on flute, clarinet, or bass clarinet.

Autumn is a straightforward ballad with a contrasting swing solo section. Although the piece does include interesting colors through Florence's orchestration, as well as a few key ensemble passages, the success of *Autumn* hinges on the tenor saxophone soloist and her ability to create expressive, melodic, and rhythmic interest.

Unit 3: Historical Perspective

Bob Florence had been composing for over twenty years and had developed his own voice when he wrote *Autumn*, although the influence of Bill Holman's music was still important. Holman's writing for his own band, as well as Stan Kenton's, is marked by polished arrangements and an almost symphonic treatment of the brass section. In addition to absorbing these elements, Florence works with a broad sound palette, and changing tone colors are often a part of his compositions.

Bob Florence was raised in Los Angeles and proudly claims to be a composer of commercial and jazz music. By 1981, both the bebop era and West Coast jazz movement had passed, but elements of each were assimilated into Florence's music. His band was filled with L. A. musicians such as Pete Christlieb, who had experience in the studio and could play music of many genres. Florence and Holman have maintained their reputations as bandleaders and composers, enabling them to keep consistent personnel in their bands. The tight performances and polished sound of these musicians have been a hallmark of the Bob Florence Big Band (and The Bob Florence Limited Edition, as it has also been called) since its inception in the late 1970s.

Unit 4: Technical Considerations

No tempo marking appears in the score for this ballad; however, Florence performs it at ♩ = 60, and the duration is 6:30 at that speed. Eighth notes should be played straight and a conductor is needed for ensemble passages.

Doubles appear in all saxophone parts, and it is imperative that the saxophonists feel comfortable on their respective instruments. Although the demands on finger technique are low, good tone and pitch are important. Intonation and blend must be addressed in sectional rehearsals.

Range should not be problematic, although a crucial D above the staff (d^2) at the tune's climax requires a strong lead trumpet, and the first trombone has some passages in the third octave (up to C [c^1]). Otherwise, ranges in *Autumn* fall in a comfortable range.

Unit 5: Stylistic Considerations

Since this piece follows in the Kenton tradition, a few elements should be considered. As it is performed by Florence, the opening of *Autumn* remains constant, without rubato. Ensemble vibrato is kept to a minimum. Section F may be an exception, where each part in the saxophone soli contains important soloistic lines. Besides sections F, H, and K, ensemble parts are always in support of the soloist. This does not mean, however, half and whole notes should lack direction or shape. Every note should be played with a warm, full tone, as well as a sense of direction. This happens when each player feels the pulse within each note and leads to the next pitch with a sense of the overall phrase.

The saxophone soloist must personalize his performance with rhythmic and melodic embellishment, building over the course of the piece. Being aware of the ballad tradition is very important, beginning with Coleman Hawkin's recording of *Body And Soul.*

There is room for embellishment in the bass part, as the written parts are largely suggestions. There are certain passages (with no chord changes) that should be played exactly as written, but other sections may be embellished to good effect.

Unit 6: Musical Elements

MELODY:

There are two important melodic components to *Autumn*. In the introduction, four voices create a single melody by connecting eighth note lines and backing off on half and whole notes. The tenor melody is straightforward and lies within a comfortable range. For the most part, the melody is presented in four-measure phrases, and both soloist and ensemble should shape them accordingly. The use of space in the solo part helps delineate the tune's phrasing, and the soloist should not shy away from rests in the melody.

HARMONY:

The form of this tune is AA'BAC and is centered in F minor, with a few passages in closely related keys. During section A' (rehearsal letter B), a subtle change of harmony is introduced under the repeated melody (F minor is replaced with D♭ major, etc.).

Since this tune seldom strays far from F minor, there is a danger of playing in only one key. The soloist is urged to delineate the chord tones in all of the ii–V^7–I progressions, emphasizing each new key center, however fleeting.

RHYTHM:

Autumn is a straight-eighth-note ballad in which the rhythmic elements are clear, for the most part. At a tempo this slow, notes that are tied to an eighth note should be released on the offbeat. Of course, ensemble rhythms, attacks, and releases must be strictly followed, while the soloist should not feel tied to the exact rhythms on the page. Rhythmic variety, syncopation, and a wide range of note lengths are necessary in the saxophone melody as well as the rhythm section, particularly when accompaniment is sparse.

During the double time feel section (which is labeled as such only in the drum part) which begins just before section G, a two-feel is created in the rhythm section, and sixteenth notes should be treated as eighth notes in swing music here. Although awkward to read at first, printed rhythms will sound familiar when students are able to sing through their parts correctly. There are no slurs in the horn parts at section H, but the rules of swing apply in terms of rhythm, legato tonguing, and accents. Ensure that these passages are smooth rather than choppy, and that the entire ensemble follows the written accents and staccato markings.

Unit 7: Form and Structure

The basic form of the composition is AA'BAC.

Section	Measure	Event and Scoring
Intro	1–8	Trombones play alone with legato articulations and no vibrato. Throughout the piece, moving lines should be heard and dissonances emphasized, so long notes should take on a supporting role. All notes should be supported, and the melody builds to a full *mezzo-forte* in the fifth measure the dynamics relaxing in measures 7–8.
A	9–16	The rhythm section enters softly in support of the tenor saxophone soloist. This first statement of the melody should be the most straight ahead, although rhythmic embellishments should be incorporated. The first four bars of the melody can be played one octave lower, allowing the piece to build more. Piano may be replaced by electric piano, and comping should be sparse, comprised mostly of sustained chords.

Section	Measure	Event and Scoring
B	17–24	Trombones enter with a homophonic background line, all four voices being heard. Baritone saxophones enter four measures before section C and should balance with the trombones, ensuring that this new color is audible.
C	25–32	Tenor saxophone plays the bridge in a soli with lower woodwinds, which must play out in order to balance with the tenor lead. The soprano saxophone should be careful to not dominate the texture until the measure before section D.
D	33–40	The section A theme returns in the saxophones with soprano lead. Trumpets enter and provide support along with the trombones. Remember to shape half notes and whole notes.
E	41–46	The form ends with the soloist and rhythm section.
F	47–54	The transition to a solo section uses material from the introduction, now in the saxophones. Style should match trombones at the opening, although soloistic vibrato may be used. Despite the softer dynamics, a full and rich sound is needed.
G	55–62	A double-time feel develops in the rhythm section two bars before section G, creating a two-feel in the bass and drums. Sixteenth notes (equivalent to eighth notes here) should be lightly swung. The soloist begins improvising here, during the B section of the form.

SECTION	MEASURE	EVENT AND SCORING
H	63–70	The full ensemble takes the lead for the first time in the piece. Playing should be strong from each section, although trumpets have the lead for the first two measures. Swing articulations should match across all sections of the band, particularly in the tutti third measure. Remember that marcato accents are accented, with space after them.
I	71–76	The tenor continues to improvise over section C with backgrounds from the woodwinds. Parts must be heard without covering the soloist.
J	77–83	New harmonic material leads to the cadenza with backgrounds in the woodwinds and trombones. Sixteenth notes in the woodwinds should be played straight, and the drummer must be sensitive and not clash with swung sixteenth notes. Only hint at the underlying swing feel. The tenor solo should continue to build, playing into the cadenza. Quarter notes leading into section K do not have to be exactly in time.
K	84–90	Material from the introduction appears again, this time the full ensemble building to a *fortissimo*. The tempo may be slightly faster than earlier in the piece, as performed on the recording. Dynamic contrast in last two measures should be drastic.

Unit 8: Suggested Listening

Coleman Hawkins, *Body and Soul*, RCA.
Bill Holman Band, *A View From the Side*, JVC.
Bob Florence Big Band, *Westlake*, Discovery Records.

Unit 9: Additional References and Resources

Owens, Thomas, "Bob Florence," in *The New Grove Dictionary of Jazz*, ed. Barry Kernfeld (London: MacMillan, 2002).

Wye, Trevor. *A Trevor Wye Practice Book for the Flute, Vol. 1: Tone* (London: Novello, 1996).

Contributed by:

Joren Cain
Assistant Professor of Music
Valdosta State University
Valdosta, Georgia

Teacher Resource Guide

Basically Blues
Phil Wilson
(b. 1948)

Unit 1: Composer

Born in Belmont, Massachusetts on January 19, 1937 Phillips Elder Wilson, Jr. began taking piano lessons at the age of four. After studying the piano for two years, his piano teacher discovered that Phil had dyslexia. Although he excelled on piano, (Phil played almost entirely by ear) his piano teacher s uggested he take up a single-line instrument that didn't require reading dense notation, so Wilson began playing trombone.

After High School, Phil attended the New England Conservatory of Music and played in Herb Pomeroy's Boston-based big band (1955–1957). Wilson left New England Conservatory after two years to go on the road with the Dorsey Brothers Band, playing trombone and later piano. In 1960, Wilson was drafted by the military and became soloist and arranger for the North American Air Defense Command (NORAD) band and studied at the Navy School of Music. After military service, Phil became the lead trombone player (1962–65) in Woody Herman's now-famous 1960's band lineup "Swingin' Herd," performing and contributing arrangements to Woody Herman's albums.

In 1966 Wilson accepted a faculty position at the Berklee School of Music, where he still teaches. Wilson has led an after-hours rehearsal band at Berklee. Originally called the Thursday Night Dues Band, the name was changed to the Rainbow Band in 1985. Past members has included drummer Terry Lyne Carrington, pianist Cyrus Chestnut, guitarist John Scofield, saxophonist Ernie Watts, and trumpeter Roy Hargrove.

Wilson has performed with Louis Armstrong, Buddy Rich, Frank Sinatra, Herbie Hancock, Woody Herman, Thad Jones, Clark Terry, and many others. Recent recordings include Wizard of Oz Suite and The Pal Joey Suite with NDR Big Band on Capri, and AC-Cent-Tchu-Ate the Positive: Arlen Songs with Paul Schmeling on Seaside.

Unit 2: Composition

Phil Wilson *Basically Blues* (1959) appears on the Buddy Rich's album *Swingin' New Big Band* (1966). This blues composition in the key of G is a Basie style easy swing. The term easy in this case does not mean simple, but makes reference to the stylistic approach. The tune opens with the rhythm section laying down the groove ala Basie. The sax section plays the riff like theme of the piece. Throughout the tune you'll hear various riffs developed in all sections of the band. The dynamic contrast of the shout chorus as well as the key change (A♭) in the third chorus of the shout section is very effective. Solo space is available for trombone, tenor sax, and piano but any instrument can be added.

Unit 3: Historical Perspective

Phil Wilson's musical development occurred during an era when some of the greatest big bands were in full bloom. As a big band member of Woody Herman, Buddy Rich, and Dorsey Brother's band, Wilson not only learned from the innovators of the genre, but also contributed by composing, arranging, and performing for these groups and others. Phil's compositions have become staples in the educational jazz repertoire. Wilson is further contributing to the jazz world through the development of the Rainbow Band a student after hours group.

Unit 4: Technical Considerations

This easy swing chart is rated Grade 4 1/2, and the recommended tempo is ♩ = 100–112, with a duration of 5:25. The lead trumpet range goes to concert D above staff (d^2), and the lead trombone range goes to concert C-flat (third octave). The saxophone soli is challenging technically and stylistically. Bass, piano, and guitar parts are not written out; only chord symbols provided. The changes are not your basic blues changes. These blues changes employ many altered chord changes throughout the chart. Soloists must understand the blues form, altered chords and the ii–V turnarounds.

Unit 5: Stylistic Considerations

This easy swing, blues-style composition is reminiscent of Count Basie's style, which emphasized a bluesy, riff-oriented approach. The articulations are very deliberate and emphasized. The opening of the piece is a very typical Basie approach with the rhythm section laying down a very relaxed swing groove. The piano player should avoid using too much left hand chords, while bass and guitar players should lock the groove by playing the four beats together. Therefore, the Freddie Green style of playing is a must for guitarist.

The wind players must be able to vocalize the correct style in order to create the feeling of swing. It is very important that the vocal inflections emphasize the blues.

This selection is a great tool for teaching student jazz groups the concept of swing style and ensemble performance. Because of the motif approach of the melody, chart also presents a great opportunity for players to further develop a jazz vocabulary.

Unit 6: Musical Elements

MELODY:
The opening melody is a 2-bar riff that is simply stated. This riff approach occurs throughout the tune with each idea introduce and developed. These melodic riffs should be learned vocally without notations to create the swinging, bluesy feel intended. Using call and response as a teaching tool and Buddy Rich Orchestra recording as a performance resource of this chart is ideal to conveying to proper performance style.

HARMONY:
The chart is a G blues. Altered chords are used to create more interest and a strong bluesy sound. The entire chart stays in the key of G except for the third chorus of the shout section where the tune modulates 1/2 step up to concert A♭. This half step movement upward creates great tension in the climactic section of the chart.

RHYTHM:
The entire band must feel the four downbeats of the pulse as well as the triple feel of the rhythm. The swing feel requires that the entire band feel the four downbeats as well as the triplet pulse on each downbeat. It may be necessary to set a metronome to quarter notes subdivided by triplets for the ensemble to hear as they sing and/or perform the rhythmic examples of the piece.

Unit 7: Form and Structure

The basic form of the composition is 12-bar Blues.

SECTION	MEASURE	EVENT AND SCORING
Intro (1)	1–12	The tempo is ♩ = 100–112. The rhythm section plays a chorus of G blues on top with the piano performing a solo. The left hand of the piano should play chords sparsely while the bass and guitar play the four beat swing *a la* Freddie Green.
13	13–24	Saxes play the melody harmonized with the rhythm section the first time through this repeated section. Trumpets join in on the repeat performing a riff-derived countermelody to the saxes melodic riffs. Sing these parts to establish good swing feel.
25	25–36	Trumpets and trombones take over the melodic responsibility with the sax playing a short response to set up the trombone solo.
37	37–48	The trombone solo continues with the tenors and bari playing a background figure that is a combination of the trumpet counter-melody and sax melody play in bars 13–24.
49	49–60	This section is a saxophone soli for traditional saxophone section instrumentation with an alto lead; the five measure of the soli is performed in one breath. Make sure the approach taken is very vocal and bluesy; all parts must line-up with everyone listening to the alto for phrasing and articulations. Rhythm section plays stop time during the first three measures. This soli is used to introduce the tenor sax soloist (the Buddy Rich recording used trumpet solo until measure 61).

SECTION	MEASURE	EVENT AND SCORING
61	61–72	Continuation of the tenor solo (in the Buddy Rich recording the tenor solo begins here). Trumpets and trombones play background figures also based on riffs.
73	73–84	Piano solo; no background.
85	85–96	Full band shout section played softly; everyone must listen to the lead trumpet player for articulation style, phrasing, and balance. Rehearse this section with the ensemble vocalizing parts with a bluesy swing approach. Everyone must internalize the triplet swing feel for this section to be effective. The rhythm section must provide a strong rhythmic pulse to anchor the band.
96	96–108	Continuation of shout chorus. The ensemble sound should be big and full; dynamic level is *forte*.
109	109–120	Shout chorus develops in a new key, concert A♭. this half-step modulation helps to create more intensity in the climactic section of the shout chorus. Brass will find the last three bars of this section very challenging. This chart pushes the range on lead and other players in the section. The dynamic contrast must be maintained.
121	121–132	To close out the chart, saxes re-introduce the melody back in the original key, concert G. The full ensemble enters four measures from the end in block style, performing a Basic style big-soft-big dynamic contrast. In the last two bars, bass, piano, and guitar play a Basie-type ending in unison. The last chord is an unexpected Gmaj^9 chord played by the full ensemble.

Unit 8: Suggested Listening

Buddy Rich Orchestra, *Swingin' New Big Band*, Capitol Records.
Woody Herman Orchestra, *Woody Herman, 1963*, UMG Recordings.

Unit 9: Additional References and Resources

Berg, Shelly, Lou Fischer, Fred Hamilton, and Steve Houghton. *Rhythm Section Workshop* (Van Nuys: Alfred Publishing Company, 2000).
Dunscomb, Richard, and Willie L. Hill Jr., *Jazz Pedagogy: The Jazz Educator's Handbook and Resource Guide* (Miami: Warner Brothers, 2004).

Contributed by:

Jose Antonio Diaz
Director of Bands
MacArthur High School
Houston, Texas

Teacher Resource Guide

Basie–Straight Ahead

Samuel "Sammy" Lewis Nestico

(b. 1924)

Unit 1: Composer

Sammy Nestico was born in Pittsburgh, Pennsylvania on February 6, 1924. He is one of the most prolific and well-known composers and arrangers in the jazz idiom and big bands in particular. Nestico received the bachelor of music education degree from Duquesne University in 1950 and has received honorary doctorate degrees from Duquesne and Shenandoah University in Virginia.

Nestico's teaching credentials include: Westinghouse Memorial High School in Wilmerding, Pennsylvania; Pierce College in Los Angeles, California; and the University of Georgia, in Athens, Georgia. In addition to these appointments, Nestico contributed to jazz music education through his 600 big band compositions that provided a foundation for the study and performance of big band literature at the secondary and university levels. Many of his arrangements were essential to teaching the basics of jazz interpretation relative to articulation, swing phrasing, feel and style. Additionally, Nestico's arrangements across various sub-styles have served as models for analysis in studying big band orchestration and composition.

Nestico's early training included a stint as staff arranger for the ABC radio station (WCAE) in Pittsburgh at age seventeen. Also, he was a member of the United States Air Force Band in Washington, D. C. as staff arranger, and later became the leader of the Airmen of Note. His extensive television credentials include writing for Julie Andrews, Merv Griffin, Mary Tyler Moore, Perry Como, *The Tonight Show*, *The Streets of San Francisco*, and many others. Other notable collaborations include recordings with Sarah Vaughn, Frank Sinatra and Nancy Wilson.

Sammy Nestico is best known as a composer/arranger for the Count Basie Orchestra from 1968 through 1984. He understands the Basie style, which has at its foundations the elements of complexity within simplicity, surprise, blues, the Kansas City rhythmic and melodic nuances, riffs, and a harmonic language identifiable with the Basie sound.

Unit 2: Composition

Sammy Nestico composed and arranged *Basie–Straight Ahead* (1968) during the sixteen years that he served as composer/arranger for the Count Basie Orchestra. This 32-bar piece is based on the AABA form in terms of its harmonic scheme. The melody of the antecedent phrase (first four bars of section A) never repeats itself exactly throughout the form. There are obvious similarities between the melodic material in bar two of the first and last A sections, bars 3 and 4 in the second A section, and bars 3 and 4 of the last A section. However, the consequent phrases (last four measures of each A section) add cohesiveness to the composition. Nestico's use of writing over the bar lines (not adhering to the delineations of the 8-bar sections) add the elements of interest, surprise, and growth throughout the arrangement. This growth is further achieved through the use of modulation (keys of E♭ and F) along with the tenor saxophone solo, piano solo, and saxophone soli, growing out of the arrangement in unexpected places within the form.

Unit 3: Historical Perspective

For a brief period from 1950 to 1952, Basie formed a small group due to challenging economic times. His payroll was reduced to seven members. The Count Basie Orchestra experienced a revival in the late 1950s and 1960s with the addition of personnel such as Thad Jones, Frank Foster, and Frank Wess, who were great soloists and composers. Collaborations with many great composers/arrangers were tempered by Basie's scrutiny. Outside arrangers who were commissioned to compose for the band often had their scores edited by Basie. He wanted to make certain that the music was not too complex or difficult for the relaxed style for which the band was known. The sixteen-year collaboration with Sammy Nestico proved to be a great match as Sammy was a major contributor to the Basie library during his last years.

Unit 4: Technical Considerations

This chart is rated Grade 4–5, and the suggested tempo is ♩ = 200 with a duration of 4:00. However, the classic performance of *Basie–Straight Ahead* (Count Basie and His Orchestra, Dot DLP-25902) is performed at a slower tempo (♩ =190). Basie's mastery as bandleader was the role that he played in determining the proper feel and tempo of a selected composition.

The lead trumpet plays up to concert E♭ above the staff (e♭²) and the lead trombone goes up to concert C above middle C (c¹).

The saxophone soli is challenging stylistically and the lead alto saxophonist must pay attention to the subtle but important nuances (bends, scoops, dynamics, etc.).

The harmonies are not complex, but soloists should be aware of the harmony, and memorize the original melody to assist in hearing the form. Take notice of Basie's approach to his solo in this piece. The beauty is a result of a great melodic approach rather than "licks" and too many notes.

Unit 5: Stylistic Considerations

This composition contains many of the elements of the Kansas City influence that forms the foundation for the Basie style. Included are riffs, call and response between the brass and saxophones, elements of the blues especially in the tenor saxophone solo, and most importantly the great swing feel of the Basie band inherent throughout this piece. It is essential to listen to this piece as well as other big band compositions in order to understand jazz from an aural perspective. All members of the band including the rhythm section should sing the melody, background figures, shout chorus, and lead line of the sax soli. This piece should be utilized as a teaching tool for the basic feel of a straight ahead medium up-tempo big band piece.

Unit 6: Musical Elements

MELODY:

This melody is simplistic, spacious, dynamic, and contains enough contrast to make it interesting without being predictable. Throughout the development and recap, the melody is shared between all of the sections from the unison saxes through the tutti sections. The eighth-note passage of the A sections serves as a spring board for the tutti transitions and shout chorus.

HARMONY:

This composition begins on the IV chord and goes through a sequence of ii–V progressions leading to C major, the key of the exposition. At the bridge, the key center shifts to the IV chord and finally cadences with a iii–V/ii–ii–V progression back to key of C before returning to the IV chord for the last A section. The second chorus begins in the key of E♭, and the final modulation to F occurs during the second A section of the last chorus. With the use of a few chromatic passing chords and the tritone substitution, the harmony is basic four-part harmony with the appropriate extensions for the Basie style (not too dense and the sparse use of minor seconds in the voicings).

RHYTHM:
Rhythmically, Nestico's arrangement remains true to the character of the Basie style. The rhythm section provides the traditional "flat four" feel which is the foundation of the Basie sound. Any variation from this rhythm section approach suggests a big band other than the Count Basie Orchestra. An effective performance of this composition requires a light approach in the rhythm section and in the horn sections. The band as a unit is responsible for providing this swing feel. As stated earlier, it is essential to sing all sections (rhythmically) while maintaining an awareness of melody. Another approach involves having the lead trumpet, lead alto, and lead bone play and then sing their parts on the tutti sections.

Unit 7: Form and Structure

The form of this composition is AABA.

SECTION	MEASURE	EVENT AND SCORING
Intro	1–12	The suggested tempo is ♩ = 200, however the classic performance of *Basie–Straight Ahead* (Count Basie and His Orchestra, Dot DLP-25902) is performed at a slower tempo (♩ = 190). This composition is based on 8-bar phrases, yet the intro is a 12-bar blues featuring Basie on piano.
A	13–20	The melody is played by the alto and tenor saxophones in unison. The first four measures state a simple spacious melody followed by a three-measure phrase of eighth-note material. The tutti brass and baritone sax figure end the first A section while introducing the second one.
B	21–28	A contrasting unison melody continues with the upper saxophones while unison trumpets play a short counter melody. The next four measures of eighth-note saxophone melody is accompanied by harmonized trombone background figures leading to the bridge.

SECTION	MEASURE	EVENT AND SCORING
C	29–36	The tutti brass plays a pick up to measure 29, and the melody of the bridge is harmonized tutti with lead trumpet on the melody doubled with the lead alto saxophone and lead trombone. The dramatic contrast in dynamics between the bridge and the second A section (*subito forte*) should be noted. The next four bars are tutti with a decreased tessitura, which allows a decrease in energy and volume to prepare for the unison saxophones to state the melody with the same light texture as the opening melody. Again, the immediate contrast between loud and soft sections, pitting small sections against tutti horns, is a basic component of the Basie style.
D	37–44	The last A section begins with saxophones in unison with a trumpet counter melody. Harmonized trombones support the melody at measure 40 as the saxes state the ending phrase of the form before the tutti pickup into the second chorus which modulates to the key of E♭.
E	45–60	This section begins tutti through bar 54, and the tenor saxophone solo begins on the second bar of the second A section of this chorus. Letter E borrows its rhythmic material from the second A section of the form, which was performed by the saxophones. This material serves as an interlude and acts as a springboard, introducing the soloist. Two measures before letter F (the bridge), the brass section provides a short interlude to support the soloist going to the bridge.

Section	Measure	Event and Scoring
F	61–76	The tenor saxophone solo continues through the bridge. It is important that the rhythm section maintain the tempo and intensity behind soloists when the horn section is silent. In too many instances, the transition between loud tutti sections and soloists with rhythm section result in sagging tempos and a lack of intensity. Students should focus on playing softly with intensity and energy. The trombones return in measure 69 (the last A section of the second chorus), playing background figures behind the soloist using rhythmic material related to the first four bars of the opening A section.
G/H	77–108	The tutti interlude which begins the third chorus sets up the saxophone soli. This soli presents a stylistic challenge. Pay attention to the accents, bends, phrasing, and the use of vibrato in the lead alto. During section rehearsals, be specific regarding turns. The brass plays figures during the rests and sustained notes of the saxophone soli. The sax soli prepares for Basie's piano solo at the bridge (measure 93). The piano solo continues through the beginning of the last chorus.
I/J	109–132	The beginning of the last chorus is also the shout chorus. In this chart and other Basie Orchestra stylings, the shout section begins softly and gradually gets louder as the development section progresses. Letter J, the second A of the form, begins with the same tutti melodic material harmonized in the new key of F. The dynamic marking in this section is *forte*, and the contrast between these sections should be emphasized in performance to reflect this growth.

SECTION	MEASURE	EVENT AND SCORING
K	133–148	The shout chorus continues for four measures after the piano solo and melodic material is restated in the saxophone section as was the case in measure 23. Another tag (turnaround) is introduced in measure 141 with a call and response figure in the trombones followed by the trumpets. This leads to an exact recap of the original bridge.
L	149–163	The fourth turnaround begins with the saxes stating rhythmic variations of a previous theme. In the final turnaround the trumpets and trombone play the theme that the saxes played in measures 17–18. Four bars before the end, a variation of Basie's classic piano endings precedes the tonic in F major. In the performance of the tags (turnarounds) in letters K and L, the performers must be aware of the musical conversation of those restatements. Each time the four-measure harmonic material repeats itself, regardless of reharmonization, the intensity should increase.

Unit 8: Suggested Listening

Count Basie Orchestra, *Chairman of the Board*, Roulette.
Count Basie Orchestra, *The Complete Atomic Basie*, Blue Note Records.
The Best of Count Basie, 1957,n Roulette/Pablo,
Count Basie and his Orchestra, *Basie–Straight Ahead*, Dot, DLP-25902.

Unit 9: Additional References and Resources

Gridley, Mark C., *Jazz Styles: History and Analysis*, 9th *edition* (Englewood Cliffs: Prentice Hall, 2006).

Porter, Lewis, Michael Ullman, and Edward Hazell. *Jazz From its Origins to the Present* (Englewood Cliffs: Prentice Hall, 1993).

Contributed by:

Ira Wiggins
Director of Jazz Studies
North Carolina Central University
Durham, North Carolina

Teacher Resource Guide

Black and Tan Fantasy

Duke Ellington

(1899–1974)

James "Bubber" Miley

(1903–1932)

transcribed by David Berger

(b. 1948)

Mark Lopeman

Unit 1: Composer

Duke Ellington was born on April 29, 1899 in Washington D. C. Duke formed a love of music and art at an early age and was offered an art scholarship to the prestigious Pratt Institute in New York. Although he was good at art, his love of music would prevail. His fondness of music and his talent surfaced as early as the age of seven, when he composed his first composition *Soda Fountain Rag*. Edward earned the nickname "Duke" because of his flair and style in the way that he dressed. He was always sharp and dapper. Duke Ellington was also the consummate gentleman and scholar and was a member of that group of artists that we like to use the phrase "intelligencia" to describe.

Unit 2: Composition

Black and Tan Fantasy is an excellent piece to teach the use of plunger technique to the brass players of your ensemble. Plunger technique takes a considerable amount of practice (trial and error) to execute and master. For the high school student you might want to play recordings of artists who mastered the plunger technique such as "Bubber" Miley, Joe "Tricky Sam" Nanton, Al Grey, Cootie Williams, and Clark Terry. The list goes on and on, but this will give you a starting point for your band. Let your students experience the sound of the open hand technique against the completely closed hand sound on their instruments playing straight quarter notes using plungers. This should help the students hear the difference in each of these sounds. *Black and Tan Fantasy* is a depiction of a funeral and a celebration at the same time, so you should try to create an atmosphere of sympathy and celebration.

Unit 3: Historical Perspective

During the late 20s, 30s and 40s in New Orleans it was customary for musicians to play at funerals. Bands would parade down the street playing solemn music in honor of the deceased. The music would continue all the way to the burial site. Once the body was laid to rest the band would break out into an all out celebration. This custom is still honored and done in some parts of the USA today. The author remembers attending a few of those parades as a youngster in South Florida.

Lots of plunger work is required throughout the piece for all brass players. "Bubber" Miley is considered the innovator of the *wa-wa* technique with the plunger so lots of listening to this style is required.

Unit 4: Technical Considerations

Although this piece doesn't call for an extended amount of range on any instrument in particular, it is worth noting that the trombone players should have a range of at least B♭ above tuning note B♭ (b♭) as the piece requires that the second and third trombone players play these notes at some point and time during the piece. You need to have at least one saxophone player who is familiar with the style, techniques and vibrato of Johnny Hodges. Although on this piece on the original recording Otto Hardwick plays the solo.

The introduction of *Black and Tan Fantasy* requires extensive plunger work within the brass section and requires that all players use plungers, growls, vibrato, and mutes. At letter B, your best saxophone player should play the solo. You might want to open-up section D to E for some of your best soloists. The section from D to E is a B♭ blues.

As always the teaching tools for all Ellington pieces (and any other swing compositions for that matter) are recordings of the original Duke Ellington bands. An excellent compilation of CDs to have is *Duke Ellington, The Essential Collection, 1927–1962.*

Unit 5: Stylistic Consideration

Black and Tan Fantasy is a straight, slow, swing piece with the exception of the introduction (measures 1–12) and the coda (or outro) in the last four bars. Your ensemble could benefit greatly from performing this piece because in order to play it well and in it's most authentic form, all players have to use vibrato and all of the brass players use plungers and mutes throughout the entire piece. This is an excellent piece to demonstrate and show-off the diversity in your brass section.

Unit 6: Musical Elements

MELODY:

The melodic structure of *Black and Tan Fantasy* begins with a 12-bar declaratory statement featuring the muted brass section. The actual melody starts at letter B with the saxophone section playing underneath the lone saxophone solo (you may wish to give this solo to your strongest saxophone player and the player that has the best tone, as this solo requires very smooth and lyrical playing). The solo is rather nostalgic and somewhat understated, however, it evokes a very endearing feeling to listeners when played correctly (think of a nice walk in the park on a Sunday evening).

HARMONY:

The clever incorporation of two different tonal centers for *Black and Tan Fantasy* is done so skillfully by Duke Ellington and "Bubber" Miley that one hardly notices it without a glance at the score. The twelve bar intro is composed of B♭m and E♭m chords with an F^7 chord in measure nine that helps to solidify the key of B♭m. The tonal center changes at measure thirteen and moves to dominant seventh chords with the occasional ♭5 and diminished chords to strengthen the character and mood change that evokes that "happy" or "nostalgic" feeling. Section D through E is a straight 12-bar blues. Section E sets up the outro of *Black and Tan Fantasy* which returns to B♭ minor.

RHYTHM:

The intro, which features the gritty sounds of the muted brasses is a 2-beat feel (*a la* boom-sop, boom-sop, with accents on "sop," or beat two) that transitions into a slow swing feel which always requires musicians to subdivide each beat to perform correctly. I like to use the syllables doo-doo-la, doo-doo-la...which I learned from the famed music educator Ron Carter. The doo-doo-la doo-doo-la system should be used to teach style and feel placing heavy accents on the "la" part of every beat.

Unit 7: Form and Structure

The basic form of this piece is ABB—(Solo section with backgrounds)—Coda/Outro.

Section	Measure	Event and Scoring
Introduction, A	1–12	The piece starts out in B♭ minor and requires all of the brass players to be ready and set to go with plungers and mutes.
B	13–20	Well-balanced ensemble playing within your sax section is needed here. Put your best saxophone player on the solo. Smooth playing with balanced playing with the addition of section vibrato is paramount here.
C	21–28	A repeat of measures 13–20 with the addition of a 2-bar brass interlude that leads into the solo section.
D	29–40	This section begins a 12-bar blues in B♭. You might want to open this section up for some of your better soloists. Be careful to select your soloist in an order that will allow one of your brass players to take the last solo because on the last solo at letter D the sax section plays a two-measure groove that could cover up a weaker soloist.
E	41–50	This section allows your last and presumably your best soloist to take an extended solo.
Coda/Outro	51–54	This section marks the return to B♭ minor and marks the only time in the piece where the full ensemble plays together.

Unit 8: Suggested Listening

Ellington, Duke, *The Essential Collection, 1927–1962*, Columbia Records.
Jazz Archives, *Talking and Preaching Trombones, 1924–1945*.
Ken Burns Jazz, *The Story of America's Music*, Complete Set.
Melton Mustafa Orchestra with Jesse Jones, Jr., *St. Louis Blues*, Bob Weinstock Productions.
Northern Illinois University Jazz Ensemble, Ronald Carter, Director, *We Came to Swing!*

Unit 9: Additional References and Resources

Gioia, Ted, *The History of Jazz* (New York: Oxford University Press, 1997).
Gridley, Mark C., *History and Analysis*, 9th *edition* (Upper Saddle River: Prentice-Hall, 2006).

Contributed by:

Reuben Cooper, Jr.
Director of Bands
DeKalb High School
DeKalb, Illinois

Teacher Resource Guide

Blues in Hoss' Flat

Frank Foster

(b. 1928)

Unit 1: Composer

Frank Foster was born on September 23, 1928 in Cincinnati, Ohio. He shares the same birthday as John Coltrane, however Coltrane was born two years earlier. During his early years, Foster played clarinet and alto saxophone, but changed to tenor saxophone in 1947 in order to develop a musical identity free from Charlie Parker's influence. Foster began playing gigs while in high school, leading his own band and writing all the arrangements. He later attended Wilberforce University and played with the Wilberforce Collegians.

At Wilberforce, Foster played lead alto saxophone, and his arrangements occupied a major portion of the band's repertoire. During his final year at Wilberforce he played tenor saxophone. Trumpeter Snooky Young, an alumnus of the Basie and Lundsford bands, hired Foster in Detroit during the summer of 1949. While in Detroit, Foster was exposed to musicians such as Thad, Hank and Elvin Jones, Kenny Burrell, Tommy Flannagan, Paul Chambers and Barry Harris to name a few. Foster played gigs in Detroit for two years with those musicians. Frank Foster was drafted into the Army in 1951 and discharged in 1953.

Upon his discharge Foster returned to Detroit. The Count Basie band was playing in Detroit at that time and needed to replace the tenor saxophone chair vacated by Lockjaw Davis. Foster auditioned for the band and was hired. His career began with Count Basie on July 28, 1953. Frank Foster was a key member of the Basie saxophone section, and became a significant composer and arranger with the Basie Band. His most noted work with the Basie band was *Shiny Stockings*, which was Basie's signature tune.

Unit 2: Composition

Frank Foster wrote *Blues In Hoss' Flat* in 1956 as a member of the Count Basie band. This composition swings with a shuffle feel, and displays characteristics of the hard-driving Kansas City blues style that Basie is noted for. It requires great rhythmic precision due to the interplay between brass and woodwinds, and syncopated accents within the ensemble. Plunger work is essential for the trombone section and trumpet soloist.

Unit 3: Historical Perspective

In the 1930s the Count Basie band was noted for riff-based patterns that were rehearsed and played by rote as a head arrangement rather than a notated arrangement. This was a characteristic of the typical Southwestern jazz band, and particularly the Benny Moten band, with whom Basie worked in 1929. The Kansas City bands were organized around their rhythm sections, which supported interplay between brass and woodwinds and provided accompaniment for soloists. Count Basie tailored his rhythm section to sensitivity toward the band and its soloists, and established the concept of four equally emphasized beats to the bar as the standard of jazz performance.

During the 1950s and 1960s the Count Basie Band maintained its characteristic swing identity as established in the 1930s, however Basie chose soloists with modern leanings in their playing style. Players such as Thad Jones, Frank Wess, Frank Foster, Marshall Royal and Eddie "Lockjaw" Davis were prominent soloists in the Basie band during this period. The sound of the Basie band changed as arrangers such as Neal Hefti, Thad Jones, Benny Carter, Frank Foster and Quincy Jones contributed their works to the band.

Unit 4: Technical Considerations

This is a medium-advanced level blues shuffle. The tempo is ♩ = 132. Attention should be paid to this tempo in order to maintain the drive of the tune without rushing or dragging. The key signature is concert D♭, which can present intonation problems, and soloists will need to be comfortable improvising in that key. Solos are featured for tenor saxophone, trumpet, trombone and piano. Hats are required for trumpet soli passages, and plungers are required for trombone soli passages. The trumpet solo is with plunger. Brasses will need to be secure with shakes. Lead trumpet range goes to concert D♭ ($d\flat^2$) and lead trombone goes to concert B♭ (b♭). The bass line is written for much of the chart except during solos and full ensemble soli sections. The guitar part consists of chord notation throughout the chart. Some pitch notation occurs on the introduction, and rhythmic notation occurs on the last two measures. The piano part also functions as a conductor score. The drum part provides rhythmic notation and cues throughout the chart, except during solo sections.

Unit 5: Stylistic Considerations

The blues feel must be emphasized at all times. It is passionate and earthy. Much consideration must be given to the feeling of time throughout the ensemble. The tempo must not rush, and the rhythm section must be rock solid in maintaining the groove. Heavy back beats on beats two and four are needed, but must be tastefully played. Eighth notes should be played with a swing feel, and the upbeats must be exaggerated in order to bring out the syncopation between four-quarter note rhythms vs. eighth note rhythms. Call and response vocal inflections emphasizing the blues feel are essential throughout each section in this piece.

Unit 6: Musical Elements

MELODY:
The trombone section at Letter A introduces the melody. Fourth trumpet at Letter B as a growl plunger solo restates the melody. A call and response effect occurs as the trumpet section (in hats) answers the call of the trombone soli at Letter A, and the trombone section (in plungers) answers the call of the fourth trumpet at Letter B.

HARMONY:
The melody and harmony of this blues progression do not modulate. It is a straightforward blues in D♭.

RHYTHM:
This is a swing feel chart. Each quarter note should be subdivided into a triplet pulse (oo-de-la) by the entire ensemble even though the shuffle feel is implied. The feeling should be of syncopated eighth notes as opposed to the dotted eighth and sixteenth note feel. Emphasizing the last syllable of the triplet pulse (la) will create the necessary accent on the upbeat eighth notes. Students should sing their parts rhythmically for accuracy in articulation.

Unit 7: Form and Structure

This composition is written in a 12-bar blues form.

Section	Measure	Event and Scoring
Intro	1–8	Tempo is ♩ =132. Saxophone soli introduces thematic material while trombones and rhythm section pedal on dominant seventh, building tension into Letter A. Strong back beats on 2 and 4 by trombones and rhythm section are important in building tension. The piano triplet fills in measure four are important in setting up the shuffle feel.
A	9–20	Trombone section states the melody, while saxophones countermelody, punctuated by trumpet accents fanning hats. A dialogue is established between brass and saxophones. Trumpets should exaggerate accents when fanning hats. "Bwop-Bwop!" "Bwop-Bwop!" Trombones need to place extra weight on accent on beat 2 and legato attack on beat 3 of the two-measure melodic riff at Letter A and its return in measures 13–14. The trombone soli is very sassy and spirited. Trombonists should listen to recordings, sing and imitate nuances as a section.
B	21–32	The fourth trumpet states the melody using plunger growl, while saxophones countermelody, creating call and response punctuated by trombone accents. Trombones fan plungers on last two bars. Pay careful attention to balance trombones under call and response between soloist and saxophone section.

Section	Measure	Event and Scoring
C	33–44	Two-measure saxophone lead in figure to fourth trumpet solo with plunger. Saxophones provide background with soli figures. Call and response between soloist and saxophones. Brasses lay out.
D	45–56	Fourth tenor saxophone solo. Trombones and baritone saxophone provide background figures.
	57–68	Tenor solo continues. Brasses provide backgrounds. Trombone 1, baritone saxophone and bass trombone are grouped together with different rhythmic figures than remainder of brasses
E	69–80	Tutti ensemble soli for two bars at *mezzo piano* followed by interplay between brass and saxophones at *forte* featuring tutti ensemble and soli sections. Careful attention should be paid to dynamics and articulation. Measure three of Letter E is *forte* and many slurs occur between eighth notes tied to triplets. There is a contrast in dynamics and articulation from the first three measures of this section and the remainder of the section until Letter F.
F/85	81–104	Second trombone solo with rhythm section accompaniment at measures 81–92. Backgrounds enter at rehearsal number 85, and enter in the following order: fourth tenor with baritone saxophone; first and second altos and third tenor; and brass section. Saxophones enter softly and brasses punctuate with stinging accents and shakes to build intensity.

Section	Measure	Event and Scoring
G	105–116	Piano solo with rhythm section accompaniment only. Refer to recordings for appropriate style. Count Basie was a very "economical" pianist.
H	117–128	Tutti ensemble soli for eight measures. Dynamic change to *piano*. Drummer should play on hi-hat only for contrast. Interplay between brass and saxophones with brass playing quarter notes against saxophones eighth notes. Brass quarter notes should be played very short, and saxophone eighth notes are swung with a legato attack. Saxophones should emphasize upbeat eighth notes. Upbeat eighth notes on the bass trombone part should be emphasized in order to create the "chugging" effect between brass and saxophones. This effect will return several times in the chart. Sixteenth notes at the end of the phrase should be played in a separated style, with the first note strongly accented.
I	129–140	Ensemble soli continues. *Mezzo piano* is the dynamic indication, however the band will *crescendo* into Letter J. The softer the band can play at this point, the more impact they will have during the upcoming shout chorus. The drummer should set up the shout chorus with eighth note triplets one measure before the shout occurs and catch the accent on the upbeat of beat four.

Section	Measure	Event and Scoring
J	141–151	Shout chorus. The lead trumpet voice should really cut through here. The entire ensemble must play nuances exactly as the lead trumpet. This is the highest point in the chart! Sing phrases to solidify style and articulation. Listen to recordings for authentic interpretation. Piano triplet fills are important here also.
Tag	152–166	The chart cools down here after the shout. The band will enter at *mezzo forte* and soften to *mezzo piano*. Roles reverse during interplay between brass and saxophones as they alternate between quarter note against eighth note patterns; recreating call and response "chugging" effect. Fourth trumpet enters conversation with plunger solo every two measures. Solo continues into last chord of chart.

Unit 8: Suggested Listening

Basie, Count, *Blues Alley*, Laserlight Digital.
Chairman of the Board, Roulette Jazz.
On the Road, Pablo.
April in Paris, Polygram Records.
Basie, Count, *The Complete Atomic Basie*, Blue Note Records.

Unit 9: Additional References and Resources

Bernotas, Bob, Frank Foster interview, 1992, revised 1999 (http://www.melmartin.com/html_pages/Interviews/foster.html).
Kernfield, Barry, *The New Grove Dictionary of Jazz, Volume I* (New York: Macmillan Press, 1988).
Sheridan, Chris, *Count Basie: a Bio-Discography*, (Westport: Greenwood Press, Inc., 1986).
Walker, Leo, *The Big Band Almanac* (Cambridge: Da Capo Press, 1989).

Contributed by:

Robert Griffin
Director of Bands
Howard W. Blake
High School of the Arts
Tampa, Florida

Teacher Resource Guide

Body and Soul

Edward Heyman

(1907–1981)

Robert Sour

(1906–1985)

Frank Eyton

(1894–1962)

Johnny Green

(1908–1989)

arranged by George Stone

Unit 1: Composers

Edward Heyman was born in New York on March 14, 1907. He studied at the University of Michigan after which he moved back to New York. Credits included Heyman who contributed songs to film scores including That Girl From Paris, Curly Top, Kissing Bandit, Delightfully Dangerous and Northwest Outpost.

Robert Sour was a lyricist and composer and also the president of Broadcast Music Incorporated (BMI). As well as writing the lyrics for Body and Soul, Sour also composed lyrics for the song Walkin' by the River.

Frank Eyton was born in London on August 30, 1894. Eyton collaborated with composer Noel Gay on many stage musicals such as Lights Up, The Love Racket, and Sweetheart Mine.

Johnny Green was born in New York on October 10, 1908. Whilst Green was studying at Harvard and bandleader Guy Lombardo heard his Harvard Gold Coast Orchestra and hired him to create dance arrangements for his nationally famous orchestra. Green wrote a number of jazz standards, including Out of Nowhere and Body and Soul. As well as being a notable pianist he wrote the scores for various films and TV programs.

Unit 2: Composition

While spending time in London, Johnny Green wrote *Body and Soul* for Gertrude Lawrence. Jack Hylton & His Orchestra recorded the ballad first in Britain, but it was Paul Whiteman and His Orchestra (Jack Fulton, vocals) who popularized it. The song follows a standard 32-bar AABA form and was written in concert D♭, modulating to D for the bridge.

Unit 3: Historical Perspective

On October 15, 1930, *Body and Soul* appeared in the Broadway revue, *Three's a Crowd. Body and Soul* was one of the revue's most popular songs, and Holman's recording rose to number three on the recording charts. Despite its popularity, *Body and Soul* was in fact banned from radio for nearly a year because of its somewhat suggestive lyrics. In spite of, or maybe because of, its racy lyrics, an astounding number of renditions made the charts in the 1930s and 1940s. Louis Armstrong was the first jazz artist to record *Body and Soul* in 1930, with his version staying close to the song's melody. Armstrong's New Orleans colleague Henry "Red" Allen's version recorded in 1935 explored the improvisational possibilities of the tune. In 1938, tenor saxophonist "Chu" Berry further explored the changes in a manner continued a year later by his mentor Coleman Hawkins. Out of all the hit recordings of *Body and Soul*, Coleman Hawkins' is the best remembered. In 1973, the National Academy of Recording Arts and Sciences inducted Hawkins's 1939 recording into the Grammy Hall of Fame. The original recording is on Coleman Hawkins's *Body and Soul* CD.

Unit 4: Technical Considerations

This chart is rated Medium Difficult, and the recommended tempo is ♩ = 120 or faster. However, this chart works well at a slower tempo too.

The lead trumpet range is very manageable and only goes up to concert F (f), and the lead trombone range goes to concert G (g). Trumpets need to double on flugelhorns. The melody is beautifully harmonized and will require players to listen carefully to their tuning. Solos appear in both the lead alto and tenor parts which are written out with chord symbols for more advanced players to improvise on the changes which feature the ii–V^7–I progression as well as tritone substitutions.

The piano part has both chord symbols and written chords and the guitar part contains both written lines and chord symbols.

Unit 5: Stylistic Considerations

This particular arrangement of *Body and Soul*, which is traditionally played as a ballad, is done in a medium swing style. The overall style of the piece is reminiscent of earlier music arranged by both the composer Gil Evans and the Canadian arranger Rob McConnell. The notated articulations should be strictly adhered to so as to play the harmonized passages accurately and with the feel that the arranger intended.

This arrangement is a great showcase for the entire ensemble with many intricate details in the phrasing and dynamics, which can be brought out in rehearsals. Lead alto and tenor saxophones also get a chance to feature as soloists.

Unit 6: Musical Elements

MELODY:

The melody along with phrasing and articulations should be learned vocally, with the entire ensemble singing their parts. It is also recommended that all players listen to several different recorded versions of the tune by different vocalists and instrumentalists. Keeping the vocal feel of the melody throughout is crucial for this tune.

HARMONY:

The melody retains its original key of D♭ major modulating to D major in the bridge. George Stone uses tritone substitutions extensively in this arrangement along with his use of altered dominant seventh chords and root suspensions. The use of these arranging tools makes the melody sound thick along with harmonic surprises for those familiar with the chord structure. Young players will benefit from playing and hearing these harmonic structures within the ensemble.

RHYTHM:

The chart begins with the drums playing a swing pattern on the snare with brushes. It is important that the band can feel both the quarter note and underlying triplet feel without hearing the hi hat and ride cymbal. Players should be encouraged to listen to the drum pattern in isolation then sing the

introduction as written. The solo sections at measure 73 have a "two" feel before the drums switch to sticks at measure 83.

Unit 7: Form and Structure

The form of the composition is AABA.

SECTION	MEASURE	EVENT AND SCORING
Melody (1)	1–16	The tempo is ♩ = 120 or faster. Lead alto and second trumpet (on flugelhorn) have the melody with lead tenor and trombone playing a counter melody with rhythm section. This first statement of the melody is exposed and players need to observe their articulations and dynamics carefully and play together as if they were in a small combo. In measure 16 the full band comes in on a triplet figure which should not be played too loudly.
Melody (2)	17–33	The full band plays the second part of the melody which is fully harmonized. There are moving inner parts which complement the melody and these should be isolated and rehearsed independently. All accents should be played strictly as written and long notes should be given a subtle *forte piano* so as not to overwhelm other moving parts.
Bridge	33–49	The saxophones have the melody which is harmonized with both rhythmic and melodic embellishments. The trumpets and trombones have separate counter melodies and backing figures which again should be rehearsed in isolation. The saxes are marked *forte* whilst the brass begin *piano* and gradually build in volume through to measure 49.
Melody (3)	49–57	Lead alto has the melody with rhythm section accompaniment.

Section	Measure	Event and Scoring
	57–65	Full band restates melody.
	65–83	Trumpets switch from flugelhorn to trumpet for this repeated section over the changes to the A section. It features the saxes, trumpets and trombones playing three separate themes respectively. In the first eight measures followed by solos from the alto and tenor saxes in the second eight measures.
	83–101	The bridge now modulates to concert F major where the trombones state the melody to the bridge for the first six bars before giving way to an ensemble theme which moves towards the D.S. for a key change back to concert D♭ major. Trumpets switch back to flugelhorn for the D.S. The dynamics from measure 97 are important to set the scene for the melody on the D.S.
Coda	101–end	Full band plays a series of block chords before a short rhythmic figure to end the chart.

Unit 8: Suggested Listening

Armstrong, Louis, The *Essential Louis Armstrong*, PolyGram Records.
Hawkins, Coleman, *Body and Soul*, RCA Records.
Holiday, Billie, *Body and Soul*, Verve Records.
Rob McConnell and the Boss Brass, *The Jazz Album*, Concord Records.

Unit 9: Additional References and Resources

Dunscomb, Richard, and Willie L. Hill, Jr., *Jazz Pedagogy: The Jazz Educator's Handbook and Resource Guide* (Miami: Warner Brothers, 2004).

Contributed by:

Eddie Severn
Freelance Trumpeter and Composer
Saylorsburg, Pennsylvania

Teacher Resource Guide

Cobblestones

Kris Berg

(b. 1961)

Unit 1: Composer

Kris Berg was born in St. Louis, Missouri on April 21, 1961. He started playing violin in the fourth grade, switching to bass the next year, when there was not a bassist in the program. The Berg family moved to Bonne Terre, Missouri when Kris was in the eighth grade. There, director Bill McCaleb introduced him to the electric bass, and jazz. In high school, other educators that had a profound impact on Berg's development include his high school band director Dennis "Bake" McBride, and noted Missouri educator Jim Widner. He earned his masters and bachelors of music in jazz studies at the University of North Texas, where he directed various jazz ensembles and taught big band arranging.

Kris has performed with many great artists including Kurt Elling, Randy Brecker, Bob Mintzer, Bobby Shew, Jimmy Heath, Doc Severinsen, Clark Terry, John Fedchock, Frank Mantooth, and Matt Harris. Kris Berg's arrangements have been performed and recorded throughout the world. A few of his arrangements include: *Narnian Dance* (1997), Pacific Coastin' (1997), Dave Brubeck's *Blue Rondo ala Turk* (2005), and the best selling arrangement of Pee Wee Ellis' *The Chicken* (2001). Mr. Berg is currently director of jazz studies at Collin County Community College in Texas, an artist clinician for Yamaha basses and is author of the book *Bass Lines in Minutes*, published by Hal Leonard.

Unit 2: Composition

Cobblestones was originally written for "The Zebras," a multi-keyboard fusion group, at the University of North Texas, directed by Dan Hearle. The melody was changed in this arrangement for obvious breathing considerations. The saxophone section introduction is actually one of the keyboard parts.

Kris was greatly influenced by the counterpoint in the Bill Holman blues, *Kingfish*, recorded by the Stan Kenton Orchestra. Due to the fact many of the charts he writes are for younger ensembles, involving various technical limitations, Berg believes in creating linear interest through this use of counterpoint. He says this creates confusion, which builds excitement. One can also hear the influence of Thad Jones and Bob Mintzer in this chart.

Another compositional tool Berg employs is the use of traditional root movements, spiced up with unexpected sonorities. The seeds of these ideas are found in the music of Jeff Lorber (who loves Bill Evans) and Ronnie Laws.

Whereas Jaco Pastorius's electric bass playing on Pat Metheny's *Bright Size Life* was an important influence on Berg, the groove on *Cobblestones* is more related to Jimmy Haslip's playing on the Yellowjackets tunes *Matinee Idol* or *Sittin' In It*, Danny Wilson's performance on the Jeff Lorber recording of *Wizard Island*, or Clint Mosley on Ronnie Laws's recording of *Always There*.

Unit 3: Historical Perspective

The growing popularity of R&B, Funk, and Rock in the late 40s, 50s and 60s, and the advent of electric guitars and keyboards, had a profound influence on the development of jazz. The music of James Brown and the British Invasion led to the jazz funk excursions of Alexis Korner, Larry Coryell, Gary Burton and Miles Davis, whose music was later informed by Sly Stone, Jimi Hendrix and various recordings from Motown. The jazz side of this cross-pollination came from the language of Coltrane, Hubbard, Hancock, Corea and Tyner. In the 70s Stevie Wonder dominated the Funk scene along with bands such as Earth, Wind and Fire, and later Steely Dan. The grooves of Jeff Lorber and Ronnie Laws were more akin to this modern funk. Throughout the 70s and 80s improvisations combined with infectious dance grooves to give fusion mass appeal.

Unit 4: Technical Considerations

This arrangement is rated Grade 3, and the suggested tempo is ♩ = 112–116; a little slower would work, however. The lead trumpet goes up to a concert B♭, (b♭^{1}) and the lead trombone up to a G (g). The saxophone soli is difficult rhythmically and does not always lay well. The bass part is a series of funk ostinati alternating with through composed passages, which are frequently rhythmically aligned with the rest of the ensemble, thus a strong bass player is a necessity.

Unit 5: Stylistic Considerations

This is a driving funk chart with elements of Jeff Lorber, Stevie Wonder, Tower of Power and The Brecker Brothers. The time feel is derived from the bass locking with the bass drum and snare drum using a sixteenth note subdivision as opposed to the triplet subdivision coming from the ride cymbal in a swing chart. The comping is static and groove oriented throughout the repetitious chord progressions found in fusion. Variation in texture from s ection to section creates excitement throughout the chart as well as helping the solo section to build.

Unit 6: Musical Elements

MELODY:
Rhythmic subdivisions and articulations are the keys to the melodic content of this chart. It is about layering and synchronization. Counting, clapping, and singing the lines with consistent articulation is a must. Some ghosting of notes (on-off tonguing in saxophones) will help the syncopated accents, and keep the rhythmic drive. Listening to the Brecker Brothers for articulation would be helpful. Due to the Mintzer-like layering, dynamics are extremely important to prevent weighing things down and help in building the anticipation.

HARMONY:
Cobblestones is basically a series of vamps primarily in F minor. Kris Berg uses altered ii–V progressions, chromatic root movement (tritone substitutions) and suspended sounds to get there. Traditional root movement, with the unexpected sonority in the ♭VI chord, gives it the necessary tension and release to make the chart thrilling, as it moves to and from F minor.

RHYTHM:
The duple subdivision of this funk chart must be internalized by the players. Thinking "one-ee-and-a, two-ee-and-a," or "su-gar-da-ddy, su-gar-da-ddy," will help set this up. It is important that the drums and bass lock together while the bassist accurately performs the part to fit rhythmically with the horn lines. The piano part is frequently with the horns; and the guitar must fit into the puzzle without bogging down the groove. Learning these rhythmic subdivisions at a slower tempo, will reap great benefits.

Unit 7: Form and Structure

SECTION	MEASURE	EVENT AND SCORING
Intro	1–4	A rhythmic ostinato in an *a cappella* saxophone section functioning as a funky keyboard with the baritone saxophone providing the left hand sets up the entire composition. Internalizing the sixteenth note subdivision, through counting, clapping, singing, and setting articulation, will help the entire band here. The saxophones need to enter with a solid sense of rhythmic integrity being careful not to rush the quarter notes on beats three and four. The conscious subdivision will help this.
A	5–16	The ostinato continues, joined by the rhythm section. They are answered by the tenor saxophones who set the style and articulation.
A (repeat)	5–18	The repeat starts with a countermelody in second, third, and fourth trombones. The lead trombone, with second, third, and fourth trumpets, join the tenor saxophones. Again, sing together for articulation and rhythmic feel- copying the tenors, giving the line dynamic shape for direction.
B	19–25	The first trumpet joins to lead an ensemble call and response. The band should listen to the lead trumpet for articulation and the electric bass, which is doubling the lead line for intonation. Trumpets and tenors answer in unison with a variation of some of the melodic ideas found in the previous section.

Section	Measure	Event and Scoring
C	26–34	A new melodic cell starts in the saxophones, which rhythmically links to the bass line. The brass joins the rest of the rhythm section for syncopated pads which must build dynamically, leading to the unison two-four figure, where the note length and articulation is dictated by the lead trumpet and electric bass. This "extra" two-to-four measures breaks things up and adds excitement to the solo break.
D	35–42	This is the solo section for the lead tenor saxophone. It is a vamp in F minor with an altered ii–V. The soloist should be comfortable with F minor pentatonic melodic material and rhythms based on the internalized sixteenth note subdivisions. Adding altered and diminished sonorities resolving to minor can add excitement. Michael Brecker was great at this. Listen to Gerald Albright, Bob Berg, Hank Crawford, King Curtis, Kenny Gorelick (with Lorber), David "Fathead" Newman, David Sanborn, and Stanley Turrentine for articulation and phrasing. Learning the written solo first would be beneficial to get an idea of the style the arranger is going for.
D	43–50	The solo continues with backgrounds. The saxophones enter with a unison line related to the tenor melody at A, while the trumpets play syncopated jabs. Starting these a bit softer and then building will give the parts forward motion. The trombones enter on the second time in contrary motion and rhythmic counterpoint. Individual shaping will add excitement and not bury the soloist.

Section	Measure	Event and Scoring
C'	51–58	The solo climaxes over different harmonic content, basically F^{7SUS} to A♭m^7/D♭ with a chromatic walk-up in measure 58. Unlike the original section C, the trumpets do not join until the fourth measure to help build to the end of the solo. Make sure the last section does not end too big, so there is still somewhere to go, the soloist also needs to be aware of this. The band articulation at 58 must be the same as it was at 33. One could open up the first solo section D and cue the backgrounds at 43.
E	59–66	The rhythm section lays out, except for the pseudo reggae in the drums with the figure on the rim. Exercises from the Louis Bellson book would help this section and the entire arrangement. Continued focus on the subdivisions will help keep the rhythmic drive. This section involves stacking rhythmic vamps which line up on the "e" of four. The trombones set the foundation with the trumpets joining in after four measures.
E'	67–74	The contrapuntal texture thickens with the addition of the saxophone soli. The lead alto saxophone dictates the shaping and articulation. Learning some pentatonic shapes and vocalization, along with the constant focus on the subdivision, will help here. Measures 59–74 is a Bob Mintzer-like section where individual shaping and careful attention to dynamics is imperative, as the thickened counterpoint creates a controlled chaos, adding tension leading up to the release with the shout chorus at 76.

Section	Measure	Event and Scoring
F	75–86	The shout chorus (a full band tutti) must be sung together for shaping, articulation, and accents. The band follows the lead trumpet for style and listens to the electric bass for intonation.
C	87–94	This is the recapitulation of measures 26–34, without the two-four measure. Be careful not to start too loud so the band can build to the end.
A'	95–104	This is the same material from measure 9 with the addition of the saxophone melody from section C.
B'	105–114	This is an extended section B. These last three sections must use the confusion of the counterpoint to build excitement, thus the individual shaping and consistency of articulation again is paramount to successfully performing this piece. Have the entire band sing the last two notes to match length and inflection, keeping in mind the subdivision so the drum fill sets up the band.

Unit 8: Suggested Listening

Berg, Bob, *Short Stories*, Denon.
The Brecker Bros, *Straphangin'*, Arista Records.
Kenton, Stan, *Kenton Showcase*, Capitol Records.
Laws, Ronnie, *Pressure Sensitive*, Blue Note Records.
Lorber, Jeff, *Wizard Island*, BMG International.
Bob Mintzer Big Band, *Incredible Journey*, DMP.
Camouflage, DMP.
Wonder, Stevie, *Songs in the Key of Life*, Motown.
Yellowjackets, *Yellowjackets* Warner Brothers/WEA.

Unit 9: Additional References and Resources

Bellson, Louis, and Gil Breines, *Modern Reading Text in 4/4 For All Instruments* (Van Nuys: Alfred Publishing Company, 1985).

Bergonzi, Jerry, *Inside Improvisation Series, Vol. 2:"Pentatonics"* (Rottenburg: Advance Music, 1994).

Crook, Hal, *Ready, Aim, Improvise! Exploring the Basics of Jazz Improvisation* (Rottenburg: Advance Music, 1999).

Erskine, Peter, *Time Awareness for all Musicians* (Van Nuys: Alfred Publishing Company, 2005).

Gridley, Mark C., *Jazz Styles: History and Analysis* (Upper Saddle River: Prentice Hall, 2006).

Lorber, Jeff, www.lorber.com.

Shipton, Alyn A *New History of Jazz* (New York: The Continuum International Publishing Group, 2007).

Contributed by:

James Kaczmarek
Band Director/ General Music Instructor
James Shields Elementary
Co-Director South Shore Youth Jazz Ensemble
Chicago, Illinois

Teacher Resource Guide

Con Alma

Dizzy Gillespie

(1917–1993)

arranged by Michael Philip Mossman

(b. 1959)

Unit 1: Composer

John Birks "Dizzy" Gillespie was one of the most important jazz figures of the twentieth century. He was especially noted for his trumpet virtuosity, his role in the development of bebop, and his influence in bringing Afro-Cuban elements into mainstream jazz. Gillespie's improvisations were very advanced in terms of chromatic harmony and rhythm. Several of his compositions are considered jazz standards, including *Con Alma*, *Groovin' High*, *A Night in Tunisia*, and *Manteca*.

Unit 2: Composition

Con Alma is often performed by jazz players in a 12/8 Latin feel with a swing bridge. Dizzy's recorded big band arrangement, from the album *Afro*, features a 4/4, even eighths Latin feel. Michael Mossman's arrangement combines these various approaches. His chart moves from cha cha (4/4 even eighths) to *bembe* (12/8) to swing. The original melody is clearly stated, and the arrangement adds many complex counter lines, particularly in the saxophones.

Unit 3: Historical Perspective

Dizzy Gillespie played with numerous swing big bands, including groups led by Cab Calloway, Earl Hines, Benny Carter, and Billy Eckstine. Gillespie first became interested in Afro-Cuban music while playing with Cuban trumpeter Mario Bauza in the Cab Calloway band. Bauza went on to become the musical director of Machito's Latin jazz group, the Afro-Cubans. Gillespie later worked with other important Afro-Cuban musicians including Chano Pozo and Chico O'Farrill. Gillespie's interest in combining bebop with Afro-Cuban music in a big band setting culminated in several recordings, including the album *Afro* in 1954, which featured the first recorded version of *Con Alma*. *Afro* combined traditional jazz big band instrumentation with a Latin rhythm section. Mainstream jazz musicians eventually embraced the fusion of Afro-Cuban rhythm with jazz forms and harmonies.

Unit 4: Technical Considerations

The difficulty level of this chart is Intermediate. The arrangement is marked ♩ = 130. The lead trumpet range goes to concert C above the staff (c^2). The lead trombone is written to A♮ (second space treble clef [a]). The rhythm section and horn parts are both rhythmically complex. Rhythm section parts are carefully notated. They are a great help in achieving authentic feels throughout the chart. There is a one-chorus solo for first tenor saxophone. The soloist will need to have the ability to interpret fairly advanced chord changes. There are no woodwind doubles. The arrangement calls for cup mutes in the trumpets for a brief passage at the end.

Unit 5: Stylistic Considerations

Authenticity of groove is very important in this chart, not only for the rhythm section but the horns as well. Printed articulations should be followed carefully, and the band should sing lines together to establish articulations and nuances that are not marked.

Unit 6: Musical Elements

MELODY:

The A section of the melody consists of long, flowing phrases made up primarily of half notes with some triplet and quarter note motion near the cadence points. This gives the melody a chorale-type character. The bridge melody is more syncopated, which fits its swing accompaniment. The counter lines are often derived from the bebop language and should be played with bebop inflections, including proper articulation and ghosting. As is typical of big band notation, the presence or lack of slurs should not be interpreted as articulation markings.

HARMONY:
Michael Mossman uses many substitute and passing chords in this arrangement. In order for these to be heard with proper balance and intonation, the band members must hear each individual note in context of its chord. Stack chords from the bottom up to let the band hear how each note fits. Make sure the students are aware of doublings across the band and who has the melody.

RHYTHM:
Time feel and groove should be addressed as soon as possible in rehearsals. The saxophone, trumpet, and trombone sections should think of their parts as orchestrated drum parts. Having each section play with the drums and percussion, or with a partial drum/percussion part, will solidify the time feel. One of the challenges of Michael Mossman's arrangement is the rhythmic variety. New rhythms and variations on existing rhythms are introduced frequently. Each new rhythm should be practiced and rehearsed until it is as comfortable as the previous rhythms.

Unit 7: Form and Structure

The basic form of the composition is AABA.

SECTION	MEASURE	EVENT AND SCORING
Intro (1)	1–5	The band has primarily unison rhythms.
Intro (2)	6–17	The saxophones have pyramid figures; trumpets and trombones have primarily unison melodic figures; climax of intro occurs at measure 14.
Intro (3)	18–21	The *bembe* groove is introduced by drum set and percussion.
Melody: A	22–29	The melody is played by unison trumpets; trombones 1–3 have a unison counter line. Guitar and piano double the above parts. Bass and drum parts could be deviated from after the written parts are comfortable.

SECTION	MEASURE	EVENT AND SCORING
Melody: A	30–37	An active saxophone counter line is introduced.
Melody: B	38–45	Bridge; trumpets, trombones, and saxophones trade melody and counter lines; make sure each section knows who has the melody at any given time—teach the entire band the melody soon after introducing the chart. Bass could improvise walking line for first four measures, but should play part as written starting at measure 42.
Melody: A	46–54	Melody is scored for all wind instruments; rhythm section supports melody; bass part should be played as written.
Tenor solo	55-85	Background figures are based on complex triplet subdivisions, so make sure band is feeling triplets or 12/8. The bridge is swing, but the rhythm section maintains a 12/8 groove, so the swing feel in the wind instruments must be very strong. The rhythm section switches to a double-time Latin feel for the second A section (measures 62–69).
	86–102	Band soli; measure 94 is a phrase extension, making the A section from measures 86–94 a nine-measure phrase.
	103–110	Bridge melody returns.
	111–118	Recapitulation of A melody in brass, with saxophone counter line.
	119–126	Drum breaks, building to next section.
	127–142	Return of intro material builds to end.

Unit 8: Suggested Listening

Dizzy Gillespie Orchestra, *Afro*, Verve Records.
Dizzy Gillespie and the United Nation Orchestra, *Live at Royal Festival Hall*, Red Ink Records.
Getz, Stan, *Sweet Rain*, Verve Records.

Unit 9: Additional References and Resources

Gioia, Ted, *The History of Jazz* (New York: Oxford University Press, 1997).
Malabe, Frank and Bob Weiner, *Afro-Cuban Rhythms for Drumset* (Miami: Manhattan Music Publications/Warner Brothers Publications, 1990).

Contributed by:

Tim AuBuchon
Director of Jazz Studies
Truman State University
Kirksville, Missouri

Teacher Resource Guide

Filthy McNasty

Horace Silver

(b. 1928)

arranged by John LaBarbera

(b. 1945)

Unit 1: Composer/Arranger

Composer Horace Silver was born in Norwalk, Connecticut on September 2, 1928. His father had immigrated to the United States from Cape Verde—and that island nation's Portuguese influences would play a big part in Silver's own music later on. When Silver was a teenager, he began playing both piano and saxophone while he listened to everything from boogie-woogie and blues to such modern musicians as Bud Powell and Thelonious Monk. Now surrounded by a devoted family in California, Silver has received much of the recognition due a venerable jazz icon. In 2005, the National Academy of Recording Arts and Sciences (NARAS) gave him its President's Merit Award.[1]

John LaBarbera started playing cornet when he was five years old. By the age of seven he was playing jobs with the LaBarbera Family Band, consisting of his parents and brothers (Pat on saxophone and Joe on drums). During the late 1960s, John performed in the trumpet section of the Buddy Rich Big Band. During this period he developed his love for composition and arranging. LaBarbera went on to write music that was recorded and performed by Buddy Rich, Woody Herman, Count Basie, Dizzy Gillespie, Sammy Davis Jr., Mel Torme, Chaka Khan, Harry James, Bill Watrous, The Glenn Miller Orchestra, Al Cohn, Bill Perkins, Phil Woods, and others. As co-producer and arranger for The Glenn Miller Orchestra Christmas recordings, *In The Christmas Mood I &*

II, John received Gold & Platinum Records. He is also a co-founder of the world famous all-female big band, DIVA.

Mr. LaBarbera is a two-time recipient of the National Endowment For the Arts award for Jazz Composition, and was nominated for a Grammy award in 2004 for his big band recording, *Fantazm*. His published works distributed by Kendor Music and Hal Leonard Publishing are considered standards in educational jazz literature.

In addition to his professional writing career, John LaBarbera is an Associate Professor of Music at the University of Louisville and serves on the faculty at the Skidmore Summer Jazz Institute in upstate New York. John spent seven years as Jazz Editor of the International Trumpet Guild, is a long standing member of the International Association for Jazz Education, and is a sought after clinician and lecturer throughout the U.S. and abroad.

Unit 2: Composition

This arrangement is scored at an accessible Grade 4 level with a recommended tempo marking of ♩ = 130, with a duration of 5:40. The source material has all the defining elements of Horace Silver's music, including a memorable melody, a strong groove, and a combination of musical styles—namely blues, gospel, and hard bop. The basic blues form does not stray far from that of the original hit recording, with first alto saxophone, first trumpet, and first trombone featured on melodic material. Improvised solo space is offered for first alto saxophone and first trumpet, with supporting backgrounds punctuating the last chorus of each solo. A first trombone solo follows before a rousing shout chorus brings this classic chart to an exciting finish.

Unit 3: Historical Perspective

During the 1980s, the number of touring professional big bands was on the decline, due primarily to economic considerations and changing musical tastes. However, jazz music continued to develop a strong presence in North American educational institutions, later gaining footholds in Europe, Japan, South Africa, and Australia. Many prominent big band writers began to compose and arrange jazz music for student and military groups, which became the last bastion of big band jazz. Although composing and arranging for these groups provided a new revenue stream, writers such as John LaBarbera were equally concerned with preserving big band music for posterity. While writing original big band charts remained important, it was, and continues to be, essential to expose developing musicians to classic jazz music such as the songs of Horace Silver. In 1983 John LaBarbera arranged Silver's popular *Filthy McNasty*. It remains a staple in big band jazz libraries to this day.

Unit 4: Technical Considerations

Lead trumpet range extends to concert B♭ (fifth octave [b♭[1]]) and trombone to G (fourth octave [g]). Drastic deviations from the suggested tempo marking may compromise the playability or effectiveness of certain rhythmic figures. The drummer is required to render a solid swing shuffle groove. Although the guitar, piano, and bass parts contain some notation, these players are required to negotiate parts that are predominantly chord changes and rhythm slashes.

Unit 5: Stylistic Considerations

Horace Silver's piano playing and writing style fuses elements of blues, gospel, and hard bop. In John LaBarbera's big band treatment, he captures the true flavor of Horace Silver's 1961 and 1962 quintet versions. These recordings (see Unit 8 below) featuring side players Blue Mitchell (trumpet), Junior Cook (tenor saxophone), Eugene Taylor (bass), and Roy Brooks (drums), will help players properly emulate the stylistic nuances of the piece.

Unit 6: Musical Elements

MELODY:

The simple, yet infectious melody has a sassy playfulness. At first glance, it appears to be set in a rock feel, but strict adherence to articulation markings will ensure a convincing shuffle groove. Key centers are well defined, as dictated by the basic blues progression.

HARMONY:

The harmonies are not particularly complex, with frequent use of basic $V^{7(\sharp 9)}$ chords reminiscent of the jazz/rock sound of the 1960s and 1970s. LaBarbera often orchestrates first and second altos in unison, employing a similar technique for first and second trumpets on occasion. Though posing some intonation challenges to developing players, this effectively compacts the voicings to produce a small group sound.

RHYTHM:

With the exception of a few sixteenth notes in the melody, the relatively simple rhythms are easy to negotiate. Even eighth-note figures in the horn parts juxtaposed with stop-time hits by the rhythm section occasionally interrupt the shuffle feel for added rhythmic dimension. Again, the suggested listening in this guide will assist players with proper assimilation of the gospel flavored jazz/rock feel commonly used during this period of jazz history.

Unit 7: Form and Structure

The basic form of the arrangement is 12-bar blues.

SECTION	MEASURE	EVENT AND SCORING
Intro	1–8	The tempo is ♩ = 130, which allows players to learn the piece up to tempo. A trio consisting of alto saxophone, trumpet, and trombone make robust musical statements, alternating with strong ensemble replies. For optimum results, be sure to faithfully observe articulation markings.
	9–21	The same trio backed by the rhythm section states the lively melody as a combo within the big band. Deliberate playing is called for during this section.
	22–32	The saxophones are assigned the melody, supported by trumpets and trombones alternating ensemble hits. This section, which also includes some staccato even eighth-note figures, should be played with meticulous precision.
	33–45	As marked, this solo section occurs six times—three times for each improviser with backgrounds occurring on the third chorus of each solo. The easily negotiated blues form ends with a predictable iii–VI–ii–V turnaround. Although guitar and piano have specific rhythms followed by rests, comping between the figures is appropriate and recommended.
	45–54	Soloists alternate two-measure phrases with the ensemble. Improvisers should edit their ideas to yield to the ensemble entrances.

Section	Measure	Event and Scoring
	55–56	The trombone soloist plays an unaccompanied solo break based on the turnaround chords. The soloist is advised to maintain a steady time feel during the break in order to guarantee a clean reentry by the ensemble.
	57–68	The trombone solo occurs three times through the form with trumpet backgrounds joining the second time and saxes the third time. Special care should be taken to defer to the soloists by playing background figures crisply but not excessively loud. Dynamic markings to this affect are provided. Listen to recordings of Horace Silver's original recordings to hear how Blue Mitchell and Junior Cook conceptualized their improvised solos for stylistic compliance.
	69–75	Tutti ensemble orchestration kicks up the excitement level a notch. Excessive overblowing could cause intonation problems here. For the same reasons, be mindful of unisons in the first and second alto saxophone parts and the first and second trumpet parts.
	76–80	The trio of section leaders returns with a brief statement supported by the rest of the ensemble. Background players should play this line with assurance, while taking care not to upstage the soli players.
	81–100	The rest of the saxes join the trio through measure 88 before making the final statement. Once again, the remainder of the horns remain in a supporting role, taking care not to eclipse the sound of the trio.

Unit 8: Suggested Listening

Abate, Greg, *Horace Is Here*, KoKo Jazz Records.
Horace Silver, *Doin' The Thing/Horace Silver Quintet Live at the Village Gate*, Blue Note.
Horace Silver, *Paris Blues*, Pabla.

Unit 9: Additional References and Resources

Jarvis, Jeff and Doug Beach, *The Jazz Educator's Handbook* (Delevan: Kendor Music, 2002).
Silver, Horace, *Let's Get To The Nitty-Gritty: The Autobiography of Horace Silver* (Berkeley: University of California Press, 2006).

Contributed by:

Jeff Jarvis
Director of Jazz Studies
California State University, Long Beach
Long Beach, California

1 http://www.horacesilver.com/silverpages/inside.php?mod=bio.

Teacher Resource Guide

Footprints
Wayne Shorter
(b. 1933)

arranged by Matt Harris
(b. 1959)

Unit 1: Composer

Wayne Shorter was born on August 25, 1933 in Newark, New Jersey. He attended Newark Arts High School where he studied art. Shorter was an average art student with an almost insatiable interest in film until he heard a radio show that presented a new style of music, "bebop." His interest was kindled and at fifteen years old he started taking private lessons on the clarinet. He later turned to the tenor saxophone and, along with his brother Allan (alto sax player turned trumpeter), joined local music groups. As a teenager Shorter competed against saxophonists Sonny Stitt and Sonny Rollins.

After graduating from New York University, Wayne was drafted into the U.S. Army. He spent two years in the army during peacetime and was able to play in the army band while continuing to compose during his off time. At the end of his army career, Shorter performed with Horace Silver and Maynard Ferguson. In 1959, he worked with and eventually became the musical director for Art Blakey and the Messengers. In 1964, Shorter replaced John Coltrane in Miles Davis's Quintet where he played with Herbie Hancock, Tony Williams and Ron Carter. Shorter, whose love for Latin, Classical and jazz was evident in his compositions, ventured more into a style labeled Fusion. He and keyboardist Joe Zawinul started the group Weather Report in 1970 and they became a premier showcase for this new style of jazz. After fifteen years with Weather Report, Shorter continued to lead bands and record and compose for many great artists.

Wayne Shorter's career of over forty years is incredibly documented in his nearly 100-album discography. He has performed/recorded with other notables such as Donald Byrd, Lee Morgan, McCoy Tyner, Steely Dan, Carlos Santana, and Joni Mitchell. In 2004, Shorter's C.D. *Alegria* 2003 received a Grammy Award for Best Instrumental Jazz Album. This album featured many musicians including drummer Terri Lyne Carrington and percussionist Alex Acuna. His quartet with Danila Perez, John Pattitucci, and Brian Blade continues to perform.

Unit 2: Composition

Footprints has been recorded more often than any other of Wayne Shorter's masterpieces. It was first recorded in 1966 on his album entitled *Adam's Apple.* That same year it was also released on Miles Davis's album *Miles Smiles.* Shorter felt that the ascending and descending melodic lines over the repetitive bass lines and accentuating percussion was indicative of Miles's expressive temperament.

Shorter originally recorded this piece as a 12-bar minor blues in 6/4 time but this arranger and many other arrangers notate it in 3/4 time stretching the form from twelve to twenty-four measures. Matt Harris gives the melodic line to the trumpet, trombone, guitar, and tenor and baritone saxophones while the bass repeats one line changing only a single note to solidify the chord progression played by the keyboard. This allows the ensemble to recreate the mood set by the original masters. The full ensemble repeats the melodic line with close harmony adding tension released only when the saxophones play the final phrase in unison against a traditional brass shout.

Unit 3: Historical Perspective

Wayne Shorter's career began to blossom in the 1950s after the end of the Korean war and in the midst of civil unrest in the United States. He attended America's first high school for the arts and New York University, two schools that nurtured freethinking, which had been a part of Shorter's spirit. Questioning the status quo had become a part of the fabric of America and this was also evident in the music of the jazz musicians. They had begun to experiment with rhythms and harmonies juxtaposing styles that created new avenues for improvisation. Small ensembles had begun to replace the big dance bands of the swing era.

At this time, Newark was known for being a difficult place to survive; however, its proximity to New York allowed for many artists to have the opportunity to learn and share their craft with the masters. From 1961–1970, Shorter recorded albums with Donald Byrd, Miles Davis, Freddie Hubbard and many other legends.

Unit 4: Technical Considerations

This chart is rated at the medium advanced level. The recommended tempo is ♩ = 160 with a duration of 5:10. The chart works best at the recommended tempo. Be careful not to drag the 3/4 time because it needs to feel more like 6/4 time but taking it any faster destroys the intended feel of the four against three (as in measures 37, 44, 76, etc.).

The first trumpet has an optional concert G one octave above the staff (g^2) and a concert C (d^2) written within the melody lines. The first trombone part has an A♭ written one octave above the staff (a♭). The first alto saxophone part has a soprano saxophone double for the first half of the chart. An optional B♭ bass clarinet part is provided for the baritone saxophone chart.

The bass part is written out until the solo section of the chart. A written bass part is not provided again until the final twelve measures of the piece. The guitar part has written melodic lines with chord symbols for the other sections. The piano chart has suggested chords for each chord symbol.

The close harmonies written for the tutti sections will challenge the players to balance out their parts while being sure that the intended sonorities remain prevalent. The solo changes are navigable by most soloists at this level.

Unit 5: Stylistic Considerations

This arrangement of *Footprints* is written as a jazz waltz; however, the intent is for the chart to be played with an up-tempo 6/4 feel. It was initially written for Wayne Shorter's combo with Tony Williams on drums. The drummer here should play loosely around the three feel without giving the feeling of a strict waltz. Williams explored rhythms especially with the cymbals while bassist Ron Carter established the time.

Soloists should feel free to explore rhythms and scales that would be more reminiscent of the styles of Wayne Shorter and Miles Davis.

Unit 6: Musical Elements

MELODY:

Harris simply writes the melody for tenor saxophone, baritone saxophone, trumpet, trombone, and guitar. He carefully ends each section alternating between two phrases: 1) a dotted quarter note and three eighth notes, and 2) four quarter notes in the space of three beats, recreating the original mood of the composition. Learning this simple but intriguing melody will help the soloist with improvisation.

HARMONY:
The melody is played over a 12-bar minor blues form (called a 24-bar blues for the remainder of this section). The tonic chord is played over a recurring bass line. The bass line continues the tonic on the first beat of the ninth measure but changes the subsequent notes in that measure to establish the subdominant chord to be played by the piano in the tenth measure. The final 8-bars uses extended chords in cycles of fours starting on F♯ before returning to the tonic to complete the phrase.

In the section that begins at measure 174, arranger Matt Harris uses the melody from John Coltrane's composition *Giant Steps*. (Coltrane preceded Shorter as the saxophonist for Miles Davis.) The melodic line is harmonized and given to different players throughout the passage.

RHYTHM:
This up-tempo swing should have more of a 6/4 feel than a waltz. The arranger indicates that the drummer should vary the rhythms of the high hat and not play consistently on the one of the second measure. This will help give the feel of a free flowing three rather than the um pah-pah um pah-pah of a waltz. The bass player keeps a consistent pattern for the band allowing the drummer to vary the rhythmic patterns adding a sense of intensity to the phrases. The band should be able to feel the one first a heavy one and than a light one without having to count three beats to a measure.

Unit 7: Form and Structure

This composition is a 24-bar minor blues.

SECTION	MEASURE	EVENT AND SCORING
Intro (1): A	1–16	The intro begins a half step above the key of the composition. Have students play notes one at a time, sustaining them, while adding other parts, starting with the baritone sax and fourth trombone. Allow them to hear the dissonance. Do this for each chord. The bass line must be played as written between the four bass parts. Play this composition slower than the indicated ♩ = 160 in order to make sure that the students are playing the correct pitches and to give them a chance to adhere to the dynamic markings.

Section	Measure	Event and scoring
Intro (2): B	17–24	The band sustains the chord decreasing the volume level while the rhythm section sets up the style.
C/D	25–28	This soli section should be rehearsed in a small group in order to insure continuity of style. The lines drawn to connect the first four measures are phrasing marks and not slurs. Each note in this grouping should be articulated with a light tongue as in the syllable "loo." Be careful not to cut the final note of the phrase too short. It works to give that note its full value.
		The next four measures comprise the rhythm section's answer to the melody. Measure 37 has a four quarter-note grouping to be played against the three beats maintained by the rhythm section. Have the band practice feeling this song in a one with first a heavy one for the first one, two, three than a light one for the second one, two, three. When the emphasis is placed on the one, it is easier to place the grouping of four quarter notes as you would four sixteenth notes on one beat and the three quarter notes as eighth-note triplets on one beat.
	49–52	This is the interlude again, establishing the rhythm section's groove.
E/F	53–68	This time the melody is harmonized for the entire horn section. Check each chord individually from the bottom up just as you did for the introduction. It is very important that each section is balanced in order for the melody in the top voices to be heard. Every voice should move at the same time with the same articulation. The tenor sax solo is every four bars but the player plays the written notes with the tutti section.

Section	Measure	Event and scoring
	69–74	This is a traditional brass shout section played against the melody. The brasses and drummer must come out of the melodic mode in order to give the hits with the proper drum set up.
	75–76	The low voices have a beautiful ending to this section with the delayed sound of the three against four. Strive to sound like one voice.
G/H	77–100	This is an open solo section for piano. The bass part is chorded for walking bass however the solo is open for bass or guitar.
I/J	101–124	The band returns with soft background work complete with muted brass and contrasting rhythms.
	125–148	The open solo section is for tenor saxophone.
	149–173	The brasses return with traditional brass hits but the saxophones enter with contrasting melodic lines.
K/L	174–196	The full ensemble plays in unison rhythmically while the bass player continues to walk the changes. Take creative license to vary the dynamic level on the repeat. Also, consider adding dynamics to the sustained notes that conclude each phrase.
	197–end	This ending should be treated the same as intro two. The chord in the horns fades away leaving only the rhythm section until the final muted chord is played.

Unit 8: Suggested Listening

Coltrane, John, *Giant Steps*.
Davis, Miles, *Miles Smiles*, Blue Note Records.
Shorter, Wayne, *Footprints: The Life and Music of Wayne Shorter*, Columbia/Legacy.

Unit 9: Additional References and Resources

Mercer, Michelle, *Footprints The Life and Work of Wayne Shorter* (New York: Penguin Group, 2004).
http://wikipedia.org/wiki/Wane_Shorter (accessed July 1, 2006).

Contributed by:

Roxanne Stevenson
Director of Bands
Chicago State University
Chicago, Illinois

Teacher Resource Guide

Georgia on My Mind

Hoagy Carmichael

(1899–1981)

arranged by Dave Bardhun

Unit 1: Composer/Arranger

From jazz music to Hollywood pictures, Hoagland (Hoagy) Howard Carmichael's artistic life parallels the glamorous rise of pop American cultures from the past century. Hoagy, whom by the forties had become nothing short of an American icon, was in fact not only a remarkable songwriter, but also a lyricist, pianist, singer and actor.

Born in Bloomington, Indiana in 1899, Carmichael's early musical influence came from his mother, who played piano at university dances and local movie houses. Hoagy's infatuation with jazz stemmed out several years later, on listening to Louie Jordan's Band, an early jazz ensemble led by Afro American musicians. While studying law in Indiana, Hoagy formed his first band, The Carmichael Syringe Orchestra and eventually met the great cornet player Bix Beiderbecke, with whom he recorded some of his own compositions such as *Riverboat Shuffle* and *Georgia on My Mind.*

Predictably, Hoagy abandoned his law training in Indiana and moved to New York where he struggled to establish himself as a musician and songwriter. Some of his compositions were progressively noticed and played by leading bands of the time. By 1930, Hoagy Carmichael had composed some of his most famous songs including the very popular *Stardust.*

Success and fame would finally come towards Hoagy's way on moving to Hollywood in 1936, where he successfully established himself as a popular songwriter, pianist/singer, actor and even TV show host. As a songwriter, Hoagy had already placed three songs on the Hit Parade by 1946: *In the Cool, Cool, Cool of the Evening*, *Lazy Bones*, and the classic ballad *Skylark*. Other memorable Carmichael compositions include *The Nearness of You*, *Lazy River*, *I Get Along Without You Very Well*, and *Ole Buttermilk Sky*, nominated for an Oscar as Best Song in 1947.

Unit 2: Composition

Hoagy Carmichael wrote *Georgia on My Mind* in 1930 on the suggestion of his friend, Frankie Trumbauer, a prominent jazz saxophonist of the time, who encouraged Carmichael to write a song about the southern United States. The poetic lyrics of the song, written by Stuart Gorell, create a charming ambiguity about whether Georgia is truly a place or a woman. The introductory verse is often omitted. The melody develops over a standard 32-bar AABA form. Dave Baudhun's arrangement for Big Band maintains the southern taste of a *bluesy* ballad with a 12/8 feel and features the first alto sax throughout the chart, with the ensemble complementing with catchy backgrounds and lines with triplet feel beneath the melody.

Unit 3: Historical Perspective

On September 15, 1930, Hoagy Carmichael assembled an orchestra of some of the most accomplished jazz musicians of the time to record *Georgia on My Mind* in a Victor studio session. Among the musicians present in the studio were some of the luminaries of early jazz, such as: Bix Beiderbecke on the cornet (who died just a year after the recording), Jack Teagarden on trombone, Jimmy Dorsey on clarinet and alto sax, Bud Freeman on tenor sax, 'Pee Wee' Russell on alto sax, Joe Venuti on violin, and Eddie Land on guitar.

The song reached number ten in the charts for the first time, however, thanks to saxophonist Frankie Trumbauer, who recorded the song just a year after this all-star session. The song has appeared on the Hit Parade several additional times since then, most notably in 1941 as recorded by Gene Krupa with Anita O'Day, and the more famous version in 1960 recorded by Ray Charles with Ralph Burns and his orchestra, finally reaching number one on the charts.

Georgia on My Mind was designated as the official state song of the state of Georgia by the Joint Resolution of the Georgia General Assembly on April 24, 1979.

Unit 4: Technical Considerations

This chart is from the *Hal Leonard Jazz Ensemble Library* (Grade 4), and the recommended tempo is ♩ = 60, which enhances its slow, 12/8 feel.

The lead trumpet range goes to a concert C above the staff (c^2), and the lead trombone to a concert A above the staff (a). No doubles are needed for this chart. Bass line parts are written out, as are suggested voicings for the piano and a suggested solo for the lead alto saxophone, which is assigned the entire melody and given the only improvisation feature of the chart.

Harmonically, the changes of this arrangement are relatively simple and do not stray from the original song, except for a brief re-harmonization of the second half of the bridge during the shout chorus section. The challenge of this chart rests more in its stylistic interpretation than in the technical level of the various sections. The chart is fairly manageable for a moderately advanced ensemble. A skilled lead alto player and drummer, however, are highly recommended for the success of this chart.

Unit 5: Stylistic Considerations

A gospel-like mood may be emphasized for an effective and colorful interpretation of this arrangement. The rhythm section should be familiar with the classic big bands shuffle styles and imply a similar 12/8 bouncing swing feel, but in a slow ballad tempo with a marked "layback" frame of reference. The lead alto player should carry and interpret the luscious and longing melody with much freedom, dynamics, and stylistically bluesy nuances reminiscent to Cannonball Adderley's approach to ballads. A more experienced player should be also encouraged to idiomatically embellish the melody throughout the charts, with exception to those few bars where the lead alto is playing in rhythmic unison with the ensemble. The ensemble parts should carry a similar "dirty" and "layback" swing feel, with much attention to locking the triplet feel phrases and articulation in sync with the rhythmic section's bouncing slow 12/8 feel.

Unit 6: Musical Elements

MELODY:

The haunting, yearning melody of *Georgia on My Mind* should be learned by rote and initially exposed to the ensemble in several of its many vocal and instrumental renditions (Billie Holiday, Ray Charles with the Count Basie Orchestra, James Brown, Louis Armstrong, etc.). The the longing and somber color of the melody is characterized by the prevalence of skips of minor thirds and perfect fourths in the A sections and the use of a minor pentatonic motive in the bridge.

HARMONY:
Section A of *Georgia on My Mind* is in F major and follows the very popular harmonic formula of several standards songs of this era, with a brief modulation to the relative minor (D minor) and a turn-around back to the major key via a pivotal ♭VII chord in the fourth measure as a connecting link. (Usually a dominant chord, the arranger treats this as a major VII chord instead, with exception of measures 44 and 68.) Section B remains stable in the relative minor key with an interesting use of an implied Dorian sound in the fourth measure, where the melody stresses a ♮6 and a ♭7over a non-resolving ii–V (Dm^7–G^7). A II^7 chord in the sixth measure of the bridge favors the harmony back to the turn around that will reestablish the major key of section A.

RHYTHM:
This arrangement requires the whole band to be extremely attuned to the rhythmic interpretation of the 12/8 swing feel. It may be challenging to maintain a steady and smooth feel at the suggested ♩ = 60. A good teaching strategy is to have less experienced ensembles play at a slightly faster tempo, and perhaps as a straightforward shuffle. When the triplet-bouncing feel is understood, agreed upon, and fully internalized across the ensemble sections, the band should then attempt to play it as a ballad while trying to maintain the same playfulness and bouncing feel of the shuffle at the slower tempo.

Unit 7: Form And Structure

The basic form of the composition is AABA.

SECTION	MEASURE	EVENT AND SCORING
Intro/A	1–8	Lead alto saxophone plays the melody freely without accompaniment. Bass and drums enter at measure 7. The conductor should mark the steady ballad tempo on measure 7, leaving the alto saxophone much freedom of interpretation in the first six bars of the melody.
	9–14	The lead alto saxophone plays the first A section of the melody in time and in a small combo setting, without any other horns. Make sure that the rhythmic session establishes the proper ballad feel with confidence and swing.

Section	Measure	Event and Scoring
	15–16	The saxophone section in unison (except for the baritone saxophone playing chord roots) and the trombone section play a two-bar phrase leading to the second A section beneath the lead alto's last melody note of the verse.
B	17–24	The lead alto saxophone plays the second A section of the melody with a simple baritone saxophone and trombone section background that becomes progressively busier rhythmically. Although not in the score, the dynamics of the background may increase gradually from measure 20 on, to prepare the sudden *crescendo* played by the whole ensemble and leading to an ***ff*** by the end of measure 24.
	25–33	The lead alto saxophone plays the bridge of the melody and the whole wind section harmonizes a counter line in rhythmic unison. Make sure to immediately drop the dynamics of the ensemble from ***ff*** to ***mf*** in measure 25. The drums should carefully match the rhythmic figures of the wind section while keeping steady time. Add dynamic contours throughout the phrasing of the wind sections and accent the upbeats with short and crisp articulation. Lock the triplet phrasing of the winds with the rhythmic section triplet swing feel throughout this section.
C/D	33–40	The full band plays most of the last A section, harmonizing and/or complementing the melody carried by the lead alto saxophone. Watch for dynamics ranging from ***ff*** to ***mf*** and back to ***ff***.

SECTION	MEASURE	EVENT AND SCORING
	41–56	The alto saxophone solo changes, AA of the AABA, form. (The suggested written solo may work well with the rhythm section's double time feel.) The rest of the wind sections lay out.
	57–64	Tutti section with first trumpet lead. Make sure all phrasing matches the lead trumpet and the section player's articulation while swinging hard at this slow tempo. Establish a "layback" interpretation across the section to enhance the bluesy mood, but make sure the energy level of this section stays up and that the rhythmic section keeps a steady tempo without dragging the time. Again, match the triplet phrasing of the winds with the rhythmic section 12/8 in measures 63–64, and make sure that the tenuto marking over the triplets is performed with a certain laid back attitude.
F	65–73	The lead alto saxophone plays the ending section of the melody with a baritone saxophone and trombone section background. There is an optional alto saxophone cadenza in between the final fermati.

Unit 8: Suggested Listening

Armstrong, Louis, *Georgia On My Mind*, Prism Records.
Carmichael, Hoagy, *Hoagy Sings Carmichael*, Pacific Records.
Fitzgerald, Ella with Pass, Joe, *Speak Love*, JVC Victor.
Holiday, Billie, The *Very Best of Billie Holiday*, Mastersong.
O'Day, Anita and Krupa, Gene, *Let Me Off Uptown: The Best Of Anita O'Day*, Columbia/Legacy.
Count Basie Orchestra and Charles, Ray, *Ray Sings*, *Basie Swings*, Concord Records.
Webster, Ben, *At the Renaissance*, JVC Victor.

Unit 9: Additional References and Resources

Dunscomb, Richard, and Willie L. Hill. Jr., *Jazz Pedagogy: The Jazz Educator's Handbook and Resource Guide* (Miami: Warner Brothers, 2004).

Lee, William F. III, *America's Big Bands* (Milwaukee: Hal Leonard Publishing Corporation, 2006).

Sudhalter, Richard M., *Stardust Memory: The Life and Music of Hoagy Carmichael* (Oxford: Oxford University Press, 2002).

Contributed by:

Marco Pignataro
Director of Jazz & Caribbean Music Studies
Puerto Rico Conservatory of Music
San Juan, Puerto Rico

Teacher Resource Guide

Jumpin' Punkins
Mercer Ellington
(1919–1996)

transcribed by David Berger
(b. 1948)

Unit 1: Composer

Mercer Ellington was born in Washington D. C., March 11, 1919. He was the son of world famous composer, pianist, and bandleader, Duke Ellington. He tried his entire life to escape the shadow of his famous father, but never did. A talented trumpet player, Mercer studied music with his father and actually wrote his first composition, *Pigeons and Peppers*, at the age of eighteen. Mercer studied music in New York at Columbia University and the Institute of Musical Arts at Julliard. He had several professions in life, including salesman, disk jockey, record company executive, trumpet player, and his father's aide.

Mercer performed in Sy Oliver's Band after World War II, led his own band for a number of years, and was music director for Della Reese in 1960. He took over as leader of the Ellington Orchestra after his father's death in 1974. In 1988 he won a Grammy with the Ellington Orchestra for *Digital Duke*. This recording pulled together many of the former greats of the Ellington Orchestra, including Clark Terry, Norris Turney, and special guest artists such as Branford Marsalis and Sir Roland Hanna.

Mercer also wrote a biography of his father titled *Duke Ellington in Person*. The book gave a personal account of Duke Ellington from a son's perspective.

Unit 2: Composition

Mercer wrote *Jumpin' Punkins* (1941) when his father asked him, to join the band as a writer. It is believed that even though Mercer composed several compositions during the following two years, Duke himself actually arranged the music for the Ellington Orchestra. This would account for the near perfect adherence to many stylistic concepts of harmony and voicing used by Duke during this period. The composition also contains the swing and style of many other Ellington Orchestra compositions recorded during this period. The parallel voicing of the chromatic clarinet and baritone sax melodies are very reminiscent of many Ellington Orchestra compositions. This 32-bar form with a 20-bar interlude still has the blues and dance as its main focus. The main emphasis of this composition still emphasizes the greatness of the individual performers in the Ellington Orchestra. With Duke Ellington on piano, Harry Carney on baritone sax, Jimmy Blanton on Bass, Barney Bigard on Clarinet, and Sunny Greer on drums, the composition was a great vehicle for soloists. It seems very obvious that this composition was specifically written as a dance composition during this era because of the traditional dance swing rhythms employed throughout.

Unit 3: Historical Perspective

During the early 1940s, there was an ASCAP strike that affected all music, especially big bands and their popularity. The broadcast industry (radio) refused to program any music written by ASCAP composers, which included Duke Ellington. This led to bands not being able to get any dance hits generated through radio, which led to a decline in touring performances. Duke asked his oldest son, Mercer to join the Ellington Orchestra as a songwriter to get songs published through a new performance rights organization established by the broadcast industry, BMI. Mercer wrote his best compositions during this two year stint (1940–41), including *Things Ain't What they Used To Be* (reported to have been won in a card game from Johnny Hodges), *John Handy's Wife*, *Blue Serge*, *Moon Mist*, and of course, *Jumpin' Punkins*.

The early 1940s saw two of the greatest soloists in the music business, bassist Jimmy Blanton and tenor saxophonist Ben Webster joining forces with the great Johnny Hodges on alto saxophone in the Ellington Orchestra. The level of compositions for the Orchestra increased tremendously because of the great talent available to perform the music. This was also the time that Billy Strayhorn, a former member of the Mercer Ellington Band joined the Duke Ellington Orchestra as well. *Jumpin' Punkins* was written as one of the compositions to specifically showcase this great talent as well as provide material for arguably the greatest of the Duke Ellington Orchestras. It also provided the compositions for one of the greatest recordings in the history of the Duke Ellington Orchestra, "The Blanton-Webster Band."

Unit 4: Technical Considerations

This chart is rated Grade 3–4, and the recommended tempo is ♩ = 120–137 with a duration of 3:41. This works well as a dance jump tempo. This chart is best for intermediate to advanced jazz bands due to the extended range of the lead trombone, which is common in Ellington arrangements.

The lead trumpet range extends to concert A in the third octave (a^1), and the lead trombone range goes to concert B♭ (third octave [b♭]).

This composition employs a very singable saxophone section introduction that recapitulates in the 8-bar ending section. The brief but effective ostinato bass line, masterfully performed by bassist Jimmy Blanton on the original recording, is very important in setting up the driving dance feel for the composition. The piano solo at section A should be played as written because it introduces the melody and because of the interplay between the melody and the open fifth bass line that drives the swing feel forward. The repetitive stylistic swing rhythms throughout the piece adds a very cohesive feel and dance intent to the composition is very playable by saxophonists of any age. The instrumentation calls for clarinet double in the tenor saxophone and no doubles in the brass section. There is the usual six brass instrumentation, which is common for big bands during this era.

There are very predictable key centers in this composition with complex, "Duke" type passing chords throughout the piece. The solo sections have predictable changes with written solos that should be learned first, chord changes, then create an original solo in the style of the referenced recording. Complete study of the transcribed solos from the original Ellington recording is suggested. The use of chromatic progressions throughout the composition adds variety, excitement, and interest to a composition that is well crafted as an exciting piece of dance oriented music.

The bass line and piano parts are fully voiced and written out for less experienced jazz bands, but include chord symbols to allow for creativity of more advanced players. The guitar part, however, does not have any parts written, just chord symbols. Be sure to imitate the guitar comping on all four beats heard on the recording because it is very rhythmic and employs the third to seventh resolutions in the voicings.

Unit 5: Stylistic Considerations

This danceable, swing-style composition is reminiscent of the hard-driving Ellington Orchestra style of the Blanton-Webster years. The articulations are very similar to the Basie/Louis Armstrong type popularized in the 1940s. *Jumpin' Punkins* is a composition that swings at a broad range of tempos and should be taken at a slower tempo until younger bands understand the style of articulations and phrasing.

This selection would also be an ideal feature for clarinet and baritone saxophone. (The original recording featured Barney Bigard on clarinet and Harry Carney on baritone sax.) There are many examples of swing rhythms that can be isolated to teach swing feel and syncopation throughout this composition. This composition also provides many examples of the importance of repetition that can used to teach style and interpretation in jazz. Because the chart doesn't demand an abundance of technique, it lends itself to teaching blues inflections and many other important jazz concepts needed to perform more complex literature. Dynamics and balance with the clarinet as lead with the saxes and even the brass section is very important. Listening to hear the orchestrated harmony is very important.

Unit 6: Musical Elements

MELODY:

The simple, but strong melody should be learned vocally, without notation, using call and response with the entire ensemble while listening to the original recording. The sequence and repetition of melodic ideas is a unifying force throughout the composition. The key centers are well defined with logical progressions. The unifying melodic rhythm is also very traditional swing for this era, and is specifically blues-oriented with swing-style syncopations. The melody was used throughout the composition as different colors in orchestration are introduced. The piano sets the melody and mood for the entire composition.

Make sure when singing the melody, all attacks, releases and specifically the blues inflections are incorporated. The attention to detail will make the performance concepts much easier.

HARMONY:

The melody and changes are very blues-oriented between the I and IV chords in section A with tritone progressions added as movement, starting in concert C. Mercer Ellington uses a tritone bridge with the B^7 chord to add contrast and a great deal of movement and excitement to the composition. He also uses chromaticism in the harmonic progressions through the use of tritone substitutions.

Chromatic dominant chord movement to D minor (ii chord) in section C in the full ensemble scoring also adds harmonic excitement to the stop-time

drum breaks. It is very obvious that Duke was either a great teacher or that he actually arranged the Mercer compositions for the Ellington Orchestra.

RHYTHM:
The swing, jump dance feel requires that the entire band feel the four downbeats as well as the triplet pulse on each downbeat. It may be necessary to encourage everyone to coordinate the feel of four quarter note beats set by the bass drum and bass guitar while feeling the triplet pulse (doo-od-la). Make sure the band starts at a moderate to slow tempo. There are concepts presented in earlier chapters that address teaching rhythmic feel in the large jazz ensemble. Make sure the entire band feels the last third of the beat pulse as they attack or sing beat one. In other words, rather than feeling 1–2–3–4, try, "ah-one, ah-two, ah-three, ah~four."

Singing stylistic and rhythmic articulations is very important in any swing composition. Have students sing rhythmic examples from the composition daily.

Unit 7: Form and Structure

The basic form of the composition is AABA (32-bar) with a 20-bar (8+8+4) interlude section (section C), framed by a 6-bar intro and ending.

SECTION	MEASURE	EVENT AND SCORING
Intro (1)	1–6	The tempo is ♩ = 137. Learn the composition at a much slower tempo until the swing and style are established. Alternate the saxophone section melody with clarinet lead and bari sax in octaves, bass included, and drums fills. Exaggerate the swing feel and phrase direction through use of appropriate dynamics. All ending notes are accented with short articulations. Listen to the use of the obvious blues inflections on the recording. Clarinet must really spend a great deal of time listening to the recording because of the lead responsibilities for the entire ensemble. Listening to learn is very important for the entire ensemble. Imitate to emulate.

Section	Measure	Event and Scoring
A	7–14	Piano introduces the main theme for the composition, while the guitarist (ala Freddie Green), bass (ala Jimmy Blanton), and drums (ala Sonny Greer using brushes) maintain the rhythmic feel and forward drive. Everyone should sing and learn the melody as it introduced stylistically correctly by Duke Ellington on the recording. This melody will be the basis for the cohesion of the composition. Bassists work the bass line as Jimmy Blanton introduces it, because the parallel moving line is a driving force in the rhythm section.
B	15–22	The hard driving jump feel has to be maintained in the rhythm section as the piano maintains the melodic theme. Continue to feel the triplet pulse and well as the four beat jump dance feel. The clarinet solo should be rooted in the blues.
C	23–30	The bridge. Piano leads with the melody and a two-measure riff is repeated throughout the saxophone section with the alto lead. This section changes key center via a B^7 chord (tritone). Make sure all lines are vocally oriented and articulated in the same manner. Add dynamic contours throughout the phrasing with everyone following the piano and lead alto and listening to the entire section. Exaggerated swing phrasing is required, tongued short and accented (dot-doo-dot-dot). Sing all phrases along with the original recording to agree on style and articulations.

Section	Measure	Event and Scoring
D	31–38	Piano maintains the melody on the return to section A section of the form. Saxophones with clarinet lead, and answer the piano in a very traditional blues tone as it relates to the history and development of the jazz language. Clarinet has the lead, so listen for balance and keep the blues and swing as the main focus. Saxes need a big swinging sound at measures 37–38 with the clarinet as lead.
E/F/G	39–62	Baritone sax solo with changes, with trombones playing backgrounds. Trombones need to sing through all rhythms with everyone singing the lead trombone line along with the original recording to agree on style of phrasing and articulations (short exaggerated notes). All ending notes are characteristically short and accented. In measures 55–62, the bridge section (B of the AABA form) employs a very rhythmic comping section in the trombones that has to be very accented and precise. Trumpets join the backgrounds as the solo returns to the A section of the form.
H	63–70	The baritone sax solo continues as the melody returns in the A section of the form with brass and clarinet leading. The clarinetist should listen to the original recording in order to better lead the ensemble. Trumpets and trombones have to really listen to balance the clarinet lead. Dynamics throughout the section are very important. The bari sax solo as played by the great Harry Carney is very important, since it was written specifically for him. Learn the original recorded and transcribed solo, then work to create your own in a similar style. Spend time at the piano studying the progressions.

Section	Measure	Event and Scoring
I/J/K	71–90	This section uses full ensemble scoring and chromatic writing to create a great stop-time environment, originally played by the great sonny Greer on drums. Make sure all articulations are the same and the clarinet is heard, because it has the lead for the entire ensemble. The bari sax and double bass have to be very confident on beat 1. The rhythms are very traditional and predictable, and should adhere to the Louis Armstrong/Cootie Williams model of articulations. Singing rhythms and individual parts is valuable for style and balance. Use very obvious dynamics contours to build to the drum breaks. In measure 87–90, the composition sets up the return to the original form and the saxophone section.
L	91–98	This section features a saxophone soli that is not technically challenging but stylistically very important to the composition. Pickups to this section have to be very aggressive and confident. The intent to swing has to be very obvious. Listen and sing along with the original recording while feeling the triplet pulse and the four-beat dance feel. Follow all dynamic contours. Rhythm section has to play a *subito piano* at the beginning of this section.
M	99–106	A repeat of the A section of the form with the entire ensemble listening and responding to each other melodically and rhythmically. Trombones have the melody while the bass begins to prepare for the next section to follow. Trumpets should remember that cup mutes are used to create a sense of urgency in the composition.

Section	Measure	Event and Scoring
N	107–114	A return to the B section or bridge, where the composer uses the entire ensemble to create the excitement of a train sound that many other Ellington compositions have displayed. The melody is in the piano, but the repletion and exaggeration of the rhythm is very important. All should feel the anticipation of the triplet pulse so that the forward motion is maintained. The cross rhythms between the brass section and the rest of the ensemble has to be very obvious.
O	115–122	This is the final A section of the composition; it uses the sax section with a clarinet lead to introduce the final version of the melody with piano answering.
P	123–128	Recapitulation of the introduction with the saxophone section and the clarinet playing the lead. The drum fills have to be in the exact jump swing style as the entire composition. Dance on the drums!

Unit 8: Suggested Listening

Count Basie Orchestra:
The Complete Atomic Basie, Blue Note Records.
April in Paris, Polygram Records.
Duke Ellington Orchestra, *The Blanton-Webster Band, 1940–42*, RCA, 1987.
Duke Ellington, *The Great London Concerts*, Music Masters Jazz.

Unit 9: Additional References and Resources

Dunscomb, Richard, and Willie L. Hill, Jr., *Jazz Pedagogy: The Jazz Educator's Handbook and Resource Guide* (Miami: Warner Brothers, 2004).

Thigpen, Ed, *Rhythm Brought to Life: A Rhythmic Primer* (Van Nuys: Alfred Publishing Company, 2000).

Contributed by:

Ronald Carter
Director of Jazz Studies
Northern Illinois University
DeKalb, Illinois

Teacher Resource Guide

Le Belleclaire Blues

James Morrison

(b. 1962)

Unit 1: Composer

James Morrison was born in Boorowa, Australia in 1962. He starting playing at nine, and was performing professionally in nightclubs when still only thirteen. He graduated from the New South Wales Conservatorium of Music in 1980 and was appointed a lecturer the following year.

After touring with Australian Jazz Legend Don Burrows for six years, James was ready to launch his own international career. He rapidly developed a reputation as a virtuosic multi-instrumentalist, playing trumpet, trombone, tuba, euphonium, flugal horn, saxophone, and piano with equal and extraordinary facility, and this led Leonard Feather to write in *Downbeat* that "James Morrison is as sure a bet for jazz superstardom as Wynton Marsalis was in 1981."

In 1987 James played with Dizzy Gillespie at the Montreux Jazz Festival and subsequently toured with the Phillip Morris Big Band and then with Ray Charles and BB King. He has also played with many other jazz legends, including Cab Calloway, Woody Shaw, Red Rodney, and Wynton Marsalis. In 1992, Morrison recorded *Two the Max* with Ray Brown, Benny Green, and Jeff Hamilton.

Morrison has performed, by invitation, for Presidents Clinton and Bush at Parliament House in Canberra, Australia and for the Queen and Princess Anne in London.

In addition to being a wonderful ambassador for jazz in Australia, Morrison also supports and sponsors the National Band Competition and his own scholarships each May at Generations in Jazz in Mount Gambier, South Australia.

Unit 2: Composition

Each year, Morrison writes the set piece for the First Division at Generations in Jazz in Mount Gambier. *Le Belleclaire Blues* is one of these set pieces, and has now also become popular with professional and student big bands around the country. The composition is a blues piece, very much in the tradition of Count Basie, but it also has Morrison's distinctive flair, energy, chord substitutions, and extensions that mark it as a contemporary composition.

Unit 3: Historical Perspective

In Australia, the big bands survived into the seventies and eighties with "The Daly Wilson Big Band" in Sydney and the "Will Upson Big Band" in Western Australia both good examples. Both groups survived by playing some commercial arrangements in addition to standard arrangements from the swing era and original compositions by writers like Ed Wilson and Graeme Lyall. Morrison, however, with his reputation and high profile, has been able to keep the tradition alive with his own big band, which he organizes together with his brother, John, on drums.

Big bands are popular in schools and there are a growing number of community big bands around the country.

Unit 4: Technical Considerations

This chart, published by Wilson Publishing, is available rated as a Grade 5+ and Grade 3+. The only essential difference is that trumpet, and, in places, some trombone parts have been taken down an octave or revoiced so that they are playable by performers with less-developed high ranges. It is the Grade 5+ chart which is closest to Morrison's recording and which is reviewed here.

The recommended tempo is ♩ = 120 with a duration of 4:13. The lead trumpet range goes to concert F (f^1) and the overall range is consistently high. The lead trombone goes to concert C (third octave [c^1]). The saxophone soli is not technically demanding, but requires appropriate *swing phrasing*, and the baritone player must sometimes be able to play an independent line at the very bottom of the instrument's range. Apart from the improvisatory sections bass line parts are fully notated (also with chord symbols). There are three quite challenging but short notated *solo breaks* for bass, which could be edited or improvised as necessary. The harmonic struckture is much more complex than found in many standard blues, and the piano part is most often fully notated, apart from the solo section (which has chord symbols). The guitar part has chord symbols and some rhythm indications. Experienced soloists will likely use appropriate harmonic generalization while playing the essential changes in the face of so many chords within a 12-bar sequence.

Unit 5: Stylistic Considerations

This medium groove composition, which moves from a "two-feel" to a standard swing "four-feel" and draws on the tradition of the early blues form, the typical driving force of the Basie band. Also present is the dynamic energy of Morrison's writing and playing, which is particularly evident in the trumpet section. The lead part has Morrison's style and hallmark all over it.

Articulation on all parts is quite detailed, and adhering to them, together with appropriate blues inflections, is essential in order to capture the style and spirit of the arrangement.

Morrison is always able to surround himself with excellent side playersThe original recording of *Snappy Duo* features Ray Brown on bass, Jeff Hamilton on drums, Herb Ellis on guitar, and Morrison on lead trumpet. Incredibly, Morrison also plays all other trumpet, trombone and saxophone parts, including the tenor solo, and piano!

Unit 6: Musical Elements

MELODY:

At both the beginning and end of the chart, the melody floats across the changes with a pentatonic and suspended simplicity. The quarter-note triplets and wider intervals sound like a fresh version of a Basie tune that we have already heard, but the music never descends to the level of cliché. The second and extended shout chorus modulates so that the melody can be finally repeated a tone higher.

HARMONY:

The introduction, first statement of the melody, and the solo and shout choruses are all in E♭. The second shout chorus, which is extended to fourteen bars, sets up the modulation to F major. Throughout, it is a more complex blues structure in the tradition of Charlie Parker, with diminished passing chords, chordal and tritone substitutions, and more complex turnarounds. Chord roots are often specified, and this, together with augmented chords and altered extensions, makes for some very pleasing chromatic movement. At times the dense harmonies in the ensemble sections are more reminiscent of Thad Jones than of Count Basie.

RHYTHM:

The initial statement of the melody throughout the first two choruses exhibits a "two-feel," but there is already an underlying anticipation of the strong "four-swing style" which follows. A solid rhythm is essential so that the brass can place "shock" notes as part of the call and response (e.g., during the second chorus). In the two shout choruses, players must be able to phrase together on the quarter-note triplet and semiquaver figures and also on the offbeats. It is important not to anticipate, particularly notes that are off the beat. Practice slowly and sing phrases as necessary.

Unit 7: Form and Structure

The basic form of the composition is a 12-bar blues.

SECTION	MEASURE	EVENT AND SCORING
Intro	1–4	Tempo is ♩ = 120—a medium groove. Full ensemble. Practise getting the *turn* together and keep the *diminuendo* very even.
Melody	5–18	Initial statement of the melody by saxophones in unison. Use no vibrato and stay slightly under the lead alto's volume. On repeat, the dynamic level will increase as a call and response is introduced with the brass section. Trumpets and trombones need to get the "jazz turn" together. The tenor solo is set up by the bass solo break and offbeats, which must be short and together in measures 17–18.
Soli	19–43	Four choruses of tenor saxophone solo. It is important for both the soloist and those playing "backing lines" to build up the intensity of the solo. The backing lines are well orchestrated, but increasing the dynamics without overpowering the soloist is essential.
Shout Chorus	44–56	Measure 44 is the pickup into a full ensemble shout-style chorus at measure 45. This is a climax at *fortissimo*, and should contrast completely to the previous sections. This is the archetypal big band sound, with the drummer locked in and phrasing with the lead trumpet, which has cues on the part.

SECTION	MEASURE	EVENT AND SCORING
Shout chorus and interlude	57–71	This section is part shout chorus and part interlude, with an extra two bars and a modulation into a recapitulation of the original melody a step higher. The style of the previous chorus continues until the last four bars (measures 67–70) when the *subito mezzo piano* and bass solo anticipates and re-establishes the mood of the first two choruses. This is actually a recapitulation of the second chorus in the new key, but now played *forte* and *fortissimo*. The bass has another solo break in measure 74.
Coda	81–90	Although not marked as such, this is the coda. Trumpets now phrase with saxophones, as trombones provide underpinning for the harmonic structure with longer tones. Listen to the lead trumpet. This is again reminiscent of a Count Basie ending, but there are no final subtle piano sounds; rather a dense chord, off the beat, and drum fills bring the music to an appropriate conclusion.

Unit 8: Suggested Listening

Basie, Count, *Ken Burns Jazz*, Verve.
So Far So Good: the Best of James Morrison, WEA Records.
Snappy Doo, Morrison Records.

Unit 9: Additional References and Resources

Berg, Shelly, Lou Fischer, Fred Hamilton, and Steve Houghton, *Rhythm Section Workshop: For Jazz Directors* (Van Nuys: Alfred Publishing Company, 2006).

Dunscomb, Richard, and Willie L. Hill, Jr., *Jazz Pedagogy: The Jazz Educator's Handbook and Resource Guide* (Miami: Warner Brothers, 2004).

Contributed by:

Brian W Copping
Jazz Coordinator
School of Instrumental Music
Perth, Western Australia

Teacher Resource Guide

Li'l Darlin'

Neal Paul Hefti

(b. 1922)

Unit 1: Composer

Neal Paul Hefti, jazz trumpeter and composer/arranger, was born October 29, 1922 in Hastings, Nebraska. He started playing the trumpet in elementary school at the age of eleven, and by high school was spending his summer performing with local territory bands to help support his family. In 1939, while still in high school, he got his start in the music world by writing arrangements for the Nat Towles Band. The Earl Hines Band also performed some of his arrangements. Two days before his high school graduation in 1941 he joined the Dick Barry Band as a trumpet player. He traveled with the band to New Jersey, but was fired because of his inadequate sight-reading abilities. When Hefti moved to Los Angeles, California in 1943, he joined Woody Herman's First Heard Band as a trumpeter. Hefti composed and arranged some of Woody Herman's most popular recordings, including *Wild Root* and *Apple Honey*. Seeing still more avenues of expression, Hefti left Woody Herman in late 1946 and began freelance composing and arranging. He wrote charts for Buddy Rich, Billy Butterfield, George Auld, Charlie Ventura, Harry James, and most notably, Count Basie.

Unit 2: Composition

Hefti wrote *Li'l Darlin'* during his tenure with the Count Basie Band (1950–62). Although not technically demanding, this chart is a great educational tool for teaching the laid-back "Basie" style and rhythmic ensemble playing. *Li'l Darlin'*, which Count Basie slowed down even more than Hefti had intended, is probably the best known of Hefti's big band charts. Listen to the many recorded versions of this chart by the Count Basie Band and you will hear that each performance is a little different. This chart is a 32-bar form with a four-measure piano introduction and a thirteen-measure coda.

Unit 3: Historical Perspective

In 1950 Neal Hefti met Count Basie and started composing and arranging for what became known as the Count Basie New Testament Band. Hefti's compositions and arrangements resulted in a new band style that was maintained for more than twenty-five years. One of Count Basie's most successful albums was called *Basie*, now commonly referred to as *The Complete Atomic Basie* (1957). This album featured eleven compositions written and arranged by Hefti, including the popular jazz standard ballad *Li'l Darlin'*, which became a signature composition for the Count Basie Band. Other Hefti masterpieces included on this album were *Fantail*, *Teddy The Toad*, *Splanky*, and *The Kid From Redbank*. Although Hefti received numerous awards for his compositions, including two Grammy Awards for *Li'l Darlin'*, *Splanky*, and *Teddy The Toad*, he is best known in jazz education for his long collaboration with Count Basie. Additionally, he occasionally led his own bands during the late 1950s, but concentrated on writing for films while still being influenced by his jazz experiences.

Unit 4: Technical Considerations

Li'l Darlin' is a professional-grade chart written for the Count Basie Band. Although this chart is best suited for an advanced high school or university/college jazz ensemble, arrangements are available for young and first year jazz ensembles. Playing time is approximately 4:30.

Li'l Darlin' is all texture. The chart has a tendency to drag if played too slowly and will sound rushed if played too fast. A good tempo is one that gives the feel of a moderate two-step dance. This composition must be performed in the laid-back "Basie" style, with precise rhythmic ensemble playing.

The rhythmic ensemble concept is stylistically challenging with staccato and sostenuto markings. The melody is harmonized for full ensemble. The lead trumpet range is E♭ concert (e♭^{1}) and the lead trombone range is concert E♭ (e♭). The piano part is written out with chord changes. Dynamics, *diminuendos*, and *crescendos* are very important. There is also a solo harmon mute for fourth trumpet with saxophone backgrounds (subtoning). The guitar part must be played in the "Freddie Green" style (four strums to the bar" "choo-chit-choo-chit").

Unit 5: Stylistic Considerations

Neal Hefti's compositions and arrangements for the Count Basie Band are a colorful part of the fabric of twentieth-century jazz. In *Li'l Darlin'*, the simplicity of the notation is the key to its persuasive rhythmic drive and Basie groove. This composition is a good example of the Count Basie laid-back style and rhythmic ensemble playing. Basie maintained a big band that possessed an infectious rhythmic beat and the distinction of being a band that swung while playing softly. This chart places emphasis on simplicity, swing feeling, and producing a warm and colorful sound.

Unit 6: Musical Elements

MELODY:

The melody is sixteen measures, repeated 8+8. The melody is harmonized for the full ensemble, tutti with a unison rhythm. The melody does not require much technical ability; however, special attention must be given to articulation (staccato and sostenuto markings), attacks, and releases. Notes marked staccato should not be played too short, but with a "do" swing feel. The lead alto saxophone should perform as the lead voice, playing slightly above the lead trumpet and the lead trombone with a good jazz vibrato. This will give the melody a warm and colorful, "sassy" sound. The lead alto saxophone leads the jazz ensemble.

HARMONY:

The voicing style used in this composition is typical Neal Hefti as developed during his composing/arranging period with the Count Basie Band. Essentially it is four-part block voicing in saxophones and trumpets with trombones doubling trumpets an octave lower. The melody is harmonized for full ensemble with a unison rhythm. This chart does not include modulations; however, there are a few tonicizations, such as secondary dominants and tritone substitutes leading to target chords. To add color and harmonic excitement, augmented V^7chords and altered harmonies are used. The F major tonal center is well defined, with logical chord progression.

RHYTHM:

The rhythm scheme for this composition is basically a unison rhythmic pattern that requires the ensemble to swing with a laid-back feel. This is also required for the dotted quarter note that is played on the upbeat of beat 1. If this note value is not played correctly the swing feel will be lost. Practice clapping and singing the dotted quarter note on the upbeat with the correct attack. To best achieve the Basie swing feel, think of the meter as 12/8 with the straight eighth notes played as quarter/eighth triplet pairs with a laid-back feel. The best teaching tool for learning to swing this chart listening to recordings of the Count Basie Band, especially this chart. Stylistic swing and rhythmic patterns are required for a successful performance.

Unit 7: Form and Structure

Basic Form: Intro-AABA-coda. Total measures: 77, including all repeats.

SECTION	MEASURE	EVENT AND SCORING
Intro	1–4	Tempo: ♩ = 80–85. Be careful with the tempo, which should not too slow nor too fast, but must produce a good laid-back feel. The intro is played by the piano, guitar, bass, and drums (brush on cymbal) but could also be performed by the piano only, in the Basie style with the rhythm section coming in at rehearsal letter A with the full ensemble.
A	5–12	Tutti section; first part of the melody (eight measures). The melody is harmonized for full ensemble (measures 5–8). Guitar, piano, bass, and drums (using brushes) enter on the downbeat (beat 1). The full ensemble, with brass using bucket mutes, comes in with a unison harmonic rhythm and blocked chords on the second half of the beat. The attack for this note (a dotted quarter) is accented/sostenuto. Special emphasis must be placed on attacking this note together. Staccato quarter notes follow. The staccato must be performed using a "swing staccato" and a "do" swing feel, and the rhythmic ensemble pattern must not be rushed. The baritone saxophone part must be substantially supported to add gusto on the harmonic bottom. Measures 9–12 are a repeat of measures 5–8 with the exception of the harmonic scheme tonicizing the chord at rehearsal letter B.

SECTION	MEASURE	EVENT AND SCORING
	13–24	Second part of melody (8 measures). This section begins with an eighth-note pickup leading to a new melodic phrase, measures 13–16. This is unison harmonic rhythm with blocked chords, and attention must be given to the attack of the accented eighth-note pickup. The phrase should have an eighth-note swing feel accenting the second half when it is tied to a down-beat. The second part of this melody (measures 17–20—the first ending) is basically the same unison rhythm as measures 9–12, with a change in the harmonic scheme to return to rehearsal letter A. Section A is repeated and then goes to the second ending, measures 21–24. The melodic material and unison rhythm are the same as measures 9–12, with the harmonic scheme going to a ii^7–V^7–I progression in the home key
B	25–40	Rehearsal letters C and D feture a harmon-muted solo for fourth trumpet with saxophone backgrounds. This solo is transcribed from a Wendell Cully solo heard on *The Complete Atomic Basie* CD. This is a killer solo if played with a sassy vibrato, a down to earth laid-back feel, and a lot of emotion. The soloist should listen to Wendell Cully's version for style, phrasing, and performance concepts. The saxophone section should play softly (subtone) behind the solo, and be felt more than heard. Have saxophone work on sectional phrasing (attacks and releases) and a sectional laid-back feel. Along with the rhythm section, this will provide a colorful cushion for the soloist. This section ends with a D.S. al Coda. The D.S. returns to rehearsal letter A, measure 5.

SECTION	MEASURE	EVENT AND SCORING
A	5–16	D.S. back to rehearsal letter A and then to the coda. The material here is the same as discussed sections A and B above. Sections A and B (four measures) are played to measure 16, followed by a jump to the coda (measure 41). Do not play the first ending.
Coda	41–53	This is a four-measure tag utilizing the material found in the second ending (measures 21–24). This tag is repeated three times with the same basic harmonic scheme. The tag should be played softer each time without destroying the swing laid-back feel. The lead alto saxophone should lead the ensemble on these phrases. On the last tag there is a rallentando and a *decrescendo*; however, do not slow the phrase down too much, because it might kill your groove.

Unit 8: Suggested Listening

Basie, Count, *Li'l Darlin'* on *The Complete Atomic Basie*, Blue Note, 1957.
Basie, Count, *The Best Of The Count Basie Orchestra On Denon*, Denon Records, 1995.
The Count Basie Orchestra Directed by Frank Foster, *The Legend, the Legacy*, A&M Records, 1989.

Unit 9: Additional References and Resources

Boras, Tom, *Jazz Composition And Arranging* (Belmont: Thompson Schirmer, 2005).
Dunscomb, Richard and Willie L. Hill, Jr., *Jazz Pedagogy: The Jazz Educator's Handbook and Resource Guide* (Miami: Warner Brothers, 2004).
"Neal Hefti," http://www.everything2.com/index.pl?Nde=Neal%20Hefti.
Gridley, Mark C., *Jazz Styles: History and Analysis* (Upper Saddle River: Prentice-Hall, Inc., 2000).

Dance, Stanley, *The World of Count Basie* (New York: Charles Scribner's Sons, 1980).

Contributed by:

Russell Thomas, Jr.
Director of Jazz Studies
Department of Music
Jackson State University
Jackson, Mississippi

Teacher Resource Guide

Manteca

Dizzy Gillespie
(1917–1993)

Walter Gil Fuller
(1920–1994)

Luciano Pozo Gonzales
(1915–1948)

arranged by Mike Tomaro
(b. 1959)

Unit 1: Composers

Dizzy Gillespie was born in Cheraw, South Carolina on October 21, 1917. Named John Birks, the youngest of nine children and whose father was a weekend bandleader, he acquired the nickname of Dizzy because of his clownish behavior. A trumpeter, composer, and bandleader, Dizzy Gillespie became one of the most important and influential figures in all of jazz history. Along with Charlie Parker, he was the chief architect of the modern jazz style known as bebop.

As a trumpet player, he continued the lineage of Louis Armstrong and Roy Eldridge, but demonstrated a level of virtuosity on the trumpet that set him apart from others. His technical prowess was often represented by an agility and command of the high register of the trumpet, as well as fast tempos that he seemed to perform with ease. As an improviser and bop stylist, he set a performance standard that became a model for modern jazz playing from the mid-1940s forward. His recordings and performances with Charlie Parker defined a stylistic and improvisatory direction for jazz that continues to be utilized today.

Dizzy was a successful bandleader of small groups and big bands from 1942 until shortly before his death. He attracted many outstanding players to his bands through the years including Charlie Parker, Kenny Clarke, Sonny Stitt, John Coltrane, Ray Brown, Milt Jackson, James Moody, Wynton Kelly, Jimmy Cobb, Lee Morgan, and Slide Hampton. In addition to writing numerous arrangements for other bands, Dizzy was a noted composer who contributed several works for his small groups and big bands that became staples in jazz repertory, such as *Con Alma*, *Salt Peanuts*, *Things To Come*, *Bebop*, *Birk's Works*, *Blue 'n' Boogie*, *Ool-Ya-Koo*, *Woody'n'You*, and Latin and Afro-Cuban works such as *A Night In Tunisia*, *Manteca*, and *Tin Tin Deo*.

Walter Gil Fuller was born in Los Angeles on April 14, 1920. He is regarded as one of the most influential music arrangers in the bebop style. His writing prowess was reflected during his high school days when he would transcribe big band arrangements and tour with local bands. After studying engineering at New York University in the early 1940s, he wrote for a number of orchestras, including those led by Jimmy Dorsey, Jimmie Lunceford, Les Hite, and Jeters-Pillars. After Fuller was discharged from the army in 1945, he returned to New York and founded a music publishing company. He began an association with Dizzy Gillespie around 1946 when he recorded his arrangements for Gillespie's sextet and big band, where Gil is heard scat singing on *Oop-bop-sh'bam*.

Most notable about Gil was that he undertook for Gillespie the orchestration of *Manteca* and a number of other Gillespie compositions. He later contributed arrangements to big bands led by Benny Carter, Woody Herman, Buddy Rich, Artie Shaw, Lucky Millinder, Stan Kenton, and Tito Puente.

Luciano Pozo Gonzales, more popularly known as Chano Pozo, was born in Havana, Cuba on January 7, 1915. A Cuban drummer, singer, and dancer, Chano Pozo's drumming and singing were rooted in the Cuban *lucumi* faith, derived from West African rituals. He was the cousin of Chino Pozo, another Cuban percussionist, who performed in the United States with Tadd Dameron, Fats Navarro, Machito, and Illinois Jacquet.

Chano Pozo's performance with Dizzy Gillespie in September of 1947 at Carnegie Hall was historic, for it represented the first time that an attempt had been made to fuse elements of jazz and Latin music at a serious artistic level. Chano Pozo contributed significantly to what became known as Afro-Cuban jazz. Additionally, he made several recordings with Gillespie and contributed to the compositions of *Manteca*, *Afro-Cuban Suite*, and *Guarachi guaro*. Unfortunately, Pozo was murdered in 1948. Nevertheless, in his brief career in the United States he helped to popularize Latin music.

Unit 2: Composition

Dizzy Gillespie collaborated with Gil Fuller and Chano Pozo on *Manteca*, which means "skin" or "greasy" in Spanish. It was among the first pieces to integrate authentic Afro-Cuban polyrhythms with the bop idiom and one of his most popular compositions. The original arrangement for Dizzy's big band was done by Gil Fuller and was a rhythmically exciting showcase for Dizzy's trumpet playing and Pozo's drumming. The composition had a rhythmic groove introduction that could be layered with riffs that built up to the theme. The form (AABBA) of the piece was intro, theme (with each section lasting eight measures), and ending, which recapitulated the intro.

This arrangement for big band by Mike Tomaro captures the rhythmic drive of the original arrangement. Set as a salsa, the rhythm section provides a strong groove that is strengthened with the entry of the horns. The harmonically contrasting bridge or B section is set as a samba before the return of section A and theme as a salsa. There is improvisational space for tenor saxophone, but the chart could be opened up easily to accommodate the soloing of any instrument. A rousing tutti section brings this arrangement to closure.

Unit 3: Historical Perspective

Dizzy Gillespie is one of the most expressive and virtuosic improvisers in the history of music. As one of the primary creators of bebop and the Afro-Cuban entry in jazz, he has secured his place in history as one of the most influential jazz musicians of all time. His improvisations as a soloist in combos or big bands changed the way jazz improvisation was done. He radically expanded the rhythmic and harmonic foundations of jazz during the 1940s. Although bebop was represented mostly by small groups, and Dizzy led several successful small bands, he extended the principles and character of the bop style to the big band, as well. He also played piano and sang on occasion, and his engaging and humorous personality made him a very popular bandleader.

Dizzy's associations with the Cuban trumpeter Mario Bauza and Cuban percussionist Chano Pozo resulted in Dizzy being credited with ushering in the Afro-Cuban component in jazz, which launched a greater Latin music presence in jazz repertoire of several notable musicians, including Charlie Parker, Tadd Dameron, Stan Kenton, Woody Herman, and Bud Powell. *Manteca* was one of the most successful Afro-Cuban works, and Dizzy enjoyed much popularity with the big band version of the tune. Other Latin-influenced or Afro-Cuban tunes associated with Dizzy are *Cubana Be/Cubana Bop*, *Con Alma*, *Tin Tin Deo*, and *A Night In Tunisia*.

Unit 4: Technical Considerations

This chart is rated Grade 3–4, and the recommended tempo is 𝅗𝅥 = 100, with a duration of 3:00. The tempo marking is good; strive to maintain that tempo.

The lead trumpet range goes to concert B♭ above the staff (b♭[1]); the lead trombone range goes to concert F♯ above the staff (f♯). Parts for saxophones, trombones and trumpets lie within practical ranges of these instruments, and there are no extreme ranges.

The harmonies and rhythms are not complex. This is a fun chart to play. Much of the writing is homophonic. The improvising space is not difficult and should afford several players the opportunity for a solo feature.

Unit 5: Stylistic Considerations

A performance of this chart should reflect the character of the Afro-Cuban style of the Dizzy Gillespie big band of the 1940s and 50s. The appropriate rhythmic feel will determine proper performance of this work. The rhythm section, which includes an optional auxiliary percussion player in addition to piano, guitar, bass, and drums, would benefit from detailed work to be certain that the rhythmic groove, salsa, and samba feels are properly executed. The rhythmic feel must also permeate the horn sections, as well.

Unit 6: Musical Elements

MELODY:

The theme is not unlike a two-measure call and response pattern that characterizes the A sections of the form. The composition is defined by a strongly rhythmic salsa groove. Although the material is melodic, it has a strong rhythmic pulse. The bridge, or B section of the form, offers contrast with more legato lines in the melody and less rhythmic drive.

HARMONY:

The harmony in the introduction emphasizes concert B♭, with A♭ offering some alternation before the return to B♭. Such is the case with the strongly homophonic orchestration of the theme.

The bridge offers a contrasting, luscious harmonic palette beginning on A♭m, which runs the cycle in fourths over an eight-measure phrase that is repeated with some alteration on the return to the A section theme.

RHYTHM:

The Afro-Cuban feel is a prerequisite for proper execution of *Manteca.* The rhythm section should work alone to establish and distinguish the salsa and samba grooves so that they feel and comfortable. This same rhythmic feeling must be executed throughout the entire ensemble.

Unit 7: Form and Structure

The basic form of the composition is intro—AABBA—Ending.

SECTION	MEASURE	EVENT AND SCORING
Intro	1–8	The tempo is 𝅗𝅥 = 100. The piano begins with a short melodic/rhythmic motive joined with punctuations by the full ensemble.
Intro	9–16	The rhythm section joins, including the optional auxiliary percussionist, who ideally should have a cowbell, high and low timbales, suspended cymbal, and cabasa. The important bass line is stated for the first time and saxophones add a riff.
A	17–24 repeated	Full band plays and saxophones have the melody. Trumpets provide the response to the saxophone call and trombones reinforce both, while the rhythm section lays down a strong salsa groove.
B (bridge)	25–40	The bridge offers a wonderful contrast to the A section and features saxophones with the legato melody in the first eight measures with occasional brass punctuations. Roles are reversed in the last eight measures when brass carries the melody. Rhythm section energy is held back somewhat, with the percussionist tacit during the bridge and a less-rhythmic piano part containing more sustained chords. The feel of the bridge changes to a samba.
A	41–48	Same as 17–24.
Solo space	49–56 repeated	First tenor saxophone improvises on the harmonies of the first eight measures of the A section theme; any soloist may be used on the repeat.

Section	Measure	Event and Scoring
	57–66 repeated	Saxophone solo continues with trombone background, joined on the repeat by saxophones. Solo ends in measure 66.
A	67–74	The return of the A section introduces a new melody instead of the original in the trombones, while other horns are tacit.
A	75–82	New melody in saxophones and trumpets, rather than the original. Trombones provide harmonic support underneath. Note that drums are tacit from 67–80, which provides more contrast within the rhythm section.
Bridge (D.S.)	25–39	Same as the previous bridge section (measures 25–40).
Coda	83–91	The piano melodic/rhythmic motive from the introduction returns.
	92–99 repeated	Strong tutti section drawing from the A section theme; reminiscent of a shout chorus.
	100–104	The final five measures begin with a *subito piano*, progress to *fortissimo*, and end with a ***fff***, bringing the chart to a rousing and highly rhythmic end. Listening to a recording of Dizzy Gillespie's Big Band playing *Manteca* will convey the spirit and energy of this chart, and hopefully inspire other performers.

Unit 8: Suggested Listening

Dizzy Gillespie Orchestra, *Things to Come*, Laserlight Digital.

Gillespie, Dizzy, *Dizzy's Diamonds: Best of the Verve Years*, Disc III: In An Afro-Cuban, Bossa Nova, Calypso Groove, Verve.

Hampton, Slide & the JazzMasters, *Dedicated To Diz*, Telarc Jazz.

Unit 9: Additional References and Resources

Dunscomb, Richard, and Willie L. Hill, Jr., *Jazz Pedagogy: The Jazz Educator's Handbook and Resource Guide* (Miami: Warner Brothers, 2004).

Gillespie, Dizzy with Al Fraser, *To Be, or Not...to Bop: Memoirs* (Garden City: Doubleday, 1979).

Maggin, Donald L., *Dizzy: The Life and Times of John Birks Gillespie* (New York: HarperCollins, 2005).

Shipton, Alyn, *Groovin' High: The Life of Dizzy Gillespie* (New York: Oxford University Press, 1999).

Contributed by:

William T. McDaniel
Professor of Music and
Director of Jazz Studies
The Ohio State University
Columbus, Ohio

Teacher Resource Guide

Moten Swing
Buster Moten
Bennie Moten
(1894–1935)

arranged by Ernie Wilkins
1922–1999

Unit 1: Composer

Bennie Moten was the pioneer of the influential style of music known as the Kansas City Swing. Moten originally began as a pianist in several of the "barnstorming," southwest-based, itinerant blues bands. By the early 1920s, he had started the first of many great Kansas City bands, the Kansas City Orchestra. The band went through several periods which eventually shaped the band's style and led to a great lineage of Kansas City bands that include The Count Basie Orchestra and the Jay McShann Orchestra. When first formed, the group was performing in a style very closely based on that of New Orleans and King Oliver. By 1926, in keeping with the times, they sounded more sophisticated, almost like Fletcher Henderson's orchestra. Finally, with the recruitment of bassist Walter Page, trumpeter Oran "Hot Lips" Page, and pianist Bill "Count" Basie, the band's signature sound was realized. Other musicians included Ben Webster and Jimmy Rushing.

Unit 2: Composition

Moten Swing set the standard for the swing tunes of the big band era and clearly defined the sound that would influence the bands of Ellington, Basie, and their followers. Too many musicians to count have recorded it, including Kenny

Burrell, Dexter Gordon, Bennie Goodman, Charlie Parker, Django Reinhardt, Oscar Peterson, Terry Gibbs, Gene Ammons, and Willie Smith. Historically, *Moten Swing* will always be remembered as one of swing's greatest anthems. What originally began as a Kansas City riff has come to fruition as a musical masterpiece in the jazz orchestra repertoire.

Unit 3: Historical Perspective

Bennie Moten and his Kansas City Orchestra were among the finest swing bands of the 1920s and 30s. Over the course of a decade, the band personnel included jazz giants such as Count Basie, Walter Page, Jimmy Rushing, and Eddy Durham. All of these members had been picked from the ranks of The Blue Devils, Moten's competition. In 1932, Bennie Moten also included Ben Webster in the band, and that same year, they recorded the world-renowned Moten Swing.

Though the composition credits have been given to Bennie and Buster Moten, Eddy Durham is cited as the unaccredited writer of the tune. Moten passed away in 1935, but immediately following the Basie band was formed with most of the same personnel and became the next giant of the big band era.

After the collapse of the band with Moten's passing, *Moten Swing* became a standard in big bands and was recorded again by the Basie band on the album *Making Whoopee* in 1948. Another recording of the tune emerged that same year, performed by the trumpeter Billy Butterfield and his orchestra.

Unit 4: Technical Considerations

This chart is rated Grade 4. "Riff" tunes are pieces based on singular melodic riffs that together create the song. Listening to the first recording of this piece reveals how hard the band swings. This arrangement by Ernie Wilkins, however, does not display all of the qualities inherent in the original recording. Wilkins orchestrated everything precisely for the Basie band of the 1950s, in which Mr. Wilkins played tenor saxophone. There are solo spaces in the arrangement for tenor and trumpet. The tune has not lost its riff-like qualities in Wilkins's arrangement. It sounds slightly modernized, possibly because of the personnel shift. However, it maintains the perspective of what it was meant to do: play the blues!

Unit 5: Stylistic Consideration

Moten Swing, as the title says, is supposed to swing, and swing hard, just as it did when played in the 1930s. Swing is the most important factor in getting *Moten Swing* to sound as it should; it is the only way to really get the feel, or vibe, of the tune across to the listener. The drums hold a constant, steady beat that is perpetually moving forward, yet comfortably laid-back, and the rest of the rhythm section follows that example. The bass, true to walking bass style, walks along just as laid-back as the drums, but still plays an extremely key part in keeping the tempo and thus keeping the feeling of the tune.

The horns also keep a similar line throughout the piece because of the riff form of writing, where a line is repeated with small changes to notes and/or rhythm.

Unit 6: Musical Elements

MELODY:
In *Moten Swing* there is no real melody. The melody comes from a collection of riffs and this, along with terraced dynamics, gives the chart its life.

HARMONY:
The melody and chord changes do not modulate. Wilkins employs the best of the Kansas City riffs and uses them in a unique way that preserves the composition's historical qualities. The harmonic inferences in *Moten Swing* were ground-breaking for their time. The intervals between the players' changes keep the listener interested in the music.

RHYTHM:
Swinging hard is the most important aspect for the band, as reflected in the title, *Moten Swing*. There should be a "four on the floor" feel from the rhythm section, with the band moving on top of that for a triplet feel. The dominant rhythm is played (doo-dot-dot-dot). It is important to observe all written articulations.

Unit 7: Form & Structure

The basic form of the composition is AABA. Please note: The section numbers and measures are not the same.

SECTION	MEASURE	EVENT AND SCORING
Intro (1) 5/5A	1–19	The tempo is ♩ = 112, a good tempo for learning how to swing. Here, the piano plays a four-measure solo in the Basie style alone; the rhythm section enters in measure five.
	15–21	The ensemble enters with a *fortissimo* lick, followed a very soft figure. Saxophones have a chordal background in the next section.
	31–34	Here the brass are in hats. Play the famous melody of this chart softly and highly articulated; saxophones are out.
	41–50	Saxophones enter. This is a fully-harmonized tutti based on a Kansas City riff.
	49–58	Saxophones take the original melody alone; It is very important to observe all written articulations.
	57–66	Trombones are in tight plungers and play a new riff over a tenor saxophone solo.
	67–82	Here is a trumpet solo with a harmonized saxophone background which uses the previous riff in a different way.
	83–98	Brass leads the figure here, starting with a soft riff. Correct articulation is very important. Next, brass rips a *fortissimo* figure based on this figure: ♫ 𝄾 ♪𝄾 ♪.

SECTION	MEASURE	EVENT AND SCORING
	107–122	This is the highlight of the chart. The ensemble begins with a half note followed by two eighth notes. This figure begins softly and builds to a rousing finish. Have fun and swing hard!

Unit 8: Suggested Listening

Basie, Count, *Basie Beginnings* (1929–1932), (1930–1932) box set, (1929–1930).
Moten, Bennie, *Moten Swing*.
Moten, Bennie, *Moten Stomp*, Rare Sequential Recordings, 1929.

Unit 9: Additional References

Driggs, Frank and Chuck Haddis, *Kansas City from Ragtime to Bebop—a History* (New York: Oxford University Press, 2005).
Pearson, Nathan W, *Goin' to Kansas City (Music in American Life)* (Chaimpaign: University of Illinois Press, 1987).
Rice, Marc, "The Bennie Moten Orchestra 1918–1935: A Kansas City Jazz Ensemble and its African American Audience," doctoral dissertation, University of Kentucky, 1998.

Contributed by:

Thara Memory
Artistic Director
Pacific Crest American Music Program
Portland, Oregon

Teacher Resource Guide

My Foolish Heart

Ned Washington

(1901–1976)

Victor Young

(1899–1956)

arranged by Dave Rivello

Unit 1: Composers

Victor Young began his career as a concert violinist, but also played in popular orchestras. His recording career included providing backing for popular singers such as Bing Crosby. In the 1930s he moved to Hollywood; there he concentrated on composing for film, the area in which he is best known.

Young received twenty-two Academy Award nominations for his film scores; he was awarded an Oscar posthumously for his 1956 score for *Around the World in Eighty Days*. Other notable scores include *Golden Boy* (1939), *For Whom the Bell Tolls* (1943), *Love Letters* (1945), *Samson and Delilah* (1949), *The Quiet Man* (1952), and *Shane* (1953). His best-known songs include *When I Fall in Love*, *Stella by Starlight*, *Sweet Sue*, *Street of Dreams*, *My Foolish Heart*, and *I Don't Stand A Ghost of a Chance With You*.

Ned Washington was a well-known lyricist that contributed to many songs for film. His best-known lyrics are *When You Wish Upon a Star*, *High Noon*, *I'm Gettin' Sentimental Over You*, *My Foolish Heart*, and *Rawhide*.

Unit 2: Composition

This composition is an excellent example of Young's creative writing within the 32-bar song form. The form is ABAC (sometimes called the "two halves" form): in this form the melody is presented in two equal halves, each beginning with the same phrase. The lyrical quality of the melody is sustained by the way in which Young masterfully uses sequence and near-sequence to continually relate each new melodic phrase to the previous one.

Unit 3: Historical Perspective

My Foolish Heart first appeared in the film of the same name in 1949. The film was a commercial flop, but the song was nominated for an Academy Award that year, losing out to Frank Loesser's *Baby, It's Cold Outside*. The song was soon a popular hit for Gordon Jenkins and Billy Eckstine. Many notable jazz artists went on to record the song, making it a popular standard tune: Bill Evans, Joe Williams, Tony Bennett, Carmen McRae, and Nat Cole all offered memorable versions of the song.

Unit 4: Technical Considerations

This chart is designed for high school and advanced junior high bands, although more experienced groups will also find the arrangement appealing to play. The recommended tempo is ♩ = 72 and should stay within a few beats per minute of that speed.

The highest lead trumpet note is a written A (a^1), and the lead trombone goes up to F (f). No doubles are required, but optional parts are included for flute, tuba, horn, and treble clef baritone.

First alto saxophone is the primary soloist; the solo may be improvised using the included chord changes or played as written. A short, seven-measure piano solo is also included, featuring both chord symbols and a written solo. The bass line is notated fully throughout but also includes chord symbols for the more experienced player.

Piano voicings are generally given in root position with the exception of the piano solo. These voicings should be learned and then augmented as experience permits with two-hand voicings such as those found in Frank Mantooth's *Voicings for Jazz Keyboard* or Bill Dobbins' *The Contemporary Jazz Pianist, Volume 2*.

Unit 5: Stylistic Considerations

The piece is a ballad and should be played with an even-eighth-note feel throughout. The drummer may find it helpful to listen to examples of recorded brushwork by such drummers as "Philly Joe" Jones, Mel Lewis, or Jeff Hamilton.

The entire band should pay careful attention to dynamics at every level from ***pp*** to ***ff***. Players should determine where their part is scored in unison and where in chord voicings; the unison sections should be played lightly and with particular attention to intonation. Players should strive for a full, legato ensemble sound, using full breath support, especially at the end of phrases.

Unit 6: Musical Elements

MELODY:
The melody is highly sequential, alternating between stepwise and arpeggiated motion. The alto soloist should familiarize herself with several different recorded examples of the tune to internalize the phrasing of the melody.

HARMONY:
The harmony of the composition consists primarily of diatonic harmonies embellished by secondary dominant chords. The original tune did not change keys, but this arrangement modulates up a perfect fourth at measure 54.

RHYTHM:
The rhythms of the chart are simple even-eighth-note figures with little syncopation. The horns should pay close attention to the rhythm section and play figures accurately without slowing down.

Unit 7: Form and Structure

The basic form of the composition is ABAC.

SECTION	MEASURE	EVENT AND SCORING
Introduction	1–5	Full ensemble: setting of tempo, mood, and key. The ensemble should be full but not loud; a smooth *diminuendo* into measure six will help the transition into the melody statement.

SECTION	MEASURE	EVENT AND SCORING
Melody (A)	6–13	Lead alto presents the melody, which should be interpreted somewhat freely (on the basis of listening to several different vocal versions of the song). Background figures occur immediately, and these figures, especially the unisons, should be played lightly and as legato as possible
Melody (B)	14–21	The melody moves into a higher register in the alto, and the legato backgrounds continue. Players should listen across sections to assure accuracy of pitch and rhythm (e.g., baritone sax and third trombone, first tenor, and first trombone).
Melody (A)	22–29	Brass provides backgrounds here, which must be played with careful articulations (note the various tenuto markings) and sensitive dynamics.
Melody (C)	30–37	The ensemble reaches its highest point so far in this phrase; be sure to begin each *crescendo* softly. It is imperative that as the drummer moves to mallets in measure 35 that the ensemble maintain tempo and forward motion. Bass and piano are tacet here, so the music must move!
Alto solo	38–53	Alto solo with backgrounds.
Piano solo	54–61	Key change to E♭ major.
Ensemble	62–69	A short saxophone *soli* begins this ensemble section. The second alto player should play with lead alto style and sound! The unison trombone line should be truly *mezzo-forte* and in tune.

Section	Measure	Event and Scoring
Final melody	70–83	The climax of the piece occurs with the final melody statement. *Marcato* accents should be "fat" at places such as measures 79–80.
Coda	84–91	The arrangement winds down with the soloist playing a melody over saxes, trombones, and rhythm section. Each moving line should be brought out of the texture, even when the passage is very soft. The trumpets will need to focus air and sound to play the final harmon mute chord precisely and in tune.

Unit 8: Suggested Listening

Bennett, Tony and Bill Evans, *The Tony Bennett/Bill Evans Album*, Fantasy.
Evans, Bill, *Waltz for Debby*, Original Jazz Classics.
McRae, Carmen, *20th Century Masters: The Millennium Collection*, Verve.

Unit 9: Additional References and Resources

Dobbins, Bill, *The Contemporary Jazz Pianist, Vol. 2* (New York: Charles Colin, 1984).
Dunscomb, Richard, and Willie L. Hill, Jr., *Jazz Pedagogy: The Jazz Educator's Handbook and Resource Guide* (Miami: Warner Brothers, 2004).
Lawn, Richard, *The Jazz Ensemble Director's Manual: A Handbook of Practical Methods and Materials for the Educator* (Oskaloosa: C.L. Barnhouse, 1995).
Mantooth, Frank. *Voicings for Jazz Keyboard* (Milwaukee: Hal Leonard, 1997).

Contributed by:

Raleigh Dailey
Lecturer in Jazz Studies
University of Kentucky
Lexington, Kentucky

Teacher Resource Guide

Oclupaca

Duke Ellington

(1899–1974)

transcribed by David Berger

(b. 1948)

Unit 1: Composer

Edward Kennedy "Duke" Ellington was born April 29, 1899. His parents, James and Daisy Ellington, created a comfortable middle-class environment for their family in a culturally vibrant African-American neighborhood in Washington D. C. Duke's boyhood enthusiasm for piano and baseball grew into a focused enthusiasm for music in his teen years. Early on, Duke demonstrated leadership: he played in small groups and booked bands under the name of Duke Ellington's Serenaders. He moved to New York in 1923 and led a band called the Washingtonians. Duke's early years in New York enabled him to hone his own compositional style and personal sound. A significant break came for Duke and his orchestra in 1927 when they were offered a steady gig at the Cotton Club in Harlem. The Cotton Club gave Duke the opportunity to perform regularly with his band and collaborate with New York's most well known composers and performers. It was then that Duke began to compose for and record prolifically with his orchestra; his reputation spread nationwide. Johnny Hodges and Cootie Williams joined the orchestra in 1928 and 1929 respectively, and played a significant role in the overall sound of the ensemble. The contexts and boundaries of Duke's compositions were heightened and expanded in the 1930s. Duke began writing extended works as well as music for film. Many critics consider the late 1930s and early 1940s to be a creative peak for Duke and the orchestra. The musicianship of the orchestra was exceedingly high, and Duke consistently conceived and developed compositions with his band members in mind.

The music and performances of Duke Ellington's music are the single best embodiment of jazz and American music in a single jazz musician or composer. His band performed a wide breadth of American music, rich with influences from all corners of the globe, night after night, for four decades.

The 1950s were not kind to the larger big bands in America; but the now-famous performance at the 1956 Newport Jazz Festival sparked a renewed fervor for Duke and the ensemble. During the 1960s, Duke continued writing more extended works for his orchestra. He embarked on many international tours at this time, and much of his music was rich with the indigenous music of Latin America, Eurasia, and the Far East. The late 1960s also saw a development in Duke's commitment to writing sacred music, notably a series of three Sacred Concerts in the late 1960s and early 70s. Duke composed and toured with his ensemble until just a few months before he died of cancer on May 24, 1974.

Unit 2: Composition

Oclupaca is the first piece of Duke's *Latin American Suite*, which was composed and performed in 1968. Much of the material of this suite was written before the Duke Ellington Orchestra's tour of South America in 1968. The suite was originally titled *Mexicanticipation*, aptly named as a composition intended to be premiered in Mexico City. The performance in Mexico City was preceded by concerts in the South American countries of Brazil, Chile, and Uruguay. The hospitality, culture, and music of South America during this tour had a deep impact on Ellington. The indigenous music of these countries and the pleasant travel experiences moved him to revise and expand and ultimately change the name ffrom *Mexicanticipation* to *Latin American Suite*.

Unit 3: Historical Perspective

Many jazz aficionados and historians consider the late 1960s a season of particular success for Duke Ellington's writing. Many of his most appreciated extended works were composed during this period. The *Latin American Suite* is one of three series of compositions specifically inspired by a particular area of the world where Duke and his band had spent time. These works, although inspired in part by music of other lands, were never intended by Ellington to represent indigenous music in any precise manner. It is noteworthy to mention there are no changes to the instrumentation of Duke's orchestra in the performance of the *Latin American Suite*—no congas, bongos, etc. Although the music is often unmistakably Latin in style, it is more consistently in keeping with the wider sensibilities of Ellington's taste and finesse.

Unit 4: Technical Considerations

One of the fascinating elements of Duke's music is the breadth of musical and technical challenge that it presents. If a band plays enough of Duke's music, successfully capturing the spirit of his intentions, they will be prepared to face every musical challenge in the canon of jazz band literature. The difficulty rating of *Oclupaca*, medium easy to medium, as rated by the publisher, is due to the absence of fast technical passages and higher brass ranges. The trumpet range extends merely to a concert A♭ (a♭[1]), and the trombone range is capped with an F above the bass clef staff (f). The most significant technical hurdle in the piece is found in a 24-bar section where trumpets play longer notes with harmon mutes. In this passage, the lead trumpet plays a concert G; good intonation here will be a challenge for trumpets. That being said, the subtle difficulties in this piece should not be underrated; the piece is demanding, both dynamically and stylistically. The importance of creating and maintaining a distinct mood within the sections of the piece is essential in keeping with the essence of the composition.

The tempo should be very similar to the original recording (♩ = 128); any other tempo would spoil the delicate character of this piece. The performance time is approximately 4:30.

Unit 5: Stylistic Considerations

This is primarily a Latin piece with a distinctly different swing/shuffle section in the middle. This swing-eighth-note section reflects two moods: a stronger, more urgent swinging feeling at letter G, and a quieter, more relaxed shuffle at letters H and I. The Latin groove and flavor make up the bulk of the piece, and the Latin mood is subtle and mysterious.

Unit 6: Musical Elements

MELODY:

The melody in the reeds at letters B–E is unique and has some surprising resolutions. It should be learned aurally and sung vocally. One challenging but beneficial exercise is to have reed players take turns singing the melody one note at a time—as in a handbell choir. To illustrate: Clarinet sings the first note; first tenor saxophone follows with the second note; second tenor saxophone sings the third note, etc. For another vocal exercise, have reed players sing the melody together in unison, holding each note as though a whole note with a fermata, singing each new note only as directed. This will help diagnose and improve imperfections in intonation.

HARMONY:

The harmony is blues-based throughout: seven choruses of F minor blues, two choruses of A♭ major blues, returning to two choruses of F minor blues. The minor blues sections are virtually devoid of the minor seventh degree in the piano voicings, fills, and other accompanying orchestrations. Instead, Duke uses the sixth, major seventh, and ninth degrees of the scale as a means of embellishing triads. This contributes to the mysterious mood of the minor tonality. Many young jazz pianists include the minor seventh in their minor chord voicings unconsciously; this is to be avoided. The two A♭ major choruses have an interesting harmonic twist: the first two bars of the 12-bar form begin with IV^7 instead of the usual I^7. This makes the transition from F minor to A♭ major more interesting.

RHYTHM:

The sharp distinctiveness between the Latin and swing sections is a defining characteristic of the piece. The Latin groove has an even eighth-note subdivision, and the swing groove employs an eighth-note subdivision based on the eighth-note triplet.

A lack of swinging eighth notes stems from a lack of internalization of eighth-note triplets. The second partial of the eighth-note triplet, although generally not played *per se,* is a mathematical and rhythmic necessity for upbeats to be played on the third partial of the triplet.

Unit 7: Form and Structure

Like so many of Duke's compositions, *Oclupaca* is a masterpiece of form and careful development. The piece consists of eleven choruses of 12-bar blues form. Harmonically speaking, the first seven are in the key of F minor, followed by two choruses in A♭ major, returning to F minor for the final two choruses. Rhythmically speaking, the first six choruses are Latin; the seventh through ninth choruses are swing; and the last two return to Latin. The seventh chorus embodies a significant change of groove and feeling, but also serves as a transitional chorus, possessing the swing feel of the two subsequent choruses while maintaining the minor tonality of the preceding Latin choruses.

Chorus	1	2	3	4	5	6	7	8	9	10	11
Groove	Latin	Latin	Latin	Latin	Latin	Latin	Swing	Swing	Swing	Latin	Latin
Tonality	Minor	Minor	Minor	Minor	Minor	Minor	Minor	Major	Major	Minor	Minor

The musical ideas in the first seven choruses develop step-by-step, carefully building and leading to each subsequent section. The changes in instrumentation, dynamics, and mood occur within the framework of each of these 12-bar choruses.

SECTION	REHEARSAL LETTER	EVENT AND SCORING
Intro (1)		Drums and bass set up a repetitive ostinato figure in F minor. The harmonic pattern changes to accommodate chord changes in the blues, but the basic ostinato remains the same for the six choruses to follow. The simplicity and rhythmic consistency of this figure is of the utmost importance to the arrangement's success. For a drummer to capture the essence of Rufus Jones' performance on the original recording, the tom figure should be played with the following accents.  A drummer will likely rush the accented notes. It will be helpful for her to play all sixteen of the sixteenth notes in the measure, perfectly evenly, and experiment with accenting three or four different sixteenth notes per measure. This will enhance the drummer's awareness of the accented notes being rhythmically connected to the sixteenth note grid. The importance of dynamic balance among the various instruments within the drum kit can best be assessed during this introductory section. The bass drum, hi-hat, and tom figures should be mixed appropriately.

Section	Rehearsal Letter	Event and Scoring
Intro (2)	A	The 12-bar blues form begins with the entrance of the piano outlining F minor blues changes, staying close to the "Charleston" rhythm (beats 1 and the second half off beat 2). The pianist should not need to play loudly to be heard over the bass and drums. Duke's use of the extreme high register of the piano creates a unique timbre as well as a pleasant contrast to relatively low register of the melody to follow. The dynamic contour set by Duke's comping serves as a model for both the melody and rhythm sections of the choruses at letters B–F and J–K. The volume builds as the harmony moves to the IV and V chords, and then recedes as the harmony returns to the I chord for measures 11–12.
Melody	B	The melodic content in the first four choruses is played by four reeds in unison: clarinet, two tenor saxophones and baritone saxophone, all one octave lower. Russell Procope's clarinet tone has a woody and mysterious quality in the recording. Capturing this timbral quality with the reed section is a challenge; the saxophonists must be concerned with the timbral dominance of the clarinet, attempting to match the articulation and dynamic contour of the clarinetist in every way, but at a much quieter volume. The rhythm section should play at a quiet and supportive volume; every subtlety in the interpretation of the melody should be perfectly transparent. The dynamic contour is simple and yet significant; as the melody ascends in pitch it should increase slightly in volume, and vice versa.

SECTION	REHEARSAL LETTER	EVENT AND SCORING
Melody	C	As the melody continues, reeds should gently accent the first note of each pick-up note. Piano switches from playing chords to playing single-note fills with reeds in a call and response pattern. Brass enters strongly at measure 9; this entrance is surely intended to be a bit of a surprise. This brass figure also foreshadows the considerable dominance and contrast trumpets will have at letter G. Reeds should *crescendo* convincingly in measure 10.
Melody	D	Reeds and rhythm section immediately return to the original *pianissimo*, and although they continue with new melodic material, there is a sense of recapitulation of the mood at letter B. Duke's piano part here was certainly at least partially improvised; the call and response nature of the piano fills are most important.
Melody	E	Reeds increase slightly in volume as they make way for the trumpets response to their melodic figures. Trumpets should play with a great sense of accent and rhythmic precision. The note on the second half of beat 2 should be played quite short. The air stream must be stopped abruptly with the tongue. Piano chords fit perfectly in the very short span of time between brass and reed figures, creating something of a three-way call and response conversation.

Section	Rehearsal Letter	Event and Scoring
Transition	F	The trombone figures at letter F function as a transition and introduction to letter G, which is the dynamic height of the piece. Trombones should attack the first note of each two-measure phrase aggressively and then carefully spread the *crescendo* over the entirety of the measure, making sure that second and third trombones do not overpower the lead trombone. The note on the second half of beat 4 is short, and should be stopped with the tongue. Again, the piano serves as a response to trombones.
Swing	G	This section is the most dynamic section for the band as a whole. The bass walks in four, playing a few extra eighth notes along the way. Drums should begin the swing eighth notes with a transitional measure one bar before letter G. Rufus Jones' example here is textbook. The drummer must swing convincingly, playing fills in between each of the two-measure phrases. The fills should be aggressive but simple, not straying from the strong triplet-eighth-note groove. The tutti passage from the trumpets and saxophones is a bit unconventional, with each phrase beginning with two sixteenth notes. The second of each of the first two sixteenth notes should be played short.

Section	Rehearsal Letter	Event and Scoring
Shuffle	H	Letters H and I are much quieter in volume than the swing section (letter G). The *decrescendo* transition one bar before letter H is an important function of the acoustic bass in this regard. Saxophones and trumpets (with harmon mutes) have mostly long notes and should subdivide and listen to the rhythm section in order to accurately play the second half of beat 3 in measures 2, 4, 6, and 8. These parts should be sung in rehearsal; this will improve the intonation of the performance. The tenor solo should be played with some *bravura*, and should be heard over the rest of the band, with careful attention being paid to the unique rendering of the blues harmony; the first two measures of the form begin on the IV chord.
Melody	J, K	The melody at letter J is an identical restatement of the melody at letter B; the mood, rhythm, and overall dynamic sensibility of the accompaniment should reflect this. Unlike letter B, which is followed by a further development of the melody at letter C, the melody at letter J is followed by another restatement of the same melody at letter K. This gives the distinct impression that the piece is nearing the end. The band should begin to *decrescendo*.
Conclusion	L	This simplification continues as the melody drops out, leaving only the piano, bass, and drums playing together as they did at letter A. The harmony is simplified as the piano and the bass remain on the F minor chord, as opposed to the minor blues progression at letter A. This allows a greater focus on the *decrescendo* as the song fades to a conclusion.

Unit 8: Suggested Listening

Ellington, Duke, *The Blanton-Webster Band*, RCA.
Ellington, Duke, *The Latin American Suite*, OJC.
Ellington, Duke, The *Afro-Eurasian Eclipse*, OJC.
More', Beny, *The Very Best of Beny More'*, Greatest Hits.
Prado, Perez, *Lo Mejor de lo Mejor*, Sony International.

Unit 9: Additional References and Resources

Ellington, Duke, *Music is My Mistress* (Garden City: Da Capo Press, 1973).
Duke Ellington: Memories of Duke, WarnerVision Entertainment DVD, 1968.
Hasse, John Edward, *Beyond Category: The Life and Genius of Duke Ellington* (Garden City: Da Capo Press, 1973).
Jazz at Lincoln Center: *Essentially Ellington*, http://www.jalc.org/jazzED/ee/index.html (April 10, 2007).
Tucker, Mark, ed., *The Duke Ellington Reader* (New York: Oxford University Press, 1993).

Contributed by:

Jim Gasior
Associate Professor of Jazz and Instrumental Studies
New World School of the Arts
Miami, Florida

Teacher Resource Guide

Say What You Mean

Mike Tomaro

(b. 1958)

Unit 1: Composer

Mike Tomaro has been the director of jazz studies at his alma mater, Duquesne University in Pittsburgh, Pennsylvania, since 1997. Prior to taking this position he served for seventeen years as a member of the prestigious Army Blues Jazz Ensemble, a unit of "Pershing's Own" United States Army Band. While a member of the Army Blues he performed on saxophone, flute, and clarinet, while also serving as the composer or arranger for much of the group's repertoire. During this time he was featured as a soloist on several recordings with this ensemble, while also earning a master of arts in saxophone performance degree from George Mason University in Fairfax, Virginia. He is a Yamaha Performing Artist on saxophone.

Tomaro is a prolific composer and arranger with more than eighty publications to his credit. Prominent jazz artists such as Grammy award-winner Nancy Wilson, Randy Brecker, Mike Stern, Ernie Watts, Bobby Shew, New York Voices, Alan Vizzutti, and many others have performed his music. As an instrumentalist, Tomaro has performed with a wide variety of artists and groups, including Ray Charles, Michael Feinstein, Terence Blanchard, Louis Bellson, the Dizzy Gillespie Tribute Big Band, the Woody Herman Orchestra, the Smithsonian Jazz Masterworks Orchestra, and the Pittsburg Symphony Orchestra.

Four commercial recordings have been released featuring Tomaro's skills as performer, composer, and arranger: *Home Again* on the Positive Music label, and *Nightowl Suite*, *Forgotten Dreams*, and *Dancing Eyes*, all on the Seabreeze Jazz label.

Unit 2: Composition

Tomaro says,

> "My motivation for writing the piece was to try and integrate some of Thad Jones's harmonic and melodic concepts into a composition for younger players. All of Thad's music is too difficult for this level, and I wanted to attempt to sound as much like Thad as possible, simply by reducing the breadth of his voicings to accommodate younger brass players and write lines that were only slightly less rhythmically and melodically complex than his."

Unit 3: Historical Perspective

Thad Jones was a brilliant cornet and trumpet player, known for his harmonically adventurous soli and writing for big band. Playing with the Count Basie band was a prominent part of his early career, and leading it was perhaps the highlight of the end of his career. Composer Mike Tomaro has incorporated both adventurous soli and big band writing in *Say What You Mean*, written in the Basie swing style while utilizing Jones's rich harmonic palette.

Unit 4: Technical Considerations

Say What You Mean is listed in the Kendor catalogue as medium easy difficulty, which is correct in terms of the range of the instruments, the tempo, and the difficulty of the rhythmic figures. However, it may lie closer to a medium level of difficulty, analogous to a Grade 4, in terms of the numerous chord extensions and the frequent use of accidentals, which provide a more pungent harmonic vocabulary than is typically found in lower grade levels. Also, the key signatures (C and Df major) may be challenging to less experienced players. The composer suggests that the tune be played no faster than the marked tempo of ♩ = 120 to maintain its relaxed swing feel. Duration is approximately six minutes. The lead trumpet range goes no higher than a written A above the staff (a^1). The lead trombone range is similarly restrained to an F♯ above the staff (f♯). Rhythm section parts are notated with chords cued, including a fully written-out bass part. The drummer is given specific parts to play at several sections, either to provide stylistically appropriate fills or help unify the background riffs from the horns.

Unit 5: Stylistic Considerations

Tomaro says,

> "Stylistically, it is imperative to adhere to the indicated tempo. Playing this chart any faster will run the intended feel. The rhythm section groove is vital to the success of the chart as well. Students should listen to recordings of Thad and Mel's (Lewis) rhythm section and strive to attain the same kind of driving swing feel that they did. Also, due to the tempo, all the horns should swing these lines very hard, with almost overemphasized back accents."

Unit 6: Musical Elements

MELODY:

Silence is an important element of the melody in this composition. Enter this silence by ending each small fragment of the melody with an extremely short note as marked. Performing in this manner is a characteristic of all great swing bands. It is appropriate to use the tongue to stop the final note of each phrase, resulting in an articulation that resembles the word "dit." Observe accents as marked to give direction to the musical line within each phrase. In measures 73-88, remember that muting the trumpet should change the tone color of the sound, not necessarily the volume. Remember to play louder when muted to balance the saxophones.

HARMONY:

Frequent accidentals and numerous chord extensions and chord substitutions enrich the harmonic vocabulary of this composition. The key signature modulates away from the starting point of C major to D♭ major in measure 81. C major returns at the D.S.; the piece maintains this tonality until the conclusion of the piece. This harmonic complexity is characteristic of Thad Jones, one of the most important figures in big band jazz composition. *Say What You Mean* was written in tribute to Jones, and draws from his composition *Mean What You Say*.

RHYTHM:

Interpretation and accurate reproduction of the swing feel is a skill that must be learned by imitating the great artists of the medium. There is no way to accurately perform music of this style without listening to, imitating, and internalizing the swing interpretations of Count Basie, Duke Ellington, and numerous other masters. The intentionally moderate tempo of this composition places a premium on swing rhythms. The few sixteenth notes preceded by sixteenth note rests incorporated into this composition are not to be swung, but interpreted literally. Syncopations are frequent, and should be performed with an accent, as marked, within the context of the performance traditions of this style. Successive quarter notes must be performed strictly in time, without rushing. Verbalizing "dat-n" on each successive quarter note, to emphasize the asymmetric subdivision within it, will help keep this seemingly simple rhythmic figure in time and swinging. The pulse in swing style moves forward, but the feel of the rhythms within that pulse lay back, creating the musical juxtaposition that is the essence and the appeal of swing music.

Unit 7: Form and Structure

The basic form of the composition is a 32-bar, AABA structure. Most phrases start with pickup notes, so adjust measure numbers given below accordingly.

Section	Measure	Event and Scoring
Intro	1–8	Triplets in the drums lead to short *fortissimo* statements by brass answered by saxophones. The rhythm section finishes the final two measures of the intro.
A	9–16	Trumpets are scored in unison on the melody trade off with the rhythm section in a conversational manner.
A	17–24	Alto and tenor saxophones are scored in unison on the melody are answered again by the rhythm section supported by trombones. Note the open and closed designations for high hat cymbal.
B	24–28	Trombones are scored in unison on the melody in section B, and are answered by all saxophones. The full band answers at the end of the statement by second trombone.
B	29–31	Saxophones are scored in octaves, performing sequential figures following descending whole tone chord changes. The full band answers at the end of the phrase.
A	33–36	Trombones scored in unison restate a modified A theme punctuated by the rhythm section and supported by saxophones.

Section	Measure	Event and Scoring
A	37–39	Alto and tenor saxophones make a final melodic statement, joined by the full band to end the phrase,
Soli	41–72	Open for soli. Background figures and rhythm section kicks are on cue. Piano and guitar parts provide chord changes and voicings, but players are asked to comp. The form is still AABA. Scale and sample solo sheets are provided as a starting point for soloists. Ideally, soloists should be trained to improvise their own original rhythmic and melodic ideas rather than merely recreate the sample soli provided by the composer.
C	73–87	Trombones and baritone saxophone play an ostinato rhythm supported by matching rhythms in the drums. Alto saxophones are paired with first and second trumpets, each using a harmon mute, scored in unison on a melodic line. Tenor saxophones are paired with third and fourth trumpets, each using a cup mute, scored in unison on a similar but contrasting melodic line.
D	89–96	Saxophone soli section with traditional instrumentation and an alto saxophone lead. Ending notes of each phrase should be played very shortly with a crisp articulation ("voo-dit"). Listen to a variety of saxophone soli sections as played by professional musicians, analyze their articulations, and then imitate in a similar style here, rather than playing everything slurred. Slur markings should in fact be interpreted as phrase markings. Observe accents as marked to give direction to the musical line.

SECTION	MEASURE	EVENT AND SCORING
E	97–103	A shout section for the full ensemble at a *fortissimo* dynamic level. Maintain balance within complex harmonic structures by altering the volume of each part as needed to fit within the chord. Tune all chords in relation the lowest sounding pitch. Match the lead trumpet for style, i.e., length of note, type and degree of accent. Use a syllable such as "bahdt" on the final quarter notes in measures 98 and 100 to maintain rhythmic integrity while providing an appropriate length and sonority to the rooftop accents (^).
Transition	104–110	Two short drum solos provide a transition from section E to the D.S., which returns to the trumpet melody in measure 9.
Coda	111–122	This composition ends with a musical reference to the Thad Jones standard *Mean What You Say*. In measure 120, the "NC" in the piano part tells the pianist to play "no chord," only written notes. Note the straight eighth notes in measure 121. The drummer should add a fast triplet figure to coincide with the release following the fermata in the final measure. This triplet should be voiced on the lowest toms, ending with the bass drum. Doing so will give a sense of finality to the ending and obscure any inaccuracy in the release.

Unit 8: Suggested Listening

Basie, Count, *Straight Ahead*, Verve.
Mike Tomaro Big Band, *Dancing Eyes*, Seabreeze Jazz.
Mike Tomaro and the Three Rivers Jazz Orchestra, *Nightowl Suite*, Seabreeze Jazz.
Vintage Orchestra, *Thad*, Nocturne.

Unit 9: Additional References and Resources

Dunscomb, Richard, and Willie L. Hill, Jr., *Jazz Pedagogy: the Jazz Educator's Handbook and Resource Guide* (Miami: Warner Brothers, 2004).

Contributed by:

Thomas Bough
Director of Athletic Bands
Northern Illinois University

Teacher Resource Guide

Shiny Stockings
Frank Foster
(b. 1928)

Unit 1: Composer

Frank Foster was born in Cincinnati, Ohio on September 23, 1928. He was a clarinetist and alto saxophonist in his youth, but he began to play tenor saxophone in 1947 to separate himself from the influence of Charlie Parker. Frank's mother was an amateur pianist, so he heard music in his home.

As a young person, Foster played in dance bands in and around the Cincinnati area. After spending some time at Central State University, he moved to Detroit, Michigan, and between 1949 and 1951 he played with Snooky Young and others. His early influences included Wardell Gray and Sonny Stitt. The military interrupted his musical career in 1951, but upon his discharge in 1953, he became a part of the Count Basie Orchestra and developed into one of Basie's primary soloists. With the Basie band, Foster was not only a key member of the saxophone section, but he also became one of Basie's most trusted composers and arrangers. His most famous composition for the Basie band was *Shiny Stockings*.

Foster became a freelance artist in New York in 1964. He began playing with Elvin Jones in the late 1960s. Also in the 60s, he created a big band called the Loud Minority that had up to twenty-five musicians and allowed Foster to experiment with spoken drama and jazz. From the mid-60s through the 80s, Foster played with Duke Pearson, Buddy Rich, Thad Jones-Mel Lewis, Clark Terry, and Jazzmobile big bands. While with Jazzmobile, the ensemble played his *Lake Placid Suite* at the 1980 Winter Olympic Games. Foster began leading the Basie band two weeks after Basie's death in June of 1986, and continued until July of 1995. He continues to compose, record and lead various groups.

Unit 2: Composition

Frank Foster wrote *Shiny Stockings* during his illustrative eleven years with Basie from 1953–64. The hard swinging chart became a mainstay for the Count and has become a jazz classic. The essence of the Basie orchestra is contained in the piece, with the strong four of the rhythm section setting up the gradual building of the chart from the softer head in the tutti brass to the stomping shout at the end. The now famous sax soli demonstrates Foster's grasp of how a sax section can build through a long soli to an amazingly exciting climax. Changes for the solo section are found in the fourth trumpet.

Unit 3: Historical Perspective

Foster's career began at a time when big band fortunes were at low ebb. His years with Basie (1953–64) saw the band go through a revival, building upon the toe-tapping swing the band is famous for. While Foster was with the band, he recorded numerous tunes that are now part of standard big band literature. During this era Basie kept his swing-style rhythm section, but many soloists with more modern leanings were hired. Foster and Thad Jones are two of the notable additions. Quincy Jones, Neal Hefti, and Foster all submitted charts to this band, which was unequaled for its relaxed precision and control of dynamics.[1]

Unit 4: Technical Considerations

Shiny Stockings is rated Grade 5–6, with a recommended tempo of ♩ = 120; the duration is 7:30. The chart seems to groove at the indicated tempo.

The lead trumpet range is to a concert B♮ (b^1); the lead trombone range is also to concert B♮ (b). The saxophone soli is classic, and is technically and stylistically challenging. There are no doubles required for the chart. The bass has both written parts and changes.

Guitar and piano parts contain only chord changes, which are straight ahead. Changes for the fourth trumpet solo are not exceptionally difficult, but require a soloist with improvisation experience.

Unit 5: Stylistic Considerations

The hard swing of *Shiny Stockings* is a perfect example of the style developed by Basie. The swing feel can be magnified by emphasizing the first note, top note, and last note of a swing phrase, and by ghosting the unimportant notes.

This chart would be an excellent choice for a band with a strong sax section and a director desiring to instill the beauty and excitement of straight-ahead swing. Foster wrote *Stockings* to swing hard, and students quickly catch the flavor of the great Kansas City big band traditions begun by Benny Moten and carried on by the Count.

Unit 6: Musical Elements

MELODY:

After an 8-bar introduction by trombones and rhythm section, brass introduces the swinging 16-bar melody. In order to achieve the correct feel, every member should be encourages to learn to play the melody with all appropriate swing inflections. Inner parts will be much stronger as each individual internalizes the melody for himself or herself. Saxophones pick up the melody for another statement of the first eight measures of the head before brass plays a slightly altered last eight prior to the saxophone soli. The soli lasts for sixty-four measures with a suggested cut to thirty-two measures indicated, if the director desires. The overall chart should build by increments from the ***mf*** brass head to the ***ff*** shout at the end.

HARMONY:

The changes are easily recognizable and flow logically using dominant chords without extensions. The head begins in concert D♭, then modulates to concert F for the trumpet solo, remaining in F to the end. The ii–V progression is used extensively, with several tritone substitutions leading back to the tonic. There are indications of the use of pedal on several chords.

RHYTHM:

The rhythm section should be encouraged to listen intently to the Count Basie Orchestra rhythm section to begin to master the seemingly simplistic, hard-swinging four for which it was noted. Each band member should internalize the subdivided triplet swing time in his body as he plays this chart (think, "doo-da, doo-da, doo-da"). Each member of the ensemble must feel the time individually. The rhythm section cannot make up for bad time in the horns if ensemble time is anything less than "in the pocket."

Brass players should be encouraged to repeatedly sing the head together several times with proper articulation and nuance, and to begin to feel the time together. Saxophones should also sing their soli slowly, and then gradually speed up until the tempo is reached to understand the placement of the various sixteenth-note runs, the feel of the triplets, and the coordination of the shakes and articulations as clearly indicated by Foster.

During the soft shout beginning at letter K the rhythm is in a two-beat feel, and must be kept light from K to M.

Unit 7: Form and Structure

Section	Measure	Event and Scoring
Intro	1–8	A hard swinging tempo of a ♩ = 120 is established by the rhythm section and trombones during the 8-bar intro. The introduction is rhythmic with trombones, bass, piano, and guitar playing punches together. Drums play a straight-ahead swing pattern.
A	9–24	Brass introduces the first statement of the harmonized, hard-hitting head. The lead trumpet must be heard over the rest of the tutti brass, so listening for that lead sound is essential. The Basie laid-back style applies to this head. The lead trumpet, with the rest of the brass following that example, establishes the feel. Listening to the original recording by the Basie band can help young players internalize the feel of the head in both the rhythm section and in the brass. This chart reminds us again and again of the importance of the lead trumpet player taking on the leadership of the band, both when the brass is playing a tutti section and when the full band is playing. Everyone in the band must keep those "elephant ears" locked on the lead trumpet sound!
B	25–40	Saxophones have the dotted quarter pickup into letter B that sets up the section to play the head in unison for the first for eight bars, after which brass again picks up the harmonized melody. Again, it is important to listen for the lead trumpet for balance, style and concept. The head needs to be played strongly by the brass into three before letter C to set up the sax soli that begins in measure 38.

SECTION	MEASURE	EVENT AND SCORING
C/D	41–72	One of the most famous saxophone tutti sections in all of big band literature begins with the section pickup in measure 38. The rhythm section lays out for two bars to allow the full impact of the saxes to hit the listener. Saxophones must blow through the line thinking that there is an arrow written over the notes from breath to breath. When the lead alto goes into the upper register, it is imperative that the rest of the section supports the upper notes with even more sound, thinking of a triangle with the lead on top and the supporting section with a fuller, fatter sound. Articulations are clearly indicated in the parts and should be followed carefully. Accents on the first note of each triplet (e.g. measure 49) will assist in helping them be together and have a stronger rhythmic feel. The shakes should be coordinated with the lead alto. In measure 65 sixteenth notes should have a slight accent on the first of each group of four to emphasize the rhythm, while still hitting the accented fourth sixteenth of each group. There is an optional cut in measure 71, two before letter E to two before letter G, that shortens the saxophone tutti sixty-four to thirty-two measures.

SECTION	MEASURE	EVENT AND SCORING
E/F	73–105	The wonderful saxophone tutti continues at letter E, and requires absolute adherence to the leadership of the lead alto. The sixteenth runs beginning in measure 80 will need extra sectional time in order to work out inner parts. Sing the lick slowly, play it slowly, and then speed it up to tempo. The wonderful writing of this tutti section is a major reason that *Shiny Stockings* is a big band classic.
G	105–112	This 8-bar transition section masterfully takes the ensemble into the key of concert F. The fourth trumpet solo has a 2-bar lead-in to letter H with the rhythm laying out.
H/I	113–144	The rhythm section should be sensitive to the dynamics behind the fourth trumpet solo at letter H. If the dynamics are softer, the solo can gradually build over these thirty-two mesures. The background in the brass (tutti riff) and saxes (repeated figure echoing the brass) should not be loud. Brass should start softly and grow on each of the repeated four eighths/quarter note licks. The background allows the solo to grow, and the balance of the solo with the rhythm section should continue to increase in volume and intensity.
J	145–154	Another 8-bar transition section copying the transition at letter G demonstrates Foster's ability to build tension with the unexpected. Each dotted quarter in the 3/4 section beginning in measure 150 should be accented to establish change of meter. The drum fill into letter K should bring the band down to the ***mp*** entrance of the quiet shout.

SECTION	MEASURE	EVENT AND SCORING
K/L	155–186	The "I" word (intensity) makes this 2-beat soft shout work. Each member of the ensemble must listen for the lead trumpet, play just under that sound, and yet completely support it. Singing this section as a band will help lock in the feel. All ensemble members should sing the first few times, and then the rhythm should play while the horns sing. The repeated eighths in measure 163 should grow as indicated, and then each repeat of the figure should grow obviously louder, so that the ***ff*** on beat 2 in measure 168 forewarns the audience of what is to come. The lead trumpet should dictate the quick *decrescendo* back to ***mp***. Letter L repeats the intense soft shout. At measure 179, the band should mimic the shake of the lead trumpet and then build to the shout chorus at letter M.
M-end	187–221	The shakes at letter M and three after M can be accomplished in several ways: The ideal, of course, is to have each member of the band copy the shake of the lead trumpet. If most of the brass is unable to shake, the lead trumpet can shake with the saxes while brass members *crescendo*. If band members are not accomplished enough to perform the shake, they can hit the note with an ***fp*** and *crescendo* into the drop on the second half of beat 4. Cutting together on four before the fall is encouraged for precision. Remember a note must be firmly established before the fall takes place. The fall should not be too short (perhaps off on beat 2.5 or 3 of the following measure). Follow the example of the Basie band at measure

195 by starting ***ff*** with a *decrescendo* over the bar, and repeat the same dynamic again in measure 197. The rip into beat 1 of measure 199 in the first ending needs to *crescendo* into the note. Again, the lead trumpet must be followed, with the band ending the rip together exactly on beat 1.

The whole-note fall two before the repeat should cut on beat 1 of the next bar. The way the figure is written in measure 204 (the second bar of the second ending) indicates the laid back feel that is expected. The 2-bar trombone soli at measure 206 should be very strong. The chart builds all the way from the second ending to the end, culminating with the famous Basie upper register piano ending and final chord. The last note should be absolutely together on four with the ***sfz***.

Unit 8: Suggested Listening

Count Basie Orchestra, *The Compete Atomic Basie*, Blue Note Records.
Count Basie Orchestra, *The Best of Count Basie*, MCA.
Count Basie Orchestra, *The Complete Clef/Verve Count Basie Fifties Studio Recordings*, Mosaic Records.

Unit 9: Additional References and Resources

Dunscomb, Richard, and Willie L. Hill, Jr., *Jazz Pedagogy: The Jazz Educator's Handbook and Resource Guide* (Miami: Warner Brothers, 2004).
Dance, Stanley, *The World of Count Basie* (Cambridge: Da Capo Press, 1980).

Contributed by:

Thomas W. Streeter
Professor of Music/Director of Jazz Studies
Illinois Wesleyan University
Bloomington, Illinois

Endnotes:

1 Barry Kernfield, editor, *The New Grove Dictionary of Jazz*, New York: The Macmillan Press Limited, 1988, 1994.

Teacher Resource Guide

Squatty Roo
Johnny Hodges
(1906–1970)

arranged by John Clayton
(b. 1952)

Unit 1: Composer/Arranger

Johnny Hodges (nicknamed "Jeep," or "Rabbit") was born in Cambridge, Massachusetts on July 25, 1907. New Orleans saxophonist Sidney Bechet, with whom he later studied, heavily influenced Hodges's saxophone playing. After a stint in Chick Webb's band, Hodges joined Duke Ellington's orchestra in May 1928 as lead alto saxophonist on the recommendation of longtime Ellington clarinetist Barney Bigard. This was the beginning of a thirty-eight-year tenure with Ellington (with a break from 1951 to May, 1955). Ellington and Billy Strayhorn wrote many songs showcasing Hodges's signature warm tone, sweeping glissandi, and gift for melody, sometimes creating pieces from a portion of a Hodges improvisation. Hodges passed away on May 11, 1970 in New York City.

John Clayton was born in 1952 in Venice, California. He began studying double bass with Ray Brown when he was sixteen, and by age nineteen was performing on Henry Mancini's television show, "The Mancini Generation." Clayton attended Indiana University and graduated with a degree in double bass performance in 1975. Soon after graduation he joined the trio of Monty Alexander (which included drummer Jeff Hamilton); two years later, he joined the Count Basie Orchestra for two years. Clayton then spent five years as the principal bassist in the Amsterdam Philharmonic Orchestra.

Upon his return from Europe, Clayton founded the Clayton Brothers Jazz Quintet with his brother, alto saxophonist Jeff Clayton. He also founded the Clayton-Hamilton Jazz Orchestra with his brother and Jeff Hamilton, a big band that has performed and recorded since 1985. John Clayton is currently a faculty member at the University of Southern California. He counts Quincy Jones, Thad Jones, Duke Ellington, Oliver Nelson, and Henry Mancini among his compositional influences. He has written for or played with Diana Krall, Whitney Houston, Joe Williams, Carmen McRae, Natalie Cole, Quincy Jones, Diane Reeves, Nancy Wilson, Dee Dee Bridgewater, George Benson, Cassandra Wilson, Dr. John, and McCoy Tyner.

Unit 2: Composition

John Clayton's arrangement of *Squatty Roo*, uses the melody from the Hodges composition *Squaty Roo*. (Note that Hodges' original spelling differs from Clayton's by the use of a single "t" instead of the double "t" preferred by Clayton.) Hodges' original piece is based on a 32-bar, AABA form. The chord changes are similar to those of *I Got Rhythm*, by George Gershwin. Other recordings of this piece can be found under both *Squaty Roo* and *Squatty Roo*.

Clayton's arrangement was first recorded on the Clayton-Hamilton Orchestra recording, *Live at* MCG. It was written in 2005 and has a Grade 5 difficulty.

Unit 3: Historical Perspective

Squaty Roo was one of more than 150 small-group recordings between 1935 and 1941 which Duke Ellington organized for members of his orchestra. These sessions were an opportunity for some of Ellington's most notable soloists to perform extended improvisations in a combo setting. These recordings, originally released on the Variety and Victor record labels, included anywhere from six to nine musicians. They were led (at least nominally) by Rex Stewart, Cootie Williams, Barney Bigard, and Johnny Hodges, with Duke Ellington playing piano as a sideman. *Squaty Roo* comes from one of the Hodges-led sessions. Johnny Hodges' original composition, *Squaty Roo*, is a vehicle for soloing over *I Got Rhythm* changes.

The Clayton-Hamilton Jazz Orchestra recorded *Squatty Roo* as the closing track for the album *Live at* MCG (MCG Jazz). This album was recorded over four days at the Manchester Craftsmen's Guild, a non-profit arts institution in Pittsburgh, Pennsylvania.

Unit 4: Technical Considerations

This chart is rated Grade 5; the recommended tempo is ♩ = 220. The lead trumpet goes up to a G♯ (g♯[1]) with one 8-bar section ranging between a B♭ (b♭) and G (g[1]). The second trumpet part tops out at a D (d). The lead trombone part goes up to a C (c). There are challenging saxophone parts as well after the solo section.

Solo changes are written out for fourth trumpet, first trombone, and first tenor sax, while the guitar, piano, and bass also have changes written. These soloists should be proficient at playing over "rhythm" changes at a fast tempo.

Aside from a few written-out melodic lines and rhythmic hits, there are only chords shown for the piano and bass parts. Pianists should therefore be proficient at creating rootless chordal voicings, and bassists should be capable of playing walking bass lines. There are numerous sections involving complex drum fills and hits, and there is a lot of high-speed interplay with the horns. A rhythmically confident, highly skilled drummer is a necessity.

Unit 5: Stylistic Considerations

Many of the most challenging sections in *Squatty Roo* occur after the solo section. Measure 111 finds the band playing a series of offbeat hits in succession, followed by a 2-bar drum solo. Many jazz bands will have to fight the tendency to rush during these repeated eight measures. A strong drummer is necessary to stabilize this section, but all ensemble members will have to be extremely focused between measures 111–119. A similar interplay occurs between measures 128–135 as well.

While the melody was written during the swing era (*Squaty Roo* was recorded in 1940), this arrangement definitely has a bebop tempo. The subsequent melodic development in the arrangement has a bebop influence, and the harmonic density in this development section is reminiscent of Thad Jones and other post-swing era composers.

Unit 6: Musical Elements

MELODY:

The melody on the head can be learned vocally, and accents will align with the upper edges of the melodic contour. The primary melody outlines the chord changes while using few passing tones. The key center of the piece stays in B♭ major.

HARMONY:
The piece is built on standard *I Got Rhythm* chord changes. During the development section following the final soloist, a shout chorus unfolds involving a series of dense, altered-dominant chords voiced across the ensemble. These chords ultimately reinforce the key center of B♭ major, moving chromatically either to or from that key. The second development chorus after the solo section involves a complex re-harmonization and non-standard augmentation of the original *Squatty Roo* melody during two extended A sections. Section B harmonizes a composed lead trumpet melody using a variety of voicing techniques across the band before simplifying to a unison piano melody for the final A section.

RHYTHM:
The closely interwoven entrances and hits require rhythmic independence across the band. The extended form of the later shout chorus and sectional interplay require a mature rhythmic awareness. Much of the challenge of this piece is found in this rhythmic complexity. Singing can be a very important part in diagnosing and fixing potential rhythmic and articulation issues.

Unit 7: Form and Structure

SECTION	MEASURE	EVENT AND SCORING
Intro	1–8	The tempo is ♩ = 220. The drummer plays eight measures of time on a loose hi-hat.
Intro (A-1)	9–16	Saxes, piano, and bass enter in pickups to measure 9. These instruments play a six-measure rhythmic motif that also serves as the conclusion to the arrangement. Saxes play a short unison line in measures 15–16 and then hand off the rhythmic riff to the brass and rhythm section in measure 16.

SECTION	MEASURE	EVENT AND SCORING
Intro (A-2)	17–24	Brass takes the riff, while saxes play a unison answer line between brass hits. Drums have a two-measure solo in measures 23–24. Directors may want to slow down measure 20 to practice the quick transition from the sax line (which ends on beat 2) to the first brass/rhythm hit (which begin on the second half of beat 2). Once students have mastery of this transition, have them play measures 20–21 slowly, and then at tempo.
B	125–32	Piano plays the melody in both hands.
B-2	33–40	Saxes, guitar, and piano play unison melody with brass playing background hits. Care is needed to get brass and rhythm hits in the correct spots in measures 33 and 35, as the hits on the second half of beat 3 may rushed or dragged. Saxes should take care to accent the high note on the second half of beat 1 in both measures 33 and 35 as well. In measures 37–38, saxes should take care to accent the tops of the melodic contour. Trombones should be prepared for the offbeat entrance in measure 39.
B-3	41–48	Piano solo.
B-4	49–60	Saxes reenter with the unison melody; brass and guitar supply background hits. Slow practice may again be necessary to help the ensemble hear how sax and brass parts fit together. The drummer should lead the band out of the fermata in measure 60 with a clean fill to set up the hits beginning on beat 4.
C-1 through C3	61–85	Open solo section over "rhythm" changes (measures 61–68 are repeated).

Section	Measure	Event and Scoring
D-1	86–94	Last soloist continues, with saxes playing backgrounds and trombones playing background hits.
D-2	95–102	Trumpets reenter with trombones in measure 95 on hits. The solo and sax backgrounds continue.
D-3	103–109	Trumpets are out as trombones take over background hits.
E-1	111–119	Tension builds as the drummer plays fills over harmonically dense ensemble hits. Measures 115–119 may take rehearsal time to keep offbeat hits in time.
E-2	120–127	Piano solos; backgrounds out.
E-3	128–135	Saxes play a different lick, while brass and rhythm play most of the same hits as in section E-1. The drummer takes a 2-bar solo in measures 134–135 to transition into section F-1.
F-1	136–148	The original melody is harmonized across the ensemble with a version of augmentation lengthening the original four measures of melody out over nine measures. This development culminates in an alto/tenor sax unison line in measure 145–148, leading into a drum solo.
F-2	149–160	The lead trumpet receives the melody, which is then harmonized across the ensemble through measure 151. The lead trumpet and unison saxes then trade the melody back and forth until measure 155, when the ensemble has hits together. Ensemble counting is very important in this section; focus on keeping the ensemble together in measures 154–156. Trombones play a held chord over a subdued drum solo to enter the last A section of the form.

Section	Measure	Event and Scoring
G-1	161–168	Piano plays melody in both hands.
G-2	169–176	Piano and bass play the opening melody and rhythm from the introduction. Saxes play a lick in measure 176 which introduces brass and rhythm hits in measure 176.
H	177–187	The band reprises section A-2 in measures 176–180, using interplay between saxes and brass/rhythm. Trombones and bass (with bow) *diminuendo* on a chord beginning in measure 183, culminating in an ensemble hit on the second half of beat 4 in the last measure.

Unit 8: Suggested Listening

Clayton-Hamilton Jazz Orchestra, *Live at* MCG, MCG Jazz.
Hodges, Johnny, *Passion Flower 1940–46*, Bluebird.
Hodges, Johnny, with Dizzy Gillespie, *Verve Jazz Masters 35*, Verve.
Stewart, Rex, and Johnny Hodges, *Things Ain't What They Used to Be*, Koch Records.

Unit 9: Additional References and Resources

Dance, Stanley, *The World of Duke Ellington* (Cambridge: Da Capo Press, 1970).
Feather, Leonard, and Ira Gitler, *The Biographical Encyclopedia of Jazz* (New York: Oxford University Press, 1999).
Hasse, John Edward, *Beyond Category: The Life and Genius of Duke Ellington* (Cambridge: Da Capo Press, 1993).

Contributed by:

Scott Mertens
Sycamore, Illinois

Teacher Resource Guide

St. Thomas

Sonny Rollins

(b. 1930)

arranged by Mark Taylor

(b. 1948)

Unit 1: Composer

Theodore Walter "Sonny" Rollins was born in New York City, New York, September 30, 1930. His career has included recording with Thelonious Monk, John Coltrane, Miles Davis, Art Blakey, as well as nearly every other influential jazz artist to emerge during his lifetime.

Rollins is the composer of several important jazz standards, including *Oleo*, *Airegin*, and *Doxy*, as well as *St. Thomas*. He also composed and recorded the influential *Freedom Suite* in 1958. His choice of improvisation material is often unusual, and includes such unlikely jazz renditions as *I'm An Old Cowhand*, *How Are Things In Guacamora?* and *There's No Business Like Show Business*.

His career has been marked by two periods of intense practice activity during which he made no recordings, emerging latter with new style characteristics in his playing. He remains one of the most influential jazz masters of the twentieth century.

Unit 2: Composition

Rollins first recorded *St. Thomas* on the album *Saxophone Collosus* in 1956. Although Rollins is credited with its composition, it was also recorded in 1955 by Randy Weston (with a slightly different form and melodic interpretation) as *Fire Down There* on his album *Get Happy* and listed as a traditional song from the Virgin Islands.

St. Thomas is typically played with a calypso style drumbeat and a bass line consisting primarily of half notes.

Rollin's improvisation on the original recording of this work is often held up as a model for motivic development within an improvisation, particularly the first few choruses, during which fragments of the melody and its articulation are fully explored.

Unit 3: Historical Perspective

Sonny Rollins is of the generation of jazz musicians that followed the creators of the bebop style. His contemporaries include musicians such as Miles Davis, John Coltrane, Clifford Brown, Bill Evans, Jackie McClean, and Elvin Jones to name a few. His work, which serves as the foundation of his immense influence, is rooted in the bebop and hard bop styles, and extends into the 1960s era of jazz experimentation and exploration. Early saxophone influences included Dexter Gordon, Coleman Hawkins, and Lester Young, but he was also significantly influenced by John Coltrane.

Rollins often employs a "tongue in cheek" type of musical humor that separates the mood of his work from the intense concentration of feeling found in the Coltrane's work.

Unit 4: Technical Considerations

This chart is rated intermediate in this edition, and the recommended tempo is ♩ = 104; the chart will, however, work well at a faster tempo. Consider the tempo marking to be a minimum, as the style and energy level found in the original composition will not be communicated by a slower tempo. It is written for soli (with solo sheets provided in the needed keys) and a percussion feature for drum set and auxiliary percussion.

The lead trumpet range extends to a concert G (g^1), but for only one measure. The lead trombone reaches a concert F (f) several times during the arrangement. The bass line is entirely written out.

Harmonies are written out for piano and include chord symbols, but the guitar part is comprised of chord symbols only. Changes are occasionally complex, but the piece remains entirely in the key of C, the same as Rollins' original recording. Although it is possible to play these harmonies on a very advanced level, *St. Thomas* is often used as one of the pieces that can be introduced to a young improviser. The straight-eighth rhythmic feel, repetitive bass line rhythm, and short formal structure make it a good fit for young musicians.

Unit 5: Stylistic Considerations

The drum part differs significantly from the calypso style beat that is found on both the Rollins and Weston recordings. Here arranger Mark Taylor provides a typical jazz samba feel. It would work equally well with either beat, and if a young drummer can accurately imitate what is found on the aforementioned recordings, a substitution would be fine.

The marked articulations for the melody portion differ slightly from the original interpretations.

This piece could easily be opened up to feature the percussion section in an extended way, and/or used as a feature for any members of the band who wish to improvise a solo.

Unit 6: Musical Elements

MELODY:

This melody is very tuneful and easy to remember, making learning it by ear an excellent option. The chart is written in unison (or octaves) throughout the arrangement. It is important to emphasize the light forward motion found in the melody, and to avoid a heavy, labored feeling.

HARMONY:

The piece is in the key of C throughout, featuring the use of secondary dominants and tritone substitutions. The harmony lends itself well to the use of blues inflections within an improvised melodic line (C or A blues scale). Another common device used to navigate these chord changes is the pentatonic scale.

RHYTHM:

Eighth notes should be played straight. The notated samba rhythm and bass line give the composition a feeling of 2/4. It is important to encourage the rhythm section to keep a light and buoyant feeling that always maintains forward motion.

Unit 7: Form and Structure

The composition is in a 16-bar chorus, divided into 4-bar melodic segments. The 4-bar sections result in an AABC form.

Section	Measure	Event and Scoring
Intro	1–16	The tempo is ♩ = 104 (slower for learning purposes, but may eventually be faster), beginning with percussion and then adding the full ensemble in tutti quarter note rhythm until measure 14. The quarter notes are marked with sharp accents, but should never be heavy and labored.
Melody (1)	17–32	The first half of the melody is presented in octaves with second trumpet, first alto, first tenor, baritone sax, first trombone and rhythm section. The second half continues the same instrumentation in harmony, alternating the lead voice.
Melody (2)	33–50	The first half of the melody is presented with the brass in octaves and saxes playing an accompaniment part in four-part harmony. The second half is fully voiced in ensemble tutti, with unison saxophone lines in the bars of rest.
Soli	51–71	The solo section has backgrounds marked second time only and is written for the full ensemble together.
Percussion solo	72–78	This section is marked as a "time solo" and could easily be extended to feature the percussion for a longer time.
Shout section	79–90	This section written in full ensemble tutti and is limited to only a few rhythms.
Coda	91–100	This section is essentially identical to measures 9–16.

Unit 8: Suggested Listening

Rollins, Theodore Walter "Sonny," *Saxophone Colossus*, Prestige Records.
Weston, Randy, *Get Happy with the Randy Weston Trio*, Riverside Records.

Unit 9: Additional References and Resources

Goins, Wayne E., *The Jazz Band Director's Handbook: A Guide for Success* (New York: Edwin Mellen Press, 2003).
Lawn, Richard J., and Jeffrey L. Hellmer, *Jazz: Theory and Practice* (Van Nuys: Alfred Publishing Company, 1997).

Contributed by:

Steven Snyder
Associate Professor of Music
Morehead State University
Morehead, Kentucky

Advanced Bands

Teacher Resource Guide

Airegin

Sonny Rollins

(b. 1929)

arranged by Michael Abene

(b. 1942)

Unit 1: Composer/Arranger

Theodore Walter "Sonny" Rollins was born September 9, 1929 in New York City. He took piano lessons for a brief period, abandoned the piano for alto saxophone, and finally studied tenor saxophone. His influences include Coleman Hawkins, Lester Young, Charlie Parker, Eddie "Lockjaw" Davis, and Illinois Jacquet. While attending high school in the Harlem Public School System, Rollins led a musical group with Jackie McLean, Kenny Drew, and Art Taylor. Also, jazz greats Thelonious Monk, Bud Powell, Duke Ellington, and Sy Oliver were all at some point his neighbors.

From the bebop period in the 1940s to the 1960s, Sonny Rollins availed himself of many outstanding opportunities, all eventually contributing to his legendary status as one of the saxophone's top innovators. From 1948 to 1949 he rehearsed with Monk and recorded with Babs Gonzales, Bud Powell, Fats Navarro, and J. J. Johnson. From 1953–1954 he recorded with Charlie Parker, Miles, Davis, The Modern Jazz Quartet, and Thelonious Monk and composed *Airegin*, *Doxy*, and *Oleo*. In 1955 he turned down an invitation with the Miles Davis Quintet and accepted a position with Max Roach and Clifford Brown. In 1956 he played with John Coltrane on *Tenor Madness* and recorded *Saxophone Colossus*. During this period he also introduced the popular practice of bopping in three-four meter (*Valse Hot*) and, motivated by influence from his mother, championed Caribbean (Calypso) themes. In the 1960s he wrote and recorded the film score for *Alfie*, excluding the title song.

Unit 2: Composition

Sonny Rollins composed and recorded *Airegin* between 1953 and 1954 in one of the Miles Davis sessions. *Airegin* (Nigeria spelled backwards) was written to commemorate the newly formed independence of Nigeria as an African state. The composition typifies the sound of the swinging hard-bop/post bop movement of the smaller groups in terms of harmony and rhythm.

Originally written for a small group, the arrangement discussed here is for big band. The arranger, Michael Abene, is very creative in his rhythmic approach and timbre assignments.

Unit 3: Historical Perspective

In the 1920s, long before the start of Sonny Rollins's professional career, Fletcher Henderson pioneered the early swing movement in New York, setting the climate for the 1930s big band. Sonny Rollins sampled this period as it waned. Later, he pursued the small group as his performance medium. His professional career began with his use of the small group medium in the 52nd Street clubs in New York. Coleman Hawkins was an important influence, followed by the groundbreaking influence of bebop innovators Miles Davis, Charlie Parker, and Thelonious Monk (1953–1954). As he experimented with small groups, Rollins found the style of some pianists restrictive and incompatible with his harmonic concepts. These encounters forced him to use a piano-less rhythm section, using only bass and drums. During the 1960s, after one of his absences from the music scene, he returned to find his style somewhat dated. As a result, he connected with the avant-garde movement through association with Don Cherry and Billy Higgins.

Unit 4: Technical Considerations

Airegin is Grade level 5–6, with the approximate suggested tempo ♩ = 240 (approximate playing time is seven minutes). Originally written for an up-tempo, post-bebop small group, the composition sounds best at the fastest tempo. Reed one requires doubles on flute or piccolo (range to high G) and soprano saxophone. The doubles make this a challenge. Reeds two and three (one double at measure 291) require improvisation. The lead trumpet range is to concert C (third octave) and trombone one is to B♮ (third octave). Piano solos plus a strong rhythm section are also required. The chord changes for the piano, guitar, and bass are challenging in that, for the most part, there are only chord symbols. Two-five, flat-five, raised-nine, and flat-nine harmonies support the F minor tonality.

Unit 5: Stylistic Considerations

This swinging, strenuous composition is typical hard-bop/post-bop style. Sonny Rollins was one of the leaders who linked Charlie Parker with John Coltrane, and it has been said that one of his major contributions to jazz is what is called "thematic improvisation." This assertion may be in need of revision, considering that the bebop players of the period paid little attention to melody but more to chord changes. To a degree, the small groups dictated the stylistic sound of the unit.

Sonny Rollins's tendency toward performing with bass and drums was innovative and, at one period, he utilized solo saxophone (*It Could Happen to You*, 1957, and *The Freedom Suite*, 1958). During this period the small group began to replace the large group. Originally composed to feature a small group, this big band arrangement of *Airegin* features rhythm section and reeds two and three as solo improvisations.

Unit 6: Musical Elements

MELODY:

The melody is in post-bop style and in a fairly standard form. This melodic standard form should be memorized as a vocal so as to internalize the sound and form. The melody is distinctive for its use of rhythm and, in terms of pitch, it moves in a reasonable, interconnected manner.

HARMONY:

The composition is in a minor key, beginning with the minor seventh, flat-five, flat-nine, raised-nine, thirteen, and raised-eleven as the focal points of harmonic movement. Later in the arrangement, chord substitutions, chord extensions, and chromatic progressions combine to achieve an individualistic effect against a hard-bop melody. The timbre-textured chords and sound are generally thin and open, except for some occasional full ensemble writing (shout sections), but the mixing of timbres for big band enhances to a different, individualistic sound.

RHYTHM:

The rhythms are typical, of swinging, stylistic hard-bop composition. The rhythm section, then, should generate enough energy to execute the style of the period; it should define harmony and keep good time. The very fast tempo

(♩ = ca. 240) requires a good, solid rhythm section that can stabilize the sound at that tempo. Listening to recordings of stylistic practices from post-bop performances of the composer will aid in understanding how to make this composition swing. Clapping rhythm and singing various parts articulated in the jazz idiom will also provide a better understanding for performance.

Unit 7: Form and Structure

SECTION	MEASURE	EVENT AND SCORING
Introduction	1–16	The introduction opens in a big band style with all wind sections in like rhythms and dissonant chords scored in close harmony. Trumpets three and four are in minor seconds, as are the lead trombone and trombone two. The tempo is ♩ = 240. Approach the performance process at a slow tempo so as to establish a foundation for the fast, swing tempo that is without rhythm section. Observe dynamics (*ff–p*) and phrasing. Observe breathing, breath marks, and articulation to enhance the full ensemble sound. Tune dissonant chords in the introduction and throughout the composition with breath support.
	17–44	The rhythm section should practice slowly as a separate unit because it is both a solo unit—for 36 measures—and the support group for the big band. The rhythm section (piano, guitar, bass, and drums) should also create excitement and interest. Establish a feel for soloist and ensemble and rehearse in isolated sectionals for a better understanding of rhythmic concepts, chord changes, style and improvisation as a unit. Listen to the rhythm sections of Sonny Rollins. Transcribe solos and accompaniment (comping, etc.).

Section	Measure	Event and Scoring
	45–52	Paraphrase the melodic and harmonic rhythms in the interlude. The interlude/transition should set up the A section of the form, with attention to dynamics. Rhythm should establish a firm and solid foundation.
	53–72	The first eight bars, the A section of the form (measures 53–60) are antecedent-consequent phrases stated with reed one (flute or piccolo), reed two, and trumpet three in unison. The B section (measures 61–72) of the form retains the same timbre and instrumentation but adds a call and response line in the reed three, reed four, reed five, and lead trombone. Observe the stylistic articulations (staccato and accent) with phrase lines in reference to the post-bop approach.
	73–90	Measures 87–90 constitute a repetition of the A section of the form with a 3-bar drum solo break. The lead is now in reed three, soprano lead in reeds four and five (measures 77–87), and the lead trombone is added (measures 81–87). Rehearse like rhythms separately so as to unify the different lines in each section. Sing lines to gain a better feel for the composition.
Shout section	91–99	This is a big band shout section. Play chords slowly to hear harmonic relationships and increase tempo to secure the rhythmic feel in the full ensemble, since the rhythm is the same throughout. Practice saxophones, trumpets, trombones, and rhythm section separately, paying attention to stylistic articulations. Attach accents with energy.

Section	Measure	Event and Scoring
	99–126	This is a section for improvisation on reed three with rhythm section accompaniment for one full chorus. Reed three should transcribe Sonny Rollins's solo on *Airegin*, study the chord changes, and rehearse with the rhythm section separately from the big band. Use scales first on chord changes, then arpeggios and stylistic rhythms.
	127–146	Reed three continues the improvisation for another full chorus (measures 127–162). Reed one is on soprano saxophone. It enters with reed two, reed four, and reed five as a quartet background, with brass accented hits in response. Reeds and brass should sing and clap parts with rhythm section. Remember to phrase and articulate: accent, slur, and tongue last staccato note (doot). Reed three continues to improvise. Brass hits should be precise with full sound. Rehearse brass separately (B section, measures 134–142) keeping a stylistic brass choir in mind.
	147–163	This section is both a repeat and a continuation of the previous section. Measures 155–162 should be rehearsed with the B section of the form as a focus.
	163–182	Reeds four and five enter in unison and sustain (at measure 166) while reeds one and two enter in unison at measure 167 with the same rhythm. They continue unaccompanied to measure 170. This call and response is based on the 8-bar A section of the form. The rhythm section should enter in a smooth, well-connected manner with the reeds. At this point, chord changes become more complex, with flat-fives, flat-nines, thirteens/

	raised-elevens, raised-nines, etc. Strive for a brass choir sound at measure 179. A series of calls from the reeds and responses from the brass occur at measures 147–148 and 178–179. Balance and blend the interlude/ transition (measures 179–182).
183–198	Reeds three, four, and five are in unison. This soli saxophone section starts the A section of the form, joined by reeds one and two, accented with brass hits (measures 185–186 and 190–191). Balance and blend when the entire ensemble is playing in measure 195.
199–226	Reed two improvises for a full chorus, with some background from the full band. Reed two should study chord changes, starting with scales and transcribing the Sonny Rollins solo before attempting to improvise on the tune. Drums must listen to and perform hits with reeds or brass. Pay attention to glissando scale approach from above.
227–254	This is an improvisation section for reeds two and three. At this stage, reeds two and three should have transcribed the original solo. Therefore, be fluent in trading fours.
255–282	This section is a return to the beginning of the form, scored with reeds and brass in mixed timbres. Call and response starts this section and should be made important in the process of music communication. Fours continue in the B section with brass hits throughout the chorus. All accents should be played musically and stylistically correctly.

Section	Measure	Event and Scoring
	283–302	The A section of the form reoccurs with reed one (back on flute or piccolo), reed two, and trumpet three. Reed three on soprano, reeds four and five, and lead trombone respond on a counter unison line. Sing and clap these contrapuntal lines separately and together.
Shout section	303–320	This shout section is rhythmically repetitive and may be viewed as a pre-coda with full big band. Sing and clap the full big band shout section. Play chords slowly, minus the rhythm, for solidarity of sound, then add the rhythm and play in time. Accents should be stylistic and musical. The drum solo break at measure 318 should be creative and exciting.
Coda	321–336	This coda is a repeat of the introduction as tag ending material. Observe the all-important dynamics and ending at *pianissimo*. Drums complete the composition without piano and bass, except for the last measure.

Unit 8: Suggested Listening

Abene, Michael, arranger, *GRP All-Star Big Band*, Verve Music Group, 1995, 011105980029.

Miles Davis Quintet, *Cookin'*, Concord Music Group, 2005, PRCD–7094–2.

Sonny Rollins, *Airegin: 1951–1956*, Giants of Jazz, 1998.

Sonny Rollins, *Saxophone Colossus*, Prestige, 1987, OJCCD–291-2 (P-7079).

Sonny Rollins, *The Bridge*, on *Roots of Jazz Funk Volume One*, MVP, 1997, 50012–2.

Sonny Rollins, *Sonny Rollins, Volume One*, Blue Note, 1988, CDP 7 81542 2.

Sonny Rollins, *The Very Best*, Blue Note, 2005, 77395.

Sonny Rollins, *Green Dolphin Street* on *Sonny Rollins On Impulse!*, Impulse!, 1987, 254 613–2.

Unit 9: Additional References and Resources

Davis, Nathan T., *Writings in Jazz,* fifth edition (Dubuque: Kendall/Hunt Publishing Company, 1996).

Feather, Leonard, *The Encyclopedia of Jazz* (New York: Horizon Press, 1960).

Kernfeld, Barry, "Sonny Rollins," in *The New Grove Dictionary of Jazz* (New York: St. Martin's Press, 1995).

Virgin Books/Muze UK Ltd., 2004.

Contributed by:

James H. Patterson
Associate Professor and
Clark Atlanta University Jazz Orchestra Director
Clark Atlanta University
Atlanta, Georgia

Teacher Resource Guide

Anitra's Dance

Edvard Grieg

(1843–1907)

arranged by

Edward Kennedy "Duke" Ellington

(1899–1974)

William "Billy" Thomas Strayhorn

(1915–1967)

Unit 1: Composer and Arrangers

Edward Kennedy "Duke" Ellington was born in Washington, D. C., April 29, 1899. He studied the piano at the age of seven or eight, but those studies didn't appear to have a lasting effect upon him. He showed an interest in art and attended the Armstrong Manual Training School until he heard a hot pianist by the name of Harvey Brooks who would change the manner in which Ellington thought about music forever. Three months short of his graduation, Ellington dropped out of school to begin his career as a professional musician. He formed his first group, The Duke's Serenaders, in 1917. In 1923, Duke became a member of Elmer Snowden's Washingtonians. After becoming the leader of The Washingtonians he moved the band to New York, where it established itself at nightclubs such as the Exclusive Club, Connie's Inn, the Hollywood Club (Club Kentucky), Ciro's, the Plantation Club and the Cotton Club. The Washingtonians was the beginning of what would ultimately become the Duke Ellington Orchestra. Duke and his orchestra created some of the most swinging and sophisticated jazz music ever. After a successful and celebrated career, Ellington died in New York City on May 24, 1974.

William "Billy" Thomas Strayhorn was born in Dayton, Ohio on November 29, 1915 but spent the majority of his early life in Pittsburgh, Pennsylvania. Strayhorn studied classical music at the Pittsburgh Musical Institute. He was a composer of extraordinary talent, demonstrated in his composition, *Lush Life*, composed at the age of sixteeen. In 1939, he joined the Duke Ellington Orchestra and became an essential arranger for the orchestra, both composing and sitting-in at the piano. He assimilated Duke's style in such a way that it was difficult to determine where Duke's arranging and composing ended and Strayhorn's began. Some of Strayhorn's compositions include *Chelsea Bridge*, *Day Dream*, *Johnny Come Lately*, *Rain-check*, and Ellington's theme song, *Take the A Train*. He died of leukemia in 1967.

Edvard Hagerup Grieg, consider one of Norway's greatest composers, was born in Bergen, Norway, June 15, 1843. He was a thought to be a humble yet innovative composer who spent his entire life developing a style of composition that was based primarily on his Norwegian background via the usage of folk melodies and impressions that were linked to the landscapes and lifestyles of the people with whom he surrounded himself. Grieg died in Troldhaugen, Norway on September 4, 1907.

Unit 2: Composition

Anitra's Dance is a movement of Edvard Grieg's *Peer Gynt Suite*. It was composed in 1867 as incidental music for the play, *Peer Gynt*, written by Norwegian playwright Henrik Ibsen. The *Peer Gynt Suite* is considered one of Greig's greatest works. In 1960, Duke Ellington and Billy Strayhorn arranged Greig's *Peer Gynt Suite* for Duke Ellington Orchestra. While maintaining the integrity of Greig's composition, Ellington and Strayhorn used the elements of jazz—rhythm, harmony, melody and timbre—to reinterpret Grieg's composition. The improvisatory sections are short, but give each soloist an opportunity to work with the thematic material.

Unit 3: Historical Perspective

Throughout his career, Duke Ellington was considered an innovator. From the early influence of jazz greats Louis Armstrong and Sidney Bechet Ellington realized the importance of individuality. As a result, his orchestras consisted of the most distinguished and unique personalities in jazz. Individuals such as Barney Bigard, Cootie William, Ben Webster, Juan Tizol, Tricky Sam Nanton, Ray Nance, Sam Woodyard, Jimmy Blanton, Jimmy Hamilton, Johnny Hodges, Paul Gonsalvez, Harry Carney, Russell Procope, and Britt Woodman, to name a few. It was through these individuals that Ellington created some of his greatest musical compositions and performances. He and Strayhorn collaborated to create original works such as *A Drum is a Woman, The Queen Suite, The Deep South Suite, Jump for Joy, Such Sweet Thunder, My People*, and interpretations of works by classical composers such as *The Nutcracker Suite* by Tchaikovsky, *and The Peer Gynt Suite* by Grieg.

Unit 4: Technical Considerations

This chart is challenging, but manageable with work. The recommended tempo is ♩ = 94, with a duration of 2:57. It works very well at this tempo. The lead trumpet range goes to concert C three octaves above middle C (c^2, but only for one note); the lead trombone range goes to concert A above middle C (a). The range of the clarinet goes to concert F three octaves above middle C (f^2). The use of the plunger mute with the pixie mute may be challenging initially, depending on the player. Bass lines are written out.

The harmonies for the soloist are very simple. Some solo experience is required in the first and fourth reed players (alto and tenor saxophones). The clarinet part may present some technical challenges due to the intervals written in the melody, but are manageable.

Unit 5: Stylistic Consideration

In this composition, Ellington and Strayhorn draw upon their experiences of the concerto grosso style of writing (solo versus ensemble) used in classical music and the New Orleans tradition, while continuing to incorporate the intense swinging tradition of the 1950s and 60s for which the orchestra was known. *The Big Four*, which is used from the first note of the piece, should be exaggerated whenever it is encountered. This arrangement illustrates the ability of Ellington and Strayhorn to incorporate the old with the new to create a style that is timeless. Accents and dynamics are sometimes written in the music, but are mostly implied, and should be added whenever needed. Ellington and Strayhorn arranged this selection as the final movement of the suite as a feature for clarinetist Jimmy Hamilton. As such, it is a great stand-alone piece for featuring a clarinetist with little improvisation experience and can work well as a strong closer for a program.

Unit 6: Musical Element

MELODY:
Grieg provides a good melodic fabric with which to work. Ellington and Strayhorn have added countermelodies, riffs and call-and-responses, making it a great arrangement. It is recommended that the performers think of the arrangement as a dialogue as they explore how each part fits with the next. Encourage the performers to be conscious of all the events that are played by the other instruments in the orchestra. This will give them a better understanding of their individual parts as well as the entire work.

HARMONY:
The harmony of this arrangement is very simple. Use this as an opportunity to focus on other elements of the music.

RHYTHM:
This is the most important element of jazz music and the music of Duke Ellington. Ellington and Strayhorn have taken Grieg's waltz, the dance of that time, and interpreted it using the dance rhythm of their own time: 4/4 swing. This piece must swing from the beginning to the end. The band should feel the 4/4 swing of the rhythm section. It is important that the band is informed of *The Big Four* rhythm that occurs in New Orleans music. *The Big Four* is simply moving the accent from the strong beat (typically beat 1 of a measure) to an unexpected beat (such as beat 4 of a measure). This concept is used throughout the arrangement. Exaggerate all syncopations. The swing rhythm should maintain intensity throughout.

Singing rhythms as a rehearsal technique is recommended.

TIMBRE:
This is another important aspect of the Ellington sound. It is very important that each musician add her personality to her individual part. This allows the music to come to life. Make sure that each performer is trying to evoke his own individual voice while playing his instrument at all times.

Unit 7: Form and Structure

The events of the arrangement are as follows:

Section	Measure	Event and Scoring
Intro	1–4	The tempo is ♩ = 94. It is important that the first note of the introduction has the correct feel. It is a syncopation that is used in New Orleans music, and is frequently referred to as *The Big Four*. It should be played *fortissimo* and with a lot of accent. *The Big Four* should be played with a full sound and placed in the center of the beat. Be careful not to play this note too short. *The Big Four* will occur throughout the piece and should be played accordingly.
A/B	5–20	The full band plays the opening theme. The dynamics should follow the contour of the melodic line. Exaggerate the syncopation whenever it occurs. After the theme there is a dialogue between saxophones and trombones. It is best if this dialogue, or call-and-response, is thought of as a conversation. Interpreting the music accordingly will allow the performers and the listeners to have a better understanding of the arrangement.
C/D	21–36	The first half of this phrase is a repeat of the opening theme. For the alto solo that follows, this is an opportunity to work with the melodic material provided or to venture out and play something that is totally unrelated melodically. In any case, the soloist should study the original solo as a reference, then work on making up his own solo.

Section	Measure	Event and Scoring
E/F	37–52	Three events occur here. First is the melody of the trombones. It should be played full and in balance. The response to the trombone melody is in the trumpet section. This should be played full as well with the dynamics following the contour of the line. Make sure to add an accent to the anticipations. The role of the saxophone line is that of a riff to add intensity as a countermelody. It should be played with a lot of accent, but not too loudly. The intensity and volume of the entire 16-measure phrase should gradually increase, then gradually decrease. The drummer should attempt to play the accented rhythms of the trumpets.
G	53–60\	This is a transition section to prepare the listener for the clarinet entrance. The call-and-response between saxophones and trombones should gradually decrease in volume. The trombone with plunger mute should be played like a vocal part. It may be helpful to have performers sing their parts, first then imitate what they have sung. In the score, the third trombone part differs from the original Ellington recording. Originally the third trombone enters on beat 2 of the first, third, fifth and seventh measures of this section. The corrections should be made and performed.

Section	Measure	Event and Scoring
H	61–71	The clarinet part should be played lightly, singing but swinging. Trombones should continue to be very vocal, but careful not to play too loudly for the clarinet. After the clarinet finishes in the fourth measure, then trombones can play out a little more. The rhythm section should set up a light pedal rhythm feeling to differentiate this section from previous sections.
I	72–83	Here the rhythm section should start swinging again with intensity. Trombone parts should be very rhythmic. Clarinet should increase in intensity as well. Saxophones and trumpets enter as a response to the clarinet. With each entrance, the intensity of the section should increase until the end of the section. Follow the contour of each melodic line for the dynamics. The rhythm section should follow the dynamics as well.
J	84–93	This is the shout chorus of the piece and should be played loudly. It is very important that the drummer plays a fill that sets up the band. Play all syncopations with a lot of accent and make all lines sound as vocal as possible. Follow the contour of the melodic lines. The clarinet should play with a lot of power and intensity, as it now has the responsibility of responding to the band.

Section	Measure	Event and Scoring
K/L	94–109	This is a full orchestration of the section performed earlier by the trombone section(letters E/F). It should be played full and with power as it is a call-and- response between ensemble and solo tenor saxophone. Do not be initially concerned about overpowering the tenor saxophone. The intent is for this response to emerge from the density of the ensemble. Saxophones should play the riff in the last four measures of letters K/L under the tenor saxophone solo with a lot of rhythm. It is important that the rhythm section plays the dynamics of this section for it to be effective.
M	110–119	This is a repeat of letter J.
N/O	120–135	This is a repeat of letter A with clarinet playing the response to the band. Trombone and saxophone parts should be played as a call-and-response to each other, but dynamically beneath the solo clarinet. The dynamics should gradually decrease because of the range of the clarinet. The clarinet should also follow the dynamics of the line and *decrescendo* gradually so that the last four measures are played at ***mf***. This will set up the finale of the piece. The rhythm section should follow the dynamics as well.

SECTION	MEASURE	EVENT AND SCORING
P	136–143	The entire band should enter at a dynamic level of *forte*, remembering to add and extra accent to *The Big Four*. With the repetition of each section the dynamics and the intensity should increase throughout the orchestra until it reaches the final phrase at an ***ff***. In the third- and second-to-the-last measures, the eighth notes should be played short and straight. Do not swing these notes. The clarinet response should be strong and clear. The final response played by the rhythm section, saxophones, and trombones should be definitive.

Unit 8: Suggested Listening

Ellington, Duke:
Three Suites, Columbia Records.
Such Sweet Thunder, Columbia Records.
The Queen Suite, Original Jazz Classics.
The Far East Suite, Bluebird.

Unit 9: Additional References and Resources

Ellington, Duke, *Music is My Mistress* (Garden City, NY: Doubleday, 1973).
Hasse, John Edward, *Beyond Category: The Life and Genius of Duke Ellington* (New York: Da Capo Press, 1993).

Contributed by:

Victor L. Goines
Artistic Director of Jazz Studies
The Juilliard School
New York, New York

Teacher Resource Guide

Bird Count
Maria Schneider
(b. 1960)

Unit 1: Composer

Maria Schneider, born in Windom, Minnesota, arrived in New York City in 1985 after studies at the University of Minnesota, the University of Miami, and the Eastman School of Music. She immediately sought out Bob Brookmeyer, under whom she studied composition. At the same time, she became an assistant to Gil Evans, working on various projects with him, but most notably, the film *The Color of Money* and music for the Gil Evans/Sting tour in 1987. Later she was invited to conduct Evans' music extensively, featuring such musicians as Jon Faddis, Wallace Roney, Miles Evans, Ingrid Jensen, and David Sanborn.

The Maria Schneider Jazz Orchestra came into being in 1993, appearing at Visiones in Greenwich Village every Monday night for a stretch of five years. Subsequently her orchestra received invitations to perform at many jazz festivals and concert halls across Europe as well as in Brazil and Macau. She received numerous commissions and invitations to guest conduct her music with orchestras in the U.S. as well as in Italy, Portugal, France, Sweden, Denmark, Norway, Finland, Belgium, Holland, Germany, Slovenia, Austria, Canada, Scotland, Australia, Greenland and Iceland. She received a commission with Norrbotten Big Band and the Danish Radio Orchestra to arrange and conduct concerts with Toots Thielemans. Other commissioning organizations include the Metropole Orchestra, Stuttgart Jazz Orchestra, Orchestre National de Jazz (Recapitulation), Carnegie Hall Jazz Orchestra (El Viento), Monterey Jazz Festival (Scenes from Childhood), University of Miami Concert Jazz Band (Three Romances), Hunter College (Concert in the Garden and Sky Blue), and Jazz at Lincoln Center (Bulería, Soleá y Rumba). She was the recipient of a Doris Duke award to compose a dance work (*Dissolution*) in collaboration with the Pilobolus dance group. It was performed with her orchestra at the American Dance Festival and Kennedy Center. She arranged a concert of Ivan Lins' music for Ivan Lins, Toots Thielemans, and the Danish Radio Orchestra for an extensive European tour in 2003.

Concert in the Garden, released only through mariaschneider.com (an ArtistShare site), won a 2005 Grammy Award and became the first Grammy winning recording with Internet-only sales. It received Jazz Album of the Year by the Jazz Journalists Awards and the *Downbeat* Critics Poll. Both also awarded Schneider Composer of the Year and Arranger of the Year, and the Jazz Journalists also named her group, Large Jazz Ensemble of the Year.

Schneider's debut recording, *Evanescence*, was nominated for two 1995 Grammy Awards: Best Large Jazz Ensemble Recording and, for its title piece, Best Instrumental Composition. Her second and third recordings, *Coming About* and *Allégresse*, were nominated for Grammys as well. Maria had two compositions from Concert in the Garden were also nominated. Her third album, *Allégresse*, was chosen by both Time and Billboard in their Top Ten Recordings of 2000, which was inclusive of all genres of music.[1]

Unit 2: Composition

Maria Schneider composed and arranged *Bird Count* (1992) as a part of the Kendor Studio Writers Series, which is now called the Jazz Summit Series. This series of Kendor compositions are for the "proficient groups," and their difficulty is rated advanced, which is the most challenging level Kendor offers. The composer indicates that this piece is in "raucous swing" style. *Bird Count* is based on a blues riff melody with a 12-bar blues in F throughout. The tenor and bari saxophones introduce the 12-bar riff, which eventually is transported through every section of the band. Many solo opportunities appear in this piece with written changes for third trumpet, first alto, and bari saxophone. A good recording of *Bird Count* can be found on the composer's album, entitled *Days of Wine and Roses* (see Unit 8 below).

Unit 3: Historical Perspective

In her score notes, Schneider suggests that the group should listen to recordings of Charles Mingus to "get the spirit that this piece intends to convey." *Bird Count* is far from the *avant-garde* style that Charles Mingus is known for. With its blues riffs, *Bird Count* relates better to Mingus' early 1950s bebop style when he was performing with Charlie Parker, Miles Davis, Art Tatun, and Duke Ellington.

Bebop (or just bop) was the first modern or post-swing style of jazz music. It developed during the late 1940s and was considerably less popular than swing because it failed to attract dancers (imagine trying to dance to the fast tempo and rhythms of *Bird Count*). Bebop-style jazz did, however, showcase impressive soloists like trumpeter Dizzy Gillespie, saxophonist Charlie Parker, and drummer Max Roach. Bebop improvisations were composed mostly of melody lines that jumped around a lot and were full of twists and turns. Bebop musicians did more than embellish the melody during their improvisation. They would frequently depart entirely from the melodies and retain only the chord progressions of the piece. Bebop musicians also routinely wrote original melodies using the chord progression of popular tunes. Melodies written over the 12-bar blues progression, like *Bird Count*, had been used this way for decades.

Unit 4: Technical Considerations

This piece is rated advanced by its publisher. The recommended tempo is 𝅗𝅥 = 110, with a duration of 5:00. In determining the performance tempo, the composer suggests "part of the character and effectiveness, though, comes from an element of rawness and sloppiness, so push your players just a little."

The lead trumpet range goes to concert C (c^2), and the lead trombone range hovers a lot around a high G (g), A♭ (a♭) and A (a). Saxophones play the riff, or main melody, more than any other section, but every section eventually gets a chance to play the riff, which consists of many fast eighth notes. They are mostly chromatic, however, and a lot of technique is not required to master the fingerings and slide positions. There is enough rhythmic variation to require good counting, but nothing hard enough to discourage the players. Unfortunately, there is very little dynamic contrast, *forte* predominating with only a reduction to *mezzo forte* during the solo sections.

Only chord symbols are provided for the guitar, piano, and bass. The drum part offers no suggested written part, just slashes with the only written rhythm appearing in the last phrase or coda of the piece.

The piece is based on a basic V–IV–I blues progression; however with the fast tempo of the piece, these changes may be a challenge for the soloist to keep up with. There are two choruses of background riffs for each open solo section; this should help the soloist keep up with the changes.

At different points in the piece, every section in the band plays the melody riffs. The composer suggests that, even though some of these riffs will be a fifth apart from each other, these riffs should be practiced together "to get everyone playing and feeling it together so they can get the line loose and swinging."

Unit 5: Stylistic Considerations

Since there are no written suggestions on the drum part, having the drummer listen to the bebop-style recordings of Max Roach will help capture that style of performing. Bebop drummers are more connected to the soloist, frequently kicking and prodding the soloist as they perform. The drummer needs to move away from keeping time with the bass drum and more to the suspended ride cymbal. A nice crisp sound is needed on the high hat as it is snapped every other beat (2 and 4). The composer calls this piece a "straight-ahead blues" piece "with very few figures to catch. This makes it an excellent opportunity for the rhythm section to focus on locking in and swinging with one another. They should come out of the gate on fire."

The comping in the piano and guitar parts should be simple and complement rather than compete with each other. These instruments should support the fast pulse of the piece without getting in the way of the fast riffs being played by saxophones, trumpets, and trombones. It would be difficult to swing the fast eighth note rhythms found in the melody riffs throughout the piece. When learning the piece at a slower tempo, players should swing the eighth note; however, when performing up to the suggested tempo, the swing feel of these eighth-note riffs will be more subtle.

Unit 6: Musical Elements

MELODY:

The melody is a fast riff that is chromatic and falls on the fingerings and slide positions well. It is in AAB form over the 12-bar blues in the key of F. Every element of this piece comes from this melody riff, so even though the riff may be difficult to play (especially at the suggested tempo), once it is learned there are very few technical obstacles remaining in performing this piece. These melodic riffs are, for the most part, written in unison with limited harmonies. Make sure that the riffs are played in a legato style ("du") with the articulation ("tu" or "dat") being prominent only on the first and last note of each phrase.

HARMONY:

The harmony of this piece is the 12-bar blues in F. The composer describes it as "a V–IV–I blues (the last four bars of the form); make sure that they don't turn it a ii–V–I blues."

RHYTHM:

With the fast tempo, the challenge rhythmically will be to perform the riffs correctly, buth stylistically as well as technically. Having the students listen to bebop-style recordings will help with this, along with singing the melodic riffs of the piece while the rhythm section plays. The biggest rhythmic challenge of this piece is when the composer breaks up the melodic riffs and spreads them around the band. This happens as background to the melody itself and during solo sections. Some of these entrances are tricky and will need to be learned at a slow tempo and gradually sped up to the performance tempo. These passages will become automatic once players hear how their part fits with others and the melody. Setting the band up in a rehearsal square, instead of the traditional set-up, would allow each section to hear the other parts better.

Unit 7: Form and Structure

Section	Measure	Event and Scoring
Intro	1–8	The tempo is 𝅗𝅥 = 110. This section features a drum solo in swing style (in time). No other instruments are scored in this section.
	9–21	The riff melody is introduced in the first and second tenor saxophone and baritone saxophone parts. The melody itself is in AAB form and is very chromatic. It would save a lot of rehearsal time to have every one in the band learn this riff at the same time, gradually speeding the tempo up to the recommended tempo. Measure 213 is a place in the piece where everyone plays this riff.
	21–33	All saxophones play the melody in unison while trombones play accompanying melody fragments in the background. These riffs in the trombone part complement the melody but should not overpower the saxophone melody. Rhythmically putting the two parts (melody and accompanying riffs) together will be a challenge throughout this piece. Practice slowly at first and have musicians listen to how their accompanying riffs fit with the riff melody. Standing alone, these accompanying riffs are rhythmically challenging, but make musical sense when played with the melody riff.

Section	Measure	Event and Scoring
	33–45	This section is the same as measures 21–33, with all saxophones playing the melody. This time the trumpets join trombones in playing accompanying riffs.
	45–57	Tenor saxophones, third and fourth trumpets, and the lead trombone take the melody while the remaining parts play the accompanying riffs.
	57–69	Introduction to the solo section. The band plays a tutti riff for seven measures that serves as an introduction to the solo sections. The chord changes are written in the fourth trumpet part beginning in the middle of the tutti riff and continuing into the first solo section.
	69–177	Solo section with background riffs. Chord changes are written out for the following solo parts: fourth trumpet, first alto, and bari saxophone. The solos are repeated with a total of four choruses for each soloist. Each solo section has background licks that contain the melody riff or fragments that build throughout each solo. These background parts will help the soloist keep up with the changes. There is also a tutti riff that introduces each solo section.
	177–201	Soli section for the trumpet and trombone section which alternates with a soli section for the saxophones. These riffs are derived from the original melody and this section serves as a transition from the solo section back to the restatement of the original melody riff. To learn this section isolate the reeds, then third and fourth trumpets with first and second trombones, and then first and second trumpets with third and fourth trombones.

Section	Measure	Event and Scoring
	201–213	The melody riff returns in the reeds and first and second trumpet. Third and fourth trumpets and trombones have accompanying riff licks. Again, isolating these parts in rehearsal and then putting them together will help learn this section.
	213–225	Saxophones and brass play the melody riff in unison. This is a great spot to rehearse when first learning this piece, with every section playing this riff from which the entire piece derives.
	225–241	Saxophones restate the melody riff one last time, with a short six-measure coda to end the piece. There is an opportunity for a drum solo before the last two notes of the piece.

Unit 8: Suggested Listening

Gillespie, Dizzy, *Greatest Hits: Dizzy Gillespie*, BMG Entertainment.
Maria Schneider Orchestra, *Live at The Jazz Standard*, Days of Wine and Roses, artistShare.com.
Parker, Charlies, *The Essential Charlie Parker*, UMG Recordings.

Unit 9: Additional References and Resources

Gridley, Mark C., *Concise Guide to Jazz*, fifth ed (Upper Saddle River: Prentice Hall, 2006).
http://www.kendormusic.com/.
Lawn, Richard, *The Jazz Ensemble Director's Manual, a Handbook of Practical Methods and Materials for the Educator* (Oskaloosa: C. L. Barnhouse Company, 1981).
http://www.mingusmingusmingus.com/Mingus/index.html.
http://mariaschneider.com/about.aspx.

Contributed by:

Todd Shiver
Director of Bands
Georgia College & State University
Milledgeville, Georgia

---

1 www.mariaschneider.com.

Teacher Resource Guide

Black Bottom Stomp

Ferdinand "Jelly Roll" Morton

(1890–1941)

arranged by Jaxon Stock

edited by Robert Curnow

(b. 1941)

Unit 1: Composer

Ferdinand "Jelly Roll" Morton was born in New Orleans, Louisiana on October 20, 1890. Morton began playing the piano at the age of ten and evolved into an entity that would inspire and change the direction of jazz.

An arguably arrogant individual, Jelly Roll claimed to be the inventor of jazz. While the validation of this statement continues to be challenged, he is certainly one of the most pivotal and innovative figures in jazz history.

A very talented (and underrated) pianist, he developed his own style that seemed to bridge the gap between ragtime and jazz. Although his music was heavily influenced by the music of New Orleans, he spent a great deal of time in Los Angeles and Chicago, where he recorded his piano solos between 1923–24. He performed and recorded band sides as well, surrounding himself with the likes of Kid Ory on trombone, cornetist George Mitchell, Johnny Dodds on clarinet, Bud Scott on banjo, drummers Baby Dodds and Andrew Hilaire, and bassist John Lindsay. With an occasional personnel change, this exciting group of musicians became known as the *Red Hot Peppers*. Their most stimulating recordings were made during 1926–27.

Morton is often thought of as the first substantial composer of jazz music. Some of his well known compositions/arrangements include *The Pearls*, *King Porter Stomp*, *Wolverine Blues*, *Black Bottom Stomp*, *Grandpa's Spells*, *Mr. Jelly*

Roll, *Doctor Jazz*, and many more. As his focus seemed to be on recording jazz music, his compositions are constructed in a very careful manner. Solo parts were notated, primarily because Morton didn't want the unpredictability of improvisation on his recordings.

While he may or may not have "invented jazz," Morton is undoubtedly one of the most influential figures in the history and direction of jazz music.

Unit 2: Composition / Arrangement

As with most of his compositions, Jelly Roll Morton wrote *Black Bottom Stomp* (1926) for recording purposes. This is evident in the notated solo sections and lack of improvisation. By writing in this manner, he was also able to capture the style of the music of New Orleans so that musicians outside of the city might authentically play it. This three-themed composition was written for a seven-piece ensemble consisting of cornet, clarinet, trombone, banjo, piano, bass, and drums. Some of the unique features of this tune include the twenty-measure solo choruses that feature stop-time breaks at varying parts of the form.

This particular big band arrangement was written for the National Repertory Ensemble by Jaxon Stock. He successfully captured the original essence of the 1920s original while adding his own creative twists. For example, the banjo solo is written out for two soprano saxes (a very hip sound!), the first trumpet solo is played by first and second trumpets, and various counter-lines and harmonies have been added to certain sections of the piece.

Unit 3: Historical Perspective

Often referred to as the birthplace of jazz, New Orleans became home to a wide variety of cultures and musical styles such as ragtime, the blues, and spirituals. At the turn of the twentieth century these various styles began to combine with one another to form what would become known as America's music: jazz.

Primarily ascending from the African-American community, jazz music emerged during the time of segregation and denial of basic rights for black people. This system of discrimination was fueled by the *Plessy v. Ferguson* decision (1896) and the *Jim Crow Laws* that followed.

In spite of these laws, countless musicians of every race were meeting to play this new kind of music. When segregation finally took its toll, New Orleans natives began traveling to more appealing destinations in the north and west. With this migration and the use of the phonograph, this "jazz" music from New Orleans began to spread rapidly across the country and eventually overseas. By the 1920s, jazz had become the new and exciting dance music of the masses.

Unit 4: Technical Considerations

Black Bottom Stomp is rated Grade 5, and the recommended tempo is 𝅗𝅥 = 150. However, this tune will still work at a slower tempo if necessary.

The lead trumpet goes to a concert E♭ (e♭^{2}) twice, and the lead trombone goes to a concert C (third octave [c^1]). The reed section is scored for one clarinet and five saxophones: two soprano, one tenor, and one baritone. The brass instrumentation includes three trumpets and three trombones. The bass line is notated throughout the piece (it is not difficult) except for one section behind the clarinet solo. If needed, the bass line for the following chorus (under the piano solo) may be used.

The piano and optional banjo parts both include some sections that are notated and some that are strictly chord symbols. The piano part (ragtime/early stride style) isn't too difficult, as the player will be able to use both hands, but the solo section is an authentic stride. The left hand covers the single note downbeats with chordal upbeats while the right hand solos.

All soli are notated (transcribed from the original recording) for clarinet, trumpet, piano, and banjo (also scored for two sopranos).

Unit 5: Stylistic Considerations

This quick piece captures the sound of the 1920s and demonstrates the ragtime influences on early jazz music. The tempo of this piece demands a light and agile approach. However, to authentically reproduce the sound of this time period, the articulations need to have a bit more punch, particularly in the ensemble hits and syncopated sections.

This piece represents a pivotal era in the development of jazz music and is the perfect vehicle for educating students about its historical and cultural significance. As there are few big band compositions/arrangements in this style available, this piece would be a wonderful "excursion" in any concert program.

Unit 6: Musical Elements

MELODY:

This chart features multiple melodies by soloists, trios, and small groups within the counterpoint sections. Morton's compositions usually featured complex melodic development, and Stock's arrangement of *Black Bottom Stomp* is no exception.

HARMONY:

The first section (intro to measure 61) is centered on the key of concert B♭. It then modulates to concert E♭ for the remainder of the piece. The chords quite often jump between the tonic and dominant (especially during the s olo sections), with a few turnarounds and transition measures between the various sections.

RHYTHM:

A descendent of ragtime music, this piece utilizes a great deal of syncopated rhythms and offbeat hits. Letting the winds hear the rhythm section alone is an effective approach. This gives them the opportunity to hear the downbeat bass line with the upbeat chord hits and lets them internalize that ongoing groove.

Unit 7: Form and Structure

SECTION	MEASURE	EVENT AND SCORING
Intro	1–8	The suggested tempo is 𝅗𝅥 = 150. It will need to be slowed down initially to master the technical aspects and nuances. This is a full-ensemble passage with the melodic theme divided primarily between reeds and trumpets. All three trombone parts need to match volume in this section; match articulations in measure 4 on unison rhythms. Identifying who plays together at any given time is crucial, since there are frequent changes.
	9–24	Dynamics drop and reeds take control on floating whole notes for the first four measures of this section. In measure 5, short, accented rhythms supported by the rhythm section contrast. This section is then repeated through measure 24. Careful attention should be paid to contrasting dynamics.

Section	Measure	Event and Scoring
	25–28	The first four measures of a question/answer section. Trumpets playing the "solo" part should match the short articulations as played in the original recording. Since reeds play a blown-up stride piano part, rehearse them with the piano to achieve stylistic cohesion. Trombones need to match the quick "wah" sound with plungers. The ensemble answers with confident, accented syncopation and a boost in volume.
	33–40	A stop-time break for the two trumpets, again followed by an ensemble answer.
	41–60	The first of the twenty-measure choruses (including a four-measure interlude at the end), starting with clarinet. The ensemble trades fours with the clarinet solo throughout this chorus. When the clarinet takes over, reeds and trombones need to bring the dynamic level down considerably. Trombones should get "bright and brassy" at measure 57.
	61–68	A collective counterpoint section. The melody is played by first soprano saxophone, first tenor saxophone, first trumpet, and first trombone. Second soprano saxophone plays a soloistic counter-line that should be played strongly to match the quartet. Trombones need to be present but not obtrusive: exaggerate the glissandi, but remain light and bouncy on the remaining notes. Baritone saxophone should imitate the bass on this section, as the parts are doubled. To achieve balance in this counterpoint section, it is imperative that the long notes do not cover up the moving lines happening simultaneously.

SECTION	MEASURE	EVENT AND SCORING
	61–68 (continued)	Second and third trumpets assume the upbeat piano/banjo role, and so need to match note lengths. The melody is again in the soprano and tenor saxophones, trumpet, and trombone.
	81–100	A clarinet solo transcribed from the original recording. The accents outline a rhythm that occurs many times throughout this piece, and should be exaggerated. Although rhythm section parts are not notated, the style must remain the same.
	101–120	An unaccompanied piano solo. The left hand covers the accompaniment while the right hand solos. An optional bass part is provided if needed.
	121–128	The trumpet solo here should be played very confidently, as it is accompanied only by ensemble hits.
	129–140	More instruments join the ensemble hits, which will make it more difficult to maintain a light sound that doesn't overpower the solo. Non-soloists need to play fairly quietly during this section.
	141–148	The original banjo solo is written out and harmonized for two soprano saxophones (it is also written in the optional banjo part). Every third note should have a slight accent, again outlining that familiar "second-line" rhythm. The rhythm section returns after laying out behind the piano solo.

Section	Measure	Event and Scoring
	149–160	The repeated eighth-note pattern is split between the two soprano saxophones while the rest of the winds play short hits. Third trombone plays an independent part for the first three measures. Measure 157 features a difficult descending pattern in the reeds and piano. Vocalizing the parts for style and nuances will be helpful.
	161–180	An ensemble counterpoint section. This time, the clarinet has the obbligato line over the rest of the ensemble. Isolate the instruments playing the same lines to match style/articulation. Tenor and baritone saxophones should put slight accents on the first notes of each slurred group in measure 179 for cohesion.
		First soprano saxophone joins clarinet on a unison line. The trombone soloist in measure 187 should listen carefully to the recording for articulations/glissandi.
	189–202	The final ensemble section. Long notes should not cover up moving lines. Maintain excitement and peak in the last two measures.

Unit 8: Suggested Listening

Armstrong, Louis, *The Complete Hot Five and Hot Seven Box Set*, Columbia/Legacy. This arrangement can be found on *Swingin' It Live* by the Northern Illinois University Jazz Ensemble, NIU.

Beiderbecke, Bix, *Singin' the Blues*, Sony.

Morton, Jelly Roll, *Red Hot Peppers*, Bluebird/RCA.

King Oliver's Creole Jazz Band, *The Complete Set*, Challenge.

Unit 9: Additional References and Resources

Cook, Richard, and Brian Morton, *The Penguin Guide to Jazz on CD: Seventh Edition* (New York: The Penguin Group, 2004).

Dunscomb, Richard, and Willie L. Hill, Jr., *Jazz Pedagogy: The Jazz Educator's Handbook and Resource Guide* (Miami: Warner Brothers, 2004).

Schuller, Gunther, *Early Jazz: Its Roots and Musical Development* (New York: Oxford University Press, 1968).

Contributed by:

Mike McMann
Instrumental Music Director
North Scott High School
Eldridge, Iowa

Teacher Resource Guide

Central Park West

John Coltrane

(1926–1967)

arranged by Jon Fedchock

(b. 1957)

Unit 1: Composer/Arranger

John Coltrane was one of the greatest innovators in the history of jazz. We often think of Coltrane as an improviser, in terms of his rapid musical development, his many tonal, harmonic, and rhythmic advances, his playing of the soprano saxophone, and also in regard to his cultural impact. We sometimes overlook the fact that Coltrane also played some beautiful ballads and wrote some notable compositions.

Coltrane recorded *Central Park West* on the album *Coltrane's Sound* in 1960, but the album was not released until 1964. Thus, it was recorded during the period immediately following the landmark recording *Giant Steps* and came before his more adventurous artistic experiments with modal music and free jazz. The album *Coltrane's Sound* is possibly best remembered for a re-harmonization of the bridge on the standard *Body and Soul*, and his interpretation of the song *The Night Has a Thousand Eyes*. The album featured McCoy Tyner on piano, Steve Davis on bass, and Elvin Jones on drums.

John Fedchock joined the Woody Herman Orchestra in 1980. He was featured with the band for seven years, during which time he also was the musical director. He is active as a performer and arranger and has toured with T. S. Monk, Gerry Mulligan, Louie Bellson, and Bob Belden, among others. Fedchock is a graduate of Ohio State University and holds degrees in music education and jazz studies. He also earned a master's degree in jazz studies and contemporary media from the Eastman School of Music in Rochester, New York. He currently teaches trombone at Purchase College in Purchase, New York and at the University of the Arts in Philadelphia, PA. He has many compositions and arrangements available through Kendor Music, Inc.

Unit 2: Composition

Central Park West is relatively demanding because of the very slow tempo and high trumpet range. It is a marvelous vehicle for a good pianist, a strong tenor saxophone soloist, and a drummer who is adept at using brushes in a ballad setting. It also requires the ability for the band to play strongly and confidently at a low volume level. It is unusual in that it consists mostly of ten-measure phrases.

Unit 3: Historical Perspective

Woody Herman was a fine clarinetist and alto saxophonist, but his legacy to jazz is primarily that of being a leader as well as his ability to develop and promote young talent. He became a bandleader in 1936, and continued to lead bands into the 1980s. His earlier bands were referred to as the "First Herd" (1944), the "Second Herd" or "Four Brothers" (1947), "Third Herd" (1950), and the "New Thundering Herd" (1950).

Among the many great musicians who performed in various Herman bands are Pete Candoli, Bill Harris, Dave Tough, Conte Candoli, Stan Getz, Zoot Sims, Al Cohn, Shorty Rogers, Gene Ammons, Lou Levy, Terry Gibbs, Shelly Manne, Carl Fontana, Bill Chase, Phil Wilson, Sal Nistico, Andy Laverne, and Alan Broadbent.

Although Herman frequently performed material that he had made famous earlier in his career, such as *Woodchopper's Ball* and *Apple Honey*, he also played and recorded newer material and sometimes performed versions of current pop tunes. Beginning with the "Second Herd," his bands had a characteristic saxophone section sound consisting of three tenor saxophones and one baritone saxophone.

Unit 4: Technical Considerations

This chart is rated Grade 4 1/2, and the recommended tempo is ♩ = 60, with a duration of 5:30. It is a challenge to maintain this slow tempo throughout the piece. The lead trumpet range goes to a high D♯ above the staff (d♯^{2}), the lead trombone to an A above the staff (a), and the bass trombone to a D below the staff (D_1). There is a counter-line in the saxophones, which is rhythmically challenging at this slow tempo. The only required double is flugelhorn.

There are relatively complex chord symbols over pedals throughout the arrangement in the piano, guitar, and bass parts. No bass lines are written out. There is no guitar part. The chord changes for the tenor saxophone require a player with advanced skills.

Unit 5: Stylistic Considerations

This slow, beautiful ballad requires smooth articulations and can utilize subtone in the saxophones. The drummer must use brushes and, if emulating the Woody Herman recording, the pianist will have ample opportunity to add fills.

Unit 6: Musical Elements

MELODY:
This simple melody needs to be played dynamically but not over-dramatically. The long notes need to be carefully shaped by the ensemble. The counter-melodies, which are much more active than the melody, need to support the melody and not overtake it. The composition itself consists of ten-measure phrases.

HARMONY:
Upon first hearing, the harmony of this piece has a distinctive Coltrane sound because of some unusual root movement that, in actuality, is simply a series of ii–V–I progressions in the keys of B, D, A♭ and F major, and a pedal point in the key of B major.

RHYTHM:
Maintaining forward motion is a major challenge with this piece because of the slow tempo. The drummer should use classic brush technique. It is important that the bass player and piano player play in such a way as to create a forward momentum while avoiding being too busy or getting in the way of the counter-melodies. It is also critical that the entire band think about shaping phrases in order to avoid having the piece become stagnant.

Unit 7: Form and Structure

SECTION	MEASURE	EVENT AND SCORING
Introduction	1–4	The tempo is ♩ = 60. Maintain this slow tempo by feeling the subdivisions. The rhythm section plays an introduction with piano fills. This should be at a very low volume level and not too busy.

SECTION	MEASURE	EVENT AND SCORING
Melody	5–9	Pickups in the brass. Trumpets have the melody; trombones have an accompanying figure that should be played very delicately and at a low volume level. The rhythmic simplicity of the melody lends itself to shaping the phrase with subtle dynamic shadings.
	10–19	This is a restatement of the theme by the brass. Saxophones have a rhythmically awkward counter-line that moves quickly in eighth and sixteenth notes and triplets. Be sure that saxophones are rhythmically accurate. Saxophones should not overbalance the melody. They may play this section in a subtone.
	20–24	Saxophones play the last part of the melody while trombones play a simple counter-line.
Send-off	24–28	A full band send-off to the solo section. This is an extension of the form over a pedal in the bass. The band needs to *crescendo* evenly into the following section.
Tenor Solo	29–39	A tenor saxophone solo begins.
	39–49	The tenor saxophone solo continues with added backgrounds. This section builds into measure 49.
Climax	49–59	This is the climax of the piece. Trumpets have the melody and saxophones and trombones have counter-lines. The entire band should cut off at measure 50, beat 2. The hits in the brass in measures 55–57 on the end of beat 2 need to be heavily accented and not released until beat 1. The fall in measure 58 should go until measure 59, beat 1.

SECTION	MEASURE	EVENT AND SCORING
Ending	59–73	This is a development of the main theme used as a coda. It is important that this section is not too loud. The tenor saxophone solo has a short section that is written out, but this can be loosely interpreted and not played exactly as written.

Unit 8: Suggested Listening

Coltrane, John, *Coltrane's Sound*, Atlantic SD1419, 1964, re-released 1990.
Herman, Woody, *Best of Woody Herman & His Big Band: The Concord Years*, Concord CCD-4557, 1981.
Herman, Woody, *Fiftieth Anniversary Tour*, Concord Jazz Records CJ-302, 1986.
Herman, Woody, *The Concord Jazz Heritage Series*, Concord Jazz CCDCD-4838, 1998.

Unit 9: Additional References and Resources

Clancy, W.D. and A.C. Kenton, *Woody Herman: Chronicles of the Herds* (New York: Schirmer Books, 1995).
Dunscomb, Richard, and Willie L. Hill, Jr., *Jazz Pedagogy: The Jazz Educator's Handbook and Resource Guide* (Miami: Warner Brothers, 2004).
Kernfeld, Barry, "John Coltrane," *Grove Music Online*, ed. L. Macy, http://www.grovemusic.com (accessed 12 March, 2007).
James, Michael and Barry Kernfeld, "Woody Herman," *Grove Music Online*, ed. L. Macy, http://www.grovemusic.com (accessed 12 March, 2007).
Nisenson, Eric, *Ascension: John Coltrane and His Quest* (New York: St. Martin's Press, 1993).

Contributed by:

Paul Scea
Director of Jazz Studies
West Virginia University
Morgantown, West Virginia

Teacher Resource Guide

Cherokee

Ray Noble

(1903–1978)

arranged by Mark Taylor

(b. 1948)

Unit 1: Composer

Cherokee was written by Ray Noble, a noted British composer, arranger, bandleader, and pianist. He was one of the first English bandleaders to be successful in the United States during the big band era of the 1930s. Noble was born in Brighton, England on December 17, 1903 and died in London on April 3, 1978. He studied music at Cambridge and won England's Melody Maker award in 1926 at age nineteen. He gained notoriety as the staff arranger for the British Broadcasting Company (BBC) Dance Orchestra, and in 1929 he became director of light music at HMV records in London, a division of RCA Victor. At HMV he led the New Mayfair Orchestra, a studio group that featured some of the best British musicians from the top hotel orchestras of the day as well as vocalist, Al Bowlly.[1]

In 1934 Noble came to America and formed a band that secured a regular engagement at the Rockefeller Center's Rainbow Room seven nights a week from 9:00 p.m. to 3:00 a.m. Because union bans prevented Noble from bringing British musicians to the United States, he employed Glenn Miller to assemble a top-notch American band. With Miller taking on many of the arranging duties, Noble embraced jazz in contrast to the straight dance music played by his British orchestra. Although jazz was prevalent in the band's book, it was on ballads that the group excelled, particularly on numbers that featured Bowlly.[2]

Among the members of his big band were artists such as Glenn Miller, Claude Thornhill, and Bud Freeman, who later went on to outstanding careers of their own. In 1937 he disbanded his band and left New York for the West Coast, where he formed another less-noted band and served as musical director and part-time actor on the Burns and Allen and Edgar Bergan and Charlie McCarthy radio programs. He also worked sporadically in Hollywood, scoring several films and appearing as an actor in two, including "A Damsel in Distress." Noble retired to England in 1959.

Noble's career in music spanned a thirty-year period. His place in the world of big bands is assured by the work he did in the HMV studios and his musical compositions.[3] His first composition, *Goodnight Sweetheart*, was written in 1931. Although his compositional output was relatively small, several of his works became jazz standards: *The Very Thought of You* (1934), *Love Is the Sweetest Thing* (1934), *The Touch of Your Lips* (1936), and *I Hadn't Anyone Till You* (1938), in addition to *Cherokee*.

Unit 2: Composition

Cherokee, also known as *Indian Love Song*, was written in 1938 as the first movement of a five-movement work called *Indian Suite*. The other movements included *Comanche War Dance*, *Iroquois*, *Seminole*, and *Sioux Sue*. Arranger Billy May created the signature instrumental arrangement of the tune for the Charlie Barnet Orchestra a year after it was written. It ultimately became the theme song for Barnet.

Mark Taylor, former chief arranger for The United States Army Band ("Pershing's Own") wrote this arrangement. During his twenty-four years of service, he composed extensively for the Army Blues. He has also written for many diverse artists, ranging from The Stan Kenton Orchestra to the country group Alabama. Mark is widely published, with over 150 compositions and arrangements to his credit.[4] His knack for writing quality charts for educational ensembles of all levels has established him as one of the most highly respected jazz composer/arrangers in the business.

Unit 3: Historical Perspective

Cherokee was a staple in the libraries of most of the big bands in the 1930s. At that time it was typically played at a medium tempo and often featured a vocalist. The lyrics, which were also written by the composer, were written with a male singer in mind, but most of the signature vocal recordings have been by female singers such as Sarah Vaughn on *In the Land of Hi-Fi* (1955) and Ella Fitzgerald on *Sophisticated* Lady (Pablo, 2001). Artists such as Clifford Brown, Ahmad Jamal, and Bud Powell also recorded it in small group settings.

Due to the length of the form, most early recordings were limited to two or three choruses with soloists limited to one or two of the sixteen-measure sections of the form. It was not considered a vehicle for improvisers until Don Byas and Charlie Parker recorded it in 1945. Since then it has become a jazz warhorse that is played at jam sessions and has been arranged and recorded by many of the jazz greats in a multitude of different settings. The 64-bar AABA form and unique chord progression have also made this tune the basis for a number of *contrafacts* (a tune based on the chord changes of another tune), including Charlie Parker's *Ko-Ko* and Buddy DeFranco's *Swinging the Indian.*

Most post-1945 versions of this tune showcase the artist's virtuoso technique at very fast tempi, and some have changed the usual swing feel to various Latin styles. Recordings by modern jazz artists Wynton Marsalis and Arturo Sandoval display unique interpretations of the tune.

Unit 4: Technical Considerations

This arrangement follows the custom of playing this tune as a *flag-waver* (a swing-style tune played at a very fast or "bat out of hell" tempo) for jazz players to display their technical prowess and improvisational technique. Because of the fast tempo, mature levels of technique are required to play this chart, which is rated as Grade 5–6. It is written in cut time for easier rhythmic understanding, but the recommended tempo marking (𝅗𝅥 = 144) makes it challenging. In any case, the tempo should be taken as fast as the ensemble can play with control and accuracy.

The beginning of the arrangement features an 8-bar drum solo that establishes the tempo. The opening statement of the melody, which has drum solos and fills interspersed, is homophonic in texture for the winds and requires a drummer with solid time, control, and considerable technique. There is also a change to a Latin samba feel toward the end of the chart.

Because the bridge of the tune modulates to challenging key centers, care must be taken with accidentals. Likewise, soli for unison brass and saxophones as well as solo backgrounds require solid technique, accurate counting, and section precision. Range considerations are a concern for the trumpet and trombone sections. First trumpet has a written E above high C (e^2), and first trombone has a B♭ above middle C (b♭).

There are solos for first alto sax, second trumpet, and first tenor sax that require the ability to improvise at a rapid pace with interesting melodic material to carry these sections of the tune. The second trumpet player must have good facility in multiple keys to solo over the bridge of the tune. Before the ending of the chart, a one-chord, 64-bar section in a samba groove features all three soloists in collective improvisation (several soloists playing at the same time).

Parts are written out for piano and bass, but not guitar and drums. Drummers need to be familiar with both swing and samba feels. Mature bass players should be encouraged to create their own bass line based on the chord changes. Pianists should be encouraged to create comping rhythms and alternate chord voicings, especially during solo sections (refer to Unit 9 below for helpful texts). The written piano part should be played during section A of the tune from measures 9–42. The piano is tacit during the brass soli from measures 145–152 and 161–168, and the drums tacit during the cross-voiced soli from measures 209–221. Chord changes are provided for the guitar player, who should play Freddie-Green-style rhythm guitar. An optional auxiliary percussion part for vibraphone is also provided.

Unit 5: Stylistic Considerations

Due to the fast tempo, articulations are crucial to the successful performance of this chart. Marcato accents should be played with full sound, but as short as possible. Dynamics are also important to this tune. Care should be taken to execute the dynamics that are written as well as introducing dynamic shaping to all long notes.

Unit 6: Musical Elements

MELODY:

The melody of the tune is diatonic and primarily pentatonic with a few chromatic embellishments. Long sustained tones comprise the original melodic rhythm. In this arrangement the drummer solos over the end of each A section phrase, which has been extended by a four-measure long note that is fully scored with altered harmony. The B melody is written in its original 16-bar form using a combination of half notes and *habanera* rhythm. The final A section makes a more sustained statement of the melody. The traditional melody is heard over a walking bass solo at a later point in the chart.

HARMONY:

The harmony of *Cherokee* is diatonic, but moves through a number of key areas. The harmonic rhythm of the chord progression is relatively slow. This arrangement includes some alterations of the original tune harmony, particularly in the opening statement of the A melody. The first statement of the melody utilizes a number of extensions and alterations requiring considerable care in tuning full ensemble chords. The solo section of this arrangement reverts to the standard form and chord changes.

The chord progression to this tune begins on the tonic with a move to IV via a ii–V progression in the third measure of the form. This is followed by a 4-bar ii–V progression in the dominant key, then a return to the tonic key via another 4-bar ii–V progression. The second A section of the form follows the same format with the exception of a return to the I chord for the last two measures.

The bridge begins with descending four-measure sequences of ii–V–I chords whereby the I chord becomes minor in the following measure to start the next ii–V–I sequence. This sequence begins in the key of B (♭II), moves to A (VII), and then to G (VI). The bridge ends with 2-bar ii–V sequences in F (V) and B♭ (I). Similar chord sequences are found in tunes such as *How High the Moon* and *Laura*. The chord progression of the last A section is the same as the second A.

RHYTHM:
Rather than the original whole note/half note melody, the arranger has used quarter and eighth notes with rests. The A section melody is written with a slight hint of hemiola rhythm. Quarter- and half-note triplets should be played evenly with each note accented. All rhythms must be played accurately so that the tempo does not drag. Vocalization using scat syllables should be used to learn the rhythms initially, and the A and B melodies should be rehearsed initially with the rhythm section playing quarter notes to solidify the ensemble precision.

Unit 7: Form and Structure

The form of *Cherokee* is AA'BA", sixty-four measures, with each section being sixteen measures long. The tonality is major throughout, and this arrangement is written in the original key of B♭ major.

It is written in cut time and the indicated tempo is 𝅗𝅥 = 144. However, you may want to initially rehearse the tune more slowly in four rather than two.

SECTION	MEASURE	EVENT/SCORING
Intro	1–8	A drum solo, which can be opened, must establish the appropriate tempo.

SECTION	MEASURE	EVENT/SCORING
A, A'	9–42	The A section of the melody is stated in stop-time fashion by the full ensemble. It is important for the drummer to fill in the rests in the melody rhythm for ensemble accuracy and to set up the ensemble adequately for reentry. The fifth note of the melody of each of the first three phrases is extended for a drum solo fill. The beginning of this long note should be accented. The ensemble should drop the dynamic level to *piano* and then *crescendo* to the release. Articulation of the accented notes is very important. The syllable "daht" should be used for the marcato accents. Lots of air rather than a heavy, percussive tongue should be used for both the regular and marcato accents.
	43–44	A short drum solo ends at measure 44, beat 1. Saxophones and guitar play eighth-note pickups into the bridge.
B	45–52	Saxophones and guitar play the melody harmonized. Be sure that the pitch of notes with indicated scoops is centered.
	53–60	Brass plays this section harmonized. Glissandi should include as many notes as possible without arriving late to the next note. Accented notes should be played full value.
A''	61–76	Full ensemble plays the melody homophonically, using the more traditional sustained note values of the original melody. Half-note triplets in measure 70 should be played evenly with slight accents so that the tempo does not drag. The sforzando in measure 71 should begin loud then get immediately soft. Instruments with moving notes should play out a little stronger. The entire ensemble should *crescendo* in measure 76.

SECTION	MEASURE	EVENT/SCORING
	77–80	The full ensemble restates the *habanera* rhythm. Stop-time rhythms with drum fills set up the solo section send-off.
A	81–96	First alto sax has an improvised solo with rhythm section on the tune's traditional changes.
A'	97–112	Alto sax solo continues with backgrounds. Backgrounds feature call and response between brass and remaining saxophones. The brass background rhythm is based on Charleston rhythm and should be highlighted by the drummer.
B	113–118	Second trumpet begins a solo on chord changes to the bridge of the tune with sustained background notes in the remaining brass.
	119–124	Trumpet solo continues with sustained backgrounds in saxophones and trombones.
	125–128	Solo continues with full ensemble backgrounds.
A"	129–136	Trumpet solo continues on the A section chord changes with full ensemble backgrounds using the Charleston rhythm.
	137–144	Trumpet solo continues on the last eight measures of the form with only rhythm section accompaniment.
A	145–153	Brass section soli begins in unison and splits into parts in measure 149. Rhythmic accuracy is crucial in this section. It should be rehearsed at a slower tempo first. The drum fill in measure 152 must set up the entrance on beat 2.

SECTION	MEASURE	EVENT/SCORING
	153–161	Harmonized sax section soli that requires careful attention to correct pitches and rhythms as well as balance between the parts. The section should sound like an organ with the lead alto sax part heard slightly above the other parts. Articulations should be very legato, and tied eighth notes should be accented. Two eighth notes prior to rests should be articulated "doo-dot," with the last note accented. The fall in measure 161 should start after the pitch is established on beat 1.
A'	161–168	Harmonized brass soli returns with two alternating rhythms. This section should begin softer and gradually grow louder, climaxing in measure 167.
	169–175	Harmonized sax soli returns. Consecutive upbeats in measures 169–70 should be articulated with breath accents and played long, as indicated by the tenuto marks over the notes. The fall in measure 175 should again begin after the pitch is established on beat 1.
	175–177	Brass sets up a new solo section with a send-off.
B	177–192	First tenor sax solo begins over changes to the bridge section. Backgrounds are primarily sustained notes in the trombone and saxophone sections that require attention to balance and blend. The rest of the ensemble joins in the backgrounds in measure 189.
A"	193–200	Tenor solo continues with full ensemble backgrounds.
	201–208	Tenor solo concludes with rhythm section accompaniment.

SECTION	MEASURE	EVENT/SCORING
A	209–224	Cross-voiced soli with third trumpet, first alto sax, second tenor sax, baritone sax, and first trombone, using half note/whole note values of the original melody. Third trumpet plays melody and should be the predominant voice. Piano and guitar also play melody. Bass should play a solo-like walking line. Drums tacit during this section until measure 222, then should sneak back in. Sax section eighth note pickups into the D.S. should be full volume.
A'	61–76	This section repeats as the D.S.
Coda	225–228	Full ensemble playing the hemiola rhythm begins the coda. Drums fills are again critical to the rhythmic accuracy.
Vamp	229–236	Eight-measure vamp repeated eight times in samba feel. First alto sax, first tenor sax, and second trumpet improvise collectively all eight times. Backgrounds enter in layers. Trombones enter the third time and should accent each note. The last note of the trombone phrase should start soft and *crescendo*. Second tenor sax and baritone sax enter the fifth time. Trumpets and second alto sax enter the seventh time. This section should start soft with more simple improvisation. Each time through and as instruments are added, dynamics should gradually get louder, and the improvisation should become more intense. Trumpets and second alto sax should use legato articulation on the first two eighth notes of the rhythm and staccato tonguing on the last note ("doo-doo-dit").

Section	Measure	Event/Scoring
Ending	237–241	Full ensemble for one measure followed by a two-measure drum solo. Then the ensemble plays two final chords, which require balance, blend, and careful tuning. The last note should be played as a sforzando, accenting the attack, getting soft, then gradually *crescendoing*. The drums should fill during the fermata on the last note.

Unit 8: Suggested Listening/Viewing

Charlie Barnet and His Orchestra, *Cherokee*, 1999, ASV 5288.
Count Basie and His Orchestra, *The Complete Decca Recordings, 1937–1939*, Decca, 1992.
GRP All-Star Band, *Dave Grusin Presents the GRP All-Star Band Live*, 1993, UMG.
Elgart, Les & Larry, *Best of the Big Bands: Les & Larry Elgart*, Sony, 1990.
Ellington, Duke, *Recollections of the Big Band Era*, Atlantic, 2005.
Hampton, Lionel, *Lionel Hampton and Friends*, Telarc, 1992.
Slide Hampton and the World of Trombones, *Spirit of the Horn*, MCG Jazz 1011, 2003.
Kansas City All-Stars, *KC After Dark: More Music from Robert Altman's "Kansas City,"* UMG, 1997.
USAF Airmen of Note, *Airmen of Note*, Altissimo, 1997.
Wynton Marsalis Septet, *Live at the Village Vanguard*, Sony, 1999.

Video:
Charlie Barnet and his Orchestra, *Jasper in a Jam*, 1946.
Gene Krupa Orchestra, *The Gene Krupa Story AKA Drum Crazy*, 1959.
Racing with the Moon, 1984.
Lush Life, 1993.

Unit 9: Additional References and Resources

Berg, Shelly, Lou Fischer, Fred Hamilton, and Steve Houghton, *Rhythm Section Workshop for Jazz Directors* (Van Nuys: Alfred Publishing Co., Inc., 2005).
Dunscomb, Richard, and Willie L. Hill, Jr., *Jazz Pedagogy: The Jazz Educator's Handbook and Resource Guide* (Miami: Warner Brothers, 2004).

Haerle, Dan. *Jazz/Rock Voicings for the Contemporary Keyboard Player* (Lebanon: Studio P/R, 1974).
Harris, Matt and Jeff Jarvis, *The Chord Voicing Handbook* (Delevan: Kendor Music, Inc., 1994).
Mantooth, Frank, *Voicings for Jazz Keyboard* (Milwaukee: Hal Leonard Publishing Corporation, 1986).
Reed, Rufus, *The Evolving Bassist* (Teaneck: Myriad Limited, 1974).
Simon, George T., *The Big Bands*, fourth ed. (New York: Schirmer Books, 1981).
www.jazzstandards.com.
www.parabrisas.com/d_nobler.php.
en.wikipedia.org/wiki/Ray_Noble.
http://great-song-stylists-uk.com/Ray%20Noble/raynoble.htm.

Contributed by:

Jerry Tolson
Associate Professor
Jazz Studies/Music Education
School of Music
University of Louisville
Louisville, Kentucky

1 en.wikipedia.org/wiki/Ray_Noble
2 www.parabrisas.com/d_nobler.php
3 http://great-song-stylists-uk.com/Ray%20Noble/raynoble.htm
4 www.halleonard.com

Teacher Resource Guide

Cottontail

Duke Ellington

(1899–1974)

transcribed by David Berger

(b. 1948)

Unit 1: Composer

Edward Kennedy Ellington was born on April 29, 1899 in Washington, D.C. Duke's parents, Daisy Kennedy Ellington and James Edward Ellington, served as ideal role models for young Duke, and taught him everything from proper table manners to an understanding of the emotional power of music. Duke's first piano lessons came around the age of seven or eight, and appeared not to have had a lasting effect upon him. It seemed as if young Duke was more inclined to baseball. Duke got his first job selling peanuts at Washington Senators baseball games. This was the first time Duke was placed as a "performer" for a crowd, and had to first get over his stage fright.

At the age of fourteen, Duke began sneaking into Frank Holliday's poolroom. His experiences at the poolroom taught him to appreciate the value of mixing with a wide range of people. As Duke's piano lessons faded into the past, he began to show a flare for the artistic. Duke attended Armstrong Manual Training School to study commercial art instead of going to an academic-oriented school. Duke began to seek out and listen to ragtime pianists in Washington, and, during the summers, in Philadelphia or Atlantic City, where he and his mother vacationed. While vacationing in Asbury Park, Duke heard of a hot pianist named Harvey Brooks. At the end of his vacation, Duke sought Harvey out in Philadelphia, where Harvey showed Duke some pianistic tricks and shortcuts. Duke later recounted that, "When I got home I had a real yearning to play. I hadn't been able to get off the ground before, but after hearing him I said to myself, 'Man you're going to have to do it.'" Thus the music career of Duke Ellington was born.

In 1923, Duke left the security that Washington offered him and moved to New York. Through the power of radio, listeners throughout New York had heard of Duke Ellington, making him quite a popular musician. It was also in 1923 that Duke made his first recording. Ellington and his renamed band The Washingtonians, and it established itself during the prohibition era by playing at places like the Exclusive Club, Connie's Inn, the Hollywood Club (Club Kentucky), Ciro's, the Plantation Club, and most importantly the Cotton Club. Thanks to the rise in radio receivers and the broadcasting industry itself, Duke's band was broadcast across the nation live on "From the Cotton Club." The band's music, along with their popularity, spread rapidly.

In 1928, Irving Mills signed an agreement with Ellington to produce and publish his music. Recording companies such as Brunswick, Columbia, and Victor came calling. Duke's band became the most sought-after band in the United States, even throughout the world.

Some of Ellington's greatest works include *Rockin' in Rhythm*, *Satin Doll*, *New Orleans*, *A Drum is a Woman*, *Take the 'A' Train*, *Happy-Go-Lucky Local*, *The Mooche*, and *Crescendo in Blue*.

Duke Ellington and his band went on to play everywhere from New York to New Delhi, Chicago to Cairo, and Los Angeles to London. Ellington and his band played with such greats as Miles Davis, Cab Calloway, Dizzy Gillespie, Ella Fitzgerald, Tony Bennett, and Louis Armstrong. They entertained everyone from Queen Elizabeth II to President Nixon. Before passing away in 1974, Duke Ellington wrote and recorded hundreds of musical compositions, all of which will continue to have a lasting effect upon people worldwide for a long time to come.

(This information was derived from http://wikipedia.org/.)

Unit 2: Composition

A swing-era jazz masterpiece, *Cottontail* was actually a collaboration between Duke Ellington and tenor saxophonist Ben Webster. Webster composed the melody of the A sections based off of the changes to *I Got Rhythm* as well as the famous saxophone soli lead line. Ellington, who gets credit for the composition, composed the remainder of the piece in addition to its orchestrated realization. The outcome served as a precursor to the bebop era and a model for hundreds (if not thousands) of large ensemble charts, including classics penned by the great Thad Jones.

Unit 3: Historical Perspective

The Swing Era, spanning from 1935–1946, was the period of time when big band swing music was the popular music of America. Though the music had been around since the late 1920s with leaders such as Fletcher Henderson, Benny Carter, and Duke Ellington, most historians believe that the Swing Era started at the Palomar Ballroom on August 21, 1935 with Benny Goodman's Orchestra. This performance is credited with bringing the music to the general public throughout the rest of the country. With the financial restraints of World War II and other factors (such as the 1942–46 recording ban, the ASCAP radio ban, and "cabaret taxes"), the Swing Era's demise began. By 1946, most of the hundreds of big bands (with the exception of Duke Ellington's, Count Basie's, and a few other popular orchestras) touring the country were forced to disband, bringing a close to the Swing Era and opening the door for smaller ensembles to take the stage.

Unit 4: Technical Considerations

This chart is rated as a Grade 5, primarily because of the up-tempo feel marked at ♩ = 234. The arrangement actually works very well as a medium-up swing, though, so this is an option. It is more important for the swing feel to come through than the blazing tempo.

Brass ranges are a reasonable concern for most ensembles. The ranges are not stratospherically stretched (High C in the trombones (c^1), high D in the trumpets[d^2]), but the range is spread out through the whole section rather equally. Therefore, make sure that the brass players support the tone with more air than normal.

Saxophones have quite a challenge with the "famous" Ben Webster sax soli at rehearsal letter Q. Reduce the tempo and rehearse with a metronome to keep the time honest. The voicing (octave block) should help, as the bari sax is doubling the lead alto melody an octave lower. In addition to the challenges of the soli, there is a clarinet background segment written in the lead tenor part. It is the lead voice and is fairly high, so if your jazz tenor is not the strongest doubler, consider having one of the two altos or the bari play the part.

Be mindful of the dissonance at rehearsal letter W. It is a good idea to rehearse this section at a slower tempo so that students learn to hear how their parts work in this type of harmony.

Unit 5: Stylistic Considerations

Stylistically, this arrangement is coming straight out of the Swing Era articulations established by Louis Armstrong and Count Basie. The only difference in this arrangement is the Duke Ellington touch. His approach to orchestration is as innovative as they come. Here, he strikes the perfect balance between ensemble and soloist. Note that it is quite important for the ensemble to stay engaged throughout the solo sections. The fact that the majority of the musicians are not actively participating at the moment doesn't mean that they are not passively participating. Everyone involved is a part of the performance, and a lack of concentration will translate into a stylistic blunder when rejoining the ensemble. Play the recording for your ensemble and encourage them to transcribe their solos from the original artists. Pay attention to inflections and articulations in addition to pitches and rhythms.

Unit 6: Musical Elements

MELODY:

As is the case with learning any new arrangement, the melody should be learned vocally. If you can sing it, you can play it. It is very common for "rhythm change" pieces to have repeated A sections with nothing more than an improvised bridge. This piece is of no exception, as the melody essentially remains the same over very slight changes to the chord progression throughout its evolution. Pay attention to the motivic sequence at the end of the phrase.

HARMONY:

The harmony employed by Duke Ellington in this arrangement doesn't stray too far from the standard "rhythm changes" progression. This arrangement is centered in the key of B♭ with the A sections revolving around a I–vi–ii–V^7 pattern every two bars. The only exception is the fifth and sixth bars, where the pattern briefly tonicizes to the IV chord. The bridge utilizes a cyclical ii–V pattern that sequences by fourths to get back to the tonal center of B♭. There are no modulations throughout the large form.

RHYTHM:

The rhythmic feel follows the same principles of every other swing chart. Subdivision is crucial. The quarter note pulse should be divided into triplets on each downbeat and should be conveyed by the whole band, not just the rhythm section. Singing rhythm is just as important as singing melody.

Unit 7: Form and Structure

The small form of the arrangement is AABA (standard rhythm change form).

Section	Measure	Event and Scoring
A	1–8	First A section melody with alto sax, tenor sax, trumpet and trombone quartet.
B	9–16	Quartet joined by brass comping for second A section.
C	17–24	Bridge with solo growl trumpet and five-part saxophone pads.
D	25–28	Last A section is replaced by a 4-bar solo send-off; ensemble tutti.
E	29–36	Tenor sax improvised solo.
F	37–44	Tenor sax solo continues.
G	45–52	Tenor sax solo continues with clarinet, two trumpets, and trombone backgrounds.
H	53–60	Tenor sax solo continues with full ensemble "pops" in bars 59–60.
I	61–68	Tenor sax solo continues (second chorus begins).
J	69–76	Tenor sax solo continues.
K	77–84	Tenor sax solo continues with brass backgrounds.
L	85–92	Tenor sax solo continues.
M	93–100	Brass shout (primarily in basic ensemble voicings. Watch out for third trumpet voiced below third trombone occasionally).
N	101–108	Brass shout continues.
O	109–116	Baritione saxophone solo.
P	117–124	Piano solo.

Section	Measure	Event and Scoring
Q	125–132	Sax soli in four-part octave block.
R	133–140	Sax soli continues.
S	141–148	Sax soli continues.
T	149–156	Sax soli continues.
U	157–164	Call and response between saxes and brass (brass in basic ensemble voicings; saxes in four- to five-note voicings).
V	165–172	Call and response continues.
W	173–180	Full ensemble tutti shout (basic ensemble voicings).
X	181–189	Final A section with original quartet.

Unit 8: Suggested Listening

Ellington, Duke, *The Blanton-Webster Band*, RCA/Victor.
Three Suites, Columbia.

Unit 9: Additional References and Resources

Feather, Leonard and Ira Gitler, *The Biographical Encyclopedia of Jazz* (New York: Oxford University Press, 1999).
Gioia, Ted, *The History of Jazz* (New York: Oxford University Press, 1997).
Gridley, Mark C., *Jazz Styles: History and Analysis* (Upper Saddle River: Prentice Hall, 2003).
Kirchner, Bill, *The Oxford Companion to Jazz* (New York: Oxford University Press, 2000).

Contributed by:

Dave Stamps
Managing Director, The Center for Jazz Composition
Visiting Assistant Professor
University of South Florida
Tampa, Florida

Teacher Resource Guide

The First Circle

Pat Metheny

(b. 1954)

Lyle Mays

(b. 1953)

arranged by Bob Curnow

(b. 1941)

Unit 1: Composer/Arranger

Pat Metheny was born in Lee's Summit, Missouri, on August 12, 1954. He is one of the most influential and original jazz-fusion guitarists and composers of the last thirty years. Pat has a unique playing style that blends loose articulations with advanced harmonies and complex rhythms. Metheny broke into the international jazz scene in 1974 as a member of the Gary Burton Quintet. In 1975 he released his first album, *Bright Size Life*, and in 1977 he founded, along with keyboardist Lyle Mays, The Pat Metheny Group, a multi-Grammy-winning band with a unique sound that blends a wide range of musical genres, including jazz, pop, rock, and Brazilian music.

Lyle Mays was born in Wausaukee, Wisconsin, on November 27, 1953. He studied jazz arranging and composition at the University Of North Texas, where he composed and played for the One O'Clock Lab Band (*Lab '75* album). In 1977, after touring with Woody Herman, Lyle formed a long-lasting musical partnership with Metheny. Lyle's musical taste has been critical in the making of the fresh compositions and unique sound that distinguishes the PMG.

Bob Curnow was born in Easton, Pennsylvania, on November 1, 1941. He is a former trombonist and arranger for Stan Kenton, and has been captivated by the music of the PMG since the early 1980s, when he began analyzing and arranging some of this group's works, such as *The First Circle* and *Minuano*. In 1994 he recorded the album: *Bob Curnow's L. A. Big Band: The Music of Pat Metheny and Lyle Mays*, which presented fresh, powerful and elegant arrangements in the Kenton style.

Unit 2: Composition

The First Circle is a composition in 22/8, with a light Latin-ish groove that creates the illusion of a regular meter. It almost sounds as if it were in 4/4. The Brazilian-flavored, even-eighth feel, with double-time rhythms on flat ride cymbals, and a mixture of different styles, represents what has become known as the ECM style.

Over a simple melody and interesting changes, the primary structure of this composition is the rhythmic pattern on 22/8 (12/8+10/8), which is grouped as follows: 3+2+3+2+2+3+3+2+2.

Unit 3: Historical Perspective

This composition appeared as the third track on the ECM album *The First Circle*, which won a Grammy award in 1984 for Best Jazz-Fusion Recording. This album is one of the most significant of the Pat Metheny Group's recordings, not only because of its level of compositions and arrangements, but because it introduced two new performers that were key elements in the development of the unique sound and grooves that now characterize the PMG: the all-around drummer Paul Wertico and the multi-instrumentalist and vocalist Pedro Aznar.

Unit 4: Technical Considerations

The piece is rated Grade 6+; the tempo is 𝅗𝅥 = 318 (♩. = 106 or ♩ = 159), with a duration of 9:16.

The lead trumpet range goes to concert E (e^2), with an optional concert G (g^2) as an ending note, while the second trumpet goes to concert D (d^2). The lead trombone range goes to B (b). The trumpet section doubles on flugelhorns and is scored for five trumpets with an optional fifth chair. Trumpets with cup mutes may be substituted for flugelhorns. The trombone section is scored for five trombones, with the fourth chair as bass trombone, and an optional fifth chair. The lead alto sax doubles on soprano saxophone for soloing, while the rest of the saxophone section doubles on flutes to play background material.

The rhythmic cycle in compound meter is the most complex element of this piece; the meter is 22/8 for the most part, but there are sections in 8/8 and 12/8. The eighth-note value should be preserved throughout the performance, so it is the common denominator between meter shifts. There is no metric modulation, just different groupings of eighth notes. In addition, the rhythm section should create a very smooth groove, with relaxed transitions and natural feel. It should create the illusion that the piece is in 4/4. In Curnow's arrangement, the 22/8 cycle is divided into two bars: one 12/8, the other 10/8. However, in the Pat Metheny Song Book,[1] this piece is notated in 22/8 for the main compound cycle, 4/4 instead of 8/8, and 6/8 instead of 12/8 for the even-meter sections. Curnow's metric simplification helps in the assimilation of the different meters contained in *The First Circle*.

Unit 5: Stylistic Considerations

The constant rhythmic pattern in 22/8 is the main characteristic of this piece; it should be internalized by all the members of the band and then be felt as a whole cycle. The melody is very tonal and should imitate the human voice, with no vibrato and lots of dynamic expression. Curnow's arrangement is very powerful and moving, and it is a great feature for the whole ensemble. *The First Circle* is now a classic at jazz festivals and competitions. It is a great piece for addressing compound meters, working on saxophone section doubles, developing ensemble balance, intonation, and blend, and working on Latin/ECM grooves with the entire ensemble.

Unit 6: Musical Elements

MELODY:

The melody of this composition should be learned in the context of the 22/8 rhythmic ostinati. The performers should listen to the way Pedro Aznar interprets it in the PMG recordings, and then sing the melody with the entire ensemble in a very legato style. Then the performers should personalize the interpretation, by adding nuance and expression to it, such as fine *crescendos* and *diminuendos* towards the end of the phrases, unified articulations, no vibrato, and different dynamic levels as the piece unfolds.

HARMONY:

The harmonic changes in *The First Circle* are simple, yet fresh and ingenious. The composers used many different harmonic devices to create a chord progression that sounds simple with clear tonal centers, and yet contains many unique features, such as the use harmonic pedals, cliché lines, and modal interchange chords.

RHYTHM:

The 22/8 rhythmic cycle is the most complex element of this composition, and it should be addressed from the start. To simplify its complexity it can be interpreted using the North Indian rhythmic system, creating a *Tala*, which is a set of syllabic patterns that are put together to convey long rhythmic cycles.

The ensemble can apply the Indian system to *The First Circle* in the following fashion:

Ta-ki-ta	=	three eighth notes
Ta-ka	=	two eighth notes
Ta-ka-di-mi	=	four eighth notes

The last four eighth notes of each bar, either 12/8 or 10/8, have a pair of groups containing two eighth notes each. This can be combined into a single group or four eighths.

The *Tala* for *The First Circle's* cycle goes like this:

22/8 = ***Ta****-ki-ta-****Ta****-ka-****Ta****-ki-ta-****Ta****-ka-di-mi-****Ta****-ki-ta-****Ta****-ki-ta-****Ta****-ka-di-mi*

Stress the ***Ta*** syllables to feel the downbeats according to the grouping subdivision. In this way performers can feel, rather than count, the cycle, keeping a constant eighth-note subdivision in mind.

The following sequence could be used to learn and internalize the rhythmic cycle:

1. Have the ensemble sing this *Tala: Ta-ki-ta-Ta-ka-Ta-ki-ta-Ta-ka-di-mi-Ta-ki-ta-Ta-ki-ta-Ta-ka-di-mi*, while clapping the rhythms for the intro, or Pattern No. 1 (see example 1), and tap with one foot the first eighth note of the different groupings.

Example 1

2. Gradually eliminate the need for tapping so that the performer internalizes the entire cycle without any physical motion.

3. Practice Pattern No. 2 (see example 2) by clapping the new rhythms while tapping on the first note of each group and singing the *Tala*.

Example 2.

Unit 7: Form and Structure

This is a through-composed piece with three main sections or themes: The first theme starts at measure 11, and repeats the second half at measure 21. The second theme appears at measure 35 with the sax soli. The third theme, which starts at measure 72, is the core melodic statement. As the most important theme, it is reused before the solo section as a send-off, and on the recapitulation.

Section	Measure	Event and Scoring
Intro	1–6	Rhythmic Pattern No. 1: The two altos, second tenor, bari sax, and first, second, third, and fifth trumpets plus percussion and drums clap the pattern. It is important that the entire ensemble gets used to the clapping pattern. The suggested *Tala* is: ***Ta**-ki-ta-**Ta**-ka-**Ta**-ki-ta-**Ta**-ka-di-mi-**Ta**-ki-ta-**Ta**-ki-ta-**Ta**-ka-di-mi*. Practicing this makes it easier to assimilate the rhythms. Sing the *Tala* pattern first, then add claps and tap the main pulses (a long pulse for a grouping of three eighths and short pulse for a group of two).

SECTION	MEASURE	EVENT AND SCORING
Intro	7–10	The C pedal on piano and guitar incorporates a counter-rhythm, adding the missing eighth notes or main pulses to the rhythmic pattern. The new rhythm for the pedal complements Clapping Pattern No. 1. In this section, make sure that the tempo doesn't rush and the two parts, C pedal and claps, blend.
First theme	11–21	First tenor saxophone and fourth trumpet on flugelhorn play this simple tonal melody over the C pedal in unison and clap ostinati. Let the flugel lead the line; watch for intonation and blend, and personalize dynamics adding fine *crescendos* and *diminuendos* on the line. Avoid vibrato.
	21–24	Bass, trombones and second tenor saxophone add color to the orchestration on this plagal cadence. The clapping pattern changes to a simplified pattern; make sure eighth notes are preserved, as there will be the tendency to rush this new pattern. The tambourine part is really important, as it helps keeping the momentum and adds energy with integrated double-time rhythms.
Second half of first theme	25–30	The second half of the first theme, again for tenor sax and flugelhorn in unison. The orchestration is richer, as low brass plays an Fmaj^9 pad. Bring the dynamic level of the melody up a notch while the pad fades out.

Section	Measure	Event and Scoring
	31–34	Pattern No. 2 with claps reappears. Keep transitions smooth, without any hesitation. The low brass plays a B♭maj^9 pad. Bring the dynamics down (to ***mf*** or less) so that the saxophone soli section has enough available dynamic range.
Second theme	35–72	This contrasting section is very melodic and quiet, but should grow and build into the next theme at measure 72. Try to personalize the dynamics and balance. Controlling the levels of the inner voices can create interesting effects. It is a through-composed passage that should be played slurred in a very legato style. This is the first time that the saxophone section plays, and, unlike the traditional saxophone soli, every voice has independent motion, creating a labyrinth of sound that should be integrated with the piano, guitar, bass and bells (auxiliary percussion). These instruments double or complement many of the sax section's lines. Unify interpretation, avoid the use of vibrato, and create dramatic effects with the use of a wide dynamic range.
	57–69	Piano and bells (auxiliary percussion) should stay together, as their rhythms shift apart from the other performers. If you are conducing, focus on cueing the areas where the rhythmic figure goes against the rest of the band (bars 58–61 and 63–69).
End of second theme		70–71 Bring the dynamic level up to ***mf*** to set up the third theme. The drum fill should be clear and fading in at measure 72. It also needs to outline the rhythmic subdivision on the 12/8 bar: 3+3+2+2+2.

Section	Measure	Event and Scoring
Third theme (antecedent)	72–80	This section is more powerful than the previous two, with a heavier orchestration, as this is the first time that the full trumpet section is playing. They are in unison, so watch for intonation problems. First trumpet leads. Make the other section players aware of it in order to allow for a good blend and interpretation.
Third theme (consequent)	80–88	The second half of this phrase is in 12/8 with even 3/8 pulses. Don't let it get too heavy. Avoid back beats on the drums the first time through. Keep the eighth-note consistent on the transitions, especially going back to measure 72.
On repeat	71–89	Third theme, second time: a fully orchestrated passage. Watch for blend and intonation across sections. Bring the alto saxophone countermelody out. Flugelhorns can bring the level up a notch. Unify articulations on the low brass; some of them should be percussive. Build into measure 84.
Interlude	90–105	This section should start very softly in order to allow for a dramatic *crescendo* going into measure 105, where the main theme is reused. Watch for rhythmic accuracy on the 8/8 with the upbeats; don't rush them. At measure 96, bring out the different lines that happen in the second and third trombone as well as the second tenor saxophone parts. These lines help to build tension into the 12/8 at measure 100. Delay the *crescendo* until the last two bars before measure 105.

Section	Measure	Event and Scoring
Main theme	105–122	This section is the strongest so far, and it works as send-off into the solo section. Bring out the countermelodies that occur in the different sections, especially the saxophones at measure 113. At measure 117, bring the dynamic level down to ***mf*** or softer to create contrast after the *crescendo* at measure 116. Build into the solo section following the dynamic marks and let the flutes lead the band at measure 121.
Solo	122–189	This is scored for soprano sax in the lead alto chair with optional solos for guitar and/or piano. The solo is, for the most part, in 12/8, with some areas in 8/8. Listen and if possible transcribe the Lyle Mays solo on the *First Circle* album to understand the concept of this solo. This section should start really soft with a very transparent texture. Listen to the original PMG recording to recreate some of the colors with percussion instruments as the solo progresses. Some members of the ensemble could collaborate by inserting some extra percussion parts. Cabazas, shakers, caxixis, maracas, etc. can be used to create some interesting effects (see example 3). The flute backgrounds should be carefully rehearsed to avoid intonation and blend problems. If the saxophone section does not double on flute, tacet flute parts.

Example 3.

First layer may be played by fifth trumpet with a cabaza in measure 126.

Second layer is in the first trumpet part: a shaker playing eighth notes in measure 130.

A third layer could be played by fourth trumpet using a smaller cabaza in measures 134–162.

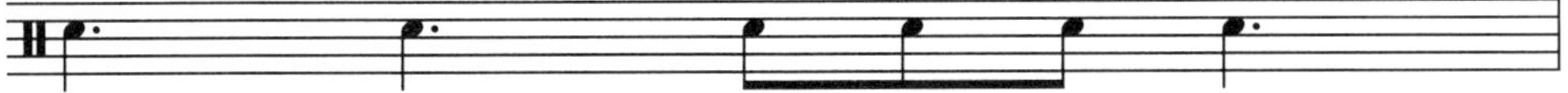

Fourth layer is played by first trombone using maracas in measures 139–151.

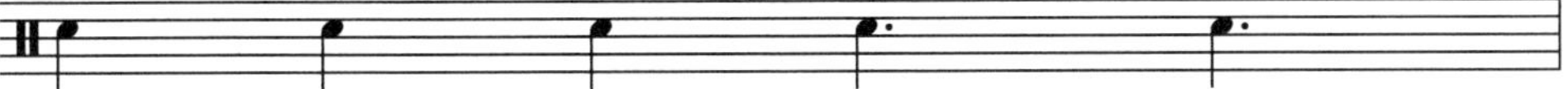

		The background material contains some difficult rhythmic figures that should be worked out first by clapping and singing: Flutes at measure 174 Trombones in measures 175–178 Fourth and fifth trumpets in measures 183–185
Breakdown	189–206	This is a powerful section for brass and rhythm section, both playing a rhythmic ostinato. Listen to the original recording to get the concept for this part. Avoiding the tendency to play it bombastically, aim for a controlled energy, creating intensity with crisp articulations, not volume. Start strong, but leave space to grow. Add more activity and volume on the auxiliary percussion and drums as you get close to measure 207.

SECTION	MEASURE	EVENT AND SCORING
	207–221	Pull back the volume a notch to build up into measure 213. Pinch the trombone bell tones at measure 211. At measure 213 make that a *subito* ***p*** to build into the recapitulation at measure 222.
Recapitulation	222–242	This is the climax of the piece. Save some energy for the very end! As this section is on the upper register of the lead trumpet, focus on pitch accuracy and melodic direction. Bring out the counter-line in the two altos and fifth trombone at measure 222. In measures 230–233 let the saxophones be aggressive with these lines.
Ending	242–248	Tag ending (three times). Keep building all the way to the end. Last note is a G in density level one (unison and octaves, no chord). Watch for good intonation within the octaves, especially on the lead trumpet.

Unit 8: Suggested Listening

Bob Curnow's L.A. Big Band, *The Music of Pat Metheny and Lyle Mays*, MAMA Foundation, MMF 1009, 1994.

The Pat Metheny Group, *The First Circle*. ECM Records, ECM 1278, 1984.

The Pat Metheny Group, *The Road To You*. Geffen Records, GEFD–24601, 1993.

Unit 9: Additional References and Resources

Clayton, Martin, *Time in Indian Music: Rhythm, Metre, and Form in North Indian Rag Performance* (New York: Oxford University Press, 2001).

Montfort, Matthew, *Ancient Traditions—Future Possibilities: Rhythmic Training Through the Traditions of Africa, Bali and India* (Mill Valley: Panoramic Press, 1985).

Contributed by:

Rodrigo Villanueva
Assistant Professor of Jazz Studies
Northern Illinois University
DeKalb, Illinois

---

1 Pat Metheny and Lyle Mays, *Pat Metheny Song Book* (Milwaukee: Hal Leonard, 2000), 160.

Teacher Resource Guide

Groove Merchant

Jerome Richardson

(1920–2000)

arranged by Thad Jones

(1923–1986)

Unit 1: Composer/Arranger

Jerome Richardson, composer, was born in Oakland, California, on November 15, 1920, and died in Englewood, New Jersey, on June 23, 2000. Primarily known as a gifted alto saxophonist/woodwind doubler, he began playing at age eight and made his professional debut at fourteen. He served briefly as replacement for Willie Smith in Jimmy Lunceford's band and toured throughout the late 1940s and early 1950s with Marshall Royal, Lionel Hampton, Earl Hines, and others. Richardson settled in New York in 1953 and freelanced with Oscar Pettiford, Lucky Millinder, Cootie Williams, Chico Hamilton, Johnny Richards, Gerry Mulligan, Gerald Wilson, Quincy Jones, and many others. He was a charter member of the Thad Jones-Mel Lewis Jazz Orchestra, serving as lead alto/soprano saxophonist, 1965–1970. Richardson moved to Hollywood in 1971 and spent the remainder of his career primarily as a very successful studio musician.

Though Richardson was a prolific composer of jazz tunes (his BMI web page lists forty titles), *Groove Merchant* is the only one to have entered the standard jazz canon. Thad Jones's arrangement, as recorded by the Thad Jones-Mel Lewis Jazz Orchestra, could certainly be described as a "hit tune" in the jazz world.

Thad Jones, arranger, was born in Pontiac, Michigan, on March 28, 1923, and died in Copenhagen, Denmark, on August 20, 1986. One of the most renowned trumpet players, arrangers/composers, and band leaders in the history of jazz, he is also from a renowned jazz family, his siblings being pianist Hank (b. 1918) and drummer Elvin (1927–2004). Though largely self-taught as a trumpet player, he began playing professionally at age sixteen in the Detroit area with brother Hank and Sonny Stitt. After a stint in the army, he performed with Billy Mitchell, Charles Mingus, and, most notably, the Count Basie Orchestra (1954–1963), the latter boasting one of the most laudable trumpet sections in the history of jazz. Jones's solo on Basie's hit, *April in Paris*, approaches Bobby Hackett's on *String of Pearls* in recorded big band jazz solo significance. Jones wrote several arrangements for the Basie band, leading to his success as a freelance arranger after settling in New York in 1963. In the fall of 1965, Jones and drummer Mel Lewis started a "rehearsal band" that took over the Monday night Village Vanguard performance spot previously occupied by Gerry Mulligan. The group evolved to become one of the best and most significant big bands in the history of jazz, primarily due to the unique, harmonically and melodically adventurous (but always swinging!) arrangements of Thad Jones.

In 1979, Jones resigned from the band and settled in Denmark, but returned to the U. S. in 1985 to take over leadership of the Count Basie Orchestra. Unfortunately, ill health forced him to retire and return to Denmark in February 1986.

Unit 2: Composition

Groove Merchant is from the relatively early period of the Jones-Lewis Orchestra, with a copyright date of 1967. It was initially recorded on June 18, 1969, and was included on the band's fifth album for Solid State, *Central Park North*. It represents one of the very few times Thad arranged one of his musicians', as opposed to his own, tunes. The music is pure Thad Jones throughout: It swings mightily *a la* Count Basie, but, in terms of melody and harmony, it is more daring and "edgy" than anything encountered in Basie. For example, note the lead trumpet line the first measure of letter H, beat three:

Example 1

A melodic line of ♭9–♭5–13–♯11 in would never be found in the music of Basie, Goodman, Ellington, Miller, etc., and rarely in Herman, Kenton, etc. Such adventurous chord functions are simply too far removed from the basic 1–3–5–7 for the traditional big band arrangement of that time.

Billy Harper, prominent tenor saxophonist with Jones/Lewis (1969–1977), recalls in a personal e-mail to the author: "This tune was usually saved [by Thad] for a special knockout, along with *Fingers* [virtuosic Thad Jones Rhythm changes chart], when putting the strongest set together."

Unit 3: Historical Perspective

Of course, the big band was *the* popular music medium in the US in the 1930s and 40s, but this quickly changed after World War II because of the emergence in popularity of small group jazz (bebop, etc.), the emergence in popularity of other forms of music, primarily rhythm and blues/rock & roll, but also country & western, etc., and the economic challenge of maintaining a big band, especially in light of decreasing interest by the public.

However, big bands did not and have not disappeared totally, but remain in existence today and even flourish in the form of university/high school big bands and "rehearsal bands."

A rehearsal band, by definition, is an organization that is not a full-time endeavor for any of its participants, but, rather, meets from time-to-time to perform music chosen by its participants, rather than music demanded by the public, dictated by commercial recording needs, etc. Though all rehearsal bands invariably begin with little thought of commercial/popular activity, the best are eventually discovered by the public, and there is no better example than the Thad Jones-Mel Lewis Jazz Orchestra. From its inauspicious beginnings on Monday nights at New York's Village Vanguard (February, 1966), the band became *immensely* popular and successful, recording many albums (one receiving a Grammy in 1979) and touring internationally (Russia, Japan, Israel, etc.) many times, all the while remaining a part-time activity for all members. Though the co-founders are long deceased, the band still exists in the form of New York's Vanguard Jazz Orchestra, and *still* plays Monday nights at the Village Vanguard (easily a longevity record!). Given that *Groove Merchant* is one of the most representative arrangements from the prototype for all modern rehearsal bands, it seems especially essential that it be included in any school jazz ensemble's library.

Unit 4: Technical Considerations

Groove Merchant is rated Grade 5, and the style is "medium shuffle." The tempo is ♩ = 132, with a duration of approximately 5:30. It could perhaps be taken a bit slower, but certainly no faster, as shuffle beats, by definition, are always laid-back, not too fast, not hurried, etc.

Lead trumpet briefly goes to high F (transposed [f²]) twice (end of intro; climax of chart four bars before the D.S.), but otherwise remains mostly below high C. The lead trombone briefly goes to high B♭ (b♭) twice, but otherwise remains mostly below G (g).

Given that the chart is Grade 5, rhythms and pitches of the brass parts should be within reach of an excellent high school or very good-to-excellent college big band. Brass sectionals will no doubt be in order for two measures before letter D and the entire brass soli at letter H.

As with anything especially challenging, the brass should master these passages *at a slow tempo*, then gradually increase to the norm.

First saxophone was originally written for soprano instead of alto, but the publisher provides a substitute first alto part. However, the first saxophonist *really should* play soprano, given that the chart includes one of the best-known sax soli in modern big band jazz (three choruses beginning at letter D), with a virtuosic soprano lead as originally recorded by the composer, Jerome Richardson. (It would seem almost sacrilege to hear this on alto!) Saxes will certainly want to have a sectional (probably several!) over this challenging, but fun, soli, beginning slowly before attempting concert tempo.

In regard to the sax soli, renowned trumpet player Marvin Stamm, who was a prominent member of the Jones/Lewis band, 1966–1973, recently shared the following reminiscence with the author:

> One truly outstanding thing [about playing *Groove Merchant*] was the sax soli with Thad playing in unison with the sax section [i.e., doubling the soprano part]. He just grabbed hold of that soli and took it right out! As effective as the soli was with only the saxes playing, it doubled in feeling and intensity when Thad played lead over them. Extraordinary!

Now, there would be a challenge for any young high school or college trumpet (flugelhorn) player!

Also, Billy Harper recalls playing the soli under Jerome Richardson, noting "The sax soli was always a 'swinger,' in that Jerome knew how to make the sax section 'lay back' on the phrasing of the passage." Note, once again, the use of that term, "lay back!"

In regard to rhythm section parts, the bass part is written out, except for the open solo section (letter G), where chord symbols only are provided. However, the changes are not difficult, so this should not be a problem for any competent young bassist. Chord symbols only (i.e., no voicings) are provided for piano and guitar. Some resources for aiding with appropriate voicings are suggested in Unit 9, which also includes references to help the drummer with a shuffle beat.

Unit 5: Stylistic Considerations

Given Thad Jones's apprenticeship in the school of Count Basie, it is not surprising that the overall feel of this chart is straight from the Kansas City/Basie/hard groove tradition. The only unique factor is the shuffle beat, fairly rare among big bands, including Basie's. In addition to repeated listening to the original Jones/Lewis recording, students (especially the rhythm section!) should seek out other big band shuffle recordings, for example: Count Basie, *Blues in Hoss' Flat* (composer Frank Foster) or Jones/Lewis, *Don't Get Sassy* (composer Thad Jones).

Also, jazz organ groups tend to play lots of shuffles, so their recordings provide a good opportunity to hear the style "close up." For example: Jimmy Smith's *Back at the Chicken Shack.*

A tip for the first trumpet player (ensemble passages) and soprano player (lead on soli): Approach your parts as a written-out, improvised jazz solo. That is, in addition to playing what's on the page, put a little bit of your personality/individuality into it. That's what all great lead players do, certainly including Snooky Young (lead trumpet) and Jerome Richardson on the original recording of *Groove Merchant.* In regard to Snooky, Marvin Stamm recalls that he was "probably the swingingest lead player ever. His time and feeling were magnificent; drummers still salivate at his time! And when he rode above the band on the shout chorus (letter I of *Groove Merchant*), it was like sailing on a beautiful sea! After it was over, you were just vibrating all over!"

Unit 6: Musical Elements

MELODY:

Groove Merchant is a straightforward mostly-diatonic 16-bar melody in ABCD form:

Example 2

Note Richardson's use of the A♭ blues scale to conclude his melody (measure 15). Also, in the arrangement, note that during the second statement of the melody (letter B), there is a four bar extension (letter C, sometimes called a "tag") due to Jones repeating measures 13–14 twice; he did not choose to do this elsewhere.

A good idea is for the director and/or students to transpose the melody for the *entire band*, and play through it tutti many times. This will help engross *everyone* in the entire arrangement. Also, require all soloists to *memorize* the melody. This will aid in "internalizing" the chord changes, correct pitches, etc., and make it easy to quote from the melody during solos—always a good idea.

Harmony:

Chord changes are relatively routine, with a lot in common with the blues (I, IV, V, etc.). Tips for soloists are included in the Solos section below.

As for ensemble chords, remember that the more complex a chord is, the greater the chance for intonation problems; that is, a pure triad is easier to tune than, for example, a $V^{13(\sharp 9 \sharp 5)}$.

A good idea: Take a complex chord that is relatively short in the chart (for example, fifth bar of letter I, the second half of beat 2—$Caug^{7(\sharp 9)}$) and have the band sustain it, *mezzo piano*. Have each section sustain its chord, individuals sustain their notes, etc., with all hearing how they fit into the whole and adjusting their intonation. Obviously, it is not reasonable to do this for every complex chord, but deliberately mastering a few will, hopefully, cause the band to "catch on" and master all.

RHYTHM:
The eighth notes are swung, of course, but are notated "straight," as is the custom. Be sure that the trombones understand that their intro eighths are swung, matching the drummer's "shuffle eighths":

EXAMPLE 3

In regard to the rhythm section, as much fun as it is to play a shuffle beat, you'll probably discover that it gets a bit tiresome chorus after chorus during the solos (letter G), etc., and also perhaps tiresome for the audience!

Try alternating between shuffle and "regular swing" beat behind soli, perhaps at letter H and/or I, etc.

SOLOS:
As stated above, the chord changes are relatively routine; players with some experience should have no problem. Novice improvisers will find it helpful to practice (even memorize!) the following practice patterns:

EXAMPLE 4

Even experienced players should practice measures 11–12 (D♭7–Ddim7); the D diminished scale (beginning with a whole step) is especially useful!

Note that the solo section (letter G) is "open" in terms of instrument(s) and length. The recording features the great pianist, Roland Hanna (note his simplicity: less is more!), but chord changes are provided for first soprano/alto, second trumpet, first trombone, and, of course, piano/guitar/bass. Billy Harper mentioned that he often soloed on *Groove Merchant*, and that he often tried to "take it further out" than one might have expected.

Unit 7: Form and Structure

The basic form is not unlike traditional sonata allegro:

Section	Rehearsal Letter
Intro	
Exposition	A
Development	
Sax soli	D
Soli	G
Brass soli	H
Shout chorus	I
Recapitulation (D.S.)	
Coda	

Unit 8: Suggested Listening

Original recording of *Groove Merchant*: Thad Jones-Mel Lewis Jazz Orchestra, *Central Park North*, Solid State SS-18058 [vinyl], 1969.

Current CD availability:

Thad Jones-Mel Lewis Jazz Orchestra, *Central Park North*, Blue Note.

Thad Jones-Mel Lewis Jazz Orchestra, *The Complete Solid State Recordings*, Mosaic box set. *Don't Get Sassy* is also included

Different recording of same chart: The Vanguard Jazz Orchestra, *Thad Jones Legacy*, New World.

Other versions of *Groove Merchant*:

Jerome Richardson Quartet, *Jazz Station Runaway*, TCB.

Thad Jones-Mel Lewis Jazz Orchestra with Monica Zetterlund,

vocalist, *It Only Happens Every Time*, Inner City [vinyl]. NOTE: This album includes an interesting rearrangement of *Groove Merchant* by Jones, featuring the late Swedish vocalist Zetterlund, lyrics by Claude Stephenson). Recorded in Helsinki in 1977, it has apparently not been released on CD.

Supplemental recordings demonstrating the shuffle beat:

Count Basie Orchestra, *Chairman of the Board*, Roulette (includes *Blues in Hoss' Flat*).

Thad Jones-Mel Lewis Jazz Orchestra, *Village Vanguard Live Sessions, Vol. 3*, LRC

(includes *Don't Get Sassy*).

Jimmy Smith Quartet, *Back at the Chicken Shack*, Blue Note.

Unit 9: Additional References and Resources

Biographical data on Jones and Richardson:

Bogdanov, Vladimir, et al, editors, *All Music Guide to Jazz*, fourth ed. (San Francisco: Backbeat Books, 2002). www.allmusic.com

Kernfield, Barry, editor, *The New Grove Dictionary of Jazz* (London and New York: Macmillan Press, 1988). www.grovemusic.com

Materials to aid rhythm section with shuffle beat:

Berg, Shelly, Lou Fischer, Fred Hamilton, and Steve Houghton, *Rhythm Section Workshop for Jazz Directors*, book, DVD, CD (Van Nays: Alfred Publishing, 2006). www.alfred.com

Soph, Ed, *Musical Time*, book, DVD, CD (New York: Carl Fischer Music, 2005). www.carlfischer.com

Materials to aid pianists/guitarists with voicings:

Bay, William, *Deluxe Guitar Chord Encyclopedia* (Pacific: Mel Bay Publications, 1971).

www.melbay.com

Christiansen, Corey, *Jazz Guitar Photo Chords* (Pacific: Mel Bay Publications, 2006). www.melbay.com

Levine, Mark, *The Jazz Piano Book* (Petaluma: Sher Music Company, 1990). www.shermusic.com

Contributed by:

Robert Morgan
Director of Jazz Studies Emeritus
High School for Performing and Visual Arts
Houston, Texas

Teacher Resource Guide

In a Mellow Tone

Frank Foster

(b. 1928)

Unit 1: Composer

Frank Foster, saxophonist/composer, was born on September 23, 1928 in Cincinnati, Ohio. Frank Foster is one of those rare triple threats: He's a saxophonist with a big, broad, rangy sound and approach; he's a composer and arranger of both tunes and long-form works; and he's a skilled leader of bands both large and small. As a saxophonist fluent on tenor, soprano, and alto saxes, he has been a welcome addition on bandstands and recording studios of vast variety. As a composer and arranger, his efforts have run the gamut, from writing such jazz standards as *Shiny Stockings* and *Simone*, to his *Lake Placid Suite*, commissioned by the 1980 Winter Olympics. As a bandleader, he has led everything from quartets to big bands, all with great aplomb and abundant skill.

Born and raised in Cincinnati, Ohio, Frank's mother was an amateur pianist, so the influence of music was always in his home. From the time he was a teenager, Frank played in dance bands in and around southern and south central Ohio. After learning music in Cincinnati schools, he matriculated to Central State University, where he joined the Wilberforce Collegians, a major collegiate training ground. In 1949 Frank moved to Detroit, where he played with both aspiring and veteran jazz musicians, including fellow Ohioan Snooky Young. Some of young Frank's early influences included Wardell Gray and Sonny Stitt.

Frank entered the Army in 1951. After his Army stint ended in 1953, he joined one of the great jazz proving grounds, the Count Basie Orchestra. This was to be one of his signature band affiliations for the next eleven years and beyond. With the Basie band he was not only a key member of the saxophone section, his keen writing skills soon came to the Count's attention, and he became one of Basie's most trusted composers and arrangers. His most-noted contribution to the Basie book was *Shiny Stockings*, which became a Basie signature. And Basie so valued his playing that Frank was also a member of the Count's occasional small band, known as the Kansas City Seven. Frank Foster's composing and arranging gifts served him well and his skills were sought by several big bands, including the Woody Herman band and the Lloyd Price Orchestra, which at the time was directed by Slide Hampton.

From the mid-1960s through the 1980s Frank Foster led his own large and small groups, including his Loud Minority big band, Living Color Band, and Frank Foster's Non-Electric Company. He was also a much sought after saxophone soloist, composer, and arranger for bands large and small. These affiliations included the Duke Pearson, Thad Jones-Mel Lewis, Buddy Rich, Clark Terry, and Jazzmobile big bands. It was the Jazzmobile Big Band that performed his *Lake Placid Suite*, at the 1980 Winter Olympic Games. Quite skilled at working with singers, Frank arranged and conducted a record date for Sarah Vaughan. He has featured such stellar vocalists as Ernestine Anderson and Dee Bridgewater in his own big bands, as well as arranging Carmen Bradford's vocals for the Basie band. Ms. Bradford even sang Frank's praises on a Basie band tune called "Papa Foss."

Frank's small ensemble memberships during the 1970s and 80s included the Elvin Jones Jazz Machine, and a quintet co-led with fellow saxman Frank Wess. Two years after Count Basie ascended to ancestry, Frank Foster took over leadership of the Basie Orchestra and swung it to good health from June, 1986 to July, 1995. He assisted mightily in upholding the proud Basie tradition, thrilling old fans and winning new converts to their distinctly swinging sound.

Since leaving the Basie organization, Frank Foster has kept busy with a broad range of small band work and jazz education. His jazz education work actually commenced years before that. He was hired as a music consultant by the New York City public schools in 1971–72. In addition to his long teaching tenure with the Jazzmobile organization, Frank has taught at the State University of New York in Buffalo and at Queens College. In 1983 he returned to his alma mater, Central State University, to receive an honorary doctorate degree.

Unit 2: Composition

Frank Foster wrote *In A Mellow Tone* for the Count Basie Band around 1957. The format of the piece is what we now associate with the style of many arrangers who were his contemporaries in the band and many who followed. The statements of the melody by the various sections of the band, the veracity of the saxophone soli and the tutti sections of the arrangement are

also associated with many of Thad Jones' compositions and arrangements. Building on the style established in the Basie Band and drawing on the types of soli sections in the Ellington and Lunceford bands, Frank creates an interesting, challenging and exciting arrangement of a classic composition that adheres to the style of the Basie band and pays homage to Duke Ellington and the arrangers who preceded him.

Unit 3: Historical Perspective

Because of World War II, there was a ban of the use of the oils necessary to produce recordings, so the recording industry became nonfunctional. In addition, there was an extra tax put on places that offered dancing, so the big bands underwent major transformations that reduced many of them to much smaller ensembles. Count Basie was down to using a seven-piece ensemble which he called the "Kansas City Seven," while others simply went out of business. The only band that was able to maintain its self during this period was the Duke Ellington Orchestra. By the late 1940s and early 50s the music had moved into the small clubs like Minton's and those on 52nd Street like the Three Deuces, etc. where people sat and no longer danced to the music. The "new music" erroneously called bebop became the music of this new era. Eventually, Count Basie and others were able to resurrect their big bands, and the young and old musicians that populated these bands became the voices of this era of big band music. which included composers, arrangers, and soloists Frank Foster, Thad Jones, Ernie Wilkins, and Frank Wess. Frank joined the Count Basie Orchestra in 1953 and stayed until 1964, a mainstay in the sound of the band with his playing and arranging skills. Two years after Basie died, Foster was called back into service to lead the Count Basie Orchestra, which he did for the next nine years, again contributing as a soloist and arranger as well as the music director and bandleader.

Unit 4: Technical Considerations

The complexity of this arrangement makes it rated at Grade 5–6, and the recommended tempo is ♩ = 120, with a duration of 6:53.

The lead trumpet range goes up to concert C (c^2) until it reaches E♭ ($e♭^2$) at the very end. The saxophone soli is challenging technically because of the sixteenth-note passages and should be practiced at a slow speed so that the complexity and phrasing are clearly understood. The full ensemble passages must be rehearsed for phrasing, balance, interpretation, and dynamics to achieve the proper swing feel.

Unit 5: Stylistic Considerations

The medium tempo and hard-swinging style of the piece is part of the tradition that defines the Count Basie Orchestra of the late 1950s, and harkens back to the beginnings of the big bands. The dynamics of the piece are very much in keeping with the style of the band, going from a whisper to a roar all within a few seconds, is also very characteristic of the band. The ensemble must be as one within each section (saxophones, trumpets, trombones and rhythm) and as a whole. Knowledge of brass players to perform shakes is critical to the overall excitement of the arrangement. Section playing is dependent on following and blending with the lead player in each section and following the lead trumpet player in tutti sections of the piece.

Unit 6: Musical Elements

MELODY:

The melody is repetitive with a few new elements introduced near the end of each 16-bar segment, and should be sung by the entire band to develop a deep sense of swing. The blues element is implicit in each segment of the melody and incorporated into the swing style of the piece.

HARMONY:

The arrangement sticks to the original compositions harmonic make-up with few exceptions. The introduction of new material either as new thematic material or as harmonized material keeps the interest throughout the arrangement.

RHYTHM:

The style and swing of the piece can only be achieved by each member of the ensemble feeling the pulse of the quarter note and triplet feel of swing eighth notes. It is important to realize that this music was dance music, and that anything that would disrupt the dancer's movement was not acceptable. Many dancers influenced the music, and many musicians influenced the dancers, so having students listen to and watch videos of the swing dance styles would also give them a better sense of how this music was played and how it functioned during the periods of live dance music. Introduce them to the idea of dancing to this arrangement or at least moving in time to the music for an added asset to its performance.

Unit 7: Form and A Structure

The basic form of the composition is ABAC.

SECTION	MEASURE	EVENT AND SCORING
Intro/first chorus	1–16	The tempo is ♩ = 120. The piece begins with rhythm section with piano hinting at the melody.
	17–32	Muted trombones and saxophones move back and forth at each other.
A	33–48	Saxophones have a unison melody with muted trumpets playing background figures.
	49–56	Saxophones continue the melody, but with open trombones playing the same background figure that trumpets played in measures 33–48.
	57–64	Saxophones continue the melody in unison with tutti brass figures.
B	65–68	An "easy" tutti section, *pianissimo* style, leading to a trombone solo with harmonized reed background.
	69–80	Trombone solo.
	81–84	Tutti figures leading to a continued trombone solo.
	85–94	Trombone solo.
	95–96	Saxophone soli 2-bar break.
C	97–112	A saxophone soli with occasional piano fills.
	113–128	Saxophone soli continues with tutti brass fills.
D	129–144	Re-introduction of the melody tutti in the "easy style" at *mezzo forte*.

Section	Measure	Event and Scoring
	145–160	Tutti continues, but with new material being introduced, getting away from the melody and leading to a build-up into the next chorus.
E	161–176	The shout chorus, where the entire band backs up the double *forte* volume and now with drum and rhythm section fills in-between the band statements, culminating with a typical Basie ending with the rhythm section leading to the last deeply harmonically rich chord.

Unit 8: Suggested Listening

Count Basie Orchestra:
Breakfast Dance and Barbeque, Roulette Jazz Records.
Basie Straight Ahead, The Complete Atomic Basie, Blue Note Records.
Thad Jones/Mel Lewis Orchestra:
New Life, A&M Records.
Groove Merchant, Solid State Records)

Unit 9: Additional References and Resources

Dunscomb, Richard, and Willie L. Hill, Jr. *Jazz Pedagogy: The Jazz Educator's Handbook and Resource Guide*. Miami, FL: Warner Brothers, 2004.

Contributed by:

Cecil Bridgewater
Professor of Music
Manhattan School of Music, New School Jazz and Contemporary Music,
William Paterson Jazz Program
New York, New York

Teacher Resource Guide

Main Stem

Duke Ellington

(1899–1974)

transcribed by David Berger

(b. 1948)

Unit 1: Composer

Edward Kennedy "Duke" Ellington was born on April 29, 1899 in Washington D. C. As an American jazz composer, pianist, and bandleader, Duke Ellington was one of the most influential figures in jazz, if not all American music.

Exposed to art and music at an early age, Duke was encouraged to study piano at age seven by his parents James Edward Ellington and Daisy Kennedy Ellington. In his autobiography, *Music Is My Mistress*, Ellington comments that he missed more lessons than he attended, feeling at the time that playing the piano was not his talent. Over time, this would change. After sneaking into Frank Holiday's poolroom at age fourteen, Duke was exposed to many great musicians, an experience that would ignite his interest in musical performance. By 1923 he had formed a small dance band known as The Washingtonians (which included drummer Sonny Greer) and moved to New York City. While there, Duke's career was transformed when King Oliver took notice of his rising success and offered him the chance to become make The Washingtonians the house band at Harlem's Cotton Club. With a weekly radio broadcast and famous clientele pouring in nightly to see him and his orchestra, Ellington's popularity was assured.

In the next several years, Ellington's orchestra grew in size and stature as many regarded as "jazz-giants" joined its ranks. Among them was the band's undisputed leading soloist, Johnny Hodges, a man who established the romantic alto saxophone style with swooping, passionate melodies. Harry Carney defined and innovated on the baritone saxophone as Duke's longest running member (1927–1974), and Barney Bigard represented a mastery over New Orleans jazz clarinet. Trombonists such as Lawrence Brown and Joe "Tricky-Sam" Nanton helped revolutionize the instrument with many unique trombone stylings, most notably the plunger mute technique. Trumpeters such as Cootie Williams and Bubber Miley added their mastery of range and muted technique, while at the same time transforming early dance-band style into a more "New Orleans," or "jungle" style.

Many of these musicians remained with Duke for decades. While many of them were noteworthy in their own rights, it was Duke's mastery of composition and arranging that melded them into one of the most influential musical ensemble of the twentieth century. Known for writing specifically for his ensemble members, Duke took advantage of each individual, unique voice in his ensemble, featuring his or her given virtuosity and allowing them to put their stamp on the masterwork.

Aside from composition, Duke Ellington is one of the twentieth century's best-known African-American celebrities. Over a career that spanned half a century, Duke appeared in several movies with his orchestra, recorded for many of America's best-known record labels, and toured the United States and Europe on several occasions. Certainly, Edward Kennedy "Duke" Ellington has left a legacy of profound music making and unsurpassed class and poise.

Unit 2: Composition

Duke Ellington wrote *Main Stem* in 1942; it was originally recorded on June 26, 1942. The piece was originally titled *Altitude*, and later was titled *On Becoming a Square* before the title of *Main Stem* was finally set. The title refers to the main street of a town where all the action takes place. A straight-ahead swing tune, this piece features the basic jazz call-and-response technique created between soloist and ensemble, as well as a riff-based accompaniment under the four-beat time pattern. Duke frequently wrote specifically for his ensemble members, and this piece served to feature several of his soloists; Johnny Hodges on alto saxophone, Ben Webster on tenor saxophone, Ray Nance on trumpet, and both Lawrence Brown and Joe "Tricky-Sam" Nanton on trombone. As the piece is a basic 12-bar blues in the key of D major, many soloists played choruses in the original ensemble. Certainly, all solo designations can vary depending on group instrumentation and skill levels.

Unit 3: Historical Perspective

In the 1940s, Duke Ellington's orchestra was at its creative peak as he wrote for distinctive voices and tremendous virtuosity. With the help of classically-trained pianist/composer Billy Strayhorn, Duke wrote many "three minute symphonies" that featured such ensemble regulars as Johnny Hodges, Ben Webster, Jimmy Blanton, Ray Nance, and Cootie Williams. *Cottontail*, *Main Stem*, *Harlem Airshaft*, *Streets of New York*, and dozens of other classic swing arrangements date from this period in Duke's career.

During this time music was commercially recorded on 78 RPM record sides, which limited its duration to just over three minutes. Ellington sought to break this paradigm of compositional form, and began branching out (later with Strayhorn), composing larger works such as *Black, Brown, and Beige* (1943). Over the course of the next two decades, Duke would add several other longer works to his repertoire.

The recording ban of 1942–43 had a serious effect on all big bands and recording artists because of the increase in royalty payments to musicians its resolution necessitated. The financial viability of Ellington's operation was threatened because of this. However, Ellington's royalty income as a composer and songwriter ultimately subsidized the Orchestra, allowing them to continue as one of the mainstream performing ensembles of the decade.

Unit 4: Technical Considerations

This chart is rated Grade 5. The recommended tempo is ♩ = 208, based on the 1942 transcription by David Berger from The Blanton-Webster Band (see Unit 8 below). The piece can be played slower or faster, but seems to find its swinging pocket at right around ♩ = 208. The lead trumpet range is modestly in the staff, but the transcribed solo parts in the second and third trumpet go to written B (b^1) and C♯ ($c♯^2$) over the staff. The first trombone part is scored only to F♯ above the staff (f♯), but the first and second solo trombone parts go to A (a) and B (b) above the staff. These soli could be adjusted down an octave for younger players or improvised in a lower register. *Main Stem* has no complicated rhythms, large intervals, or awkward fingerings. The difficulties evolve from the bright swing tempo and the rhythmic feel and placement. All of the riff inflections must be executed correctly for this music to energize properly. Due to lack of playing experience in the key of D major, some students will struggle with intonation.

Unit 5: Stylistic Considerations

This is, in many ways, a classic swing style arrangement. It presents a bright tempo with a solid four-feeling supported by simple blues riffs, brass response figures, steady and consistent drumming, and moaning and expressive blues solos using the entire range of muted effects. Conductors should identify the lead voices and melodies in each chorus and make sure that all of the players adjust their parts appropriately to the melody as it moves from voice to voice. Rhythmically, the music needs to feel light enough to not drag. If everyone thinks in two large beats per measure (as if they are marching) the music should maintain its forward momentum. The drummer can help the feel by "knocking" (crossover rim shot; be sure to find the sweet spot where the tone is rich) on beats 2 and 4 as often as possible.

Unit 6: Musical elements

MELODY:

The melody is simple and repetitive. It should be sung like a standard blues riff with inflection and rhythmic drive. Swallow the lower neighbor and push into the beats. The fast tempo suggests simple melodic improvisation within this riff-like quality. The call-and-response nature of this melody is excellent for teaching this very basic jazz concept. Jazz melodies should be played with a legato tongue technique. Phrase markings do not indicated slurring. A connected "da" tongue will produce the best results. Swing jazz also needs strong accents on all long notes. Accent and inflection, rather than volume, creates the swing.

All soli in this arrangement are connected to the structure of the piece, and in order to sound convincing, students must be well connected to the numerous accompaniment riffs.

HARMONY:

Many students will not be comfortable in the key of D major initially, but the study of this work can eventually lead to the learning of blues in all keys. The focus of the improvisation should be on moaning and crying in the blues tradition. Students should learn chords and transcribed soli first, and then develop their own solo ideas. Learning the third and seventh guide tones is very important to hearing the blues chord changes.

RHYTHM:

Main Stem is filled with some of the most basic and fundamental rhythm patterns in jazz; studying this piece enables students to learn and internalize these important rhythmic figures. The rhythm section must be able to improvise a blues accompaniment that remains light and on top of the time. Busy playing will cause the tempo to drag, and the music will lose energy.

The interplay between the rhythm section and horns is the key to making this chart work well. However, the rhythm section should not dominate or overplay. The bass needs to walk in four, but feel two large beats per measure (like marching), so as to generate the forward momentum that the music requires.

Unit 7: Form and Structure

The basic form of the composition is a large ABA.

SECTION	MEASURE	EVENT AND SCORING
A	1 – 12	The first of seven blues choruses in the key of D. The tempo is ♩ = 208. Learn at a much slower tempo until the style and nuances are mastered. The first two measures introduce the call-and-response pattern that permeates all seven choruses of the A section. The lower-neighbor eighth notes should be swallowed or ghosted, but practice singing the triplet subdivision (doo-dul-la) so as to place the swallowed notes in the correct upbeat position. Trombones should play an ***fp*** accent followed by a *crescendo* on their line, and feel the accurate jazz eighth note placement "inside" the sustained notes.
A-B	13 – 24	The melody of the second chorus is played by the second tenor and baritone saxophone. The melody is in thirds, initially based on the seventh and ninth of the D^7 chord. The transcribed solo for third trumpet responds to the main melody using a contrasting "big four" rhythm pattern. This solo can be improvised as long as the primary motif is retained in its basic structure.

Section	Measure	Event and Scoring
B-C	25 – 36	The third chorus is a riff style alto saxophone solo in the Johnny Hodges tradition.
C-D	37 – 48	The fourth chorus is a solo for third trumpet with accompaniment figures in trombones and baritone saxophone. Be careful to line up the offbeat eighth notes in the baritone saxophone against the detached quarter notes on all four beats in the trombones. This is not easy to do!
D-E	49 – 60	The fifth chorus is similar to the second chorus, with second tenor and baritone saxophone stating the primary melody. A second trumpet solo responds in a call-and-response manner, while trombones offer an "amen" choral accompaniment. This "amen" figure should be accented.
E-F	61 – 72	The sixth chorus features the four saxophones in a voiced variation of the main melody. The baritone sax plays lead in this choir. First and third trumpets respond while clarinet solos in riff fashion above the entire texture. The introduction of passing chords in the guitar suggests a slightly denser harmony.
F-G	73 – 84	The seventh and final blues chorus in this large A section continues the call-and-response idea between the trumpets and saxophones, while first trombone solos on top with plunger and pixie mute. All of the muted brass soli throughout must be played with a vocal guttural quality. This requires a lot of listening and study on the part of the soloists. The Ellington brass players are very important in the evolution of pixie-and-plunger brass pedagogy.

Section	Measure	Event and Scoring
Transition (G-H)	85 – 90	This is a six-measure modulation to the subdominant key of G major. Proper ensemble balance is a challenge, as the lead trumpet is scored in the low register.
B (H-I)	91 – 99 100–118 (I-J)	The B section consists of two 18-bar extended blues choruses. The first features a tenor sax solo; the second, a trombone solo. The dynamic swells set up the soloists on the C major IV chord, followed two measures later by C minor. The scrunch on the 14th measure of each chorus should be played as a ***fp*** *crescendo*. The dotted quarter on the second half of beat 3 followed by the quarter on beat 1 of the next bar is a jazz rhythmic cliché that all students must learn to feel.
A (J-K)	119 – 130	The key of D major returns for the recapitulation of the original blues theme and orchestration. As in the beginning, trumpets are playing with pixie and plunger mutes combined. Careful attention to intonation is required in this unison figure. Increase the trumpet dynamic by one level in order to project this line with the two mutes.
Coda	131 – 138	This is an eight-measure coda beginning on a G^7 chord reminiscent of the B theme, and then cadencing with melodic fragments from the main theme in D major. Make sure the baritone saxophone plays the solo low B up to pitch in the second bar from the end. Brass balance in the coda is also based on the trombones not overblowing the trumpets, which are scored in a lower tessitura range respectively. Note the secondary dominant chords in the

Section	Measure	Event and Scoring
	131 – 138 (continued)	harmony, which will require careful tuning, especially with muted trumpets. The "Charleston Rhythm" found in the coda was also used at letters D, F, and G. Derived from the "clave", this rhythm is basic to all of the rhythmic language of jazz.

Unit 8: Suggested Listening

Ellington, Duke, *The Blanton Webster Band*, RCA/Ariola International, 5659–2-RB, Victor, 072438–1.

Duke Ellington and his Orchestra, *Centenary Celebration 1999 Volume 3 CD*, Parker, 2001.

Duke Ellington and his Orchestra, *Duke Ellington: At the Hurricane*,, Storyville Records, 1998.

Duke Ellington and his Orchestra, *The Duke Box*,, Storyville Records, 2007.

Unit 9: Additional References and Resources

Berger, David, *Main Stem* (score transcribed for Jazz at Lincoln Center (Miami: Warner Bros. Publications, 1999).

Collier, James Lincoln. *Duke Ellington* (New York: Oxford University Press, 1987).

Dance, Stanley, *The World of Duke Ellington* (Cambridge: Da Capo Press, 2001).

Ellington, Duke, *Music Is My Mistress* (Cambridge: Da Capo Press, 1973).

Ellington, Mercer K., *Duke Ellington In Person* (Boston: Houghton Mifflin, 1978).

Tucker, Mark, *Ellington, The Early Years* (Champaign: University of Illinois Press, 1991).

http://en.wikipedia.org/w/index.php title=Duke_Ellington&action=history (accessed April 22, 2007).

Contributed by:

Stephen C. Massey
Director of Music
Foxboro Public Schools
Foxboro, Massachusetts

Teacher Resource Guide

Moanin'

Charles Mingus
(1922–1979)

arranged by Sy Johnson
(b. 1930)

Unit 1: Composer

Charles Mingus was born at a military base on the United States side of the Mexican border in Nogales, Arizona on April 22, 1922 to a Swedish African-American father and a Chinese African-American mother. Shortly afterwards, his father moved the family to the Watts area of Los Angeles, California to seek medical treatment for his ailing wife. Nonetheless, Mingus' mother died when he was not quite two years old. His father soon remarried, and Mingus was raised by his stepmother. The chaos of his early life would be reflected in his compositions, but unlike his childhood, he would be the master of his music.

Early influences that were to prove formative in his future musical life included listening to Duke Ellington on the radio, experiences with his stepmother in black church music and his study as a young man of twentieth-century classical composers such as Schoenberg and Stravinsky. Beginning on the trombone and cello before switching to bass, Mingus aggressively pursued his music, practicing and hitting all of the jam sessions he could. During the 1940s he performed and toured with a number of bands and leaders, including Louis Armstrong and, in particular, Lionel Hampton. He also was a member of the famed Red Norvo trio in the late 1940s, and as a part of that ensemble made the move to New York City in 1951. The 1950s saw him performing with all of the most influential jazz musicians, including Charlie Parker, Miles Davis, and Duke Ellington. His historically volatile and unpredictable personality may have contributed to his firing by Duke over a spat with Juan Tizol.

Although undoubtedly one of the virtuoso jazz bassists of all time and a member of many of the prominent bebop combos of the day (he was part of the famous Jazz at Massey Hall concert in 1953 with Dizzy Gillespie, Charlie Parker, Bud Powell and Max Roach), his reputation as a band leader and composer quickly came to the fore beginning in the 1950s. Compositionally, he straddled all historical periods of jazz, combining traditional elements such as brass plunger mutes and traditional jazz with the most cutting edge *avant-garde* tonal and rhythmic qualities as heard in his collaborations with Eric Dolphy into the 1960s. As noted jazz historian Ted Gioia says in his book, *The History of Jazz*, "The miracle of Mingus's music was that he could develop a coherent and moving personal style out of this hodgepodge of influences."[1]

It was in the mid- to late-1950s that Mingus began his legendary Jazz Workshop sessions in New York City. During this time and into the mid-1960s, some of his best-known compositions were created, including, *Goodbye Pork Pie Hat*, *Fables of Faubus*, *Ecclusiastics*, *Peggy's Blue Skylight*, and *Moanin'*. After a brief hiatus from the music scene in the late 1960s, Mingus came back stronger than ever as a composer, bassist, and teacher. Even though diagnosed with Lou Gehrig's Disease in 1977, he remained active to the end with all of his endeavors, even to the point of singing into a tape recorder when he was too weak to write down his compositions. Some of his last work was with Joni Mitchell, who spent time tape recording him in his apartment in preparation for her tribute album, *Mingus*. He died on January 5, 1979 in Mexico, where he was seeking a cure via alternative medicine.

Unit 2: Composition

Charles Mingus initially composed *Moanin'* in the late 1950s and recorded it in 1959 on the Atlantic album *Blues and Roots*. According to the original liner notes on the album, there weren't any printed charts on the session, and Mingus taught the lines to the musicians from the piano, utilizing a compositional practice common to musicians including Duke Ellington and Jelly Roll Morton. The distinctive bari sax opening is played by the great Pepper Adams and the soloists are Jackie McLean, Pepper Adams, and Booker Ervin. The instrumentation for the original version of *Moanin'* as played on the recording was two alto saxes, tenor sax, bari sax, two trombones, piano, bass, and drums.

The big band version of *Moanin'* addressed here was arranged by Mingus' longtime friend, arranger and orchestrator Sy Johnson and is recorded on the album *Mingus Big Band '93: Nostalgia in Times Square.* Johnson manages to retain all of the gospel and highly improvisational characteristics of the original chart.

Unit 3: Historical Perspective

Mingus was at the apex of an astounding career when he composed *Moanin'*. It was also during this time that he recorded arguably his most important recording, *Mingus Ah Um*. Unfortunately, in the early sixties, Mingus' impact on the music scene began to recede due to changing musical forms, the disappearance of jazz clubs and his outspoken views on racism.

Throughout his career he was an ardent black activist, not only in what he said, but through his actions. He began his own record label, Debut, in part out of frustration with the white-controlled recording industry. The first record released by his company was the live recording he had made of the Jazz at Massey Hall concert. Probably his most significant musical anti-racism statement was made with his composition *Fables of Faubus*. Named for Governor Faubus of Arkansas who, in 1957, sought to deny nine black students entrance to a public high school in Little Rock, it featured lyrics that Columbia Records refused to release on the album.

Since Charles Mingus' death in 1979, his wife, Sue Mingus, has continued to promote his music by the establishment of the Mingus Big Band, the Mingus Orchestra, and the Mingus Dynasty. Through her publishing company, Jazz Workshop, Inc., she has published several books about the music of Mingus as well as over a dozen big band arrangements of his music, distributed by the Hal Leonard Corporation.

Sue Mingus has also produced seven recordings of the Mingus Big Band on which the big band arrangement of *Moanin'* is found (*Mingus Big Band 93: Nostalgia in Times Square*).

The popularity of Mingus' music has been ever increasing since his death, due to its wide-ranging appeal among factions as diverse as jazz traditionalists, jazz neoclassicists, and fans of the avant-garde.

Unit 4: Technical Considerations

Definitely at the Grade 5+ level, *Moanin'* should first and foremost be considered a bari sax feature. The bari sax player on the 1959 recording was none other than the legendary Pepper Adams, and the bari player on the Mingus Big Band '93 recording is the great Ronnie Cuber. Not indicated in the chart but featured prominently on the recording is a huge "preacher testifyin'" bari sax cadenza out in front of the chart. Stamina is also an issue for the bari player, because once the chart starts, the bari sax lays down the main theme the entire time from start to finish. Played correctly, meaning low, loud and fast, this is a showcase for the bari player.

The indicated tempo on the published arrangement is fast at ♩ = 216, but seems sluggish once you listen to the recording, which is closer to ♩ = 236. Tempo isn't everything in this chart, but it adds to the excitement.

Although the written brass ranges aren't high by any stretch, there are opportunities for the lead trumpet to "ride up high" over some sections in which the entire ensemble is really blowing. Almost more of a consideration is the bottom end of the brass ranges. Unison trumpet parts routinely feature low A (A) and B♭ (B♭) played *fortissimo*, and the tuba (bass trombone) part calls for a *fortissimo* pedal F (F_2).

After the bari sax lays down the main theme there are three additional unison lines that are layered on top as the chart progresses. It's important that, even though the dynamic marking is *fortissimo*, the unison lines are played in tune. Any dissonance should be from the play of lines against each other and not from intonation deficiencies.

The one phrase that will probably take extra "shed" time to work out will be the 4-bar unison phrase that all horns play at the end of section B. It simply "lays" uncomfortably, but should come together nicely after some slow work.

Chord changes for soloing are indicated in all parts. Music at this level really requires solid soloists, as the form is long and the intensity, not necessarily from dynamics, must be maintained.

Unit 5: Stylistic Considerations

As with much of the music of Charles Mingus, the Sy Johnson big band arrangement of *Moanin'* is a true musical *mélange* of jazz styles and periods. The original recording on which *Moanin'* appears the *Blues and Roots* recording of 1959. In that context, Mingus' gospel and church roots come "moanin'" through. These gospel qualities are juxtaposed over some serious, hard-driving bop playing and writing for the rhythm section. The composed horn lines are always edgy and border on maniacal. At the end of each 16-bar phrase, the composed lines descend into group improvisation, each time adding more players to the mix in an *avant-garde* frenzy. In the big band tradition of Ellington and Basie, more players are added on different lines each time through the repeated A section.

It is important to note that the written backgrounds to the solos in the published arrangement aren't exactly what is heard on the *Nostalgia in Times Square* recording. A common practice in the heyday of the big bands was to make up backgrounds on the fly during performances. It would be a great exercise to transcribe the missing parts on the recording for use in performance.

Although Mingus' music sometimes seems to border on chaos, Mingus scholars will affirm that in performance he kept firm control over all aspects of his compositions.

Unit 6: Musical Considerations

MELODY:

There are four distinct melodic lines running through the first eight measures of the A section of *Moanin'*. Starting with the solo bari sax, each line enters and is layered on top of the previous line, building intensity. In addition to layering, more instruments are added to each motif, thickening the texture as well. The second eight measures of each repeat of the A section has the bari sax continuing with a composed line with group improvisation in the other instruments. The increasing melodic tension from the building interplay of the lines in subsequent repetitions of section A is what increases the excitement that culminates finally in the movement to section B.

One of the melodic surprises in section B is the last note of the unison line, played by all horns in the final four measures. The last note of the line is the one harmonized note of the entire phrase, and it outlines a G♭^{13} chord, which is the tritone substitution of the V chord, placing it a half step above the tonic of F. During the piece this resolves to a final A section before the soli, but at the end of the piece, this is the final chord at the *Fine*.

The rhythm section parts all are standard slash notation, with the exception of a couple of hints at a bass line and the indication for fanning the hi-hat at the beginning of the chart.

HARMONY:

Moanin' is in the key of F minor, which any jazz player will tell you makes a great key over which to solo. The first eight measures of section A follow a repeated i–VI–ii–V^{7} in a harmonic rhythm that has chords changing each measure. The second eight measures of section A maintains the F minor triad with the bass line descending each measure on the F natural minor scale, the final measure turning things back around with a C$^{7(\sharp 9)}$. This, combined with the group improvisation for the second eight measures of section A, raises the excitement level exponentially each time it comes around.

Section B moves to the iv chord (B♭m^{7}) and alternates every two measures with a G♭^{6}/F, finally ending in the very cool tritone substitution of G♭^{13}. The substitution is not used during the soli, which simply goes to a C$^{7(\sharp 9)}$.

RHYTHM:
This is a hard bop "in-your-face" chart from start to finish. All of the eight-note phrases in the horn lines are bebop in nature; all of the articulations and phrasings are well marked. The melodic line which appears in the saxes has quarter note triplets that, if played accurately, give the effect of being very laid-back eighth notes.

Horn players really need to be aggressive when playing all of the anticipated eighth-note figures in the backgrounds. This is especially a factor for the trumpets using plungers.

Unit 7: Form and Structure

The form of *Moanin'*, as derived from the solo changes, is AABA, although the actual tune is comprised of multiple repetitions of section A, culminating in one last time though sections B and A. The entire chart ends, however, with the angular unison line at the end of section B.

SECTION	MEASURE	EVENT AND SCORING
A	1–8	***ff*** bari sax solo at a very aggressive tempo of ♩ = ca. 216 or better.
	9–16	Bari sax solo continues for four measures with the tuba (bass trombone) and loosely closed hi-hat entering in measure 13. Drums should enter at ***pp*** and *crescendo* into the swing pattern at measure 17.
	17–24	Bari sax and loose hi-hat continue. Trombones enter in octaves with the first countermelody. The longer "smeared" melodic texture of this line is in direct contrast to the aggressive bari sax line.
	25–32	Bari sax continues with the written solo while the two trombones play separate soloistic, but notated, lines.
	33–48	Dynamics drop back to ***mf*** and saxes add the second countermelody to the mix. There is an additional sax solo during the group improvisation. It is important for the band to keep intensity through the end of each 16-bar phrase so that the energy doesn't die.

Section	Measure	Event and Scoring
	49–64	The entire band continues playing the same phrase set up in the previous sixteen measures, adding instruments and thickening texture. The entire rhythm section plays straight-ahead time. First tenor sax blows an improvised solo over the entire band.
	65–80	The entire ensemble now plays, adding alto saxes and lead trumpet playing yet a third countermelody. The entire band is at *forte*.
	81–96	The dynamic level steps up to ***ff*** and lead alto and lead trumpet improvise in the upper register. (Note: The published arrangement has the bari sax playing through measure 96 although on the *Nostalgia in Times Square* recording, the entire ensemble plays measure 96, beat 1, and then is silent for the rest of the measure).
B	97–112	Finally, the tension is relieved by section B played at ***mp***. *Crescendo* in the last eight measures with the entire band playing the unison figure in measures 109–112.
A	113–128	One last statement of the melody in the bari sax is followed by unison saxes and trombones on the same line. Group improvisation occurs for the last eight measures.
AABA	129–176	The solo section is open for any instrument, with backgrounds at the discretion of the director. D.C. al fine after the last solo.
D. C.	1–112	D.C. and then play as written to measure 112. There is a fermata on the final $G\flat^{13}$ with "wild, thematic improvisation" by the entire band.

Unit 8: Suggested Listening

Mingus Big Band 93, *Nostalgia in Times Square*, Dreyfus Jazz.
Mingus, Charles, *Blues and Roots*, Atlantic.

Unit 9: Additional References and Resources

Aebersold, Jamey, "Historically Significant Recordings," http://www.jazz-books.com/miva/documents/handbook/08_historically_signfcnt_recrdings.pdf (accessed July 15, 2006).

Bayles, Martha, *Hole In Our Soul: the Loss of Beauty and Meaning in American Popular Music* (New York: The Free Press, A Division of Macmillan, Inc., 1994).

Collier, James Lincoln, *The Making of Jazz* (New York: Delta Publishing Company, 1978).

_____, *Jazz, The American Theme Song* (New York: Oxford University Press, Inc., 1993), newportal.wowway.net.

Gioia, Ted, *The History of Jazz* (New York: Oxford University Press, Inc., 1997).

Mingus, Charles, *Beneath the Underdog* (New York: Vintage Books, a Division of Random House, Inc., originally published in hardcover by Alfred A. Knopf, Inc., New York, 1971).

Mingus, Sue, with musical analyses by Andrew Homzy, *Mingus: More Than a Fake Book*, New York: Jazz Workshop, Inc., distributed by the Hal Leonard Corporation, 1991).

Yurochko, Bob, *A Short History of Jazz* (Chicago: Nelson Hall Publishers, 1993).

Russell, Ross, *Bird Lives* (New York: Charterhouse, 1973).

Other authentic Mingus charts, as played by the Mingus Big Band, published by Jazz Workshop, Inc., and distributed for jazz ensemble by the Hal Leonard Corporation:

Title	Arranger	Product Number
Opus 4	Boris Kaslov	07011279
Gunslinging Bird	Steve Slagle	07010394
Song With Orange	John Stubblefield	07011279
Boogie Stop Shuffle	Sy Johnson	07010844
Children's Hour Of Dream	Sy Johnson	07010957
Duke Ellington's Sound Of Love	Charles Walrath	0701024
Ecclusiastics	Sy Johnson	07010518
Fables Of Faubus	Steve Slagle	07010704
Goodbye Pork Pie Hat	Sy Johnson	07010398
Haitian Fight Song	Sy Johnson	07010516
Nostalgia In Times Square	Ronnie Cuber	07010396
Sues' Changes	Sy Johnson	07010634

Jazz Workshop, Inc. also publishes a series called *Simply Mingus*, distributed by Hal Leonard. All arrangements are by the noted Mingus scholar, Andrew Homzy, and more accessible to less experienced bands at a Grade 4 level. Features of this series include written-out piano voicings and bass lines, written solo samples and optional soli features, moderate brass ranges and optional parts for flute, clarinet and horn. Titles include:

Title	**Product Number**
Boogie Stop Shuffle	07011215
Goodbye Pork Pie Hat	07011217
Haitian Fight Song	07011219

Contributed by:

Ben L. Huntoon
Director, Otterbein College Jazz Ensemble
Jazz Education Consultant, Stanton's Sheet Music
President, Ohio IAJE
Columbus, Ohio

---

1 Ted Gioia, *The History of Jazz* (New York: Oxford University Press, Inc., 1997).

Teacher Resource Guide

Once Around Thad Jones

(1923–1986)

Unit 1: Composer

Thad Jones was a harmonically advanced trumpeter/cornetist and a prolific arranger/composer with a distinctive sound both as a player and composer. He was the younger brother of Hank and older brother of Elvin, who both had very productive and successful careers. Self-taught on trumpet, he started playing professionally when he was sixteen with Hank Jones and Sonny Stitt.

After serving in the military (1943–46), Jones worked in territory bands in the Midwest. During 1950–53 he performed regularly with Billy Mitchell's quintet in Detroit and he made a few recordings with Charles Mingus (1954–55). Jones became well known during his long period with Count Basie's Orchestra (1954–63), taking a *Pop Goes the Weasel* chorus on *April in Paris* and sharing solo duties with Joe Newman. While with Basie, Jones had the opportunity to write some arrangements and he became a busy freelance writer after 1963. He joined the staff of CBS, co-led a quintet with Pepper Adams, and near the end of 1965 organized a big band with drummer Mel Lewis that played Monday nights at the Village Vanguard from February, 1966 on.

During the next decade, the orchestra (although always appearing each Monday evening at the Vanguard) became famous, giving Jones an outlet for his writing. He composed one standard, *A Child Is Born*, along with many fine pieces, including *Second Race*, *Groove Merchant*, *Don't Git Sassy*, and a host of many others. Among the side players in the Thad Jones/Mel Lewis Orchestra (which started out as an all-star group and later featured younger players) were trumpeters Bill Berry, Richard Williams, Marvin Stamm, Snooky Young, and Jon Faddis, trombonists Bob Brookmeyer, Jimmy Knepper and Quentin Jackson, the reeds of Jerome Richardson, Jerry Dodgion, Eddie Daniels, Joe

Farrell, Pepper Adams, and Billy Harper, pianists Hank Jones and Roland Hanna, and bassists Richard Davis and George Mraz.

In 1978 Jones surprised Lewis by suddenly leaving the band and moving to Denmark, an action he never explained. He wrote for a radio orchestra and led his own group called Eclipse. In late 1984 Jones took over the leadership of the Count Basie Orchestra, but within a year, bad health forced him to retire. His music is known for its powerful, Basie-derived swing, as well as his use of complex harmony and unique voicings.

Unit 2: Composition

Thad Jones wrote *Once Around* (1966) during his ten-year stint at the Village Vanguard. This composition illustrates his intense ensemble writing and featured use of the drums, which relies on complex harmonic sounds and rhythmic permutations. The tune is built on an 8-bar form with mainly one chord, Cm^7. The first solo section starts with an open solo for trumpet immediately after the typically dense beginning of the tune. The second open solo was written for Pepper Adams with a send-off from the brass section. The third and final open solo features piano. His creative genius is apparent throughout, as the tune is built on a melody over primarily one chord. Jones's use of exaggerated dynamics makes this relatively simple tune sound much more difficult than it really is. Within the last eight bars a 5/4 bar is thrown in to send off into the signature drum solo ending, which featured co-leader Mel Lewis. It is obvious that this tune was written as a vehicle for soloing, but as simple as it is, Jones's signature comes through loud and clear.

Unit 3: Historical Perspective

The big band era is generally regarded as 1935–45. It was the only time in history that the popularity of jazz music eclipsed all other forms of music in the U. S. Rightly or wrongly, the appearance of Benny Goodman and his big band at the Palomar in Los Angeles in August of 1935 is often referred to as the official start of the swing era. While Benny Goodman undoubtedly had a great big band, it should be clear by now that his may not have been the "best" or even most original big band playing hot jazz music at the time. Just as Benny Goodman did not start, conceive, or bring to fruition the big band era on his own, no one incident can be cited as the very beginning of the swing era. Rather, many circumstances, incidents, conditions, and inventions seemed to work together and should be taken into account when viewing the era's conception.

On the morning of "Black Thursday," October 24th, 1929, a great sell-off on the New York Stock Exchange occurred, triggering investor panic. While the market bounced back a bit that afternoon, it plummeted again on the ensuing Monday and Tuesday; soon America was in the midst of the Great Depression. On December 11, 1931 the New York Bank of the United States collapsed. These incidents helped bring to an end the prosperity, frivolity, and gaiety of the Roaring Twenties. Money began to be extremely tough to come by. The public was not able to afford going out to see live music performed or to buy records. Work was hard to find for everyone, let alone musicians. Record sales were at an all-time low. Many talented players worked the studios of radio networks and stations or were hidden in the confines of the few "sweet" dance orchestras able to stay afloat. Enter the free entertainment provided by radio.

After the 1940s, the popularity of the big band began its decline and started its journey to radio orchestras, hotel bands, and the institution of the Jazz Repertory Big Band. Much of the music performed in the 1940s by big bands was considered pop music, and was racially divided. The Glenn Miller band was considered primarily a "white" band, and the Duke Ellington band was considered primarily a "black" band. This divisive way of thinking and treating performers has given way to a much more diverse and healthy way of thinking.

Unit 4: Technical Considerations

This chart is rated Grade 5, and the recommended tempo is 𝅗𝅥 = ca. 120, with a duration of 3:45, depending on the open soli. The lead trumpet range goes to concert D (d^2); the lead trombone range goes to concert B♭ (third octave [b♭]). Bass lines are written out for ensemble voicing except on the improvisatory sections.

Although the tune is based primarily on one chord, there are complex substitute harmonies throughout. Guitar and piano parts provide only chord symbols. The changes for soloists are simple, and provide an excellent opportunity to introduce Jones's music to young improvisers. Having a strong jazz drummer is highly recommended for the performance of this chart.

Unit 5: Stylistic Considerations

This relatively bright swing spotlights the drummer loosely in the "cute" style of Oliver Nelson. Exaggerated use of dynamics is a must, as well as the use of a bebop-style articulation. Most of the musicians in the Thad Jones/Mel Lewis Orchestra were famous bebop players. No matter what, it has to swing! This selection is an ideal feature for trumpet, baritone saxophone, piano, and drums.

Unit 6: Musical Elements

MELODY:
The melody, although simple to sing and sometimes difficult to execute depending on player maturity, can be used to emphasize the call-and-response element that is prominent throughout this solo vehicle. The use of this vocal approach lends itself to getting the band to swing and realize what is going on throughout.

HARMONY:
The changes are simple, as they are built on eight measures of Cm^7. Within the ensemble shout sections and backgrounds, altered chord changes occur reflecting the sax and/or brass orchestration. Although complicated at sight, it is well within the idiom to have the piano/guitar player "lay out" or play sparsely while the ensemble is playing.

RHYTHM:
The swing feel requires that the entire band feel beats 2 and 4 throughout the piece, concentrating on this swing feel. Players will have to count, as it is a relatively challenging rhythmic feel with trading/filling in the drums at times throughout the piece. Singing this piece and making note of how the melody is passed off from one section to the other will help solidify the performance of the tune.

Unit 7: Form and Structure

The tune is an 8-bar form.

SECTION	MEASURE	EVENT AND SCORING
Intro-Tune:	1–16	The tempo is 𝅗𝅥 = c.120. Learn it at a much slower tempo until the swing and style are established. The alternating jazz trio should make sure the phrases are not slurred, but played in a smooth swing style, moving the air through each phrase. Careful attention to long and short notes is a must.
Solo (1): A	17–24	Open solo for trumpet based on Cm^7.
B	25–32	Saxophones play a repeated bebop-type countermelody. This line must sound easy and flowing. Brass must emphasize articulations and dynamics.

Section	Measure	Event and Scoring
C	33–40	A repeated full band shout chorus—the first one. Start at ***mf*** and build toward ***ff*** in measure 37. Drums must fill toward the middle of the phrase and bring things back down. Saxophones need to bring out the moving line at the end of the phrase while bringing to dynamics down to ***p***.
D	41–48	Open solo for baritone saxophone based on Cm^7.
E	49–56	Brass builds coming out of the baritone solo. Pay particular attention to articulations and dynamics. Saxophones stay behind, but support and build from ***mp*** to ***ff*** going into the second ending and a piano solo.
F	57–64	Open solo for piano based on Cm^7.
G	65–80	A *pianissimo* stop-time section subtly emphasizing the call-and-response between saxophones and brass.
H	81–88	Repeated with first and second endings. The last big shout section emphasizing dynamics articulation and subtlety.
I	89–96	Question-and-answer between saxes and brass continues. Be careful to make sure the brass answer doesn't overplay the saxophones' question.
J	97–104	Continue bringing down the band. Keep control of the drummer and see to it she doesn't overplay.
K	105–112	There is a *subito* ***ff*** and 5/4 bar in measure 107 which sets up a drum solo. This solo does not need to be super-busy and/or loud. Emphasize subtlety, and, most of all, make sure the entire band gets to hear a recording of the Thad and Mel band playing this piece.

Unit 8: Suggested Listening

Thad Jones-Mel Lewis Big Band, *Opening Night*, Vanguard Jazz Orchestra, *Thad Jones Legacy CD*, New World Records.

Unit 9: Additional References and Resources

Dunscomb, Richard, and Willie L. Hill, Jr., *Jazz Pedagogy: The Jazz Educator's Handbook and Resource Guide* (Miami: Warner Brothers, 2004).

Contributed by:

Robert Parton
Associate Professor of Jazz Studies
Chicago College of Performing Arts
Roosevelt University
Chicago, Illinois

Teacher Resource Guide

Pools

Don Grolnick

(1948–1996)

arranged by John Fedchock

(b. 1957)

Unit 1: Composer

Jazz is an art in which the risks are great, the rewards subtle.

—Don Grolnick

Grolnick grew up in Levitown, New York and became enamored with the sound of jazz. In an interview he once said, "My father took me to see Count Basie, and I just went crazy. I didn't know why or what it was, it was just swinging so hard—and I didn't even know what swinging meant." His first instrument was the accordion, although he soon switched to the piano, and while still a teenager began to write songs and arrangements. He attended Tufts University, majoring in philosophy, and during this time he met up with saxophonist Michael Brecker.

Don Grolnick has several gifts as a pianist and composer. At the top of the list is his subtly and flexibility, traits that made him well known to his fellow musicians. Michael Brecker asked him to join the seminal jazz-fusion band Dreams after Grolnick returned to New York in 1969; he was with them from 1969–1971. He went on to work with the Brecker Brothers beginning in 1975, and in the early 1980s with Steps Ahead. Often he was busy as a session musician for pop singers. In the 1980s, Grolnick was with many groups, including Joe Farrell, George Benson, Peter Erskine, David Sanborn, John Scofeild, Mike Stern, and the Bob Mintzer big band.

In 1988 Grolnick decided to take a complete break from commercial music and producing to make time to write and record his own music. This resulted in the album *Weaver of Dreams* with an all-star ensemble, including Michael Brecker, Randy Brecker, Barry Rogers, Bob Mintzer, Peter Erskine, and Dave Holland. Grolnick later said "It was the most fun I've had in my whole life." Blue Note picked up the recording and released it in 1990, to critical acclaim. "Five stars," said *Downbeat*, "...a gem of uncut jazz...startlingly fresh and full of soul."

In the 1990s he brought his own music to New York clubs as well as the concert stages of Europe and Japan. He continued to perform with James Taylor and other pop luminaries, and found new interest in Latin jazz. During his lifetime he made many contributions to jazz and pop music as well as leaving an important musical legacy.

Unit 2: Composition

Don Grolnick wrote *Pools* for the first *Steps Ahead* recording in 1983, and it instantly became one of the most popular tracks of the session. Jon Fedchock arranged the piece for the Woody Herman Big Band in 1985 and it was recorded on the *50th Anniversary Tour* (Concord Records, CJ-302). This arrangement stays very true to the original *Steps Ahead* recording. The chart is in the fusion style and is features soprano saxophone, tenor saxophone, and bass. It opens quite sparsely, with the bass handling the melody. Although not featured in this arrangement, the rhythm section is integral to the successful performance of the piece.

Unit 3: Historical Perspective

The 1980s saw the jazz community split into two distinct factions. These can be defined as those who retained an interest in traditional straight-ahead styles and those who favored more experimental jazz styles that fused together many idioms. The music of *Steps Ahead* falls into the later category while keeping the spirit of straight-ahead jazz. The music of Don Grolnick always manages to appease both camps because of its well-thought-out structure, harmony, and melody, of which this piece is a shining example. A testament to the broad appeal is the fact that shortly after its release, *Pools* was recorded by one of the seminal big bands of the twentieth century.

Unit 4: Technical Consideration

Pools is rated at Grade 5 with a tempo of ♩ = 80, with a duration of just under 7:00. The tempo of the piece needs to be very close to this marking, as it is critical to the feel of the performance.

The saxophone doubles are B♭ soprano in the first alto part and flute for the second alto part. The lead trumpet range technically goes to F♯ (f♯²), but that is misleading. The range tops out at C♯ (c♯²) for all but two measures of the piece, and is very performable without the two measures involving the high F♯. The first trombone part goes to A (a).

The rhythm parts are written well, but require a more seasoned group to pull off. Drummers will need to be able to read to make the most of the exceptional drum part.

Unit 5: Stylistic Considerations

This medium-tempo fusion composition is in the modern straight-eighth style. The need for rhythmic accuracy makes it critical that the ensemble be as tight as possible. Articulation when in a tutti situation is also very important. The solo section's forward movement is dependent on interaction between soloist and rhythm section.

This tune makes a great tenor saxophone feature, as the solo section can be repeated from measures 81–97 (sixteen measures) with backgrounds laying out until the final pass. *Pools* is a good choice for the second song of a set, as it challenges both audience and players, yet is still assessable.

Unit 6: Musical Elements

Melody:

The angular melody of section A is presented in four distinct phrase groups of unequal length. The first three are two measures long, while the final statement is four measures in length. Each phrase except the third ends with a punch on the lowest note of the melody on the fourth sixteenth note of beat 3. The absence of the punch in the third phrase is important; drums should take the opportunity to make the statement. Each time the A theme is stated, a very important secondary or countermelody is present. This syncopated phrase pushes the feel forward by emphasizing the anticipation of beat 1 with numerous events on the fourth sixteenth note of beat 4. The B section melody remains angular, is sixteenth-note based, and is an even phrase that is eight measures long. The use of longer notes separated by punch figures makes this sound more like a transition than an actual melody.

The sixteenth-note structure of the melody makes thinking subdivisions very important to properly playing it. It has a smooth overall shape, but this quality is hidden by the separation of the phrase groups.

HARMONY:
Harmony in this piece is quite complex but slow-moving. The basic harmonic vocabulary is a combination of modal and chromatic elements, the chromatic elements achieved through the use of altered extensions. The arrangement utilizes intervals of a second (on the bottom of the voicing) and fourth, often separated by a third or fourth. This is definitely an influence of the writing of the Brecker Brothers and produces a very contemporary sound.

All of this combines to give the soloist a plethora of choices for approaching the arrangement. Anything from modalism to blues-based to chromatic (digital patterns) techniques can be employed.

RHYTHM:
The sixteenth-note element of *Pools* requires great rhythmic accuracy on the part of the entire ensemble. The following exercise can help players feel where the sixteenth notes are:

1. Set a metronome to 88 beats per minute.
2. Have players clap quarter notes for one minute, working to stay as one.
3. Without stopping, change to eighth notes for one minute.
4. Without stopping, change to sixteenth notes for two minutes.

This subdivision exercise will help immensely with rhythmic accuracy, and is useful for inexperienced as well as seasoned ensembles.

Unit 7: Form and Structure

The basic form of this composition is AAB.

SECTION	MEASURE	EVENT AND SECTION
Intro	1–5	The tempo is ♩=88; do not deviate from this too much. The full ensemble should be in full voice and then decrease to almost nothing in these five short measures.
First A	5–15	The bass takes the melody. The precise rhythmic quality of the sixteenth-note line can be softened by the use of more subtle articulation.

Section	Measure	Event and Section
Second A	15–25	Tenor saxophone joins the bass on the melody, and should try to imitate the articulation of the bass player. Both should try to sound as one.
B (transition)	25–33	The full ensemble re-enters, with brass handling the primary melody (along with second alto on flute) and saxophones taking the countermelody. This section is definitely about rhythm, as before, but the dimension of texture is also introduced and should be emphasized through attention to balance.
Soprano Solo	33–49	This is the beginning of a long build in intensity, so the soloist should be aware of this and play accordingly. A modal approach with longer notes helps achieve this.
Bass Solo	49–65	There are no backgrounds here, so the forward motion is up to the soloist and rhythm section. For the soloist, a blues-based concept works nicely here, as it lays well on the bass and provides an easily digested point of reference for the audience.
Solo send-off	65–69	Brass articulation on the short notes in this section and throughout the piece should be extreme.
Tenor Solo	69–98	This section builds to the shout, so it should increase dramatically in intensity. A good way for the soloist to accomplish this is to use a chromatic/digital pattern concept.
Shout	98–106	The full band enters. Attention to articulation and rhythm is essential.
Sax Soli	106–114	Saxophones are joined by a flugelhorn for added texture.

Section	Measure	Event and Section
B section	114–124	This is a variation on the original B section and is intended as a transition to move back to the A section melody.

The overall shape of this piece is an arc. This should be emphasized through dynamics on the part of the whole ensemble, but is most affected by the insanity level of the drummer.

Unit 8: Suggested Listening

Steps Ahead, *Steps Ahead*, Wea International.
Woody Herman Big Band, *50th Anniversary Tour*, Concord Records, CJ-302.
Steps Ahead, *Holding Together*, NYC.

Unit 9: References and Resources

Dunscomb, Richard, and Willie L. Hill, Jr., *Jazz Pedagogy: The Jazz Educator's Handbook and Resource Guide* (Miami: Warner Brothers, 2004).

Contributed by:

Rick White
Director of Instrumental Music
Olympic College
Bremerton, Washington

Teacher Resource Guide

Spring Can Really Hang You Up the Most

Thomas J. Wolf, Jr.
(b. 1925)

Frances "Fran" Landesman
(b. 1927)

arranged by Frank Mantooth
(1947–2004)

Unit 1: Composer/Arranger

Tommy Wolf was born in 1925 and began playing piano at age three. Following high school graduation, he started college in Columbia, Missouri, only to be drafted into the Army. A sensitive young man torn from the security of his family at the age of eighteen, he fought in the Battle of the Bulge and was deeply marked by the experience.

In 1948, at the age of twenty-three, Wolf attended St. Louis Institute of Music and appeared on a daily television show with his trio and female vocalist. One evening when Wolf was playing piano at the Jefferson Hotel antique dealers Jay and Fred Landesman and their wives, Fran and Paula, dropped in for drinks, requested a series of esoteric show tunes, and were delighted by Wolf's interpretations. Frustrated by the lack of hip hangouts in St. Louis, the Landesmans rented a store front on Olive Street, stripped the interior to its brick walls, painted them black, decorated the room with chandeliers and antiques, and hired Wolf as house pianist. Their club, The Crystal Palace, quickly became the watering hole of choice for local artists and sophisticates.

In 1956, Wolf went to Chicago to record Wolf At Your Door, an album of eleven songs for Fraternity Records. Spring Can Really Hang You Up The Most, released by Fraternity the following year, contained thirteen more songs, with Wolf backed by bassist Monty Budwing and drummer Shelly Manne. The Crystal Palace flourished, occasionally showcasing young singers and comedians.

In the early 1960s, Wolf worked in L. A., where, recommended by drummer Jackie Mills, he was hired as a rehearsal pianist at 20th Century Fox. He soon became the most sought after and highest paid rehearsal pianist in town, working on the Andy Williams and Red Skelton television shows, and numerous musical specials, most memorably the award-winning Evenings with Fred Astaire. He founded Choreo Records (later Ava Records) with Mills and Astaire, , functioning as a producer and A&R man on albums by Irene Kral, Carol Lawrence, Charles Cochran, and Ruth Price, all of which included Wolf compositions.

With the arrival of the rock era in the mid-sixties, Wolf decided that his style of music was outdated and switched to writing lyrics, collaborating with Astaire on Life Is Beautiful and Victor Feldman on A Face Like Yours. He wrote When Jeremiah Sang the Blues, an oratorio for orchestra and chorus, with bassist and composer Alf Clausen, and Joan Baby, a musical allegory that interweaves the life of Joan of Arc with a contemporary story of a young woman who, disguised as a man, plays quarterback on a football team.

Wolf continued to work on television shows and, following a series of exhausting rehearsal sessions with Donnie and Marie Osmond in Utah, was diagnosed with an inflammation of the pericardium. He died January 9, 1979. Mary Wolf Davidson remembers him as a man of unshakeable integrity, a stubborn workaholic who compulsively pushed himself without regard for his health (from http://www.franlandesman.com/).

Frank Mantooth was born in Tulsa, Oklahoma on April 11, 1947. He was a pianist, composer, arranger, clinician, and educator. He grew up with his mother, who was a pianist, and earned his bachelor of music degree from North Texas State University in 1969.

Mantooth was a member of the Air Force Academy Falconaires (1969–73) and contributed his talents as pianist and arranger to the group. He lived in Austria for seven years following (1974-80). During his life in Europe, he studied piano in Vienna and began producing and arranging for Austrian national radio. In 1981 he moved back to the United States and recorded with the Ashley Alexander Big Band, Phil Wilson Big Band, and Kirsten Gustafson. He composed and arranged for Louis Bellson, Art Farmer, and Carla Helmbrecht. Mantooth recorded five of his own big band albums: *Suite Tooth*, *Persevere*, *Dangerous Precedent*, *Sophisticated Lady*, and *A Miracle*. He received a total of eleven Grammy nominations, both as a writer and player.

As an author, Mantooth published five volumes of *The Best Chord Changes for the World's Greatest Standards*, 165 works for combo and jazz ensemble, and *Voicings for Jazz Keyboard*. He composed works commissioned for the Kansas City Symphony, the Madison Symphony Orchestra, Doc Severinson, Peter Christlieb, Louis Bellson, the United States Air Force Airmen of Note, and numerous colleges throughout the world. In the 1980s and 90s Mantooth served as an adjunct faculty member at Northern Illinois University and DePaul University. He died of natural causes at his home in Garden City, Kansas, on January 30, 2004.

Unit 2: Composition

Frank Mantooth arranged *Spring Can Really Hang You Up The Most* in 1981 while a member of the Ashley Alexander Big Band. It was recorded on the album *Ashley Alexander Plays Frank Mantooth*. A solo vehicle for jazz trombone, this American ballad turns into a very fast-swinging piece reminiscent of the great Buddy Rich Big Band. The 32-bar AABA form is expanded to sixty-four measures during the fast swing section. The piece is in F major, providing a ponderous mood during the ballad and a triumphal celebration during the fast swing solo. The piece returns to the ballad setting to close. The accompanying sections capture the essence of modern big band with the use of five-part saxophone harmonies and rhythmic sectional brass hits in unison. The use of a pedal point creates suspense in both the ballad and fast swing sections.

Unit 3: Historical Perspective

As the popularity of big bands diminished through the decades, big band jazz has become an institution most prevalent in high schools and colleges. At the time this piece was arranged, many of the name bands (the Woody Herman Orchestra, the Buddy Rich Big Band, the Count Basie Orchestra, and Maynard Ferguson) were still traveling the world with full-time schedules. Frank Mantooth had lived a life in Europe for several years. During this time he began to develop his skills as an arranger. Most specifically he designed methods for learning about music through voicings and practical ways to write for musicians of varying levels. This piece represents his knowledge of the quintessential big band styles, arranged to be accessible for school groups and professional bands. While the recording of Ashley Alexander's trombone solo sounds very advanced, this arrangement can be performed by students.

Unit 4: Technical Considerations

This arrangement is rated Grade 4, and the recommended tempo begins at ♩ = 63, moving to a fast swing at 𝅗𝅥 = 138, with a duration of 6:25. This author finds the piece playable at a slower tempo during the fast swing section.

The lead trumpet range goes to concert C (c^2); the lead trombone range goes to concert A (third octave [a]); the solo trombone range goes to a concert B (third octave [b]). The published version has a prepared solo part for flugelhorn as an alternate to the trombone solo.

The slow sections demand a sensibility to melodic interpretations idiomatic to a jazz ballad. Originally recorded with a Rhodes keyboard, the piece also sounds strong with an acoustic piano. There are no woodwind doubles in this arrangement. The guitar, piano, and bass parts are fully notated, including chord symbols. Solo changes are very standard, including turnarounds through the natural progression. This arrangement works well with an experienced improvising solo trombonist.

Unit 5: Stylistic Considerations

Since two jazz styles are present in this arrangement, it challenges the ensemble to be able to temper articulations and aggressiveness. Beginning and ending in a ballad style, the rhythm section needs to be able to keep a very steady pulse to allow the soloist freedom to embellish the melody. Wind sections demand control of attack and volume to provide a bed of sound for the melody. Straight eighth notes are used throughout the ballad section.

When the piece switches to fast swing, the soloist is prepared with a send-off. This builds intensity and requires winds to articulate with clear and pronounced attacks. The rhythm section turns into a small group interacting with the soloist. The trombone (or flugelhorn) soloist should possess the ability to play in a bebop style over the fast swing section.

Unit 6: Musical Elements

MELODY:

The melody is very tuneful, like all great songs from the American songbook. The melody is diatonic throughout. The soloist should learn the words to the melody and master an effective interpretive style.

HARMONY:

The harmony during the entire piece is mostly tertian, with the use of pedal points to add suspense and build intensity. The A sections cycle through chords in the key of F major with the exception of the first four measures, which alternate between F and E♭ major. The bridge cycles around the subdominant (B♭) and uses a tonicization to E♭ to prepare a turnaround back to the last A section, which begins on C instead of F major. Overall, the voicings include some extensions and alterations of the dominant chords so as to not sound too dense. A very practical approach for learning how to play the chords throughout this piece is Frank Mantooth's *Voicings for Jazz Keyboard*. Both rhythm section and soloist will benefit from the study of his miracle voicings. Soloists should also be able to arpeggiate through each chord quality.

RHYTHM:

The 4/4 rhythmic feel prevails in both ballad and fast swing sections. During the ballad, the eighth notes are straight, as if playing a popular show tune. The fast swing section demands each ensemble member to feel the syncopated beat. The balance of downbeats and upbeats creates the excitement. Slow the tempo during rehearsals if there is difficulty with syncopated rhythms. Encourage students to identify beats 1 and 3 in order to divide the measure in half. When playing at a tempo of 𝅗𝅥 = 138, the swing feel has less of an implied triplet feel.

Unit 7: Form and Structure

The basic form of the composition is AABA.

SECTION	MEASURE	EVENT AND SCORING
Intro (1): A	1–4	The tempo is ♩ = 63, piano only.
Melody: B	5–15	Trombone soloist plays the melody with interpretation, accompanied by piano, guitar, bass, and drums. Saxophones lead into the bridge at the second ending.
Bridge: C	16–23	Saxophones accompany the soloist with rhythm section. The rhythmic unison in measure 20 should be cleanly articulated.
D	24–32	Melody continues with the trombone approaching a ritardando into a final fermata. Soloist plays a cadenza.

Section	Measure	Event and Scoring
E	33–48	This section is a send-off for the soloist. The change in tempo to fast swing provides a vehicle for the ensemble to play with excitement. Articulations in the winds are written to display the standard style for these phrases. The pedal point in the rhythm, lower saxophones, and trombones creates suspense. Be careful to play with good intonation. In measure 47 there is a stop-time break for the soloist.
F	49–112	This is an improvised solo for trombone with an extended 64-bar solo form. The form is still AABA, but it appears to be twice as long. Background figures are written in for brass to assist the soloist in building intensity on the second chorus.
G	113–114	All time stops for a drum solo. The drummer ends her solo with suspended cymbal and prepares the ensemble to return to the ballad style. The trombone soloist plays pickups to the melody.
H	115–128	The trombone soloist returns to the melody with accompaniment provided by the trombone section using bucket mutes. Trumpets join with a subtle harmon mute sound. Saxophones enter in rhythmic unison with trombones while the rhythm section pedals on a B♭^{SUS} chord. In measure 123, the entire ensemble is playing for the first time during the ballad style. Trumpets and trombones play with bucket mutes, and saxophones play in very comfortable ranges. In measure 128, the ensemble comes to a fermata.

SECTION	MEASURE	EVENT AND SCORING
Last A	129–138	After a slight pause, time begins and the piece comes to a close with a *ritard* and final fermata. The final F major chord rests as a bed for the soloist's short cadenza.

Unit 8: Suggested Listening

Ashley Alexander Big Band, *Ashley Alexander Plays Frank Mantooth.*, Mark, MUS-57601.
The Buddy Rich Big Band, *Big Swing Face*, Blue Note Records.
The Woody Herman Orchestra, *Giant Steps*, OJC.
The Stan Kenton Orchestra, *Kenton 76*, Creative Music.

Unit 9: Additional References and Resources

Kernfeld, Barry, *The New Grove Dictionary of Jazz* (New York: Oxford University Press, 2006).
Mantooth, Frank, *Voicings for Jazz Keyboard* (Milwaukee: Hal Leonard Corporation, 1997).
www.frankmantooth.com
www.allmusic.com

Contributed by:

Scott Hall
Director of Jazz Studies
Columbia College Chicago
Chicago, Illinois

Teacher Resource Guide

There's the Rub

Gordon Goodwin

(b. 1954)

Unit 1: Composer

Gordon Goodwin (b. 1954) began his musical education at California State University, Northridge with Joel Leach and Bill Calkins. He wrote his first big band chart when he was in the seventh grade, called *Hang Loose*. After graduation he was recruited to play in Louie Bellson's big band, where he worked with the likes of Pete Christlieb and Don Menza. He went on to play under Les Hooper and Grant Geissman.

Since then, Goodwin has risen to prominence in the American jazz scene with his big band, the Big Phat Band. Under Goodwin's direction, the band has released three albums: *Swingin' For The Fences*, which received two Grammy nominations, and *XXL*, which received three. Their newest album, *The Phat Pack* was released on June 13, 2006.

As a film scorer, Goodwin has worked on such films as *Fern Gully*, *The Majestic* and *Enemy of the State*. His work in television includes music for the TV series *The Animaniacs*. His recording history includes performances with artists as diverse as Mel Torme, Ray Charles, and Christina Aguilera. Goodwin himself has received many individual awards, including a Grammy for Best Instrumental Arrangement for his work on the feature film *The Incredibles*. He is also a three-time Emmy winner.

Goodwin is a talented conductor as well, having worked with such groups as the London and Seattle Symphony Orchestras.

Unit 2: Composition

Gordon Goodwin wrote *There's the Rub* in 2003 and recorded it with his *Big Phat Band* on the CD, *Swingin' for the Fences*. It is a half-time shuffle with strong blues and funk influences. The piece, though not harmonically difficult, requires very accurate rhythmic placement of figures and excellent intonation. The overall feel of the tune should be tight and relaxed. Solo changes are found in the alto, tenor, and rhythm section, but could be opened up to any soloist.

Unit 3: Historical Perspective

Goodwin's Big Phat Band, an eighteen-piece jazz ensemble, celebrates and personifies the best of the big band tradition with a very contemporary and original sound. Through Goodwin's writing, SRO audiences have enjoyed one of the most craftsman-like, hard-swinging, large jazz ensembles comprised of L. A.'s finest musicians. Gordon's insightful arrangements propel the listener on a journey through a myriad of styles: Latin, blues, swing, classical, hard-hitting jazz, and even an homage to Looney Tunes! The band has two Grammy-nominated albums out as well as a recent June, 2006 release, *The Phat Pack*. Members of the Big Phat Band have distinguished themselves as recording artists and soloists in the jazz field, including Eric Marienthal, Wayne Bergeron (also a Grammy nominee), Andy Martin, Bob Summers, Luis Conte, Bernie Dresel, and Grant Geissman.

Unit 4: Technical Considerations

The chart is rated Grade 6, and the recommended tempo is ♩ = 108. The published chart differs a bit from the version recorded at measure 67. On the recording, the band cut the post-solo vamp and went right to the shout chorus. This section could be cut, included, or even extended for another soloist.

Bass, piano, and guitar parts all include sections with written lines as well as sections with chord changes.

Unit 5: Stylistic Considerations

Subdivision of the quarter is essential to this type of funk/shuffle for correct placement of notes. The piece is reminiscent of some of the classic recordings made by Tower of Power.

The lead trumpet range goes to concert E (third octave [e^2]); the lead trombone range goes to B (third octave [b]). Brass kicks should be played

detached but not too short. There are a number of lines that operate independently, so strong individual playing is required by on all parts.

Some of the melodic lines are written as unisons or octaves; therefore good intonation is critical to the success of this chart. In addition, players must be able to ghost notes during figures, or the lines will be too cumbersome.

Unit 6: Musical Elements

MELODY:

The melody line, which first appears with two altos and two trumpets in unison, is eventually played in full by the entire horn section. The melody contains scoops, ghost notes (which are not indicated and need to be determined), and syncopated short notes. The timing of the scoops, determination of which notes are to be ghosted, and the length of short notes will need to be addressed. Time must be spent mastering the ghosting technique and identifying which notes are to be ghosted within the lines. Though the figures are visually complex, they need to be played in a relaxed manner without rushing the tempo. Singing the lines together can save a lot of time in rehearsals.

HARMONY:

Harmonies are fairly constant, since this is mostly a "jam groove" tune. Solo sections stay primarily in either E^7 (concert) or G^7.

RHYTHM:

This is a very important part of this piece. The entire band must feel the sixteenth-note subdivision of the quarter note in order to place figures correctly. Drums and bass need to play fairly simply, with a relaxed but precise feel. It is too easy to get too busy in the rhythm section on this type of tune. The "groove" must be the priority for the rhythm section.

Unit 7: Form and Structure

It is an ABA form that contains groove interludes for vamps and solo sections.

SECTION	MEASURE	EVENT AND SCORING
Intro	1–4	Repeated opening rhythm vamp, which sets up the entrance of the melody in measure 5.

SECTION	MEASURE	EVENT AND SCORING
Melody	5–20	Entrance of melody, which is stated by altos and third and fourth trumpets in unison. Brass punctuates with short fill-in kicks. As with the entire chart, players must subdivide to the sixteenth note in order to place the figures correctly and together. Note articulation markings!
Melody (2)	21–28	Full saxes playing unison melody interspersed with brass kicks that are more involved than previous kicks. Saxes are sometimes joined by trumpets reinforcing the main line. As with any unison line, volume should be kept down to help accuracy and maintain the groove.
Vamp	29–32	Guitar/drum groove for four Bars on E^7 to set up a solo section.
Interlude	33–42	Drums and horns only, playing the rhythm groove. Throughout the piece, the drummer needs to understand that less is more in this type of chart and that every band figure does not need to be set up; go for the simple groove instead. In this section, as well as later, it is important that the baritone sax be able to operate independently from the other players.
Solo	43–66	Solo (alto, tenor, guitar, piano, or other). Backgrounds are written any may be played any time and in various combinations (saxes only, all play, etc.). May be repeated for other soloists. Backgrounds need to be certain not to overpower the soloist.

Section	Measure	Event and Scoring
Post-solo vamp	67–91	This is the section that was cut on the recording. Begins with rhythm only, then instruments join in a few at a time with rhythmic punch figures. Builds to the restatement of the melody at next section.
Head	91–98	Saxes and trumpets stating Melody in octaves with bari and trombones in counter line.
	99–110	Altos and tenors continue with melody while brass plays background figures.
Solo vamp	111–118	Vamp for soloist (E^7) with brass background kicks.
Ending	119–133	Saxes begin with rhythmic statement that matches guitar groove. Brass answers with kicks. Full ensemble to end.

Unit 8: Suggested Listening

Goodwin, Gordon, *Swingin' for the Fences*, Silverline Records.
Any recordings made by Tower of Power.

Unit 9: Additional References and Resources

Dunscomb, Richard, and Willie L. Hill, Jr., *Jazz Pedagogy: The Jazz Educator's Handbook and Resource Guide* (Miami: Warner Brothers, 2004).

Contributed by:

John Davis
Director of Jazz Studies
University of Colorado
Boulder, Colorado

Teacher Resource Guide

Three and One
Thad Jones
(1923–1986)

Unit 1: Composer

Thad Jones was born in Pontiac, Michigan on March 28, 1923. He was the brother of pianist Hank and drummer Elvin. A talented, self-taught trumpet player, Thad started playing professionally with Hank Jones and Sonny Stitt at sixteen.

Thad performed throughout the Midwest with several territory bands, including Billy Mitchell's quintet in Detroit. He also recorded with the virtuoso bass player Charles Mingus in 1954. However, Thad's big break came later that same year, when he joined Count Basie's big band. His famous solo quoting *Pop Goes the Weasel* on Basie's *April in Paris* made Jones a well-known soloist. Thad later joined the staff writers at CBS and co-lead a group with Pepper Adams. In 1965 he and drummer Mel Lewis organized a big band that played every Monday night at the Village Vanguard in New York. Thad composed music for the band, including the standard *A Child Is Born* as well as *Fingers*, *Little Pixie*, *Tiptoe*, and many others.

In 1979 Thad moved to Denmark for five years, where he organized the band Eclipse and continued to compose and arrange music. In 1984 Thad returned to the United States to direct the memorial Basie orchestra, but retired in 1986 because of poor health. His music is known for its powerful, Basie-derived swing, as well as his use of complex harmony and voicing.

Unit 2: Composition

Thad Jones wrote *Three and One* (1970) during his ten-year stint at the Village Vanguard. This composition displays all the swing and style of Count Basie and the virtuosity of Thad's ensemble writing, which relies on complex harmonic sounds. He maintains inventive details in the 32-bar form while still making the blues a central focus. The solo shared by the baritone saxophone, flugelhorn, and bass is unexpected, but accents the interplay within the ensemble. The trio instruments have the melody.

Unit 3: Historical Perspective

During the late 1940s, the decline in the popularity of big bands in America affected even the best groups. Thad Jones was part of the revival of the great Count Basie Orchestra, which was known for its hard-driving swing. As a band member from 1954–63, Jones arranged and recorded tunes that have since become standards. Even during the turbulent 1960s, Thad was able to pull together great musicians, arrangers, and composers from the great bands of Basie, Kenton, and others to foster a creative energy at the Vanguard. Jones sought to continue the feel of the blues and the swing of Louis Armstrong while pursuing the harmony of the contemporary big band. Bebop and post-bop players were given an opportunity to experience and learn from the many great swing musicians still in New York.

Unit 4: Technical Considerations

This chart is rated Grade 5–6, and the recommended tempo is ♩ = 160, with a duration of 5:50. However, this chart works well either faster (if the band is up to the challenge) or slower.

The lead trumpet range goes to concert E♭ ($e\flat^2$); the lead trombone range goes to concert B♭ (b♭). The saxophone soli is technically and stylistically challenging. Flugelhorn is the only double needed. Bass lines are written out except on the improvisatory sections.

There are complex harmonies throughout in the guitar and piano parts, with only chord symbols provided for both. The changes for soloists are complex, but manageable because they are used in the turnaround sections of the 32-bar form. However, all three solo parts require experienced improvisers.

Unit 5: Stylistic Considerations

This bright, swing-style composition is reminiscent of the hard-driving Kansas City (Count Basie Orchestra) style. The articulations are very similar to the Basie/Louis Armstrong type popularized in the 1940s. Due to tempo considerations, bebop-type articulations, such as ghost notes, should be added whenever needed to keep the feel and swing consistent. Most of the musicians in the Thad Jones/Mel Lewis Orchestra were bebop players of great reputation. Vocal inflections, emphasizing the blues in all lead parts, are very important.

This selection is an ideal feature for bass, trumpet, and baritone saxophone. (The piece was originally written for Thad Jones on trumpet, Pepper Adams on baritone saxophone, and Richard Davis on bass.) *Three and One* is also a good change-of-pace tune featuring a jazz trio of flugelhorn, baritone saxophone, and bass at a moderate tempo.

Unit 6: Musical Elements

MELODY:

The simple, strong melody should be learned vocally, without notation, using call-and-response with the entire ensemble. The sequence of melodic ideas is a unifying force throughout the composition. The key centers are well defined with logical progressions. The unifying melodic rhythm is also bebop-oriented with swing-style syncopations.

HARMONY:

The melody and changes do not modulate, but go through a series of transient keys, starting in concert E♭. Thad Jones uses tonicization, in which any chord can be a temporary tonic (except the diminished seventh chord), to add a great deal of movement and excitement to the composition. He also uses chromaticism in the harmonic progressions through the use of tritone substitutions.

Altered dominant chords also add to the distinctive complex harmonic writing Jones employs. He is a master at using dense harmonies in the large ensemble portions of the composition.

RHYTHM:

The swing feel requires that the entire band feel the four downbeats as well as the triplet pulse on each downbeat. It may be necessary to encourage everyone to coordinate the feel of four dance beats while feeling the triplet pulse (doo-od-la). Make sure you start at a moderate to slow tempo.

Singing stylistic and rhythmic articulations is very important in any swing composition. Have students sing the following rhythmic examples from the composition (suggested syllables and feel the four-beat measures and the triplet pulse of each beat).

① Do da do un doo dot

② Da do un doo dah__

③ Da doo od la do da do un do da do dot

④ Dah doo od la doo dah__

⑤ Doo dot dot dot dot__ dah

⑥ Doo dah doo dot

⑦ Dah dot dah dot

dah dot dah dot doo doo dot

⑧ Doo dit dot do dot dot doo dit dah__ dot

Unit 7: Form and Structure

The basic form of the composition is ABAB.

SECTION	MEASURE	EVENT AND SCORING
Intro (1): A	1–16	The tempo is ♩ = 160. Learn the piece at a much slower tempo until the swing and style are established. An alternating jazz trio (baritone saxophone, flugelhorn, bass) has the melody with the full ensemble answering confidently, urging on the trio melody. Make sure phrases are not slurred but played in a smooth swing style, moving the air through each phrase. All ending notes are accented with short articulations.
Intro (2): B	17–24	The full band plays the question part of the melody, harmonized with the jazz trio answering in like manner. Personalize dynamics in this section to ensure forward melodic movement.
	25–28	The jazz trio takes the lead on the melody while the full band answers with authority.
	29–30	The entire ensemble harmonizes the melody. Sing this entire phrase to agree on style and articulation.

Section	Measure	Event and Scoring
C/D	33–64	This is a saxophone soli for traditional saxophone section instrumentation with an alto lead. Make sure all lines are vocally oriented and smooth but not slurred. Add dynamic contours throughout the phrasing with everyone following the lead alto and listening to the entire section. Bebop-style phrasing with ghost notes and stylized accents are helpful to keep phrases from slowing. The final notes of phrases should be tongued, short, and accented (doo-dot). Remember: slurs are written for those who do not understand the need to listen to jazz to be able to play stylistically correct. Lines are phrase markings and not slurs. Sing all phrases to agree on style and articulations.
E/F	65–96	Baritone saxophone solo changes, ABAB, 32-bar form; flugelhorn solo changes with saxophone and band backgrounds on the repeat. Learn the melody vocally and on each instrument. Transcribe the original solos from the recording and use the piano to play through to hear the sounds and key centers indicated.
G/H	97–128	Bass guitar solo changes; ABAB form with no backgrounds.
I/J	129–160	A full band shout section with dense harmonic writing. Have everyone listen to the lead trumpet for balance and tune from the bass guitar up. All should sing the rhythms and internalize the triplet swing. Create and personalize all dynamics throughout the section.
Coda	161–162	Flugelhorn, baritone saxophone, and bass end the coda.

Unit 8: Suggested Listening

Count Basie Orchestra, *The Complete Atomic Basie*, Blue Note Records.
Count Basie Orchestra, *April in Paris*, Polygram Records.
Ellington, Duke, *The Blanton-Webster Band*, RCA.
Ellington, Duke, *The Great London Concerts*, Music Masters Jazz.

Unit 9:Additional References and Resources

Dunscomb, Richard, and Willie L Hill, Jr. *Jazz Pedagogy: The Jazz Educator's Handbook and Resource Guide* (Miami: Warner Brothers, 2004).
Thigpen, Ed, *Rhythm Brought to Life: A Rhythmic Primer* (Van Nuys: Alfred Publishing Company, 2000).

Contributed by:

Ronald Carter
Director of Jazz Studies
Professor of Music
Northern Illinois University
DeKalb, Illinois

Vice President
International Association For Jazz Education

Teacher Resource Guide

Told You So

Bill Holman

(b. 1927)

Unit 1: Composer

Bill Holman was born Willis Leonard Holman on May 21, 1927 in Olive, California. He began to play the clarinet in Junior High School and Tenor Saxophone in high school, by which time he was leading his own band. In the Late 1940s, after serving in the Navy, he decided to compose for big bands.

In 1949 he played with the Ike Carpenter Band, in 1951, he was writing for Charlie Barnet, and in 1952 he began his association with Stan Kenton, for whom he wrote and played for many years. During the 1950s he was also active in the West Coast jazz movement, playing in small bands led by Shorty Rogers and Shelly Manne, and co-leading a quintet with Mel Lewis in 1958. Holman started The Bill Holman Band in 1975. Since, 1980, Holman has been increasingly active in Europe, writing, conducting and playing lengthy works for the West German Radio Orchestra in Cologne, Germany, and the Metropole Orchestra in Holland, that feature such soloists as Phil Woods, Sal Nistico and Lee Konitz.

Unit 2: Composition

Bill Holman wrote *Told You So* (1976) for the Count Basie Orchestra. This composition is very reminiscent of the Count Basie swing style. The form and harmonic changes are very closely related to *Doxy* by Sonny Rollins. The combination of trombones and flute is a nice addition, as well as the longer saxophone soli. Though not a true blues form, the changes and the melody both give the impression of the blues. This composition is a great example of the virtuosity found in Holman's writing.

Unit 3: Historical Perspective

During the late 1940s, the decline in the popularity of big bands in America affected even the best groups. In the 60s, Holman widened his writing associations, and eventually contributed pieces to libraries and recordings of bands led by Louie Bellson, Count Basie, Terry Gibbs, Woody Herman, Bob Brookmeyer, Buddy Rich. Gerry Mulligan, Doc Severinsen, and others. He has also written for such singers as Natalie Cole, Tony Bennett, Carmen MacRae, Mel Torme, Woody Herman, Anita O'Day, Sarah Vaughn, June Christy, and the Fifth Dimension. His arrangement of *Take the "A" Train* for Severinsen's Tonight Show Orchestra earned Holman a Grammy for Best Instrumental in 1987. Holman's compositions and recordings have contributed to the renewed excitement in fans about the possibilities to be found in the big band genre.

Unit 4: Technical Considerations

This chart is rated Grade 4–5, and the recommended tempo is ♩ = 116, with a duration of 6:30.

The lead trumpet range goes to concert D (d^2); the lead trombone range goes to concert D (third octave [d^1]). The saxophone *soli* is challenging stylistically, but technically accessible . The flute is written in the second tenor saxophone part.

There are complex harmonies throughout in the guitar and piano and bass parts, with only chord symbols provided for both. The changes for soloists are complex, but manageable because they follow the 16-bar AABA form. However, both solo parts require experienced improvisers.

Unit 5: Stylistic Considerations

This medium swing-style composition is reminiscent of the Count Basie Orchestra style. The articulations are very similar to the Basie/Louis Armstrong type popularized in the 1940s. Vocal inflections, emphasizing the blues in all lead parts, are the key to achieving the most authentic interpretation of this piece. Trombone players need to be able to use a variety of mutes, including hand mutes.

This selection would be an ideal feature for trombones and a good saxophone/flute doubler. *Told You So* is a good change-of-pace tune featuring trombones and saxophones at a moderate tempo.

Unit 6: Musical Elements

MELODY:
The melody should be learned aurally, using call-and-response with the trombone and flute. Though the melody is only heard three times, it sets the stylistic basis for the solos and soli that follow. The melody utilizes both duple and triple feels throughout.

HARMONY:
The harmonic changes are the unifying force throughout the composition. As stated earlier, the changes in this tune are an illusion to *Doxy* by Sonny Rollins. The use of tritone substitutions is common in every section of the piece.

RHYTHM:
The swing feel requires that the entire band feel the four downbeats as well as the triplet pulse on each downbeat. It may be necessary to encourage everyone to coordinate the feel of four dance beats set by the bass drum and bass guitar while feeling the triplet pulse (doo-od-la).

Singing stylistic and rhythmic articulations is very important in any swing composition. Have students sing rhythmic examples from the composition.

Unit 7: Form and Structure

The basic form of the composition is the tradtional 16-bar blues.

SECTION	MEASURE	EVENT AND SCORING
Intro:	A-H	The tempo is ♩ = 116. An ensemble shout is followed by a bluesy sax soli leading into the melody. Be sure to follow the written articulations carefully. All ending notes are accented with short articulations.
A	1–8	The first statement of the head, in the trombones. The rhythm section plays time underneath.
	9–12	Stop time adding the saxes. Trombones have a rhythmic figure played with hand mutes, answered by trumpets played with cup mutes.

Section	Measure	Event and Scoring
	13–16	Trombones end the phrase using plungers. A piano fill leads into the second statement of the head.
B	17–24	Second statement of the head. Again, trombones have the lead. Flute is added.
	25–28	A repeat of measures 9–12.
	29–32	Repeat of measures 13–16.
C	33–48	Solo section changes for second tenor (flute); 16-bar blues form. Trombone backgrounds at measure 41.
D	49–56	Solo continues. One chorus, 16-bar blues form, with hand-muted trombone backgrounds.
	57–60	Solo continues. Ensemble background hit.
	61–64	Solo continues with no backgrounds. Rhythm section plays time.
E	65–73	Ensemble lead into second solo section. Full ensemble.
	74–80	Second solo section changes in first trombone with plunger. No backgrounds. Rhythm section plays time.
F	81–96	Solo continues. Saxophones in background; rhythm section plays time.
G	97–108	Sax soli. Be sure to follow the written articulations. Rhythm section plays time.
	109–112	Soli continues with trombone backgrounds; rhythm section plays time.
H	113–120	Soli continues with trombone backgrounds; rhythm section plays time.

SECTION	MEASURE	EVENT AND SCORING
	121–128	Soli continues with brass hits in the background; rhythm section plays time.
I	129–140	Brass soli with saxophone in the background; rhythm section plays time.
	141–144	Piano solo fill; rhythm section only.
J	145–160	Ensemble shout section. This is an allusion to the introduction. Full ensemble.
K	161–168	Return of the head. Trombone and flute have the melody; rhythm sections plays time.
	169–171	Stop time adding the saxes; trombones have a rhythmic figure played with hand mutes.
	172	Ensemble hit; full ensemble.
	173–177	The ending phrase. Trombone and flute only, with rhythm section playing time; ensemble hit on the last beat.

Unit 8: Suggested Listening

Count Basie Orchestra, *I Told You So,* Original Jazz Classics.
Count Basie Orchestra, *The Complete Atomic Basie*, Blue Note Records.
Bill Holman, *A View from the Side*, JVC.
Northern Illinois University Jazz Ensemble, *We Came to Swing*, NIU.

Unit 9: Additional References and Resources

Holman, Bill, *Biography*, http://www.opendoormanagement.com/billholman/ (accessed 10 May, 2007).

Kernfeld, Barry, "Bill Holman." *The New Grove Dictionary of Jazz*, 2002 ed., Vol. 2–3 (London: MacMillan, 2002).

Walker, Leo, *The Big Band Almanac, Revised Edition* (New York: DaCapo Press, Inc., 1978).

Contributed by:

Peter M. Muller, Jr.
Graduate Assistant
Northern Illinois University
DeKalb, Illinois

Appendix

Jazz Method Books:
A Review of Currently Available Resources for Jazz Education

Joe Parisi
Lindsey Williams

This appendix presents a comprehensive, though not exhaustive, reference list of texts pertaining to jazz improvisation pedagogy. It functions as a guide to the contents of various jazz method texts. An annotated bibliography outlining the contents and perceived focus for each of the method books is included.

These resources can be used in conjunction with various approaches to teaching improvisation within a jazz ensemble rehearsal setting based on the type of piece, the changes, and possible performance approaches for jazz educators. In addition to brief annotated bibliographies of the resources included, a series of charts have been developed as a quick, efficient reference tool showing the reader the presence or omission of various pedagogically-related areas salient to teaching jazz improvisation within each resource.

The annotated bibliography gives a brief narrative description of the perceived focus of each resource as well as its contents. These charts aid in identifying, more specifically, the contents included within each resource. The charts focus on four areas of concern:

SCALES

Addresses scales specifically covered within each text. Scales included are:

- Aeolian
- Altered
- Bebop
- Blues
- Diminished modes
- Diminished whole-tone
- Dorian
- Locrian no. 2
- Lydian
- Lydian augmented
- Major
- Minor (natural, harmonic, melodic)
- Mixolydian
- Pentatonic (major, minor)
- Phrygian
- Whole-tone

CHORDS

Addresses various chords that occur within changes. Some of the chords included are:

- Major
- Major 7
- Major 7(♭5)
- Major 7(♯5)
- Minor
- Minor 7
- Minor (maj. 7)
- Augmented
- Diminished
- Half-diminished
- Dominant 7
- Altered dominant
- Dominant 7(♭5)
- Dominant 9(♯11)
- Substitution

FORMS

Shows various forms such as:

- ii–V–I
- ii dim^{7}–V^{7}–I
- Blues
- Rhythm changes
- Four-note groupings
- Intervallic improvisation
- Sectional forms

PEDAGOGY

Gives specific emphasis on:

- Comping
- Patterns
- Rhythm
- Style
- Transcriptions

Resources are listed in the far left column. Numbers beneath each category refer to chapter number(s) or pages (when noted), within each resource containing specific information pertaining to that category. Some categories are marked "throughout." For example, in Scott Reeves' *Creative Jazz Improvisation* (3rd ed.), the pedagogy section lists "all" under Style and Transcriptions because the format of the book directly addresses all of those categories in every chapter.

The authors would like to thank the instrumental staff at Wingert-Jones Publishing of J. W. Pepper and Luyben Music Co. for their support and assistance throughout this project.

Contributors

Dr. Joe Parisi
Assistant Director of Bands
Assistant Professor of Instrumental Music Education
University of Missouri–Kansas City
Conservatory of Music and Dance

Dr. Lindsey Williams
Assistant Professor of Music Education
University of Missouri–Kansas City
Conservatory of Music and Dance

Bibliography

Aebersold, Jamey. *How to Play Jazz and Improvise.* 6th ed. New Albany, IN: Jamey Aebersold Jazz Inc.

Jamey Aebersold's name is synonymous with jazz improvisation. Volume 1 is aimed at players with some experience. It is a comprehensive improvisation overview with a great deal of information and verbiage. The sixth edition surveys many fundamental topics, including:

Articulations	Modes
Bebop scales	Patterns
Blues scales	Pentatonics
Chromaticism	Related scales
Ear training	Repertoire
ii–V^7 progressions	Scale choices
Licks	Style
Melodic development	Tune learning

Although the text is not in chapter format, it does contain a wealth of information that may be intimidating to the novice.

Aebersold has a number of resources available for younger students that work progressively and introduce material in a slower, consistent manner (see Peter Blair's *Jazz Basics: The Fundamentals of Improvisation For the Young Musician*). Aebersold's text serves as a valuable resource for individual instruction or as a supplement to a more fundamental resource.

Baker, David. *Jazz Improvisation.* Van Nuys, CA: Alfred Publications.

David Baker is one of the principle founders of the jazz education movement, with a long list of innovative, analytical, and pedagogical books and articles to his credit. Jazz improvisation has long been a standard in music departments and libraries. This book has served as a foundation for many great players and a model for many other authors in the field. The revised Fireside edition serves as a valuable resource for every instrument and level. Foreword by Gunther Schuller; 133 spiral-bound pages.

Berg, Shelton. *Chop Monster 1 & 2*. Verdugo City, CL: J. Fraser Collection.

The *Chop Monster* series comes in two volumes and is sub-titled *Jazz Language Tutor*. Book One is organized into twenty-two units and moves progressively by using ear training, singing, call-and-response, and simple major/minor tonalities as a foundation towards improvisation. A conductor's book includes transparency masters, teaching suggestions, and full performance scores. The text utilizes the B♭ concert major scale as the foundation for all the exercises. For example; the Mixolydian mode is introduced but not identified.

Book Two follows the same format with twenty-one units and moves similarly with ear training, singing, and call-and-response being emphasized throughout. The key signatures B♭, E♭ and F are utilized throughout, and V–I cadences are introduced and serve as a foundation for further scale development and improvisation. More emphasis is placed on minor tonalities, scales, and modes. The blues scale and the use of blue notes is realized, as well as using further chromatics. Book Two also includes transparency masters, teaching suggestions, and full performance scores. Both texts are designed for the beginning to intermediate ensemble class usage and include pieces for the ensemble utilizing the techniques covered.

Berg, Shelton. *Jazz Improvisation: The Goal-Note Method*. Delevan, NJ: Kendor Music Inc.

Berg states that "*Jazz Improvisation: The Goal-Note Method* is intended as a programmed text for a 2-4 semester improvisation program. The approach is consonance-based, emphasizing structural pitches and harmonic considerations as opposed to scale-derived melody. The premise is that when consonant tones are surrounded with characteristic jazz formula (cliché), successful improvisation results."The text contains five sections:

Section 1: *Introduction*

Bebop melodic construction	Goal-note method
Changes	Licks
Consonance	Off-beat starts and endings
Formula	Practice techniques
Functional harmony	Swing eighth notes
General style	Time

Section 2: *Primary Chord Types*

- 12-bar blues
- Auxiliary tones
- Chromaticism and turnaround progressions
- Dominant (ninth) seventh chords
- Major seventh (ninth) chords
- Minor seventh (ninth) chords

Section 3: *Chromatic Harmony*

- Turnarounds in several applications
- Diminished seventh chords
- Scales
- Rhythm changes

Section 4: *Advanced Principles*

- Blues revisited
- Expanded major and minor harmony
- I–VI progressions
- Modal and quartal jazz
- Outside playing
- Polyharmony
- Substitutions
- Tritone substitutions

Section 5: *Appendix*

- Circle of fifths
- Formula recap
- Glossary
- Sample solos
- Scale preferences
- Transposed tunes
- Turnaround lines

Berg provides a hierarchy at the beginning and throughout each chapter of successive approximations that should lead the student to successful task completion. Each task (for example, practicing) is presented in a step-by-step manner that can easily be analyzed and synthesized. All material is expanded upon as the book progresses.

Bouchard, George. *Intermediate Jazz Improvisation.* New Albany, IN: Jamey Aebersold Jazz Inc.

Bouchard states "*Intermediate Jazz Improvisation* is written to organize, codify, and demonstrate useful information which has proven to be helpful in learning to play improvised solos in the jazz idiom. The manuscript has been prepared for the player with some experience, who is looking for a deeper and more complete understanding of chord progressions and tune structures." The author accomplishes this by basing the structure of the book on learning standard tunes and methods to play over the changes to these.The text is divided into two main parts.

Part One contains "short essays which serve as background information, followed by text chapters and exercises which correspond to the theoretical aspects of the music, and specific tune formats and guidelines that function as a detailed method for practicing each tune. The majority of material is based on the development and use of pentatonics.

Part Two is the play-along section, which includes two CDs that contain:
Specific exercises to be played in all keys.
Particular information correlated with the source material from the Aebersold catalog.
Chord charts with key sequences for all instruments.

This exercise portion is followed by short excerpts from the tunes being discussed.

Coker, Jerry. *Improvising Jazz*. Fireside Books.
Jerry Coker has published many texts on the jazz and improvisation and is among one the most respected authorities on jazz pedagogy. *Jazz Improvisation* is an excellent treatise on the subject of jazz improvisation. It covers all the improviser's basic tools, including melody, rhythm, ear-development, swing, functional harmony, and much more. The emphasis is on is on basic scale theory and melodic devices. The entire book is valuable resource, especially to younger players who have never been exposed to these ideas. The chapters on melody and functional harmony are particularly useful to a beginning improviser.

Crook, Hal. *Ready, Aim, Improvise!* Rottenburg, North Germany: Advance Music.
This book comes with the following recommendations:
One or more years of practice on a musical instrument, preferably under the instruction of a private teacher.
An ability to read music.
A familiarity with early styles of jazz improvisation acquired through listening and/or performing.
Information and exercises on various topics from the music textbooks *How to Improvise** and *How to Comp* (published by Advance Music), for which this book is recommended as a study guide.

The text is divided into six parts:

Part I: *Preparation*
A primer of basic theory, harmony, ear training history. Serves the beginning and intermediate students who need a more complete musical background before beginning the process of improvisation.

Part II: *Jazz Vocabulary*
Contains the main musical material of the book and provides extensive coverage of jazz execution and content regarding the basic elements of an improvised solo.

Part III: *Target Practice*
Provides approaches to practicing improvisation in which individual aspects of jazz execution and content are targeted.

Part IV: *Extra Help*
Contains a tune file comprised of over 300 standard titles categorized by difficulty and two play-a-long CD's that cover relevant exercises contained throughout the text.

Part V: *Practicing*
Provides suggestions for successful practice and improvement.

Part VI: *Final Thoughts*
Presents some of the author's personal views and thoughts on his personal experiences as a jazz musician and educator.

The text is well written and provides a wealth of musical examples, exercises, and practice routines. It is strongly recommended that this book be used in conjunction with the companion texts *How to Improvise* and *How to Comp*. This series is recommended for the individual who is interested in investing a great deal of time reading, analyzing and practicing.

Crook, Hal. *How to Improvise: An Approach to Practicing Improvisation*. Advance Music.

Levine, Mark. *The Jazz Piano Book*. Petaluma, CA: Sher Music Co.
This is an excellent reference for anyone wanting to learn the key ingredients to becoming a Jazz player. The book is broken up into five parts:

Chords and Scales
Focuses on major, melodic minor, diminished, and whole tone harmony, and suggests a method of practicing these scales.

Playin' the Changes
Explains how these scales can be used in a musical way, how to play the blues, "rhythm changes," how to play "outside" the changes, and how to increase your musical vocabulary with bebop and pentatonic scales.

Reharmonization
Focuses on chord substitutions and the Coltrane matrix. Illustrated with the reharmonization of three tunes.

Tunes
Includes how to read a lead sheet, tune memorization, song form and composition, and necessary tunes of the Jazz repertoire.

Getting it together
Introduces Latin and salsa concepts; includes what to listen to with a

fairly compete discography.

This is a very complete and comprehensive resource.

Reeves, Scott. *Creative Jazz Improvisation*. 3rd ed. Upper Saddle, NJ: Prentice-Hall, Inc.

This book is generally well formatted. This resource is divided into five primary parts:

Part 1: The Art of Improvisation
Part 2: Diatonic Chords and the Modes in the Major Scale
Part 3: Chord Substitutions, Harmonic Structures, and Forms
Part 4: Altered Chords, Diminished Modes, Whole-tone and Harmonic Minor Scales, and Melodic Minor Modes
Part 5: Pentatonic Scales and Intervallic Improvisation.

Part 1 provides an introduction and overview of how the book is formatted and gives operational definitions of the terms contained in the book. Consists of three chapters: How to Practice, Creatively Improvise, and Teach Jazz Improvisation; Whom to Listen To; and Rhythm.

The remaining four parts consist of several chapters each with a common format for each chapter. Each chapter is divided into five sections:

Section 1: Introduction

Section 2: Theory/Ear Exercises
Includes examples of ear training exercises that can be complete either alone or with another musician.

Section 3: Gaining Facility with . . .
Aids in gaining facility with whatever the chapter specific topic entails. This section contains patterns and may be used with either the companion CD for *Creative Beginnings: An Introduction to Jazz Improvisation* (Prentice-Hall, Inc.) or with specific Jamey Aebersold play-along series.

Section 4: Improvising on Jazz Compositions Based on...
Includes a partial list of jazz compositions which the chapter topic occurs frequently. Locations of these compositions are provided from several sources:

The New Real Book, Vol. 1
The New Real Book, Vol. 2
Creative Beginnings: An Introduction to Jazz Improvisation
Various volumes of Jamey Aebersold's New Approach to Jazz Improvisation).

Section 5: Transcription

The final section of each chapter contains a complete transcription of a recorded improvised solo and a summary of the composition and the solo. Concert pitch treble, bass, Ef, and Bf versions of the transcription are provided.

This seems to work well as an intermediate, self-directed study guide. The chapters are well written and clearly formatted. The solo transcriptions provided are solos by significant jazz artists (e.g., Louis Armstrong, John Coltrane, Miles Davis, Charlie Parker) and of high-quality jazz compositions (e.g., *So What*, *Giant Steps*, *Now's the Time*, etc.).

Scales

Title	Author	Scales/Modes (general)	Major	Minor	Dorian
Creative Jazz Improvisation	Reeves, Scott		4		6
Jazz Improvisation	Baker, David	4, 6	2, 6	2, 6	6
Improvising Jazz	Coker, Jerry	6	1, 6	1, 6	1, 6
The Chop Monster 1	Berg, Shelton		1, 6	7	
The Chop Monster 2	Berg, Shelton		4		
How to Play Jazz and Improvise	Aebersold, Jamey	pp. 46–47, 52–54, 60–61			
Jazz Basics	Blair, Peter				
The Jazz Theory Book	Levine, Mark	5 (harmonic)	2, 3	2, 3	2, 3

Title	Phrygian	Lydian	Mixolydian	Locrian	Aeolian	Bebop
Creative Jazz Improvisation	9	9	5	8	8	5
Jazz Improvisation	6	6	6	6	6	6
Improvising Jazz			1, 6	1, 6		
The Chop Monster 1			13			
The Chop Monster 2			4			7
How to Play Jazz and Improvise						p. 28
Jazz Basics						
The Jazz Theory Book	2, 3, 7	2, 3	2, 3	2, 3	2	7

Title	Blues	Pentatonic Major	Pentatonic Minor	Whole-tone	Diminished Modes
Creative Jazz Improvisation	10	19	19	15	
Jazz Improvisation	6, 11	6	6	6	2, 6
Improvising Jazz	1			6	8
The Chop Monster 1					
The Chop Monster 2	8, 9				
How to Play Jazz and Improvise	p.40	p. 30	p. 30		
Jazz Basics					
The Jazz Theory Book	9, 10	9	9	3	3

Title	Lydian Augmented	Harmonic Minor	Melodic Minor	Locrian	Locrian no. 2
Creative Jazz Improvisation	18	16	16		17
Jazz Improvisation	6	6	6		6
Improvising Jazz		6	6	6	
The Chop Monster 1					
The Chop Monster 2					
How to Play Jazz and Improvise					
Jazz Basics					
The Jazz Theory Book	3		3	3	3

Title	Diminished Whole-tone	Augmented	Altered	Patterns/ Sequences	CD
Creative Jazz Improvisation	17			Throughout	•
Jazz Improvisation	6	2	6	4, Throughout	
Improvising Jazz	8			6	
The Chop Monster 1					•
The Chop Monster 2					•
How to Play Jazz and Improvise				p. 62	
Jazz Basics					
The Jazz Theory Book	3			4, 5, 7, 8	

Chords

Title	Author	Major	Major 6	Major 7	Major 7(♭5)
Creative Jazz Improvisation	Reeves, Scott			4	9
Jazz Improvisation	Baker, David	1, 2		1, 2	1, 2
Improvising Jazz	Coker, Jerry	1	6	1, 4, 6	
The Chop Monster 1	Berg, Shelton	2		3, 8, 9	
The Chop Monster 2	Berg, Shelton	2, 3, 4		3	
How to Play Jazz and Improvise	Aebersold, Jamey	p. 41		p. 41	p. 64
The Jazz Theory Book	Levine, Mark	2, 3		2, 3	

Title	Major 7(♯5)	Minor	Minor 6	Minor 7	Minor (maj. 7)
Creative Jazz Improvisation	18		6	16	
Jazz Improvisation	1, 2 1, 2		1, 2	1 ,2	
Improvising Jazz		1	6	1, 4, 6	6
The Chop Monster 1			4, 8, 9		
The Chop Monster 2					
How to Play Jazz and Improvise	p. 64	p. 41		p. 41	p. 64
The Jazz Theory Book	3 2, 3	3	2, 3	3	

Title	Augmented	Diminished	Half-Diminished	Dominant 7
Creative Jazz Improvisation	15	14		5
Jazz Improvisation	1, 2	1, 2	1, 2	1, 2
Improvising Jazz	6	6	6	1, 4, 6
The Chop Monster 1				12
The Chop Monster 2				2, 3, 4
How to Play Jazz and Improvise		p. 41		p. 41, 54
The Jazz Theory Book	3	2, 3	2, 3	2, 3 3

Title	Dominant 7(♭9)	Sus. Chords	Altered Dominant	Dominant 7(♭5)
Creative Jazz Improvisation			15	
Jazz Improvisation				
Improvising Jazz				
The Chop Monster 1				
The Chop Monster 2				
How to Play Jazz and Improvise				
The Jazz Theory Book	3	3	3	

Title	Dominant 9(♯11)	Substitutions	Slash Chords
Creative Jazz Improvisation	18	10, 12	
Jazz Improvisation		15	
Improvising Jazz			
The Chop Monster 1			
The Chop Monster 2			
How to Play Jazz and Improvise			
The Jazz Theory Book	3		5

Forms

Title	Author	ii–V-I	iidim^7–V^7–I	Blues	Rhythm Changes
Creative Jazz Improvisation	Reeves, Scott	7	8, 17	10	11
Jazz Improvisation	Baker, David	2, 5, 7		16 (piano) 17 (bass)	
Improvising Jazz	Coker, Jerry			1, 4	
The Chop Monster 1	Berg, Shelton			14	
The Chop Monster 2	Berg, Shelton	12, 13, 14, 15, 17	12, 13, 14, 15, 17	9	
How to Play Jazz and Improvise	Aebersold, Jamey	p. 46		pp. 36–39	
The Jazz Theory Book	Levine, Mark	2, 3		10	11

Title	Free Forms	Four-note Groupings	Intervalic Improvisation	Sectional Forms
Creative Jazz Improvisation	13	20	21	11
Jazz Improvisation				
Improvising Jazz				
The Chop Monster 1				
The Chop Monster 2				
How to Play Jazz and Improvise				
The Jazz Theory Book		6		

Pedagogy

Title	Author	Style	Nomenclature	Ear Training
Creative Jazz Improvisation	Reeves, Scott			
Jazz Improvisation	Baker, David	3, 9	1	10
Improvising Jazz	Coker, Jerry	7	1	5
The Chop Monster 1	Berg, Shelton	Throughout		
The Chop Monster 2	Berg, Shelton	Throughout		
How to Play Jazz and Improvise	Aebersold, Jamey	p. 15, 42–50	p. 51	p. 29
The Jazz Theory Book	Levine, Mark		Introduction	

Title	Circle of Fifths	Intervals	Extensions	Transcriptions
Creative Jazz Improvisation				
Jazz Improvisation	2, 7			
Improvising Jazz	11		10	
The Chop Monster 1				Throughout
The Chop Monster 2				Throughout
How to Play Jazz and Improvise	p. 65			
The Jazz Theory Book	2	1		Throughout

Title	Rhythm Section	Melodic Improvisation	Playing Outside
Creative Jazz Improvisation			
Jazz Improvisation	9, 16 (piano) 17 (bass) 18 (drums)	12, 13	
Improvising Jazz	3	2, 9	
The Chop Monster 1			
The Chop Monster 2			
How to Play Jazz and Improvise			
The Jazz Theory Book			8

Index by Composer, Arranger, or Transcriber

Key:
Dev = Dev • Int = Int • Adv = Advanced

Index by Title

Key:
Dev = Dev • Int = Int • Adv = Advanced